DATE DUE

DEC 0 9 2008	
MAR 0 4 2009	
JUL 0 1 2009	
JUL 2 9 2009	
NOV 1 6 2009 2010	
Oct. 31, 2013	

BRODART, CO.   Cat. No. 23-221-003

FROM THE PALMER RAIDS

TO THE PATRIOT ACT

From the Palmer Raids to the Patriot Act

A History of the Fight for Free Speech in America

CHRISTOPHER M. FINAN

Beacon Press
BOSTON

Beacon Press
25 Beacon Street
Boston, Massachusetts 02108–2892
www.beacon.org

Beacon Press books
are published under the auspices of
the Unitarian Universalist Association of Congregations.

10 09 08 07   8 7 6 5 4 3 2 1

This book is printed on acid-free paper that meets the uncoated paper
ANSI/NISO specifications for permanence as revised in 1992.

Composition by Wilsted & Taylor Publishing Services

Library of Congress Control Number: 2007922269

For Pat

CONTENTS

In July 2005, four Connecticut librarians defied the United States government. The Federal Bureau of Investigation had issued a National Security Letter demanding information about a patron who had used one of the library's computers. Fearing that a government search of library records would have a chilling effect on free speech, the librarians contacted the American Civil Liberties Union, which obtained an injunction blocking the order. This was not the first time the FBI had run into a stonewall in its effort to obtain information from a library. Only the year before, a library in Whatcom County, Washington, had gone to court to suppress an FBI subpoena that sought the names of patrons who had checked out a biography of terrorist leader Osama bin Laden. In January 2003, the American Library Association, representing over sixty thousand librarians, demanded that Congress restore the safeguards for reader privacy that had been eliminated by the USA Patriot Act. The Justice Department was stunned. Attorney General John Ashcroft accused the librarians of "hysteria." Privately, FBI agents complained that they had to fight both the terrorists and the librarians. One agent criticized the Justice Department's Office of Intelligence Policy and Review (OIPR) for knuckling under to the librarians by blocking wider use of the Patriot Act. "While radical militant librarians kick us around, true terrorists benefit from OIPR's failure to let us use the tools given to us," the agent wrote. "This should be an OIPR priority!!!"[1]

Since when did librarians become champions of free speech? At the beginning of the twentieth century, they prided themselves on protecting the public from "bad" books. (In 1908, an Atlanta librarian revealed that she hid trashy novels in the stacks in the hope that her patrons wouldn't find them.) It isn't only librarians who changed. There has been a revolution in our attitude toward free speech over the course of the last century. Prior to World War I, freedom of speech was something most Americans took for granted. Yet there had always been censorship in America. Only a few years after the adoption of the First Amendment in 1791, Federalists threw newspapers editors into jail for criticizing the government. Defenders of slavery killed the abolitionist editor Elija Lovejoy and banned members of Congress from raising the issue of slavery on the floor of the House of Representatives. A northern critic of the Civil War was sentenced to two years in prison for making a speech that might "demoralize the troops." But censorship was not widely seen as a problem until World War I. It was then that the rapidly expanding federal government crushed criticism of the war, convicting more than a thousand Americans of making statements that allegedly harmed the war effort. Immediately following the war, Attorney General A. Mitchell Palmer launched nationwide raids that rounded up thousands of suspected Communists who were guilty of nothing more than belonging to the wrong political party.

The civil liberties movement in this country was born in the outrage over the abuses committed during World War I and the Red Scare. In the beginning, the fight for free speech was waged by a handful of men and women who believed that the greatest threat to American government came not from radicals calling for its overthrow but from patriotic officials intent on suppressing "dangerous" beliefs. Many of the early civil libertarians were radicals themselves. Roger Baldwin, a draft resister, emerged from prison to found the American Civil Liberties Union in 1920. But from the beginning, the civil liberties movement had the support of important establishment figures, including U.S. Supreme Court justice Oliver Wendell Holmes Jr. In 1919, the seventy-eight-year-old Holmes turned aside the earnest pleas of his wife and his fellow justices to protest the jailing of a radical for his beliefs. In his dissenting opinion in *Abrams v. U.S.*, Holmes explained:

When men have realized that time has upset many fighting faiths, they may come to believe even more than they believe the very foundations of their own conduct that the ultimate good desired is better reached by free trade in ideas—that the best test of truth is the power of the thought to get itself accepted in the competition of the market, and that truth is the only ground upon which their wishes safely can be carried out.

In succeeding years, civil libertarians fought to establish a free trade in ideas. Slowly, battle by battle, they fundamentally changed the relationship between the American people and their government. "The censorial power is in the people over the Government, and not in the Government over the people," James Madison said during a debate in the House of Representatives in 1794. This is the story of our triumph over government censors. But, as any librarian will tell you, the battle will never be won. The fight continues.[2]

CHAPTER I

Ground Zero

On the evening of November 7, 1919, Mitchel Lavrowsky was teaching a class in algebra to a roomful of Russian immigrants at the Russian People's House, a building just off Union Square in New York City. The fifty-year-old Lavrowsky was also Russian. He had been a teacher and the principal of the Iglitsky High School in Odessa before emigrating to the United States and now lived quietly with his wife and two children in the Bronx. Lavrowsky had applied for American citizenship. But that didn't matter to the men who entered his classroom with their guns drawn around 8 P.M. They identified themselves as agents of the Department of Justice and ordered everyone to stand. One of them advanced on Lavrowsky and instructed him to remove his eyeglasses. He struck Lavrowsky in the head. Two more agents joined the assault, beating the teacher until he could not stand and then throwing him down the stairwell. Below, men hit him with pieces of wood that they had torn out of the banister.[1]

Lavrowsky soon had company on the stairs. There were several hundred people in the Russian People's House that night, most of them students. After they were searched and relieved of any money they might be carrying, the students were ordered out of their classrooms and into a gauntlet of men who struck some of them on the head and pushed them down the stairs toward the waiting police wagons. Students were grabbed as they approached the school and dragged inside. Some were beaten in the street. Meanwhile, with the help of New York City police detectives, the Justice Department men began to tear the place apart, breaking furniture, destroying typewriters, and overturning desks and bookshelves until the floor was covered in a sea of paper. When they judged that there was nothing useful left, they carted off two hundred prisoners to the Department of Justice's offices in a building across from City Hall. The Russians were questioned about their connection to the Union of Russian Workers, which rented a room in the Russian House. The agents discovered that only thirty-nine were members of the group and released the rest. Mitchel Lavrowsky was sent home at midnight with a fractured head, shoulder, and foot.

The roundup of Russians continued through the night and into the next day. The police burst into apartments and dragged people from their beds. Sometimes they had arrest warrants, but usually they simply arrested everyone they found. In the end, the Department of Justice had grabbed more than one thousand people in eleven cities. Approximately 75 percent of those arrested were guilty of nothing more than being in the wrong place at the wrong time, and many were quickly released. Others were not so lucky. Nearly one hundred men were locked up in Hartford, Connecticut, for almost five months. Many of them were denied access to a lawyer or even knowledge of the charges against them. Probably half were Russian workers whose only crime was that they could not speak English. When a lawyer finally succeeded in getting inside the jail, ten of the men were released with no bail.[2]

America cheered the November raids. World War I had ended a year earlier, and the country was enduring a wrenching conversion to peace. Unemployment surged as returning veterans sought to reclaim their old jobs. Many of them had been eliminated as the economy was retooled for war production, and now the war workers, too, were out of work. In the transition between war and peace, there were too few consumer goods. No new housing had been built in over eighteen months. As a result, at the moment when they could least afford it, Americans found themselves facing high inflation. It isn't surprising that at a time when they were feeling so vulnerable, people began to worry about the danger of foreign radicalism. Radicalism was nothing new. The Socialist Party had existed here for many years. But the success of the Bolshevik Revolution in 1917 appeared to have launched a worldwide revolutionary threat that many people easily connected with the growing number of strikes in the United States—over 3,600 in 1919 alone. Although these strikes were driven by inflation, not radical ideology, employers did their best to paint their workers as subversives. The threat of revolution seemed to be confirmed in June when eight bombs exploded outside the homes of prominent men, including the new attorney general A. Mitchell Palmer. The nation demanded swift action. "I was shouted at from every editorial sanctum in America from sea to sea; I was preached upon from every pulpit," Palmer recalled. "I was urged—I could feel it dinned into my ears—throughout the country to do something and do it now."

The November raids were the result. Launched on the second anniversary of the Russian Revolution, they were followed by a second, even larger series of raids in January that seized over three thousand members of two new American parties, the Communist Party and the Communist Labor Party.[3]

Although the Palmer Raids generated a lot of good publicity for the Department of Justice, they accomplished little. The government never discovered who was behind the June bombings. The radicals who were arrested in November and January were not charged with any crime. The Department of Justice would have been unable to take any action at all if Congress had not made it a deportable offense for an alien to belong to a group that advocated the violent overthrow of the government. The people who were arrested during the Palmer Raids were picked up not because of anything they had done but because of what they might do. In fact, many of those arrested and held for deportation did not believe in violence. The Union of Russian Workers had declared its belief in revolution when it was founded in 1907, but by 1919 it had largely become a social club whose members were unaware of its founding principles. The Department of Labor later canceled thousands of deportation orders issued to members of the Communist Labor Party on the grounds that it, too, was not a truly revolutionary party. In the end, the government succeeded in deporting only eight hundred of the more than four thousand people it had arrested.

But the government raids did achieve something important. They raised the issue of what freedoms are protected by the First Amendment to the U.S. Constitution. The First Amendment bars government from "abridging the freedom of speech, or of the press, or the right of the people peaceably to assemble, and to petition the Government for a redress of grievances." By targeting people for deportation based on their beliefs, the Palmer Raids had violated the First Amendment. Emma Goldman made this point during her deportation hearing in October 1919. Born in Russia, the fifty-year-old Goldman was one of the country's most notorious radicals. Like many anarchists, she believed that violent acts were a legitimate response to capitalist oppression. Her lover, Alexander Berkman, served fourteen years in prison for attempting to assassinate the manager of the Carnegie Steel Mill during a bitter strike in Homestead, Pennsylvania, in 1892. Goldman herself once horsewhipped a political opponent. But mostly Goldman used her great oratorical gifts to apply the lash. Although she was short, stout, and far from beautiful, Goldman was a powerful and charismatic speaker who thrilled her audiences with a vision of a new society in which there would be equality between the sexes as well as between the classes. Conservatives had longed to send "Red Emma" packing for years, and the Red Scare gave them their chance. As she was released from a prison term for opposing the war, Goldman was arrested again and held for deportation under the law passed following the McKinley assassination that banned advocacy of the overthrow of the government. The proceeding had been recommended by John Edgar Hoover, a twenty-four-year-old official of the Justice Department who was helping plan Palmer's antiradical campaign. Hoover was listening intently as the government's attorney made the case against Goldman during her deportation hearing.

If he hoped to hear Goldman plead for mercy, he was disappointed. She refused to speak during the hearing. Instead, in a statement that was read on her behalf by her attorney, Goldman attacked the effort to deport foreign radicals as an assault on free speech. "Ever since I have been in this country—and I have lived here practically all my life—it has been dinned into my ears that under the institutions of this alleged Democracy one is entirely free to think and feel as he pleases," Goldman said.

> What becomes of this sacred guarantee of freedom of thought and conscience when persons are being persecuted and driven out for the very motives and purposes for which the pioneers who built up this country

laid down their lives? ... Under the mask of the same Anti-Anarchist law every criticism of a corrupt administration, every attack on Government abuse, every manifestation of sympathy with the struggle of another country in the pangs of a new birth—in short, every free expression of untrammeled thought may be suppressed utterly, without even the semblance of an unprejudiced hearing or a fair trial.

Goldman warned that the government was making a terrible mistake by confusing conformity with security. "The free expression of the hopes and aspirations of a people is the greatest and only safety in a sane society," she said. "In truth, it is such free expression and discussion alone that can point the most beneficial path for human progress and development." Two months later, Hoover was standing on the dock as a decrepit government ship, the *Buford,* departed for Russia, carrying Goldman and 248 other deported radicals under heavy military guard. Goldman remained abroad until her body was returned for burial in 1940.[4]

While the government succeeded in silencing Goldman, the controversy over free speech continued to grow. Only weeks after Goldman's hearing, Oliver Wendell Holmes Jr., the most prominent member of the U.S. Supreme Court, indirectly endorsed her view that radical criticism of American institutions must be protected. This marked an important change in Holmes's thinking. In March, he had written the decision upholding the imprisonment of Eugene V. Debs, the leader of the Socialist Party, for making a speech critical of America's participation in World War I. But by November, Holmes had changed his mind. In a case involving the distribution of radical pamphlets, he urged his countrymen to recognize the importance of protecting free speech:

> When men have realized that time has upset many fighting faiths, they may come to believe even more than they believe the very foundations of their own conduct that the ultimate good desired is better reached by a free trade in ideas—that the best test of truth is the power of the thought to get itself accepted in the competition of the market, and that truth is the only ground upon which their wishes safely can be carried out.

Holmes was unable to persuade his colleagues on the Supreme Court. Only Louis Brandeis joined his opinion. But an important turning point had been reached: free expression was no longer an issue for radicals alone; the fight for free speech had entered the political mainstream.[5]

This was not the first time that freedom of speech had become a political issue. In 1798, when war with France appeared imminent, Congress passed the Alien and Sedition Acts to punish French sympathizers. The Sedition Act provided a fine of up to $2,000 and two years in jail for anyone who published "any false, scandalous and malicious writing" about the U.S. government, Congress, or the president. Twenty-five people were prosecuted, and ten editors and printers were sent to jail. Opposition to the suppression of free speech was intense, and both laws soon expired. Between 1836 and 1844, northern abolitionists strenuously protested a gag rule that barred the House of Representatives from debating antislavery petitions. In 1863, the Union commander in Ohio imposed martial law and outlawed "declaring sympathies for the enemy." A former Ohio congressman, Clement Vallandigham, was tried by a military commission and exiled to the Confederacy for violating the law. The arrest of Vallandigham was condemned as a violation of freedom of speech by Democratic newspapers throughout the North.[6]

The first peacetime restriction on freedom of speech was passed in 1865 when Congress banned the mailing of obscene books and magazines. This law was broadened by Anthony Comstock in 1873 to ban advertisements for obscene material, which was also widened to include information about birth control. The passage of the Comstock Act did not generate the kinds of protests that had greeted the Alien and Sedition Acts or the arrest of Vallandigham. However, in 1902, a small group of radicals founded the Free Speech League to assert the First Amendment right of unpopular groups. Created in the aftermath of the assassination of President William McKinley by an anarchist in 1901, the Free Speech League opposed legislation restricting the right of anarchists to promote their views. It also came to the defense of those who were prosecuted under the Comstock Act for advocating free love and the use of birth control. But there was little sympathy for radicals, atheists, and advocates of open marriage. It took a world war to reveal that censorship threatened the rights of all Americans.[7]

When war broke out in Europe in 1914, the overwhelming majority of Americans believed that it had little to do with them. It seemed to concern only the territorial ambitions of countries that were an ocean away from the United States. The fact that modern weapons made the war unimaginably bloody—nearly one million men were killed and wounded in the Battle of Verdun alone—deepened the revulsion of the American people. Over the next three and a half years, however, America's isolation eroded. German submarines attempted to strangle Great Britain by sinking any ship that might be carrying armaments. More than one thousand civilians, including one hundred Americans, lost their lives when a U-boat sunk the British liner *Lusitania* in 1915. In response to American demands, Germany agreed not to sink civilian ships without warning, but in January 1917 it announced the resumption of unrestricted submarine warfare. President Woodrow Wilson urged Congress to declare war in April. The war was about more than the freedom of the seas, Wilson said. In challenging the German autocracy, America was making the world "safe for democracy." Later, he would propose a League of Nations, which he believed would eliminate the need for war. America would fight for nothing less than an end to all wars.

Many Americans remained unconvinced. There were deep divisions in the population. The growth of industry had produced vast wealth, but it was unevenly distributed, and the great mansions that graced New York's Fifth Avenue were shadowed by slum districts where tuberculosis, alcoholism, and industrial accidents exacted a heavy toll. Many workers saw the clash of European powers as a capitalist struggle between countries attempting to extend their markets. The United States was also divided between immigrants and natives. Thirty million immigrants arrived between 1845 and 1915, and many of them had opinions on the war. The more than five million Germans included tens of thousands who still cherished memories of the fatherland, while not a few of the more than three million Irish immigrants hungered for the defeat of England.

President Wilson believed there was a serious threat of disloyalty, particularly among immigrants. As early as 1915, he told the Daughters of the American Revolution that he was looking forward to the time when disloyalty would be exposed. "I am in a hurry for an opportunity to have a line-up and let the men who are thinking first of other countries stand on one side and all those that are for America first, last, and all the time on the other," he said. On December 7, Wilson's annual message to Congress charged that

> the gravest threats against our national peace and safety have been uttered within our own borders. There are citizens of the United States, I blush to admit, born under other flags but welcomed by our generous naturalization laws to the full freedom and opportunity of America, who have poured the poison of disloyalty into the very arteries of our national life.

The next day, the members of Wilson's cabinet agreed to cooperate more closely in their investigations of potentially disloyal groups and ordered the attorney general to draft legislation to curtail espionage and the right to express disloyal views. Although the legislation was introduced in June 1916, America was still at peace, and there was little support for drastic new measures. Once Congress declared war on April 6, 1917, however, the proposed "Espionage Act" moved to the top of the legislative agenda.[8]

America's newspaper publishers were shocked by the proposed Espionage Act. It included a fine of up to $10,000 and a prison sentence of up to ten years for anyone who published information that would be useful or possibly useful to the enemy. The president himself would decide by proclamation whether the information fit the definition of the crime. The American Newspaper Publishers Association (ANPA) protested strongly that the provision would destroy freedom of the press, for the president could condemn any story as useful to the enemy, including criticism of his administration. Several influential senators agreed. "To attempt to deny to the press all legitimate criticism either of Congress or the Executive is going very dangerously too far," Senator Henry Cabot Lodge of Massachusetts said. Wilson refused to back down. Press censorship was "absolutely necessary to public safety," he told the *New York Times.* But weeks of hostile editorials finally persuaded the House to kill the provision, 184-144.[9]

The press censorship provision was only one of several that potentially affected free speech. The bill criminalized "willfully" making "false statements with intent to interfere with the operation or success of the military or naval forces." The punishment was a fine of up to $10,000 and twenty years in prison. This provision occasioned little controversy, perhaps because it seemed to threaten only enemy agents. But the Espionage Act also gave the post office broad new powers to exclude from the mails any material "advocating or urging treason, insurrection, or forcible resistance to any law of the United States." Leaders of the Free Speech League, who had seen how the post office abused its power under the Comstock Act, urged Congress to amend this provision. "I know what a tremendous instrument of tyranny this rather innocent looking provision of the bill will become," a league attorney wrote Senator Robert La Follette of Minnesota. But no other organization expressed concern. The nation's newspapers did not see either section as a threat to their interests, and they became law when the Espionage Act was passed in June.[10]

Postmaster General Albert S. Burleson immediately began using his new power to exclude from the mail any material that was critical of the war. In July, post office officials notified the editors of *The Masses,* a lively literary and political magazine with Socialist leanings, that they could not mail their August issue. When Max Eastman, the editor, demanded to know what articles violated the Espionage Act, the officials refused to tell him. A delegation of lawyers headed by the famed defense attorney Clarence Darrow traveled to Washington to urge the postmaster to establish clear standards so that editors would not inadvertently violate them. But Burleson, a Texan whose father had been a major in the Confederate army, was not impressed by a group of radical lawyers. The postmaster was one of the most powerful officials in the federal government because he controlled thousands of jobs. After more than a decade in Congress, Burleson knew his power and knew how to use it. He told his visitors a folksy story and sent them on their way.[11]

The Masses finally forced the government to reveal the reasons for rejecting the August issue by challenging the post office in court. The truth was worse than anything they had imagined. The government lawyer pointed to four articles and four cartoons. The articles included a poem that eulogized Emma Goldman and Alexander Berkman, anarchists who had recently been arrested; an editorial that mentioned the arrests; another editorial about the importance of maintaining individualism during a time of war; and a collection of letters from imprisoned conscientious objectors in Britain. One cartoon, "Conscription," showed the evils of war. "War Plans" revealed a group of businessmen studying plans in a congressional meeting room, while members of Congress, watching from the sidelines, asked, "Where do we come in?" The post office also objected to a cartoon of a crumbling Liberty Bell. U.S. District Court judge Learned Hand rejected the postmaster's claim and ordered him to accept the magazine, but his decision was immediately stayed and later overridden by a federal appeals court.[12]

As a result, it was Burleson who decided what the American people could read during the war. In October, he felt confident enough to describe some of the things he was forbidding:

> For instance, papers may not say that the Government is controlled by Wall Street or munitions manufacturers, or any other special interests.... We will not tolerate campaigns against conscription, enlistments, sale of securities [Liberty Bonds] or revenue collections. We will not permit the publication or circulation of anything hampering the war's prosecution or attacking improperly our allies.

Socialist newspapers were the main target, and the post office banned at least one issue of twenty-two Socialist publications. Burleson successfully suppressed *The Masses* by arguing that it had ceased to be a "periodical" when its August issue was banned and had therefore forfeited the right to be distributed as second-class mail. The magazine hoped to save itself through newsstand sales but was forced to fold. The post office tried the same tactic against the *Milwaukee Leader*, a Socialist paper published by Victor Berger, a member of Congress. The post office even refused to deliver first-class mail to the *Leader*, a tactic that was occasionally employed against other "disloyal" parties, although it lacked any legal authority to do so. Postal authorities also threatened mainstream publications on occasion. After receiving a warning from the post office, *The New Republic* refused to carry an ad soliciting money to defend the Industrial Workers of the World (IWW), a radical labor union charged under the Espionage Act. *The Nation* had to appeal directly to President Wilson when the post office refused to accept an issue that was critical of

Samuel Gompers, an administration supporter. Meanwhile, the foreign-language press generally abandoned any commentary on the
war in order to win a license to publish under the Trading with the
Enemies Act.[13]

The Justice Department was also busy. In early September, its agents
obtained search warrants for IWW offices all over the country. The
IWW's goal was to organize unskilled workers who were generally
ignored by the unions that belonged to the American Federation of
Labor. The "Wobblies" believed in a day when the power of organized labor would destroy capitalism, clearing the way for a more just
social order. The Wobblies talked tough and were often engaged in
violent conflicts with employers who would do anything to prevent
their workers from organizing. (Their leader, "Big Bill" Haywood,
was acquitted of charges that he had participated in the assassination
of a former Idaho governor.) Like the Socialists who kept them at
arm's distance, the Wobblies opposed the war. But their goal was to
create "one big union," not to disrupt the war effort. Nevertheless,
on September 26, 1917, federal agents rounded up 166 IWW leaders
and charged them with violating the Espionage Act. They were indicted under the section that banned making false statements in an
effort to disrupt the war effort. Nearly 100 were convicted, including Haywood, who was sentenced to twenty years by U.S. District
Court judge Kenesaw Mountain Landis. "When the country is at
peace, it is a legal right of free speech to oppose going to war. . . . But
when once war is declared, this right ceases," declared Landis, who
soon resigned to become the first commissioner of baseball, delivering the same stern justice to errant baseball players that he had shown
the "reds."[14]

The prosecution of the Wobblies was the largest one carried out
under the Espionage Act, but it was only the tip of the iceberg. Despite the best intentions of Attorney General Thomas W. Gregory,
who was more sensitive to civil liberties concerns than Burleson, the
Justice Department indicted 2,168 people under the Espionage Act
and convicted 1,055. The victims included leaders of the Socialist
Party like Rose Pastor Stokes, who was convicted for a letter to the
editor of a St. Louis newspaper defending the right to dissent from
the war. She was indicted for writing, "I am for the people and the

government is for the profiteers."[15] Eugene V. Debs, the four-time Socialist Party candidate for president, was sentenced to ten years for a speech he made in Canton, Ohio, in June 1918. Although Debs chose his words carefully, knowing that government stenographers were present at every speech, he was convicted for saying, "You need to know that you are fit for something better than slavery and cannon fodder." Debs served two and a half years in prison. In 1920, while serving his sentence, he ran for president for a fifth time and received over 900,000 votes. But his health was deteriorating. He died five years after his release at the age of seventy.[16]

The overwhelming majority of prosecutions involved ordinary people. The country was in a war fever, and the Justice Department was under tremendous pressure to take action against every manifestation of disloyalty. This spirit of intolerance was encouraged by the government. "German agents are everywhere," warned a magazine ad placed by the Committee on Public Information, a government agency. "Report the man who spreads pessimistic stories...cries for peace or belittles our efforts to win the war." Such propaganda was hardly necessary. Every day the newspapers published lists of dead and wounded Americans, and local officials of the Justice Department were flooded with reports of traitorous words. The son of a chief justice of the New Hampshire Supreme Court was convicted for mailing a chain letter that asserted Germany had not broken its promise to end unrestricted submarine warfare. Thirty German Americans in South Dakota went to jail for sending a petition to the governor urging reforms in the draft laws. The producer of a film, *The Spirit of 76,* which depicted many patriotic scenes from the Revolutionary War, was sentenced to ten years in prison for including scenes portraying the atrocities committed by the British troops during the Wyoming Valley Massacre. "History is history, and fact is fact," the judge acknowledged, but "this is no time" for portraying an American ally in a bad light. An Iowa man received a twenty-year term for circulating a petition urging the defeat of a congressman who had voted for conscription. Another Iowa man was sent to jail for a year for being present at a radical meeting, applauding and contributing twenty-five cents.[17]

Many Americans believed the government needed their help in policing disloyalty. They joined dozens of private organizations that hunted spies, captured "slackers" who had not registered for the draft, and demanded that everyone purchase their fair share of Liberty Bonds. The American Protective League had 250,000 members who carried badges that said they were members of the "Secret Service." Attorney General Gregory explained that their job was "keeping an eye on disloyal individuals and making reports of disloyal utterances." In practice, they acted as vigilantes, pulling people off the street for questioning and searching homes without warrants. Whether acting through organized groups, in mobs formed at the spur of the moment, or as outraged individuals, the patriots often used violence against their enemies. Mobs tarred and feathered those they thought to be disloyal, many of whom were German. Charles Klinge was beaten and forced to kiss the flag in Salisbury, Pennsylvania, for remarks he had made about the war; George Koetzer was tarred and feathered and tied to a brass cannon in a park in San Jose, California. Robert Prager, a German immigrant and Socialist, was lynched by a group of drunken miners in Collinsville, Illinois.[18]

Protests against violations of civil liberties began within weeks of America's entry into the war. At first, the critics hoped they would be able to make some headway through direct appeals to the administration. Lillian Wald, a pioneering social worker who had founded the Henry Street settlement house in New York, knew Woodrow Wilson personally. Less than two weeks after Congress declared war, she wrote the president that free speech was already under heavy assault: "Halls have been refused for public discussion, meetings have been broken up; speakers have been arrested and censorship exercised, not to prevent the transmission of information to enemy countries, but to prevent the free discussion by American citizens of our own problems and policies."

Over the next eighteen months, there would be frequent appeals to Wilson and other members of the administration. Like Wald, the protesters were liberals who often knew Wilson or other highly placed government officials, including the leaders of the War Department and the Justice Department. But the president and his assistants were charged with winning the war and responsible for enforcing the Espionage Act and the other repressive measures passed by Congress. While frequently acknowledging their own concern about the violation of the right of free speech, there was little they could do to help.[19]

Wald could do more than write letters to the president, however.

She was the chair of one of the largest peace groups in the country, the American Union Against Militarism (AUAM). The AUAM had been founded in 1915 in an effort to prevent the United States from being drawn into the war. Now that war had come and Congress had instituted a military draft, it was assisting the growing number of conscientious objectors who were refusing to fight. Most of these men were Quakers and Mennonites, who were inducted despite the fact that their religions opposed violence. Religious scruples did not impress military officers, and conscientious objectors were imprisoned and subjected to harsh punishments in an effort to force them to fight. In April 1917, the AUAM had welcomed a new staff member, Roger Baldwin, a young man from Massachusetts who had made a name for himself as a reformer in St. Louis. Baldwin immediately threw himself into the task of negotiating fair treatment for the conscientious objectors. Two weeks after the passage of the Espionage Act, the AUAM put Baldwin in charge of the new Civil Liberties Bureau (CLB) to act as a clearinghouse for information about the rights of war resisters. However, the CLB's mandate soon grew to include challenges to free speech.

The thirty-three-year-old Baldwin was well suited for his new job. Born in Wellesley Hills, a suburb of Boston, he had grown up in a family with enough wealth to free him from any concern about making a living. It was also a family that encouraged free thinking. Wellesley Hills was only fifteen miles from Concord, the home of Ralph Waldo Emerson and Henry David Thoreau, who were the foremost advocates of the view that the individual conscience was superior to organized religion and every other institution in determining truth. "I was aware of Emerson, Thoreau and the Alcotts about as soon as I was aware of any intellectual figures," Baldwin said. "They were household names." Not all Baldwins admired individualism. One of Roger's great-uncles who lived in Lexington, Massachusetts, shocked the boy by calling Thoreau "that loafer." But Roger's father, Frank, a leather merchant who owned several factories, was a fan of Robert G. Ingersoll, a renowned lecturer who called himself "the great agnostic." Not surprisingly, Roger hoped to emulate men who had defied convention. "I sought character, personality, uniqueness," he said.[20]

The Baldwins' individualism was disciplined by a strong social conscience. Roger attributed this to Unitarianism. "Doing other people good seemed the essence of Unitarianism," he said. As a boy, he participated in church projects raising money for a hospital ship and gathered wildflowers for the sick in Boston hospitals. "The Unitarian Church was my social center," he explained. Several of Roger's relatives were deeply involved in movements for reform. His grandfather William H. Baldwin had established the Young Men's Christian Union in Boston in 1870 to provide adult education, recreation, and other social services. His uncle William H. Baldwin Jr. was the president of the Long Island Rail Road, but he was also the chairman of the Committee of 14, a group that was fighting widespread prostitution in New York City. He served as president of the New York City Club and as director of the National Child Labor Committee. His uncle's wife, Ruth, was a Socialist and a founder of the National Urban League.[21]

Roger's reform proclivities first announced themselves when he was a student at Harvard College. He was soon teaching at the Cambridge Social Union, which offered adult education classes for workers, and he later organized the Harvard Entertainment Troupes to provide entertainment to Boston's settlement houses. At the end of college, Roger sought career guidance from a family friend, the prominent attorney Louis Brandeis. Brandeis had become known as the "people's attorney" because of his willingness to challenge the corruption fostered by streetcar franchises and misconduct in the insurance industry. Brandeis urged Baldwin to devote his life to public service. He also told the young man to get out of town. "Leave Boston," he said. "I started my career in St. Louis, and I don't regret it—it's the center of democracy in the United States." Baldwin packed his bags.[22]

He arrived in St. Louis in 1906, at the high tide of the period that became known as the Progressive Era. The issue of reform had moved to center stage in response to the crusading journalism of reporters who became known as "muckrakers" for their willingness to criticize the pioneering capitalists who had been widely hailed as the paragons of American civilization. The muckrakers revealed to a horrified nation that the rapidly expanding corporations had grown as a result of ruthless tactics used to suppress competition and the corruption of elected officials whose duty it was to protect the public interest. The outrage had helped generate a movement to expand the power of government to regulate business and to solve the many problems created by unrestrained industrialism and the rapid growth of urban areas. Although the "Progressive movement" appeared to have sprung into existence almost overnight in the first years of the new century, reformers had been hard at work for many years. A new profession of social work had been organized to meet the needs of people who lived in dire poverty in the nation's cities. When government refused to address the problems of the nation's slums, social workers created privately run settlement houses to offer people help in adjusting to urban life.

For Baldwin, public service meant social work His aunt Ruth was overjoyed by his decision. (Even his father had welcomed the news, which surprised him.) She immediately arranged introductions to some of the leading social workers of the day, including Lillian Wald. Baldwin also met Jacob Riis, the former police reporter whose 1890 book, *How the Other Half Lives,* had shocked the nation's conscience, and Owen Lovejoy, head of the National Child Labor Committee, which was fighting the employment of children in factories. The reformers embraced the twenty-two-year-old Baldwin. E. M. Grossman, a St. Louis lawyer who was also a Harvard alumnus, was looking for someone to head a settlement house as well as to establish a department of sociology at Washington University. One of Baldwin's professors had recommended him to Grossman on the basis of his work at the Cambridge Social Union. Baldwin had never taken a single course in sociology, but he gladly accepted the job offers and set off for St. Louis "full of enthusiasm, ignorance and self-assurance."[23]

Roger Baldwin never lacked self-assurance. He was the oldest child of one of the country's oldest families. As the proprietor of his own business, Frank Baldwin was used to being in charge and ruled his seven children firmly. But in a house where unorthodox ideas were welcome, there was room for self-expression. Roger also received reinforcement from social relationships that he developed with adults far more easily than with other children of his age. Several of his teachers became close friends. Combined with a social status that gave him access to the "best families," Baldwin's strong confidence in himself and his abilities was irresistible. He took on the challenge of two jobs about which he knew little without a second thought.

His willingness to accept new challenges served him well in St. Louis. The Gateway City had not always been "the capital of democracy." It had been ridiculed by one of the nation's leading muckrakers, Lincoln Steffens, in a 1902 article, "Tweed Days in St. Louis." But Steffens's article had helped to launch a municipal reform wave that had made significant progress by the time of Baldwin's arrival. There may have been no better city in the world for a talented young man looking to make a name for himself as a reformer. Just a year after his arrival, in 1907, the judge who headed the city's new juvenile court offered Baldwin the chance to become the court's first chief probation officer. The movement to treat juvenile crime differently from adult crime was one of the most important initiatives of the Progressive Era, and Baldwin eagerly accepted a role in it. To meet the challenge of overseeing the rehabilitation of two thousand children, Baldwin assembled a staff of fifteen probation officers, most of whom were older than he was. Some members of the state legislature thought he was too young to handle so much responsibility and passed a law setting twenty-five as the minimum age of a probation officer. However, the law did not affect Baldwin, who had just turned twenty-five.

Baldwin's talent for organizing developed quickly in his new job. The year after he became a probation officer, he helped establish the National Probation Officers Association. In St. Louis, he created the Social Service Conference for social workers, the Council of Social Agencies, and an association of neighborhood civic groups. Baldwin was also a key player in the organization of the first group of St. Louis social workers to enroll both whites and African Americans. Baldwin possessed enormous energy and displayed a willingness to turn every social occasion into an opportunity to advance his cause. It didn't hurt that he was also attractive. "Tall, wiry, handsome and vigorous," he was one of the city's most eligible bachelors and was invited to all the important social events. Baldwin was also on the rise professionally. In 1910, he left the juvenile court to become the leader of the St. Louis Civic League, a leading reform group, where he led the fight for the reform of municipal government.[24]

But the new job did not halt a growing dissatisfaction with the reform movement. Baldwin began to believe that the problems created by industrial society ran deeper than the measures that reformers were pursuing to correct them. Social workers and probation officers attempted to help people without recommending any way to eliminate the poverty that was the source of their problems. Many liberals came to believe that capitalism itself would have to be eliminated. But Baldwin was not attracted to socialism. Socialists were obsessed "with a scheme of salvation." They were "too doctrinaire, too German and too old," he said. Indeed, he was skeptical of all radicals until he was dragged by friends to hear a speech by Emma Goldman. The speech was a revelation. "Here was a vision of the end of poverty and injustice by free association of those who worked, by the abolition of privilege, and by the organized power of the exploited," Baldwin recalled many years later. Baldwin was particularly attracted by Goldman's exposition of anarchism. His native belief in individualism responded strongly to the demand for the abolition of government and the free development of the potential of every man. He arranged to meet "Red Emma" and helped organize several speaking engagements for her.[25]

Baldwin would never lose his attraction to radicalism. He had been raised to care about those who were less fortunate than him. "I was for the underdog, whoever he was, by training and instinct, and I had an endless capacity for indignation at injustice," Baldwin told an interviewer fifty years later. "Any challenge to freedom aroused me and I was not satisfied until I acted."[26] It was this passion that led the respectable leader of the St. Louis Civic League to provide bail for Wobblies who had been jailed for refusing to pay for their meals in local restaurants. (They told the owners to bill the mayor.) It also prompted him to take up his first free speech case. When Margaret Sanger, the birth control advocate, was barred from speaking at a private hall, Baldwin persuaded her to present her address on the steps of the building. With a large contingent of police standing by, Baldwin introduced Sanger, who proceeded to give her speech. Baldwin was driven not just by his sympathy for the underdog. He believed that it was people like Emma Goldman and Margaret Sanger who moved humanity forward. "I am dead certain that human progress depends on those heretics, rebels and dreamers...whose 'holy dis-

content' has challenged established authority and created the expanding visions mankind may yet realize," Baldwin said.[27]

One reason that Baldwin admired radicals so much was that
he knew he could not do what they did. Some could plunge themselves into the proletarian movement, cutting their ties to family and
friends. While Baldwin would later pose as a working man to experience industrial life directly, he could never permanently "unclass"
himself. He acknowledged that he felt guilt about this. Yet there was
more involved than an unwillingness to deprive himself of the com-
forts of an independent income. Baldwin felt a strong sense of responsibility to the organizations that he worked for. "I have long had
the failing, if it is that, of accepting the philosophy of the lesser evil
up to the point of a clear collision with principles I couldn't surrender," he said. Roger Baldwin was not a prophet. He was an idealist
who gave up the promise of utopia for incremental gains in social
justice. He was the perfect man to lead the fight for free speech.[28]

Baldwin embarked on his civil liberties career in April 1917. A pacifist, he had been appalled by the country's rapid transformation from
a nation "too proud to fight" to one that was preparing to fight the
war "to end all wars." Although he was active in the peace movement in St. Louis, he was impatient to join a national organization.
He volunteered his services to Crystal Eastman, the executive secretary of the AUAM. "How and where in your judgment could you
use me?" he asked in a letter. He also said he would work for free. A
short while later, he arrived in New York. Although America's entry
into the war seemed inevitable by then, there was still important
work to do. After Congress passed a conscription act in May, thousands of pacifists found themselves in dire need of help. The Selec-
tive Service Act exempted from military service only members of
the three "historic peace churches" (the Quakers, the Mennonites,
and the Brethren). Other pacifists were being inducted and sent to
military training camps, where they were beaten and jailed in an
effort to force them to fight. The AUAM was soon being bom-
barded with requests for legal advice. In addition to pleas from the
men who were already in the military, it counseled those who hoped
to win exemption. AUAM lawyers took on the cases of hundreds of
men every week.[29]

Baldwin brought to his new job all of the energy and self-confidence that had been his trademark in St. Louis. He felt sure that he would be able to influence high Washington officials. Many of them were wellborn like him, and not a few were former Harvard classmates. The Wilson administration also included men like Secretary of War Newton Baker, who had been leaders in the reform movement. Baldwin assumed that he shared certain values with these officials: certainly, no one wanted to see conscientious objectors abused, and everyone agreed on the importance of free speech. He did everything he could to assure them that he wanted to cooperate with the government in resolving the problems created by the draft. "We don't want to make a move without consulting you," Baldwin wrote to Frederick D. Keppel, the assistant secretary of war. Above all, Baldwin was confident in his own considerable skill at public relations. He recognized that in a time of war government critics had to be particularly careful to present themselves as loyal to the nation's traditions. To an organizer of an antiwar rally, Baldwin recommended: "We want also to look like patriots in everything we do. We want to get a good lot of flags, talk a good deal about the Constitution and what our forefathers wanted to make of this country, and to show that we are really the folks that really stand for the spirit of our institutions." Baldwin was certain that breeding, contacts, and public relations would go a long way toward minimizing wartime repression.[30]

His confidence was entirely misplaced. He did indeed enjoy extraordinary access to high officials of the Wilson administration. He met with the secretary of war himself in June and kept up a regular correspondence with his assistant, Keppel. But once war had been declared, the Wilson administration became entirely focused on winning, and everyone who wasn't loudly prowar was suspected of disloyalty. The AUAM and other pacifist organizations inevitably came under suspicion for their defense of conscientious objectors. In May, Baldwin had called together the representatives of other pacifist groups and created the Bureau for Conscientious Objectors (BCO), which operated as a division of the AUAM. Although Baldwin strongly denied it, many government officials suspected that the purpose of the BCO was not to defend the rights of the conscientious objectors but to obstruct the draft, which was now a crime. Justice

Department agents visited the AUAM office in Washington on more than one occasion as part of an inquiry into its loyalty. Although the organization was told that its activities "would not be interfered with," the *Washington Post* reported in June 1917 that the AUAM was under government surveillance.[31]

Lillian Wald and Paul U. Kellogg, the cochairs of the AUAM, were alarmed that they might have come under suspicion of disloyalty. "We cannot plan continuance of our program which entails friendly government relations . . . and at the same time drift into being a party of opposition to the government," Wald warned. She wanted the Bureau for Conscientious Objectors to be removed from the AUAM. Baldwin objected. "Having created conscientious objectors to war, we ought to stand by them," he said.[32] A majority of the board supported Baldwin. To placate Wald, however, they renamed Baldwin's project the Civil Liberties Bureau in the hope that this would make it more acceptable to the government. Crystal Eastman, who proposed the compromise, argued that no one would deny the importance of protecting the civil liberties of all Americans. Baldwin opened the new Civil Liberties Bureau on July 2, just two weeks after the passage of the Espionage Act.

The Civil Liberties Bureau reflected the pacifist background from which it had emerged. Its directing committee was made up largely of men and women who opposed war for religious reasons. Its chairman was a Quaker lawyer, L. Hollingsworth Wood, and the committee included several clergymen, Norman Thomas, a Presbyterian; John Haynes Holmes, a Unitarian; and Judah L. Magnes, a rabbi. The first concern of the religious members was the treatment of the conscientious objectors who were suffering for their religious beliefs. However, the committee also included two social workers, Baldwin and Eastman, and was soon joined by two lawyers, Walter Nelles and Albert DeSilver, who would quit their successful practices to devote themselves to civil liberties work.

The committee held long meetings over lunch at the Civic Club on West Twelfth Street every Monday. As the weather grew hotter, the meetings were adjourned to a picnic table in the club courtyard. There the committee members reviewed the growing list of cases involving the violation of civil liberties. In addition to news of the mistreatment of conscientious objectors, every week brought new reports of mob violence against Socialists, immigrants, and others suspected of being disloyal. There were also a growing number of acts of suppression by government. Meeting permits were denied to critics of the war, and meetings that did occur were often broken up by the police or with their connivance. Prosecutions under the Espionage Act were also increasing rapidly. There wasn't much the Civil Liberties Bureau could do about mob violence, but it worked hard to make Americans see the importance of civil liberties. It issued a pamphlet written by Norman Thomas, *War's Heretics,* which attempted to win sympathy for conscientious objectors by stressing the importance of liberty of conscience. The Civil Liberties Bureau also assisted the victims. At a time when most lawyers were refusing to take on the cases of people challenged under the Espionage Act, the Civil Liberties Bureau compiled a list of cooperating attorneys who would help them. It also solicited contributions to help clients make bail and pay for their defense. "We make no distinction as to whose liberties we aid in defending, except that we do not handle any cases of enemy aliens, spies or draft dodgers," the Civil Liberties Bureau explained in an early publication.[33]

But the launching of the Civil Liberties Bureau did not succeed in removing suspicion of the AUAM. Doubts about its loyalty grew in August when the AUAM agreed to send delegates to a "peace" convention sponsored by the People's Council of America for Democracy and Peace, a coalition of radical groups. This decision prompted the resignation of Lillian Wald as cochair of the organization. In one last effort to placate her and other social workers in the group, the AUAM board agreed to cut its ties to the Civil Liberties Bureau. On October 1, the Civil Liberties Bureau became a separate organization, the National Civil Liberties Bureau (NCLB).

The founding of the NCLB gave Baldwin the freedom to pursue more aggressive efforts to dramatize the widespread violation of civil liberties, but he quickly discovered that he could not count on the support of many liberals. He wanted to dramatize the problem of mob violence, and he thought he had found the perfect case in late October when the Reverend Herbert Bigelow, a Cincinnati pacifist, was kidnapped, whipped, and ordered to get out of town. Bigelow was a prominent Progressive reformer, and President Wilson himself condemned the attack. Baldwin attempted to organize a protest meeting in New York, but the National Association for the Advancement of Colored People and other liberal groups refused to participate. Historian Charles A. Beard feared the meeting would be more "an anti-war than a pro-liberty meeting." William English Walling, a prowar Socialist, believed the purpose of the meeting was "not the protection of free speech but the propaganda of an immediate or German-made peace." Charles Edward Russell, another Socialist, condemned it as "anti-American and anti-democratic."[34]

The program, American Liberties in Wartime, was held anyway and drew a large crowd to the Liberty Theater. It received extensive and sympathetic coverage in New York's Socialist newspaper, *The Call*. The audience listened breathlessly as Bigelow described his kidnapping. "The murderers!" a man shouted when Bigelow paused. Norman Thomas, a member of the NCLB board who would succeed Debs as the nation's most prominent Socialist leader, demanded an investigation into the treatment of conscientious objectors in military camps. It was left to Dr. Joseph McAfee to address the free expression issue raised by the Bigelow case. "It is supremely important that the American people have the right to think," McAfee said. "There was never so much need as now of sturdy thinking, clear thinking, unhampered thinking.... We demand that the government of the United States be buttressed by the free public discussion of every issue." But good coverage in a Socialist newspaper would not influence many Americans. The brief article in the *New York Times* sent a more powerful message. "Most of the people present apparently were in hearty disagreement with the Government's ban on seditious criticism of the war," the reporter wrote. One of the speakers was Lincoln Steffens, the most famous of the muckraking journalists who had helped launch the Progressive movement. Steffens had grown dissatisfied with reform, however, and had come to believe that capitalism was the root of the country's troubles. He also believed that capitalism had caused the war, a conviction he shared with the audience at the Liberty Theater. To the *Times* reporter, this remark and the reaction to it confirmed the disloyalty of both the speaker and the audience. "It cheered to the echo a remark...by Lincoln Steffens, who declared that the 'Kaiser did not start the war.'" Baldwin abandoned the idea of holding any more public programs during the war.[35]

The NCLB soon lost any chance of capturing public approval.

When the leaders of the IWW were brought to trial in April, NCLB published a pamphlet called *The Truth about the IWW,* which defended the radical group as a legitimate labor organization and rejected the charges of sedition that had been filed against its leaders. Baldwin had worked hard on the report, and historians would later uphold his argument that the IWW had never constituted a revolutionary threat. But Americans believed their government as the prosecutors laid out their case. Meanwhile, other federal officials were outraged that the NCLB would defend an organization that was obviously bent on the country's destruction. The government had had mixed feelings about Baldwin and his civil libertarians. Some officials considered them outright traitors, but their high-level contacts with others in the Wilson administration prevented the foes of the NCLB from taking action. For his part, Baldwin was doing everything he could to allay the concerns of his government friends. Conceding that the NCLB may have inadvertently crossed the now vague line between legal and illegal conduct, Baldwin assured Keppel of the War Department, "We are entirely willing to discontinue any [illegal] practices." He went even further, sending the Justice Department the names of financial contributors, cooperating attorneys, and the people on the NCLB mailing list, exposing all of them to potential prosecution if the NCLB was ever declared in violation of the Espionage Act. Such a disclosure would undoubtedly have led to outraged protests if the NCLB's supporters had been aware of it. But the issue soon became moot. On August 31, the FBI raided the NCLB headquarters at 70 Fifth Avenue, seizing all its records.[36]

Baldwin was shocked. Obviously, he would not have volunteered the NCLB records if he thought there was any possibility that they might be used against the organization and its supporters. His view had always been that the NCLB and the government had a common interest in protecting individual rights. Suddenly, the NCLB was confronting agents who were under orders to find anything that "either directly or indirectly, consciously or unconsciously, might tend to hinder winning the war, especially letters to or from anarchists, socialists, IWW's or any other God-damn fools." Walter Nelles, one of the NCLB attorneys, rejected the search warrant handed to him by agent R. H. Finch, telling him the warrant was not in proper legal form. Finch replied by drawing his gun and ordering Nelles to

stand aside. Nelles then called Baldwin, who arrived in a highly excited state. He "told us that he 'did not give a damn about anything—go ahead, lock him up, shoot him, hang him or anything
else,'" Finch reported. Nelles later described the scene to the directing committee, emphasizing the humor in it. "It was all Gilbert-and-
Sullivanesque, and no one on our committee was greatly alarmed,"
Lucille Milner, a committee member, recalled later.[37]

But the situation of the NCLB was no laughing matter. Only
two weeks before the raid, the post office had notified Baldwin that
it was banning fourteen of his pamphlets. A post office lawyer acknowledged privately to the Justice Department that the pamphlets
did not violate the Espionage Act but insisted that defending the
IWW did. Therefore, all NCLB activities were illegal. To make
matters worse, the NCLB was about to lose its leader. In August,
Congress had expanded the draft to include men between the ages of
thirty and forty-five. Baldwin was thirty-four, and the signs of his
impending conscription were everywhere. In early September, the
American Protective League (APL) had launched a nationwide hunt
for men of military age who had not registered for the draft. The
largest "slacker" raid detained more than twenty thousand young
men in Manhattan. The APL men were searching the streets when
Baldwin wrote a letter notifying the draft board that he would not
report for a physical:

> I am opposed to the use of force to accomplish any end, however good. I
> am therefore opposed to participation in this or any other war. My op-
> position is not only to direct military service, but to any service what-
> soever designed to help prosecute the war. I am furthermore opposed to
> the principle of conscription in time of war or peace, for any purpose
> whatever. I will decline to perform any service under compulsion re-
> gardless of its character.

Baldwin asked for no favors except a speedy trial. He would refuse
bail and share the fate of the indigent draft resisters who could not
afford to post bond. He intended to plead guilty and expected to be
sentenced to a year in jail.[38]

The government investigation of the NCLB raised the prospect
that the members of the directing committee would join Baldwin in

jail. One director urged the organization to reduce its activities at least temporarily and thus avoid doing anything to "otherwise aggravate the situation." The other members of the committee were also worried about being indicted, but they were more concerned that Baldwin might be the only one charged with violating the Espionage Act. "If they indict some and not all, I shall be greatly disappointed," Albert DeSilver wrote to his wife. "'Taint fair any other way because we are all equally responsible." Instead of retreating, they decided to counterattack. The NCLB had already filed a lawsuit challenging the post office's ban on its publications. The committee agreed to press ahead with its case and to file a new one in an effort to force the government to return its records. The committee members also agreed to intensify their efforts to draw press attention to their activities to make it as difficult as possible for the government to prosecute them. At the same time, to represent them in their dealings with the government, they hired attorney George Gordon Battle, a conservative southerner who had good connections with Tammany Hall, the Democratic machine that ran New York City.[39]

The strategy worked. The official who was leading the investigation, U.S. Attorney Francis G. Caffey of New York, told the attorney general that the NCLB could be indicted for many of its activities, including its defense of men who had been convicted for sedition. But other Justice Department officials urged caution. "As the avowed purpose at least of this Bureau is the protection of civil liberties . . . it is of the first [importance] that no action be taken by arrest, suppression or otherwise unless it be based upon facts showing a violation of the express provisions of the law," John Lord O'Brian, an assistant to the attorney general, wrote Caffey.[40] After reading Caffey's final report, O'Brian concluded that the NCLB had not violated the law. "The organization of defense of persons accused of a crime" is not "in and of itself a crime," he said.[41] The Justice Department also indicated at this time that it had no objection to the mailing of NCLB pamphlets, a move that cleared the way for a judge to order the post office to resume their delivery. These decisions, coming on the eve of the signing of the armistice in November 1918, were the first significant free speech victories during World War I. With the end of the war, the civil libertarians looked forward to an easing of repression, but things were about to get rapidly worse. Instead, the fear of communism began to grip the country. As the Red Scare got under way, they searched desperately for someone to stand up for individual rights. The one place that they were sure they would never find help was the courts.

The American courts had played an abysmal role in protecting free speech since 1917. Swayed by their own strong support for the war, judges sent more than one thousand people to jail. They argued that the First Amendment barred censorship of written speech only prior to its publication. Once a book or pamphlet had been published, the government could punish its author if it was socially harmful. This test of whether speech had a "bad tendency" became the major benchmark in Espionage Act cases. When the U.S. Court of Appeals upheld the conviction of a man whose book criticized the war but did not directly advocate illegal acts, it explained:

> It is true that disapproval of the war and the advocacy of peace are not crimes under the Espionage Act; but the question here ... is whether the nature and probable tendency and effect of the words ... are such as are calculated to produce the result condemned by the statute.... Printed matter may tend to obstruct the ... service even if it contains no mention of recruiting or enlistment. The service may be obstructed by attacking the justice of the cause for which the war is waged, and by undermining the spirit of loyalty which inspires men to enlist or to register for conscription in the service of their country.

The question of what the effect of antiwar speech would be was to be left to the jury to decide. But in the absence of a requirement that speech directly advocate illegal acts, it was clear how jurors, whose sons were fighting in France, would vote. In retrospect, it is remarkable that they didn't convict everyone charged under the Espionage Act.[42]

The U.S. Supreme Court had the power to reverse these decisions. But when the first Espionage Act cases finally arrived on appeal in March 1919, the Court gutted the First Amendment. In three cases, it endorsed the use of the bad tendency test during wartime and upheld long jail sentences for opponents of the war who had urged people to exercise their democratic rights. Justice Oliver Wendell Holmes wrote the opinions in all three cases for a unanimous court. A veteran of the Civil War, the seventy-seven-year-old Holmes, who sported a luxuriant, white handlebar mustache, was the oldest justice. Despite his age, he was known to possess one of the best legal minds on the Court. In 1905, he had rejected the deep conservatism of his colleagues by voting to uphold a pioneering New York statute that limited the labor of bakery workers to ten hours per day. It was in part because Holmes was the Court's most distinguished justice that his opinions in the Espionage Act cases were so disappointing to civil libertarians. In the first one, *Schenck v. United States,* Holmes observed that the First Amendment's protection of the right of free speech was obviously not absolute. "The most stringent protection of free speech would not protect a man in falsely shouting fire in a crowded theater, and causing a panic," he wrote. There were additional limitations in wartime. Congress had passed the Espionage Act to protect the government's ability to successfully prosecute the war. It had a right to limit words that posed "a clear and present danger" of disrupting the war effort. A week after deciding the *Schenck* case, the Supreme Court handed down similar rulings in *Frohwerk v. U.S.* and *Debs v. U.S.,* making it clear that the government was free to suppress dissident speech during wartime.[43]

But the issue of free speech during wartime was being rapidly eclipsed by new threats to First Amendment rights. As the fear of communism grew during 1919, many voices were raised to demand a continuation of the censorship of the war years. Rioting had broken out in several cities on May 1 when workers gathered to celebrate May Day, an international holiday for labor. Although most of the rioting was started by ex-soldiers and other "patriotic" citizens, many state legislatures responded by banning the display of red flags, which they saw as a symbol of revolution. Politicians also called for the suppression of radical speech. Oregon and Oklahoma passed laws that made it a crime to advocate unlawful acts "as a means of accomplishing...industrial or political ends, or...industrial or political revolution, or for profit." The mayor of New York wanted to ban meetings that tended "to incite the minds of people to a proposition likely to breed a disregard of the law," and the mayor of Toledo, Ohio, prohibited any meeting anywhere in the city "where it is suspected a man of radical tendencies will speak." In Washington, Congress was giving serious consideration to a bill providing ten years' imprisonment for anyone who encouraged resistance to the United States, defied or disregarded the Constitution or laws of the United States, or advocated any change in the form of government except in a manner provided for by the Constitution. Under the bill, almost any protest against government could be treated as a federal crime.[44]

Yet, even as the Red Scare grew, there were signs of a new awareness of the importance of free speech, particularly among lawyers. In fact, the legal profession had never been unanimous in its view of the Espionage Act. In the first months of the war, U.S. District Court judge Learned Hand had ordered the post office to resume the delivery of *The Masses*. Hand conceded that the magazine's antiwar articles and cartoons might well undermine support for the war, even causing men to resist the draft. "Political agitation . . . may stimulate men to the violation of the law," he wrote in his decision. However, nothing in the magazine expressly urged illegal acts. There is a difference between political advocacy, which is a safeguard of free government, and violent resistance, which undermines government. This "distinction . . . is not a scholastic subterfuge, but a hard-bought acquisition in the fight for freedom," Hand said.[45] Six months later, George Bourquin, a federal judge in Montana, also refused to punish antiwar speech. The government had indicted Ves Hall for saying that Germany would "whip" the United States and that "the United States was only fighting for Wall Street millionaires." Bourquin ordered the jury to acquit Hall because his remarks were clearly statements of opinion, not an attempt to cause insubordination in the armed forces. The Espionage Act was not intended "to suppress criticism or denunciation, truth or slander, oratory or gossip, argument or loose talk," he declared.[46]

Hand and Bourquin paid a price for their independence. Hand's decision was quickly appealed and reversed, and he was passed over for promotion when the next opening occurred on the appeals court. Bourquin's ruling led to howls of protest locally where mine operators were eager to use the federal government to suppress the Wobblies. There were calls for Bourquin's impeachment and removal from office, and the governor convened a special session of the legislature to pass a law that would suppress the speech of people like Ves Hall. Many in Congress were also outraged, and at the suggestion of the Justice Department an amendment to the Espionage Act was passed in May. The Sedition Act made it a crime to speak, print, or write "any disloyal, profane, scurrilous, or abusive language . . . as regards the form of government of the United States."[47]

If a few judges could not hold back the wave of suppression, however, their defense of free expression inspired others to question the legal arguments that were being used to suppress the antiwar movement. There were at least a handful of lawyers who were willing to challenge the status quo. In addition to NCLB board members Walter Nelles and Albert DeSilver, there were those who answered the NCLB's call for "cooperating attorneys" who were willing to take on the highly unpopular task of defending antiwar protesters. A number of law school professors were also sympathetic. In the summer of 1918, a thirty-two-year-old professor at Harvard Law School began a systematic study of the use of the Espionage Act to suppress political speech. Zechariah D. Chafee Jr. was a very unlikely candidate to emerge as the champion of the First Amendment rights of Socialists, Wobblies, and other radicals. Born in Providence, his father was a wealthy iron manufacturer, and his mother was a descendant of Roger Williams, the founder of the Rhode Island colony. "My family is a family that has money," Chafee would say later. "I believe in property and I believe in making money."[48] A graduate of Brown University and Harvard Law School, Chafee practiced law in Providence for several years before he joined the Harvard Law School faculty.

Although a member of the establishment, Chafee had an instinctive sympathy for the underdog. At Brown, a classmate recalled, "his sense of justice did impel him to spring to the defense of any who he felt were unjustly oppressed."[49] He was also an independent thinker. A colleague on the Harvard Law School faculty remembered him making a commotion in the library. "Every now and then there was a great noise, and I would turn around and Chafee had discovered a new idea and was shouting his pleasure," he said.[50] Chafee was also eager to establish a career as a writer. Herbert Croly, the editor of *The New Republic,* gave him his first assignment. Harold J. Laski, a well-known English political scientist, taught at Harvard and knew

Chafee. He told Croly that Chafee was working on a scholarly article about freedom of speech during wartime. Croly invited Chafee
to submit a summary of his longer work that would be suitable for a
general audience. Chafee's article, "Freedom of Speech," appeared
in *The New Republic* on November 16, 1918, five days after the war
had ended. It was the opening shot in a campaign to create a legal
and political defense of free speech that would make it possible to
protect dissent in peacetime and enable it to withstand the rigors of
the next war.

Chafee said that the country had made a mistake. "Under the
pressure of a great crisis," it had allowed the desire to win the war to
become an attack upon freedom of speech. "Judges . . . have interpreted the 1917 Act so broadly as to make practically all opposition
to the war criminal," he said. As a result, they threatened a freedom at the core of democracy. "One of the most important purposes
of society and government is the discovery and spread of truth on
subjects of general concern," Chafee wrote. "This is possible only
through absolutely unlimited discussion." Chafee acknowledged that
government had other purposes that potentially clashed with free
speech—maintaining order, educating the young, and providing for
national defense. Yet he insisted that protecting freedom of speech
was as important as any of the other functions of government. "Unlimited discussion sometimes interferes with these purposes, which
must then be balanced against freedom of speech, but freedom of
speech ought to weigh heavily in the balance," he argued. "The First
Amendment gives binding force to this principle of political wisdom." During the war, judges had not attempted to strike a balance;
they had suppressed any speech that could undermine the war effort.
But speech must be free even in wartime, Chafee insisted. "The
pacifists and Socialists are wrong now, but they may be right the next
time," he said. "The only way to find out whether a war is unjust is
to let people say so."[51]

The Supreme Court's decisions upholding the Espionage Act
in March 1919 prompted more lawyers to speak out. The Court's
refusal to free Eugene Debs was particularly shocking because unlike the defendants in the other cases, Debs had carefully avoided
saying anything that could be construed as an effort to disrupt the
draft. Ernst Freund, a distinguished legal scholar at the University of

Chicago, was incensed by the *Debs* decision. "To know what you may do and what you may not do, and how far you may go in criticism, is the first condition of political liberty," Freund wrote in *The New Republic*. The "bad tendency" test failed because it allowed judges and juries to decide for themselves what speech was illegal. The Supreme Court had now accepted that standard, Freund said, pointing his finger directly at Oliver Wendell Holmes, who had written the opinions. "Justice Holmes would make us believe that the relation of the speech to obstruction is like that of the shout of Fire! in a crowded theater to the resulting panic," Freund said. But the parallel was "manifestly inappropriate." "The peril resulting to the national cause from toleration of adverse opinion is largely imaginary," he concluded. "In any case it is slight as compared with the permanent danger of intolerance to free institutions."[52]

Holmes was wounded by the criticism directed at the *Debs* decision. He wrote an acquaintance that the case had caused "a lot of jaw about free speech." He even drafted a letter to the editor of *The New Republic* responding to Freund's article that he decided not to send. But his conscience was also bothering him. "I hated to have to write the Debs case and still more those of the other poor devils before us the same day and the week before," he wrote in his unsent letter to the editor. "I think it is quite possible that if I had been on the jury I should have been for acquittal."[53] He believed he had taken the only position possible given the facts that were presented to him. Over the next six months, however, the seventy-eight-year-old justice began to change his mind about the importance of free speech. As the panic of the Red Scare climbed rapidly, he corresponded about the issue with Judge Learned Hand and others. When Chafee's scholarly article "Free Speech in Wartime" was published in June, Harold Laski sent it to Holmes and later arranged for the justice to meet the young man for tea at his home. The path was cleared for a remarkable reversal by a member of the Supreme Court and a critical turning point in the growth of free speech.

On November 10, the U.S. Supreme Court handed down another decision affirming the power of the government to punish speech under the Espionage Act. In the case of *Abrams v. U.S.,* it upheld long prison terms for four immigrants who had printed and distributed a pamphlet calling on workers to strike in protest over the use of American troops in Siberia, which they interpreted as an attempt to undermine the Russian Revolution. But this time the decision was not unanimous. Holmes wrote a dissenting opinion joined by Louis Brandeis that questioned the danger posed by "the surreptitious publishing of a silly pamphlet by an unknown man." The other justices saw nothing silly about it, and they were so disturbed by the prospect of a dissent by Holmes that three of them visited him at his home and tried to dissuade him. Holmes's wife, Fanny, joined the discussion and urged her husband to change his mind. But the old man politely declined.[54] In the *Schenck* case, Holmes had first enunciated the idea that speech could be restricted when it posed "a clear and present danger" to the country. In his dissent, he made it clear that such a threat would exist only under very narrow circumstances. "It is only the present danger of immediate evil or an intent to bring it about that warrants Congress in setting a limit to the expression of opinion," he wrote.[55] That danger did not exist in the Abrams case, Holmes said. Although he did not say so, there was a clear implication that he no longer believed that threat had existed in the vast majority of the Espionage Act cases.

The dissent by Holmes and Brandeis didn't help the defendants in the Abrams case. They were sent to prison and eventually deported. But it meant a great deal to those who were fighting to expand protections for free speech. In the final paragraph of his opinion, Holmes embraced the view advanced by Chafee and others that unfettered debate is the only way to attain truth. He called for "a free trade in ideas." "The best test of truth is the power of the thought to get itself accepted in the competition of the market," he said. He acknowledged that there was a risk involved. But it was a risk that was inherent in democratic government:

> It is an experiment, as all life is an experiment. Every year if not every day we have to wager our salvation upon some prophecy based upon imperfect knowledge. While that experiment is part of our system I think that we should be eternally vigilant against attempts to check the expression of opinions that we loathe and believe to be fraught with death, unless they so imminently threaten immediate interference with the lawful and pressing purposes of the law that an immediate check is required to save the country.

At the end of his opinion, Holmes wished he could say more. "I regret that I cannot put into more impressive words my belief that in their conviction upon this indictment the defendants were deprived of their rights under the Constitution," he wrote. But free speech advocates were overjoyed. Chafee called it a "magnificent exposition of the philosophic basis" of the First Amendment. Roscoe Pound, the head of Harvard Law School, described it as "a document of human liberty."[56] Holmes had given the cause of free speech two things it badly needed: prestige and an eloquence that would inspire others to take up the fight.

The civil libertarians needed all the encouragement they could get. The Justice Department had launched its first national roundup of radicals just three days before the *Abrams* decision was announced. As it prepared for even bigger raids early in the new year, it took care of some long-unfinished business by putting Emma Goldman and 248 other foreign-born radicals on a boat and sending them to Russia, a move that drew wild acclaim throughout the country. It was in this atmosphere of frenzied assault on Bolshevism that the lower house of the New York legislature, the assembly, committed one of the most flagrant acts of suppression during the entire Red Scare. Soon after the opening of the first session of the year, Speaker Thaddeus Sweet summoned the assembly's five Socialist members to appear before him in the well of the house. As the five men stood under the watchful eye of the sergeant-at-arms, Sweet made a speech accusing them of being unfit to serve in the legislature because they belonged to an organization that was committed to the overthrow of the government. He then made a motion that they be suspended pending further investigation. Although they were not permitted to reply to Sweet, the Socialists were allowed to return to their seats and vote on the motion. It was approved 140-6.

The suspension of the Socialist assemblymen caused a storm of protest from people across the political spectrum. Naturally, the Socialists were outraged. But so were many respectable men and women who were totally opposed to their views. This opposition was symbolized by the eminent lawyer Charles Evans Hughes Jr. Hughes was a Republican who had served two terms as governor of New York and served briefly on the U.S. Supreme Court before resigning to run for president in 1912. Hughes had been a reformer during his governorship, but no one doubted him when he described himself as "utterly opposed to Socialism." Nevertheless, Hughes became the leader in the fight to reinstate the Socialists. Two days after the suspension, he wrote an open letter to Sweet that condemned the suspension as "absolutely opposed to the fundamental principles of our government." The fact that all the Socialists in the assembly had been removed was proof that "the proceeding is virtually an attempt to indict a political party and to deny it representation in the Legislature," he said. Such a course was politically unwise. "Is it proposed to drive the Socialists to revolution by denying them participation in the means we have provided for orderly discussion of proposed changes in our laws?" Hughes asked. Such a course was not only politically unwise but showed a lack of faith in American institutions. "I have sufficient confidence in our institutions to believe that they will survive all the onslaughts of discussion and political controversy. But democracy cannot be preserved if representation is denied," Hughes concluded.[57] Hughes carried his fight to both the New York City and New York State bar associations, where he won the approval of resolutions condemning the assembly by solid majorities and then led a delegation of lawyers to Albany, where he tried unsuccessfully to intervene in the "trial" of the Socialists.

Opposition to the excesses of the Red Scare was growing in other places as well. Less than a week after the New York Assembly committed its act of infamy, some of the leading critics of the Palmer Raids gathered at the Harvard Liberal Club in Boston. "We should imitate the courage of our ancestors," Zechariah Chafee announced. "What are we afraid of? Have we not faith in our institutions and the common sense of our people?" In a letter read to the meeting, Oliver Wendell Holmes also played down the danger of the moment. "With effervescing opinions, as with . . . champagne, the quickest way to let them get flat is to let them get exposed to the air," he wrote. George W. Anderson had been a federal prosecutor during the war, charged with ferreting out pro-German plots and espionage. Now a federal judge, he told the meeting that not one-half of 1 percent of the alleged plots had been real. The true danger was posed by "the prating pseudo-patriots," Anderson said. "It is time that we had freedom of speech for the just contempt that every wholesome-minded citizen has and should have for the pretentious, noisy heresy hunter of these hysterical times."[58]

The "heresy hunters" were unpersuaded. Despite an outpouring of criticism and open ridicule, the members of New York Assembly "convicted" and expelled the Socialists. They also joined with the Senate to pass a number of antiradical measures called the Lusk laws. The laws had been drafted by a special committee of the legislature that had been appointed just as the Red Scare was getting under way in early 1919. Led by Senator Clayton Lusk, the committee pursued its investigation of the Bolshevist "threat" through raids and arrests of dubious legality. Not surprisingly, its legislative recommendations showed little respect for individual liberty or due process. One law required public school teachers to obtain a license from the state commissioner of education showing that they supported the state and federal constitutions and were loyal to "the institutions and laws" of the country; the license could be revoked without benefit of a hearing. The state board of regents was given the power to deny accreditation to any private school whose course of instruction was "detrimental to the public interest." Another measure authorized the courts to remove from the ballot any political organization whose doctrines violated the state or federal constitution or "imperil or destroy the government of the country."

The veto of the Lusk laws seemed a foregone conclusion by the time they reached the desk of Governor Alfred E. Smith in May 1920. Over the strong opposition of Democratic legislative leaders, Smith had condemned the suspension of the Socialists only two days after the assembly vote. His veto messages roundly condemned the Lusk bills. The teacher-licensing bill "deprives teachers of their right to freedom of thought," Smith said. "It limits the teaching staff of the public schools to those only who lack the courage or the mind to exercise their legal right to just criticism of existing institutions."[59] The school-licensing bill gave the state the power to ban the teaching of any controversial opinion, including the importance of a minimum wage or child labor laws. Echoing Holmes, Smith observed that "the clash of conflicting opinions, from which progress arises more than from any other source, would be abolished by law, tolerance and intellectual freedom destroyed, and an intellectual autocracy imposed upon the people."[60] Smith's most eloquent words were saved for the veto of the bill providing for the disenfranchising radical political parties:

This country has lived and thrived from its inception until today . . .
upon the fundamental principles set forth in the Declaration of Independence, one of which was the declaration that all men are created
equal. No matter to what extent we may disagree with our neighbor, he
is entitled to his own opinion, and, until the time arrives when he seeks
by violation of law to urge his opinion upon his neighbor, he must be
left free not only to have it but to express it. . . . It is a confession of the
weakness of our own faith in the righteousness of our cause when we attempt to suppress by law those who do not agree with us.[61]

Smith's vetoes on May 20 marked a symbolic end to the Red
Scare. The economic recession following the end of the war had
been sharp, but it proved to be short-lived. Factories were hiring
again, and inflation was disappearing. The Red hunters also had
themselves to blame. They had clearly oversold the threat of radicalism. Attorney General Palmer had boldly predicted that the country
would see new disturbances on May Day. When these failed to ma-
terialize, newspapers that had once been terrified by his warnings
began to make fun of him, and his once promising prospects of winning the 1920 Democratic nomination plummeted. Roger Baldwin,
Zechariah Chafee, and the other civil libertarians had also helped.
With the encouragement of Oliver Wendell Holmes, they had gathered support for the idea that free speech plays a critical role in the
democratic process. The importance of free speech was central to the
criticism of abuses like the expulsion of the New York Socialists and
the passage of the Lusk laws. Having experienced some success, the
civil libertarians showed no interest in disbanding. In January 1920,
the National Civil Liberties Bureau changed its name to the American Civil Liberties Union. The fight for free speech had just begun.

CHAPTER 2

Mob Rule, 1921–1930

On a drizzly spring afternoon in May 1920, Sid Hatfield, the twenty-eight-year-old police chief in Matewan, West Virginia, attempted to arrest thirteen men working for the Baldwin-Felts Detective Agency who had just finished a hard day's work evicting union miners from housing owned by the Stone Mountain Coal Company. Hatfield had asked Mayor Cabbell Testerman, the town druggist, to authorize the arrest of the Baldwin men for possessing firearms in the town limits. There was no question that they were carrying guns—each man had a high-powered rifle, and some of them were wearing sidearms as well. But the Baldwin men had been deputized by officials in a neighboring town at the company's request. They refused to recognize the Matewan warrant and told Hatfield he was under arrest for obstructing them. They handed Mayor Testerman a warrant, which he rejected as bogus. There is still a debate about who fired first. Albert C. Felts shot the mayor; Hatfield shot Felts and his brother, Lee. Miners opened fire on the other Baldwin men, killing seven and forcing the others to flee across the Tug River into Kentucky. Ten men died, including Testerman and the Felts brothers.[1]

The Matewan "massacre" triggered a civil war in West Virginia. The governor sent the state militia into the town to disarm "Two-gun" Sid and the miners who had supported him. Hatfield and twenty-three others were indicted for murdering the Baldwin men, but a jury of miners acquitted them. They had become heroes to men who had been oppressed for decades: the miners lived in company houses and were paid in scrip that they were forced to spend in company stores that charged inflated prices; they worked in one of the most dangerous occupations in the nation, but wages were low, and the pay was cut whenever there was a glut in the market. Their only hope to improve their condition was to join a union, but the coal companies adamantly refused to bargain with union representatives. The companies created private armies to intimidate the miners and made widespread use of spies to ferret out any evidence of efforts to unionize. "I joined the union one morning in Williamson, and when I got back to the mine in the afternoon I was told to get my pay and get out of my house before supper," one miner explained. The Baldwin men who were attacked in Matewan had been ousting recent recruits to the United Mine Workers Union. Hatfield was a former miner himself, and his refusal to allow the eviction of miners in the Matewan town limits was the real cause of the deadly conflict. Hatfield's example inspired the miners in the southern part of the state. Union membership grew, and so did the evictions. More than ten thousand people evicted by the Stone Mountain Coal Company were soon living in tents.[2]

Violence also grew. When the company refused again to meet with union leaders, the United Mine Workers declared a strike. The company answered by bringing in African Americans and immigrants to work in the mines. Members of the state police attacked one of the largest tent colonies, killing an unarmed striker and destroying tents and the strikers' food supplies. High-powered rifles were smuggled to the strikers, who were equipped mostly with squirrel guns and other small-caliber weapons. Strikers exchanged more than 100,000 shots with mine guards in a three-day battle in the spring of 1921. "Passengers on the Norfolk and Western trains went through the battle zone crouching on the floors of the cars while glass crashed overhead," according to one report. Then, on August 1, the Baldwin-Felts Agency company got its revenge on Sid Hatfield, gunning him down as he walked unarmed up the steps of a county courthouse with his wife. Thousands of miners declared that they had had enough and began marching on Logan County, an antiunion stronghold. President Warren G. Harding sent in federal troops, including General Billy Mitchell, the head of the army air corps. "How will you handle masses of men under cover in the gullies?" Mitchell was asked. "Gas," Mitchell said. "You understand we wouldn't try to kill these people at first. We'd drop tear gas all over the place. If they refused to disperse then we'd open up with artillery preparation and everything."[3]

The country appeared to be on the brink of a new cycle of industrial violence. The conflict between capital and labor had generated some of the most horrific acts of violence in American history. In 1892, striking steelworkers had opened fire on barges that were being used to bring nonunion men to the Carnegie mills in Homestead, Pennsylvania. Two years later, thirty-eight were killed during a strike against the Pullman Palace Car Company. Open warfare between miners and the state militia killed men on both sides during the Ludlow strike in Colorado and culminated in the "Ludlow massacre," an attack on a tent colony that took the lives of 19, including 2 women and 12 children. Labor unrest subsided during World War I as unions agreed to postpone wage demands in return for recognition by the companies. However, once the war was over, attitudes hardened on both sides as the companies again refused to bargain with the unions and working men demanded higher wages. More than four million men participated in 3,600 strikes in 1919 alone. "Is violence the way out of our industrial disputes?" the Reverend John Haynes Holmes asked in 1920.

> Capital is outraged when a bomb is thrown or a torch kindled, but thinks nothing of throwing a bullet, or a bayonet, or even an injunction, against the workers. Labour on the other hand is never tired of denouncing lock-outs, and constabularies, and deportations, but declares a strike, assaults a scab, or coerces the general public, with perfect equanimity. It is the philosophy of nearly all of us, in other words, that that violence is all right provided it is used by ourselves, in our wisdom, for the interests which we regard as indispensable to human welfare.[4]

The leaders of the new American Civil Liberties Union (ACLU) were not sanguine. "Never before in American history were the forces of reaction so completely in control of our political and economic life," the ACLU proclaimed in September 1921.

> Never before were the civil rights guaranteed by constitutional provision so generally ignored and violated.... Political democracy as con-

ceived by many of America's greatest leaders does not exist, except in a few communities. This condition is not yet understood by the public at large. They are drugged by propaganda and blinded by a press necessarily subservient to property interests. Dazed by the kaleidoscopic changes of the last few years, the rank and file citizens accept the dictatorship of property in the name of patriotism.

There was one slim hope of avoiding an escalation of labor violence. If Americans would put their faith in civil liberties, it might be possible to find compromises that would eliminate the need for violence. Workers must be allowed to join unions, hold meetings, strike, and picket. It was true that the Carnegies and Rockefellers possessed great power and would not surrender it soon. "However, the mere public assertion of the principle of freedom of opinion in the words or deeds of individuals, or weak minorities, helps win it recognition, and in the long run makes for tolerance and against resort to violence." Again and again in the 1920s, the ACLU would send its representatives into dangerous labor conflicts to assert the constitutional right to protest. To many, it seemed a quixotic dream. They were locked up, assaulted, and driven out of town. But the union was right. Civil liberties began to assume a substance that they had never possessed before, and the promise that they might one day provide a counterbalance to the power of the mob began to come true.[5]

By 1920, the underlying causes of industrial violence were well known. They had been laid out in a government report in 1915. After hearing more than seven hundred witnesses, the United States Commission on Industrial Relations had identified four major problems. Workers had not shared in the fruits of the enormous economic growth that the country had experienced. Between 25 and 33 percent of working families received too little to support "anything like a comfortable decent condition." Workers were also haunted by the threat of a sudden layoff. A majority were unemployed for up to ten weeks in any twelve-month period. These men and women did not view the government as their friend. On the contrary, they believed that every agency of the government operated to uphold the power of their bosses and thus to degrade them further. The best proof of this was the refusal of government to offer them any support in their efforts to organize.[6]

Reformers were particularly critical of the role of the courts. During the Progressive Era, the courts had blocked laws to protect the health and safety of workers, declaring it to be unconstitutional to establish a minimum wage for women and to ban child labor. The courts had also routinely intervened in labor disputes on the side of capital. "Our courts are the most pernicious part of our political institutions," Theodore Schroeder, the head of the Free Speech League, told the industrial commission during his testimony. There is an "absolute incapacity of any judge in the United States to understand what free speech means," Schroeder insisted. "It is my opinion that we have today, in spite of our Constitution, more varieties of penalized opinion than any other country in the world."[7]

Schroeder identified the many ways that courts violated the First Amendment rights of workers and their advocates. The main weapon of the employer in labor disputes was the injunction. While judges argued that injunctions were necessary to preserve public peace, their prohibitions often made it impossible for striking workers to defend their rights. Schroeder cited an injunction in a Seattle case that barred strikers from

> using in any way any language tending to incite the defendant's auditors, or the public, to lawlessness, or tending in any way to arouse the anger and incite the antagonism or wrath of the citizens; and also from using any violence or abusive language of any kind toward the United States Government, the State of Washington, or the city of Seattle, or its public officials, and from using language ridiculing the institutions of this country and holding them up to ridicule.

Injunctions often limited picketing to the point where the public was unaware that a strike was under way. But injunctions were only one of the weapons that the courts had used against labor. Federal laws against mailing obscene material and anything with scurrilous or defamatory words on the exterior had been used to suppress radical publications. Companies used the libel laws to silence critics, and sedition laws to shut down radical publications that contained threats of violence. Meanwhile, the courts ignored the threats that appeared in material disseminated by employers.[8]

The problem, Schroeder said, is that the courts and the police failed to appreciate that freedom of speech needed protecting, too. "The unconscious assumption of the courts and policemen always is that the purpose of their existence are [*sic*] the maintenance of peace at the expense of freedom of speech and the press rather than the maintenance of peace in spite of such freedom," Schroeder explained. The police had broken up over one hundred meetings because they feared that Emma Goldman might start a riot. They arrested the writer Upton Sinclair for silently marching in front of the Rockefeller headquarters in New York on the pretext that he might be attacked by outraged Rockefeller employees. The courts refused to punish the police for these abuses. "Of the thousands of men who have thus been wrongfully deprived of their constitutional liberties, I do not know of one who has ever secured any redress through courts," Schroeder said.[9]

Seven years later, in 1922, the nation's courts demonstrated that they remained deeply hostile to freedom of speech. In July, the 400,000 skilled craftsmen who maintained railroad engines and other equipment that kept the nation's transportation system running refused to accept a 12 percent wage cut and went out on strike. The public was overwhelmingly against the strike, which threatened to paralyze the economy just as the country was recovering from the postwar recession. Attorney General Harry M. Daugherty secured a sweeping injunction that prohibited the six striking unions from engaging in any acts that interfered with railroad operations. The order banned picketing and any effort to persuade railroad workers to leave their jobs, including "threats, violent or abusive language, opprobrious epithets ...jeers, entreaties, arguments, persuasion, rewards or otherwise." Union officials were forbidden to engage in any strike activity "by letters, telegrams, telephones, word of mouth."[10]

Some members of the press objected to the suppression of the strike. William Allen White was editor of the small but influential *Emporia Gazette* and a man of influence in the Republican Party at both the state and national level. He had spoken out strongly in support of free speech on many occasions in his long career, lately opposing the expulsion of the Socialists by the New York Assembly. When a Kansas court ordered merchants to remove signs from their windows indicating their support for the strikers, White took their side. He put the sign in the *Gazette*'s window and dared Governor Harry J. Allen, who was a friend, to arrest him. "I think your order restricts the liberty of utterance," White said. Allen had White arrested. The editor explained himself in an editorial, "To an Anxious Friend":

> You say that freedom of utterance is not for time of stress, and I reply with the sad truth that only in time of stress is freedom of utterance in danger. No one questions it in calm days, because it is not needed. And the reverse is true also; only when free utterance is suppressed is it needed, and when it is needed, it is most vital to justice.

The charges against White were later dropped, but two other journalists were not so lucky. Jacob Cohen, the editor of a small prolabor newspaper in Memphis, was sentenced to six months in jail for violating an injunction by denouncing strikebreakers as "snakes," "traitors," and "dirty scabs." When the editor of a Memphis daily newspaper attempted to defend Cohen's right to free speech, he was charged with contempt, too.[11]

The attack on free speech symbolized by the arrest of three editors produced a strong public protest. Liberal newspapers denounced the administration. "Liberty is not dead, and the right to free speech, a free press and unhampered assemblage will not be lightly surrendered," thundered the *New York Globe*. Even mainstream journalists worried about violating the injunction by publishing stories that were favorable to the unions or critical of the railroads. "The constitutional guarantees of a free press and free citizenship were taken away last Saturday when the First Amendment to the Constitution was abridged by Federal Injunction," *Editor and Publisher,* a newspaper trade journal, lamented. President Harding himself attempted to reassure the public that the injunction would be used only to suppress violence. But Attorney General Daugherty was clearly of two minds. When the strike was over, he insisted that he supported free speech. But the free speech that he supported was "not that freedom of speech which incites mob violence, destruction of life and property and attacks on the government."[12]

For the ACLU's Roger Baldwin, nothing was more important than helping labor win its fight for recognition of the right to collective bargaining. Emma Goldman had riveted Baldwin's attention on the fate of the working class, and he had not lost that concern when he began his fight for free speech during the war. Nor did it diminish when he went to prison in 1918 for refusing to be drafted. Even in prison, Baldwin had enjoyed the privilege that he had known throughout his life. The warden and many of his guards were Irish nationalists, and, therefore, sympathizers with anyone who refused to fight at the side of the British. The warden had allowed Baldwin to enjoy every comfort that the prison could offer, including leaving his cell door open at night so that he could continue reading and writing in the corridor.[13]

When Baldwin emerged from prison in July 1919, he was more determined than ever to pursue the fight for the working class. He took off a few weeks to marry Madeleine Z. Doty, a well-known journalist, lawyer, prison reformer, and feminist, with whom he exchanged self-authored vows. Doty promised a marriage of total freedom that might serve as a model "for the new brotherhood for which we strive, when all men shall live together in love and harmony, bound by no laws, subjected to no force—dominated wholly by love." Baldwin expressed the hope that the marriage would advance "my primary interest and joy . . . the great revolutionary struggle for freedom, so intense, so full of promise." Only a few weeks later, he left his new wife to get a taste of the life of a working man. Many of his friends opposed his plan. Big Bill Haywood complained that Baldwin's time would be better spent raising funds to pay the IWW's legal bills and told him to stay out of the kitchen in the IWW's camps. "Our boys like to eat good," he said. But Baldwin could not be dissuaded. In Chicago, he joined the Cooks and Waiters Union and marched on picket lines outside steel mills. He jumped on a freight train headed for St. Louis; shoveled ore into the smelter at a lead mine in Missouri; worked for a railroad for a couple of days in Youngstown, Ohio; and ended up cleaning ovens in a steel mill in Homestead, Pennsylvania. After several months, Baldwin returned to New York. He was ready to resume the fight for civil liberties, and he was convinced that the biggest battle would be the one for workers' rights.[14]

He made this clear in a memo outlining the goals of the ACLU that he presented to the board soon after his release from prison. In his absence, the organization had been busy fighting for the repeal of the Espionage Act and to obtain amnesty for the hundreds of people who were still in prison for their opposition to the war. But Baldwin was looking forward. "The cause we now serve is labor," he wrote. Its chief weapon would be publicity. The ACLU would join the battle where it was being fought—in the field. It would send "a few well known liberals" to challenge restrictions on union meetings in the Pennsylvania coal fields, where their arrests "would dramatize the situation effectively." The board approved the plan on January 12, 1920, a time when public opinion about free speech couldn't have been much worse. The second and largest of the Palmer Raids had just swept up thousands of radicals. Nevertheless, the ACLU opened for business a week later, operating on the ground floor of a three-story brick house on West Thirteenth Street in New York.[15]

The first major battle of the new organization would prove to be one of its severest tests. Baldwin had been reading about the struggle that the United Mine Workers (UMW) was waging to organize the miners of Mingo County, West Virginia. In March, he hired journalist John L. Spivak to go to West Virginia, meet with union officials, and make recommendations to the executive committee on the ways that the ACLU might support the organizing efforts there. Spivak was horrified by what he saw and urged the union to produce leaflets, posters, and bulletins denouncing the coal operators in the strongest possible language. Spivak sent along a draft bulletin that demanded, "The thugs and gunmen of Logan County must go!" The executive committee hesitated to endorse an approach that wasn't of a "quasi-judicial nature." Only a week later, West Virginia authorities were counting the dead in Matewan. Spivak urged Baldwin to get the executive committee to see things as they really were. "They are still under the impression that there is some semblance of legal procedure here," Spivak fumed. "There is not. You can't hold a meeting here, get pinched and then fight it out in the courts. If you try to hold a meeting in the southern counties you'll never live to see the courts." Baldwin told Spivak that he thought the bulletins should be even more radical than what he had proposed and promised to get the committee to agree. In the meantime, he should help the UMW officials in any way he could.[16]

The Matewan massacre was the ACLU's first opportunity to project itself into a national controversy, and Baldwin seized it. To this day, there remains a doubt about whether Albert Felts or Sid Hatfield fired the first shot, but Baldwin had no trouble believing Hatfield's story. The ACLU wired protests to the West Virginia governor, President Wilson, and the U.S. Department of Labor. After Hatfield was indicted for murder, Baldwin told his attorney that the ACLU would handle publicity during the trial, doing everything possible to build public support for the miners. Meanwhile, the union pressed for a congressional investigation of the West Virginia situation. It stepped up its efforts in the spring of 1921 when new violence led Governor Ephraim Morgan to declare martial law. State militia finally put an end to the exchange of fire across the Tug River. However, they also prohibited union meetings, suppressed the UMW newspaper, and arrested twelve union leaders on a charge of unlawful assembly. The Senate Committee on Education and Labor finally opened hearings in July.[17]

The ACLU's effort to make a public case for the West Virginia miners soon ran into difficulty. Baldwin was disappointed in the new publicity man he had hired, who made a poor showing in testifying before the Senate committee. But the bigger problem was the negative public reaction to the march of armed miners on Logan County following Sid Hatfield's assassination. The country's newspapers reacted with alarm to the prospect of insurrection. Although the men were finally persuaded to return home without bloodshed, grand juries in several counties issued hundreds of indictments for insurrection. Baldwin strove mightily to turn the situation around, taking over the publicity job himself and persuading the UMW to hire new counsel for the Senate hearings. But the Senate report was a major disappointment, laying equal blame on both sides. A year later, the strike in Mingo County was lost, and so was some of the credibility of the new civil liberties group. When Baldwin suggested a new free speech fight in West Virginia in 1923, a union lawyer told him the UMW had lost faith in the ACLU's methods.[18]

The limits of the ACLU's strategy became apparent again the first time that it sent one of its lawyers into Pennsylvania to protest the ban on union meetings in coal-mining towns. In the spring of 1922, Baldwin telephoned New York attorney Arthur Garfield Hays to tell him that the Pennsylvania miners had gone out on strike and asked him to participate in a protest in a closed town with UMW officials. Baldwin downplayed the difficulty of the assignment, Hays later recalled. "No, it won't take long," Baldwin said. "You'll arrive in the early morning, hold your meeting and be back in the evening." Hays had a pleasant drive down through the mountains of eastern Pennsylvania, but the union officials told him the job wouldn't be easy. They chose the town of Vintondale because they had been unable to get a foothold there. One of their men had been escorted out of town at the point of a shotgun a couple of weeks earlier. A reporter from the *New York Herald* had also been turned away. Hays told union officials that he would be happy to accompany them and make sure that the police did not disrupt their meeting. This was not received with much enthusiasm. "But when some one suggested that Attorney Hays do the talking, there was unanimous and spirited approval," Hays said.[19]

Hays, several union officials, and two reporters set off in two cars. Amid beautiful scenery, they passed "squalid villages" dominated by mountainous coal dumps. On reaching Vintondale, the union drivers gunned their engines, rushing by a swearing sentry. They soon heard the clatter of hooves as they were pursued into the center of town by armed horsemen. Their pursuers were members of the Coal and Iron Police, a state police force that was paid by the coal operators. "We know you, you ————," one yelled. "You're union organizers.... Get the hell out of this town." Hays emerged from his car full of fire. "Who are you men?" he demanded. "Where is the Post Office?" "Where is the Mayor's office; we'd like to see the ordinances of this town." Instead, one of the troopers pointed to a sign that said the sheriff would arrest anyone who created a public disorder. "I see it—what of it?" the lawyer asked. "I'm going to stand here as long as I damn please." Hays recalled the reaction:

> "Bust this up or we'll bust you up," shouts one, while hoots, threats and curses come from the others. Finally, one Arbogast, the Coal Company Comptroller, with the assistance of one of the troopers and a bystander, grabs me by the nape of the neck and the seat of the trousers while others are busy with my companions. There was then impressed on me a clear conviction, verified by other experiences, to wit—When one is in that position he may talk constitutional law, insist upon his rights as an American citizen, he may proclaim the Declaration of Independence, but all the dignity is on the side of the authorities.

Hays and his party were forced to beat a strategic retreat to a nearby union town, where a justice of the peace issued a warrant for the arrest of the men who had evicted them. Accompanied by a police officer, they returned to Vintondale. But the Coal and Iron Police were not impressed. One shook his club at Hays. "You needn't think you can intimidate me," he said.[20]

Hays's visit to Vintondale did not accomplish much, but elsewhere the ACLU's confrontational tactics were creating openings for political discourse in some of the most unlikely spots, including Los Angeles. The City of Angels was one of the most relentlessly hostile environments for unionism in the entire country. Since 1890, the city's businessmen, led by Harrison Gray Otis, the reactionary publisher of the *Los Angeles Times,* had rejected the idea of collective bargaining and had spent heavily to prevent the spread of unionism in their town. City officials banned picketing and encouraged the police to use California's notorious criminal syndicalism law, which made it a crime to advocate illegal acts, to imprison members of the IWW who were attempting to unite the workers. In 1910, bitterness at the intransigence of Otis and the rest of the business community led two union organizers to bomb the offices of the *Los Angeles Times,* killing twenty-one workers. The harassment of unionists resumed with a vengeance following World War I when the American Legion formed a "military branch" that raided radical bookstores, beat up Wobblies, and pressured the landlord of the IWW meeting hall. Men who wanted a job in Los Angeles were forced to register in company-controlled hiring halls where they were screened for union sympathies. The names of the men rejected in these "Fink Halls" were placed on blacklists that were circulated to potential employers.[21]

Nevertheless, union sentiment was growing in Los Angeles in the early 1920s. The IWW had been crippled by the wartime prosecutions, but it remained a force in the West. Its commitment to organizing unskilled workers led to gains in California's agricultural and construction industries. In Los Angeles, the IWW found converts among the port workers in the San Pedro section of the city. Three thousand longshoremen struck in April 1923 in an effort to win recognition for their union, higher wages, abolition of the Fink Halls, and repeal of the criminal syndicalism law. The police struck back by raiding Wobbly meeting places and seizing literature. On

one day, they arrested four hundred Wobblies for vagrancy, traffic violations, and criminal syndicalism, creating such pressure on the
city's jail facilities that "bull pens" had to be constructed to handle
the overflow. They also banned public meetings by the union men.
"Any attempt by I.W.W. members or sympathizers to start street
meetings or demonstrations of any sort [would] be dealt with immediately," Police Chief Louis D. Oaks announced.[22]

Oaks's announcement was the final straw for Upton Sinclair. He
had moved to California with his new wife in 1915 partly in the
hope that he could limit his political activities. His best-selling 1906
novel, *The Jungle,* had exposed the filthy conditions in the Chicago
meatpacking district and helped pass the first federal regulation of
the food and drug industry. The success of his book made him a
celebrity and propelled him into the fight for social justice. But
when he had settled in Pasadena, he promised his new wife that he
would abstain from politics and concentrate on his writing. This
proved increasingly difficult as the battle in San Pedro heated up. A
member of the ACLU's national committee, Sinclair found it impossible not to sympathize with the strikers. When their meetings
were banned, he led a delegation to Mayor George E. Cryer's office.
Although Cryer would later deny it, Sinclair said the mayor gave his
permission to hold a meeting on Liberty Hill, a spot overlooking the
harbor where the police had forbidden meetings notwithstanding
the fact that it was privately owned by a union sympathizer.

When the delegation met with Oaks, the police chief refused to
permit the meeting. He grew angry when Sinclair referred to the
ACLU: "American Civil Liberties Union? What's the American
Civil Liberties Union? What's it got to do with Los Angeles? Did it
tell you to come here? How did it tell you to come? Where's the letter it wrote you? What business have you got at the harbor?" Sinclair
insisted that he had the right to conduct a meeting on Liberty Hill.
When he tried to read the First Amendment, the chief ordered him
to "cut out that Constitution stuff." Oaks promised the writer that
he would be arrested if he showed his face on Liberty Hill. "You will
be arrested and will go to jail, and let me tell you—you will stay
there," he said. "There will be no bail." On the evening of May 15,
Sinclair and a small party climbed Liberty Hill. Passing through police lines that kept the closest onlookers far from the site of the
demonstration, they took turns attempting to speak. Reading by

candlelight, Sinclair spoke only a few words of the First Amendment before he was arrested; his brother-in-law tried to protest the arrest; and a third man asserted they had come in peace. A fourth man, a young English journalist, figured there was no point in being serious. "This is a most delightful climate," he managed to say before he, too, was carted away. The fifth speaker was Kate Crane Gartz, but the police had been ordered not to arrest women. They departed with their prisoners, who were held incommunicado for the next eighteen hours despite the best efforts of their lawyer to find them.[23]

There was a national backlash against the arrest of Sinclair and his party. A reporter for the *Baltimore Sun* described California as a "retrograde" state, and left-wing magazines and newspapers poured scorn on Chief Oaks. "When we contemplate the antics of the chief of police of Los Angeles we are deterred from characterizing him as an ass only through fear that such a comparison would lay us open to damages from every self-respecting donkey," *The Nation* wrote. Meanwhile, Sinclair and his friends were holding protest meetings at Los Angeles's Walker Auditorium. City leaders capitulated. The managing editor of the *Los Angeles Examiner* approached Sinclair on their behalf. The controversy was giving Los Angeles a "black eye," he said. Only two weeks after the arrests, Sinclair climbed Liberty Hill again and addressed a crowd of over two thousand people. (A few months later, Oaks was fired when he was discovered in the backseat of his car with a half-gallon of whiskey and a young woman who was not his wife.)

The most lasting achievement of the San Pedro fight was the establishment of the Southern California chapter of the ACLU. Sinclair launched the membership campaign with a letter that was sent to people who had signed attendance sheets at protest meetings as well as members of various women's groups and people who had purchased Sinclair's books. In short order, the ACLU of Southern California, which would grow to be the largest chapter in the nation, launched a weekly lecture series that introduced Southern Californians to radicals like Eugene Debs, who had never felt welcome before. The title of the new weekly newsletter, *Open Forum,* neatly summarizes what Sinclair and his supporters had begun to achieve.[24]

Once the ACLU began to experience some success, unions began to look to it for help. In 1924, striking silk workers in Paterson, New

Jersey, sent a telegram to the ACLU after police arrested over one hundred pickets on a single day. "Police terrorism launched here today," a union official wrote on September 4. "Request your organization take a hand in the situation and help protect our rights." The ACLU answered with a letter to the Paterson mayor and a press release. It also promised the union that it would provide speakers to help boost morale at strike meetings. When Chief of Police John M. Tracey closed Turn Hall, the union meeting place, the ACLU announced that it would hold a protest meeting there on October 6. Roger Baldwin and union officials planned carefully for the meeting, and when police cordoned off Turn Hall, two young sisters carrying an American flag led the way to City Hall Plaza, where hundreds of strikers gathered to hear a reading from the Constitution. Baldwin had chosen the Constitution to ensure that no one could be arrested for sedition, but as one of the workers began to read, the police demanded to see his meeting permit. "This is my permit," he shouted, raising the Bill of Rights. Hundreds of angry voices shouted at the police, leading at least fifty officers to charge the crowd with their nightsticks. Several people were badly beaten, and eleven were arrested.[25]

Despite his best efforts, Baldwin was not arrested at the demonstration. The next morning he showed up at the police station with a reporter for the *Newark Evening News* and demanded to see the police chief. When he was finally introduced to Tracey, he identified himself as the organizer of the demonstration and demanded that he be arrested. The chief put his hand on him in a fatherly way. "Boy, you are in the wrong," he said. "Chief, I am not near so wrong as your men are for that disgraceful spectacle last night," Baldwin replied. Baldwin challenged the chief's authority to ban meetings. "Chief, you talk as if you were the censor of who could talk in this town, what they can say and where they can say it," he said. "Well, I am," Tracey agreed. "Say, Chief, you talk as if you were the law," Baldwin said. "I am the law," Tracey confirmed. Baldwin got what he wanted. His arrest and the arrests at City Hall Plaza were widely condemned. Tracey was forced to reopen Turn Hall, and the ACLU organized another protest involving an Episcopal bishop and a decorated navy officer. This one was unmolested: the reading of the First Amendment continued, and later a resolution condemning Tracey and police brutality was approved. Similar tactics prevailed in another strike in Passaic in 1926 when ACLU board member Norman Thomas was arrested for violating a meeting ban. Arthur Garfield Hays, who joined board member John Haynes Holmes in violating a ban in a neighboring town, recalled the 1920s as a period when ACLU leaders "were all ex-jailbirds together."[26]

At the end of the 1920s, Roger Baldwin estimated that nine out of ten of the fights that the ACLU had taken on since its founding had involved the rights of labor. He continued to believe that the workers were fighting the most important civil liberties battle:

> However important or significant may be the struggle for the political rights of 15 million Negroes; however important or significant the defense of religious liberties; of academic freedom; of freedom from censorship of the press, radio, or motion pictures, these are on the whole trifling in national effect compared with the fight for the rights of labor to organize. For a larger point of view, these secondary issues dissolve into the primary.

This did not mean that the ACLU was not actively fighting on all of these fronts. Its uncompromising advocacy of free speech demanded it. "There should be no control whatever in advance over what any person may say," the ACLU had stated in *The Fight for Free Speech,* its first annual report. "There should be no prosecutions for the mere expression of opinion on matters of public concern, however radical, however violent." To give this view even more point and to borrow some of the prestige of a Founding Father, the report quoted Thomas Jefferson on its cover: "It is time enough for the rightful purpose of civil government for its officers to interfere when principles break out into overt acts against peace and good order." The ACLU could not just defend the First Amendment rights of its friends. It had to protect the rights of people whose views were directly opposed to the liberalism of its members, even those who used their right of free speech to advocate violating the civil liberties of others. In the 1920s, that meant defending the rights of the Ku Klux Klan (KKK).[27]

In September 1921, at almost the same moment that armed miners were marching on Logan County, the *New York World* published a three-week exposé of a new threat to the public peace. The newspaper reported that 500,000 Americans were members of a newly reorganized secret society, the Ku Klux Klan. The original Klan had arisen in the South to restore white supremacy following the Civil War. The new Klan was also deeply racist, but its strongest appeal was to people who feared the influence of "foreigners," the nearly eighteen million immigrants who had arrived in the United States between 1890 and 1914. The old Klan had accepted all white men, but its successor was obsessed with the fear that Catholics and Jews were plotting to take over the country. In fact, the *World* exaggerated the Klan's strength, but it had not overstated its appeal. In the following months, in part as a result of the publicity it received from the *World* exposé, it grew with phenomenal speed, reaching one million members a year later. Originally confined to the South, the new Klan had as many members in Ohio, Indiana, and Illinois as there were in the South and Southwest combined. It also spread to the cities. "Indianapolis, Dayton, Portland, Youngstown, Denver and Dallas were the hooded capitals of the nation," a historian of the urban Klan has written.[28]

The Klan presented itself to the world as the defender of Protestant morality, often announcing its arrival in town by marching into a Baptist or Methodist church and presenting the pastor with a large donation. It encouraged its members to practice "Klannishness" by patronizing the businesses of other Klansmen and boycotting those run by Catholics and Jews. But the Klan was not just another reform group or business association. Klansmen wore masks for a reason. They intended to intimidate adulterers, bootleggers, gamblers, and Sabbath breakers, and they were prepared to use violence against those whom they couldn't scare. William J. Simmons, the founder of the new Klan, made this clear when he spoke to new recruits, melodramatically emptying his pockets of weapons, including two large pistols, before he spoke. "Now let the Niggers, Catholics, Jews and all others who disdain my imperial wizardry come on," Simmons would say. The *World* credited the Klan with 152 acts of violence, including 4 murders, 41 floggings, and 27 people tarred and feathered. In Medford, Oregon, Klansmen hung an African American bootblack and a Mexican farmhand, then cut them down at the last minute. In Mer Rouge, Louisiana, they kidnapped five men in broad daylight, intending to whip them. When two of the men recognized their abductors, they were taken deep into a forest and killed.[29]

Not surprisingly, the enemies of the Klan often responded with violence of their own. A few miles outside the Klan stronghold of Youngstown, Ohio, members of an anti-Klan group, the Knights of the Flaming Circle, confronted Klansmen as they arrived to participate in a parade. Armed men searched cars for Klan robes, wrecked the cars of some Klansmen, and shot others, although no one was killed. In Pennsylvania, five thousand Klansmen defiantly marched into the heavily Catholic town of Carnegie and were met by a shower of rocks and bricks, and one Klansman was shot to death. A Klan meeting in Perth Amboy, New Jersey, was surrounded by a hostile crowd that smashed the windshields of cars, threw rocks, and refused to let police remove the shaken Klansmen until the following morning. Fourteen hundred Klansmen who were given permission to participate in a Memorial Day parade in Queens, New York, found themselves surrounded by a booing crowd. Following several attempts to block their progress, fighting erupted and the Klan was driven from the parade.[30]

The effort to suppress the Ku Klux Klan in 1922 and 1923 gave the ACLU its first real chance to test its commitment to free speech for all. Certainly, there could be no question that the ACLU and the Klan despised each other. Shortly before the publication of the New York World exposé of the Klan in September 1921, Albert De-Silver, the codirector of the ACLU, drew attention to the violence of the Klan in an article in The Nation that was later reprinted by the ACLU. He described a series of nineteen mob attacks that the Galveston, Texas, Daily News had characterized as Klan-related, beginning with the kidnapping of an African American bellboy in Dallas by masked men who used acid to burn the letters KKK into his forehead and ending with the abduction of a young white woman by white-robed men who tarred and feathered her. Klan officials in Texas attempted to dissociate themselves from this violence by revoking the charters of chapters that were suspected of brutal acts. But DeSilver believed that violence was inherent in the organization. "It is a child conceived in the tradition of a lawless past and brought forth in the extravagant obscurantism of present-day prejudice," he wrote. "Its life cannot and should not be a happy one.

The modern Ku Klux Klan does not deserve to live and it had much better die."[31]

The Klan's reputation for violence did nothing to stunt its rapid growth or stop it from exercising its political muscle. By the end of 1922, the elected officials who had condemned the Klan a year earlier had fallen silent in the face of its obvious electoral success. The Klan helped elect governors in four states that year, put one of its Texas members in the U.S. Senate, and almost managed to defeat Senator James Reed of Missouri. In addition to helping elect the new governor, the Oregon Klan played a role in passing a state initiative that sought to close all Catholic schools. Bills were introduced in the Oregon legislature to remove the Catholic chaplain from the state penitentiary, ban the wearing of any Catholic garb in public schools, and prohibit the use of sacramental wine in religious ceremonies. The fight to limit Catholic influence was even more intense at the local level. In Akron, Ohio, a Klan-dominated board of education attempted to fire all Catholic teachers working in the public schools.[32]

Not all public officials were afraid to confront the Klan. In Kansas, Governor Henry Allen swore to run the Klan out of the state after the mayor of the town of Liberal was whipped for refusing to allow the Klan use of a public hall. "If we allow this organization to take the law into its own hands, then we break down all the safeguards of society," Allen said. The Klan's position was particularly precarious in the large cities of the East and Middle West where Catholics and Jews were in the majority. In Chicago, the Board of Aldermen launched an investigation to determine whether any city employees were members of the Klan. Things went hardest for the Klan in New York City, where two grand juries investigated whether Klan members had broken any laws. Mayor John Hylan decided not to wait for any evidence of a crime to turn up. He ordered the New York City Police to "ferret out these despicable disloyal persons who are attempting to organize a society, the aims and purposes of which are of such a character that were they to prevail, the foundations of our country would be destroyed." Police began breaking up meetings of the Klan, and just two weeks after Hylan's call to action, they turned over the names of eight hundred Klansmen to the district attorney.[33]

It wasn't easy to stand up for the rights of a group whose organizing principle was prejudice. An editorial in the *New York Times* condemned the "sympathetic 'intellectuals'" who "prattle about the rights of the opprest invisible imperialists." Even Governor Al Smith, who had fought the Red Scare, could not be counted on to defend the civil liberties of the Klan. In 1923, the New York legislature passed a bill that required all membership organizations whose members swore an oath to provide the secretary of state with a list of its officers and members. While the legislation did not name the Klan directly, it contained so many exemptions that it did not appear to apply to any other group. Its purpose was plainly to frighten Klan members with exposure, a tactic that had been very successful in fighting the Klan in Chicago. In signing the bill, Smith refused to acknowledge the threat to the Klansmen's First Amendment rights. "No harm can come to any such membership organization if its intentions and purposes are honest," he said. Consequently, it was left to the leader of the New York Klan, who was known as the King Kleagle, to make the case for free speech at a late-night rally of eight thousand masked Klansmen in a field outside Eastport, Long Island. Standing in a spotlight beneath a large American flag and in front of an altar that was draped in another flag, the Kleagle attacked the new law as an infringement of First Amendment rights:

> The act was plainly unconstitutional, picking out the Ku Klux Klan and not making its provisions applicable to the Knights of Columbus and similar organizations. It is class legislation and will not be obeyed by the Ku Klux Klan, but will be contested in the courts, if necessary to the Supreme Court of the United States.

The Supreme Court wasn't sympathetic either. It rejected the Klan's First Amendment claim in 1928.[34]

But for the leaders of the ACLU, who had witnessed the crushing of dissent during the war and were now fighting for the rights of labor, it was clear that the principle of free speech had to be upheld for all groups. In 1920, Albert DeSilver told the leader of the National Association for the Advancement of Colored People (NAACP) that it was "a great mistake" to ask the post office to ban KKK literature from the mails. "We do not think that it is ever a good policy for an organization interested in human liberty to invoke repressive measures against any of its antagonists," DeSilver said. "By doing so it creates a danger of making a precedent against itself." The ACLU also opposed the NAACP's campaign to ban D. W. Griffith's racist classic *Birth of a Nation,* a film that glorified the deeds of the original Klan. In 1923, the ACLU criticized the New York Klan registration law and challenged a ban on Klan meetings imposed by Boston mayor James Curley. In arguing against the meeting ban, it again warned that repression was a two-edged sword. If Curley could ban the Klan in Boston, "there would be considerable parts of this country in which religious intolerance would prohibit Catholics, Jews, and indeed, the representatives of some Protestant sects, from holding meetings or speaking at all," the Massachusetts Civil Liberties Union wrote the mayor.[35]

The Ku Klux Klan was one of many right-wing groups that were active in the 1920s. The war and the Red Scare had demonstrated that there was money to be made by fanning the fears of the American people over the threat of Communist subversion, and more than a dozen "patriotic" groups emerged to lead the fight against radicalism. For a few years, these professional patriots worked closely with William J. Burns, the head of the Justice Department's Bureau of Investigation. Burns, whose well-known detective agency had engaged in strike-breaking activity and espionage on behalf of large corporations, was alive to the danger of radicalism. In 1922, his agents joined Michigan authorities in raiding a secret Communist meeting in the small town of Bridgman, despite the fact that the Communists were not violating any federal law. But the Justice Department soon withdrew from the fight against communism. In 1924, Harlan Fiske Stone, the former dean of the Columbia University Law School, was appointed attorney general, replacing Harry M. Daugherty, who had been forced to resign during the scandal over the government's leasing of oil reserves at Teapot Dome, Wyoming. Stone fired Burns and ordered an end to the department's spying on radical groups. "There is always the possibility that a secret police may become a menace to free government and free institutions," Stone warned.[36]

The professional patriots were outraged by Burns's dismissal and nearly apoplectic when President Calvin Coolidge took the additional step of pardoning the remaining prisoners who had been convicted under the Espionage and Sedition Acts. "Is it any wonder that right-minded Americans should feel that reasoning is rapidly reaching the limit?" asked the Better America Federation of Los Angeles. The Better America Federation and the American Constitution Association, which was based in West Virginia, were regional groups that defended the interests of the businesses that created them. At the national level, the National Civic Federation, the National Security League, and the American Defense Society competed to be the preeminent voice of ultrapatriotism. They were often supported by the Daughters of the American Revolution, the Sons of the American Revolution, the Daughters of 1812, trade groups like the National Association of Manufacturers, and veterans' organizations like the American Legion, the Reserve Officers' Association, and the Military Order of the World War. While there were a number of one-man patriotic groups, some of the larger groups commanded considerable resources. At a time when the ACLU was spending between $20,000 and $30,000 annually, the combined budget of the most active patriotic groups was estimated at $250,000.[37]

The conservative groups shared a hatred for anything Russian. Even seemingly charitable causes like aid to the victims of the Russian famine were condemned as covert attempts to support the Bolshevik regime. "If the people who are contributing to the Russian Famine Fund understood that their money was going to be used by Lenin and Trotsky, contributions would soon cease," Ralph M. Easley, the National Civic Federation chairman, said. The patriots were suspicious of all forms of liberalism. Pacifism was condemned as a Soviet plot to disarm the United States. "I would drive every damn Quaker out of America," Easley said. While they denounced unionism and all other forms of collective action by workers, they also rejected social welfare legislation, including efforts to enact a minimum wage for women and a ban on child labor. Nor were they prepared to accept any government regulation of the economy. "We believe that public ownership and public control of business through a multiplicity of boards and commissions is socialistic and bolshevistic in tendency," the Better America Federation said.[38]

The patriots spent a lot of time worrying about children. They believed that the youth of the nation were a target of subversion. "The bomb-throwing, bullet-shooting anarchist does not worry me much," said a spokesman for the Better America Federation. "But when I find a slow poison being secretly injected into our body politic, I do worry—*and so should you.*" "A great many of our members write that radicalism has obtained a toe-hold among teachers in public schools," another Federation publication revealed. But the conservative groups also recognized that the public schools offered a wonderful opportunity to disseminate their message that Americans must reject the influence of all foreign ideas and maintain the centrality of the institution of private property. They were well aware that, far from being hotbeds of dissension, public schools were places where teachers were afraid that any expression of unorthodox opinion, either in or out of school, would result in their instant dismissal.[39]

The plight of teachers with controversial opinions had never been a happy one. Public education in the United States was perceived as a tool for disseminating a common culture in a country of immigrants. Teachers were expected to promote democratic values and love of country, and their obligation to serve as model citizens did not stop at the schoolhouse door. As public employees, they were expected to refrain from endorsing unorthodox opinions in their private lives as well. Their situation worsened during the war as the schools became a tool for instilling loyalty. Teachers were dismissed for being opponents of the draft, religious pacifists, Quakers, Socialists, and economic radicals. South Dakota, Texas, and New York passed laws requiring patriotic instruction. Many schools instituted ceremonies where the flag was saluted and patriotic songs were sung. In an effort to suppress the German language, laws were passed requiring the teaching of all subjects in English, and foreign-language instruction was banned in primary schools.[40]

This repressive climate actually worsened after the war. During the Red Scare, the New York legislature approved a law requiring that "applicants for teachers' licenses . . . be loyal and obedient" and that "no such certificate . . . be issued to any person who . . . advocated a change in the form of government of the United States or of this state, by force, violence or any unlawful means." Smith vetoed the law, but it was repassed in 1921 after he lost his bid for reelection. Eighteen states demanded some sort of loyalty statement by teachers. Professional patriots sought to purge the schools of "radical" literature, including magazines like *The Nation* and *The New Republic,* books by Upton Sinclair, Henry George, and Jane Addams, and history texts that seemed to be pro-British. The American Legion published its own two-volume history textbook to "inspire the children with patriotism, preach on every page a vivid love of America and preserve the old patriotic legends." One critic wrote that *The Story of Our American People* was "so maudlin and sentimental about 'our' virtues and 'our' superiority to the rest of the world that if universally used 'our' next generation would behave like an insufferable cad toward the rest of the world."[41]

The ACLU objected to these efforts to suppress liberal ideas. "The teaching of patriotism is of course an entirely legitimate activity," the ACLU noted in its 1931 report, *Gag on Teaching.* "But to confound it with capitalism, as is too often done, is not to teach about patriotism, but acceptance of the present economic system as loyalty to the United States, and all dissent from it as disloyalty. Much of the teaching of patriotism is aimed at alleged radicalism, at pacifism and internationalism." At times business groups used the schools to directly advance their economic interests. In 1920, utilities magnate Samuel Insull helped launch a national propaganda campaign that sought to defeat the growing pressure for government regulation of electricity and gas companies. Under the aegis of the National Electric Light Association, spokesmen for the utilities industries engaged in a highly effective effort to use the public schools to disseminate their views: they challenged the authors and publishers of textbooks that they disapproved, attempted to force the adoption of books that were more sympathetic to the industry, and flooded the schools with pamphlets and paid lecturers.[42]

Some public officials had the courage to challenge the effort to turn the schools into propaganda mills. Will C. Wood, the superintendent for public instruction in California, fought the efforts of the Better America Federation to distribute its pamphlet *America Is Calling.* Al Smith secured the repeal of the New York loyalty oath on his return to office in 1923. College teachers also fought back. The American Association of University Professors, which had been founded in 1915, emerged as the main defender of academic freedom in colleges. The American Historical Association and the American Sociological Society and other professional groups began to raise their voices against the historical distortions that the professional patriots were attempting to introduce into the curriculum. In 1924, the ACLU created the Committee on Academic Freedom, made up of prominent professors, writers, and scholars, to lead the fight for freedom of speech in the schools. The next year, while searching through newspapers from around the country for civil liberties violations, ACLU secretary Lucy Milner discovered a small article about the introduction of a bill in the Tennessee legislature that made it a crime to teach evolution in the public schools. When the bill passed and was signed into law, the ACLU immediately issued a press release to Tennessee newspapers offering to defend any teacher who defied the law. A short time later, a science teacher named John Scopes stepped forward to accept the offer and launched what became known as the Trial of the Century.[43]

Efforts to add religion to the curriculum of the public schools had been growing since the end of the war, particularly in the South. This reflected the rise of a new fundamentalism in the Protestant churches that was, in turn, a response to a "modernist" trend among the clergy. The modernists, who were attempting to reconcile religion with scientific discoveries, including evolution, argued that the Bible was not the literal word of God but rather the creation of men who, inspired by the holy spirit, were nevertheless ignorant of the facts of the natural world. Fundamentalists rejected these efforts and insisted on the literal truth of the Bible. Ministers like the Reverend Billy Sunday attracted enormous crowds with his demands that religion return to the basics and his attacks on evolution. "Teaching evolution. Teaching about pre-historic man," Sunday said during a Memphis address. "No such thing as pre-historic man." "Pre-historic man," he repeated, then gagged as if he was about to vomit.[44]

But the ministers alone could not have turned hostility to evolution into a political crusade against evolution. It was only when "the Great Commoner," William Jennings Bryan, made himself the leader of the campaign to outlaw the teaching of evolution in the public schools that the movement began to make progress. At sixty-five, Bryan was bald and pot-bellied, a far cry from the fair-haired boy he had been when he made his famous "Cross of Gold" speech and swept the delegates to the 1896 Democratic Convention off their feet. But he remained the hero of the Protestant heartland. The Democratic standard-bearer in three presidential campaigns, he had always spoken for the interests of the farmers and small business men of rural America.

In the early 1920s, Bryan took up the antievolution cause with the same enthusiasm he had devoted to attacking eastern capitalists, militarists, and alcohol. Beginning in 1921, he wrote and lectured hundreds of times about how teaching evolution would undermine religious faith and create moral collapse. "I object to the Darwinian theory because I fear we shall lose the consciousness of God's presence in our daily life, if we must accept the theory that through all the ages no spiritual force has touched the life of men and shaped the destiny of nations," Bryan explained. His campaign struck a responsive chord in legislatures throughout the South. In 1923, six states actively considered antievolution proposals. Two years later, the Tennessee legislature made it a crime punishable by a $500 fine for any public school teacher "to teach any theory that denies the story of the Divine Creation of man as taught in the Bible, and to teach instead that man has descended from a lower order of animals."[45]

Because the courts were so reactionary, the ACLU was generally averse to filing lawsuits. However, it was deeply concerned about the growing attack on intellectual freedom in the schools. Eighteen states had recently passed laws that either permitted or required prayer in the schools, and the movement appeared to be gaining momentum. Idaho, Iowa, Oklahoma, and Florida passed laws in 1925; the Idaho and Florida laws made school prayer mandatory. "It is not generally known that restrictions on public teaching by legislative acts have been more numerous within the last year than at any time in American history," the ACLU reported in July 1925. Anxious to file a test case that might help block further legislation, it had been following the progress of the Tennessee antievolution bill from the beginning. "When we read press reports of what seemed to us a fantastic proposal pending in the Tennessee legislature to make the teaching of evolution a crime, we kept our eye on it," Baldwin said later. The ACLU was ready to swing into action as soon as the governor signed the bill into law. Its press release, which was printed in full in the *Chattanooga Times* and other state newspapers, sounded like a help wanted ad: "We are looking for a Tennessee teacher who is willing to accept our services in testing this law in the courts. Our lawyers think a friendly test case can be arranged without costing a teacher his or her job. Distinguished counsel have volunteered their services. All we need now is a willing client." Baldwin believed that almost any teacher would do. Both the ACLU and the prosecutors hoped to keep the trial focused narrowly on the issue of the right of the majority to dictate what could be taught in the public schools. Everyone assumed that Scopes would be quickly convicted and that the argument over academic freedom would occur during the appeal.[46]

However, lawsuits are not just about the law, and Roger Baldwin fully recognized the publicity value of the case for his organization. Shortly after Scopes's indictment, the ACLU brought him east for a couple of appearances in New York and Washington. At first glance, John Scopes was nobody's idea of a martyr for academic freedom. He had been recruited for the role by the leaders of the small town of Dayton, Tennessee, who saw in the case an opportunity to put their town on the map. He wasn't even the regular biology teacher at Rhea County High School, but a general science teacher who had occasionally filled in for the regular teacher. But in every other way, he was perfect for the role. Tall and slender, the twenty-four-year-old Scopes was both boyish and academic in his horn-rimmed glasses. A bachelor without a family to support, he could afford to take the risk of losing his job. The ACLU made sure he was photographed in carefully staged shots in front of the Statue of Liberty and the Constitution. He was an instant sensation, according to the *New York World*. "Under the banner of liberalism, to the blaze of page headlines, with the aid of special interviews, posed photographs and human interest incidents, the conglomerate host of liberals is falling in about the lanky, grave-eyed Tennessee high-school teacher," it reported. At an ACLU dinner at the Civic Club in New York, Scopes was surrounded by "feminists, birth-control advocates, agnostics, atheists, free thinkers, free lovers, socialists, communists, syndicalists, biologists, psychoanalysts, educators, preachers, lawyers, professional liberals and many others, including just talkers."[47]

The Scopes case made it possible for the ACLU to secure the support of some of the most prominent people in American life. It established an advisory committee to assist it in raising funds for the case, inviting twenty leading educators to join. All twenty accepted, including Charles W. Eliot, the former president of Harvard. The Scopes case captured the attention of George Bernard Shaw and Albert Einstein, who said that limiting academic freedom "heaps coals of shame upon the community." No less thrilling to an organization whose main weapon was publicity was the sudden interest of the mainstream press. "Our office was filled with all the top journalists," Baldwin remembered. More than two hundred reporters showed up in Tennessee for the opening of the trial on July 10; their stories would appear in over 2,300 dailies. The *New York Times* alone employed five telegraphers to transmit copy from Dayton, and more than two million words would be transmitted by the end of the eight-day trial. Americans didn't just read about the case. Although radio was still in its infancy, microphones were installed in the courtroom, and Chicagoans could listen to the trial on WGN.[48]

Yet, by the time of the trial, the ACLU had largely lost control of the case. Its hope to keep the trial confined to the issue of academic freedom had probably never been a realistic one because what interested people the most was the clash between science and religion. Bryan had portrayed evolution as an attack on religious faith, and when he volunteered to join the prosecution, he made this the central issue in the case. "The contest between evolution and Christianity is a duel to the death," Bryan said. "The atheists, agnostics and all other opponents of Christianity understand the character of the struggle." His challenge was immediately taken up by Clarence Darrow, a notorious agnostic and the most prominent defense attorney in the country. "Scopes is not on trial. Civilization is on trial," Darrow said. "Nothing will satisfy us but broad victory, a knockout which will have an everlasting precedent to prove that America is founded on liberty and not on narrow, mean, intolerable and brainless prejudice of soulless religio-maniacs." When Darrow offered to represent Scopes for free, Baldwin and other ACLU leaders attempted to dissuade the teacher from accepting the services of a man whose religious views would alienate most Americans. They wanted the defense to be led by a constitutional lawyer with impeccable credentials. But Scopes wanted Darrow. "It was going to be a down in the mud fight, and I felt the situation demanded an Indian fighter rather than someone who graduated from the proper military academy," Scopes recalled.[49]

Ultimately, the Scopes case did not succeed in establishing the principle of academic freedom. The prosecution was able to persuade the judge to exclude weeks of testimony by the ACLU's scientific experts. Darrow attempted to salvage his case by calling Bryan himself to the stand as an expert witness on the Bible. During his relentless examination, Darrow forced Bryan to admit that even he did not accept everything in the Bible as literal truth, a concession that opened the door to the possibility that other interpretations of the Bible, including those that accommodated evolution, were equally valid. But Scopes was convicted anyway. When Bryan died suddenly less than a week after the trial, many of his supporters blamed Darrow's tough questioning. Later, a myth would grow that Bryan had died of a broken heart. Some liberals criticized the strategy of the case, too, arguing that the ACLU had watered down its arguments by attempting to show that evolution was compatible with religious faith. Then the Tennessee Supreme Court ruled not only that the law was constitutional but that a technical error by the judge gave the state the right to dismiss the case, which it promptly did. As a result, the ACLU lost the chance to appeal to the U.S. Supreme Court, and the antievolution crusade continued. The Mississippi legislature banned the teaching of evolution the next year, and Arkansas voters enacted a ban in a 1928 referendum.[50]

But even though the ACLU did not win the war, the Scopes case had been an important battle for public opinion. It had allowed civil libertarians to identify their fight with the struggle for liberty that had begun centuries before when Galileo had challenged the authority of the church. They also invoked the memory of the Founding Fathers, men who had put everything at risk to win the right to think freely. During the trial, defense attorney Dudley Field Malone had demonstrated that even the people of Dayton, who supported the prosecution, were strong believers in individual freedom. Although he had spoken little during the trial, Malone was a skilled courtroom lawyer. He had been assigned the task of arguing for the admission of expert testimony, but he denied any desire to discredit the Bible. It was the defenders of the law who were being intolerant.

These gentlemen say: "The Bible contains the truth. If the world of science can produce any truth or facts not in the Bible as we understand it, then destroy science but keep our Bible." And we say: "Keep your Bible. Keep it as your consolation, keep it as your guide. But keep it where it belongs, in the world of your own conscience, in the world of your individual judgment.... Keep your Bible in the world of theology, where it belongs, and do not try to tell an intelligent world and the intelligence of this country that these books, written by men who knew none of the accepted fundamental facts of science, can be put into a course of science."

As Malone spoke, expressions of support began to be heard around the courtroom. His persuasiveness owed a great deal to his stage presence and the power of his voice. But he was also evoking the American tradition of the separation of church and state. His listeners could not help being moved.[51]

Yet it was his defense of individual freedom that brought down the house. He turned the prosecution's opposition to expert testimony into a symbol of the fear of new ideas. "What is this psychology of fear?" he asked. Old ideas had led to world war and the death of over twenty million people. Perhaps, if children were free to learn, they might avoid future catastrophes. "For God's sake, let the children have their minds open," Malone said. Scatterings of applause began to worry Darrow, who feared the possibility of a hung jury. But Malone charged on. He picked up Bryan's description of the case as a duel and threw it back at him. "There is never a duel with truth," Malone said. "The truth always wins, and we are not afraid of it. The truth is no coward. The truth does not need the law. The truth does not need the forces of government. The truth does not need Mr. Bryan." Malone turned to Bryan to deliver his final remarks:

We are ready. We are ready. We feel we stand with progress. We feel we stand with science. We feel we stand with intelligence. We feel we stand with fundamental freedom in America. We are not afraid. Where is the fear? We defy it! We ask your honor to admit the evidence as a matter of correct law, as a matter of sound procedure, and as a matter of justice to the defense in this case.

The courtroom erupted. "Dayton thundered her verdict at the end of the speech of Malone," a reporter wrote. "Women shrieked their approval. Men, unmoved even by Darrow, could not restrain their cheers." Reporters violated their outward neutrality and joined in the standing ovation. Even one of the sponsors of the antievolution law called Malone's address "the finest speech of the century."[52]

The Scopes case gave Americans a new appreciation of the vulnerability of free speech in a democracy. "The most ominous sign of our time...is...the growth of an intolerant spirit," Charles Evans Hughes, the former presidential candidate, governor of New York, and U.S. Supreme Court justice, told the American Bar Association several months after Scopes had been convicted. Equal rights were no guarantee of freedom, Hughes warned. "Democracy has its own capacity for tyranny.....The interests of liberty are peculiarly those of individuals, and hence of minorities, and freedom is in danger of being slain at her own altars if the passion for uniformity and control of opinion gathers head." Without calling the superpatriots by name, Hughes condemned the "false Americanism which professes to maintain American institutions while dethroning American ideals." But the main focus of his address was the importance of academic freedom. "I desire in a non-controversial spirit to emphasize the vast importance of the freedom of learning in the hope that our people instinct with the spirit of liberty will not lay hands on our public schools and State universities to set obstacles to the path of knowledge," he explained. Education and scientific inquiry were far more important to human progress than government. Indeed, "governments and statesmen have too often stood in the way.... Freedom of learning is the vital breath of democracy and progress."[53]

The rising public concern about freedom of speech was clearly worrisome to conservatives. They were well aware that civil libertarians were attempting to broaden the protections for free speech by making the same kind of patriotic appeals that had worked so well for the superpatriots themselves. Nor could they deny that freedom of speech, freedom of the press, and freedom of assembly were explicitly guaranteed by the Bill of Rights. So, rather than attack free speech directly, they accused the civil libertarians of being "free speech fakers" whose real goal was a radical reconstruction of American society along Soviet lines. In March 1924, the American Legion called on its state chapters to oppose the efforts of the ACLU. "These people are advocating 'free speech,' speech of the kind that would allow the advocacy of the overthrow of our government by force of arms," a legion official explained. "Free speech up to a certain point is an excellent thing, but free speech that would destroy our nation and the servicemen who defended it cannot be tolerated." "If the founders of the American Civil Liberties Union...had been frank, they would have called it the 'Unamerican Criminal License Union,'" Francis Ralston Welsh, a Philadelphia stockbroker, wrote Representative Thomas L. Blanton, who published the remarks in the *Congressional Record*. "It is a communistic organization whose subversive methods are aimed at the undermining of our government." The rest of Welsh's letter was a detailed description of the "radical" sympathies of members of ACLU's National Committee.[54]

The efforts to portray the ACLU as a radical organization succeeded for a time. In 1921, the New York City Board of Education, citing regulations that banned appearances on board property of anyone who was not "loyal to American Institutions," refused to allow executive board member John Haynes Holmes to speak in one of its schools. Five years later, it denied the ACLU the use of Stuyvesant High School for a forum on "old fashioned free speech" out of a fear that it would incite students to "revolt against regulations." The opposition of conservatives and school board officials did not stop the ACLU from growing stronger, however. Bolstered by the publicity surrounding the Scopes case, its membership grew significantly during the 1920s, although it still numbered fewer than 2,200 in 1928. Perhaps more important, it had acquired some prominent admirers among the mainstream press. "The Civil Liberties Union is the only organization of its kind in the United States, if not the world," the *St. Louis Post-Dispatch* observed in a 1926 editorial. A review of the ACLU's annual report "discloses an amazing record of activity in all parts of the country in behalf of the civil rights of man," it read. The press that the ACLU was receiving was so good that some of its old friends like the *New York World* believed that it was safe to criticize it when necessary. In 1927, the *World* tweaked the ACLU over its announcement that the American Legion had supplanted the Ku Klux Klan as the most active repressive force in the nation. Attacking the legion for the misbehavior of some of its chapters "is the kind of thing more than anything else which has earned the union the reputation of being 'radical,'" the *World* read.[55]

The efforts to suppress "radical" groups like the ACLU continued throughout the 1920s. As the threat of communism receded somewhat, the professional patriots found a new focus for their efforts in an attack on pacifism. In the wake of a horrific world war, it is not surprising that support was growing for disarmament and efforts to resolve international conflicts peacefully. But the conservatives viewed pacifism against the backdrop of the worldwide Bolshevik conspiracy, assailing pacifists as either willing Soviet agents or dupes. Pacifism would disarm the nation, making it an easy prey for the overthrow of the government. As Fred R. Marvin, the head of the Keymen of America, explained:

> "Brotherly Love," "Internationalism," "No More War," "Peace and Freedom," "Industrial Democracy," are all beautiful expressions in the abstract, but not one of these slogans originated in the mind of an American. All of them are manufactured in other lands and sent across the water to this country to destroy the morale of the American people that we, in the end, might as a nation be destroyed.

If pacifism had not originated in the United States, there was no question in the minds of the superpatriots that it was spreading rapidly and infecting many groups, including national women's groups, that had never been suspected of disloyalty before. Lucia R. Maxwell, a librarian in the War Department's Chemical Warfare Service, produced an elaborate Spider Web Chart that purported to show that pacifists had their hooks in the National Farmers' Union, the League of Women Voters, the National Women's Trade Union League, the American Association of University Women, the General Federation of Women's Clubs, the Women's Christian Temperance Union, the YWCA, the National Congress of Mothers, and parent-teacher associations.[56]

The superpatriots fought hard to keep the contagion of pacifism from spreading any further. In 1924, the Women's International League for Peace and Friendship (WILPF), a group headed by the pioneering social worker Jane Addams, announced that several of its representatives would undertake a speaking tour in a special railroad car, the Pax Special. However, a mob of armed Klansmen was waiting for them in Cincinnati, and their train had to be diverted. Businessmen forced the cancellation of meetings in Dayton and Chicago.

Over the next several years, patriot groups spent much of their time trying to deny their opponents an opportunity to be heard. The Daughters of the American Revolution (DAR) circulated a blacklist that included more than sixty organizations and two hundred men and women whom it branded as undesirable because they were "communist," "socialist," "radical," or "pacifist." The American Legion's Americanism Committee urged legion members to pressure the "owners of halls and auditoriums in which radical meetings might be held." Such efforts often succeeded. A 1928 exposé in the *New York World* documented more than twenty occasions on which pressure had forced the cancellation of speeches. The American Legion managed to cancel so many meetings by Sherwood Eddy, a leading Protestant and pacifist, that he traveled to Indianapolis to meet with the national commander, Edward Spafford. "I told him that I believed in our constitution and in the right of free speech," Eddy said. "He claimed that he also believed in this right but that he would do all in his power to prevent people coming to hear me and also to have my engagements cancelled."[57]

But the campaign of suppression backfired on the superpatriots. Their attacks impugned the reputations of widely admired Americans like Addams, making them vulnerable to counterattack. In 1927, the suffragist leader Carrie Chapman Catt unleashed a broadside against the DAR over its attacks on Addams and other outstanding women leaders. More than two thousand of Chicago's leading citizens had recently attended a dinner in Addams's honor. A telegram from President Calvin Coolidge had been read at the dinner, praising her for giving "her life and strength to the services of humanity." "Is President Coolidge a dupe?" Catt asked. Others focused their criticism on the use of blacklists. Helen T. Bailie, a member of the DAR from Cambridge, Massachusetts, assailed "the un-American blacklist" that ensured that DAR chapters would hear only one side of certain questions of national and international importance. The DAR did not improve its reputation for open-mindedness when it censured, suspended, and finally expelled Bailie. Some members of the American Legion also spoke up in defense of free speech. "How can the Legion pledge itself to support the Constitution of the United States, and then deny one of the fundamental things in that Constitution?" a former post chaplain in Raleigh,

North Carolina, wrote Spafford.[58] Other critics assailed the policy of the American Legion.

Far more damaging to the DAR and the legion than the direct attacks of their critics was the ridicule that their policies aroused. William Allen White, the Kansas editor, explained that the Daughters had been "lured into Red-baiting by the tea gladiators of Washington . . . apoplectic old gentlemen in red flannels who escape the boredom of their rich wives by sitting in club windows and bemoaning the decadence of the growing world." Elsewhere in his editorial, which was widely reprinted, White described the DAR president as "a lovely lady with many beautiful qualities of heart and mind, but in her enthusiasm she has allowed several lengths of Ku Klux nightie to show under her red, white and blue." *The Nation* decided that the best answer to the blacklist was a party and issued invitations to every individual and organization that had been proscribed. "You may bring your friend if you can prove that his name appears on any blacklist," the invitation read. "Otherwise, he will not be admitted. . . . The only thing your friends can do is to commit a dangerous or subversive act before next year's party." More than eight hundred people showed up at the Level Club on May 9, 1928, where they listened to humorous telegrams from writers, lawyers, and politicians. Bailie was among the throng that witnessed the "trial" of a libel lawsuit by the writer Heywood Broun against the DAR for not including him on its list. Clarence Darrow and Arthur Garfield Hays served as counsel. Unfortunately, the remarks by Groucho Marx, a character witness, have been lost in time.[59]

CHAPTER 3

Banned in Boston

Roscoe Arbuckle was on top of the world on September 3, 1921. As "Fatty" Arbuckle, he was one of the country's most celebrated movie stars at a time when the movies were drawing more than sixty-five million people to the theaters every week. Like Douglas Fairbanks, Charlie Chaplin, and Mary Pickford, he earned an enormous salary—$4,500 per week. With that kind of money, at the age of thirty-three, he could afford every luxury, including a $25,000 custom-built automobile that featured a full bar and toilet. Nevertheless, the work could be grueling. Movies were shorter than they are today, and it was not unusual for a star to be working on several films simultaneously. Arbuckle's schedule had been particularly hectic after he signed a new contract with Paramount Pictures earlier in the year. With the approach of the Labor Day weekend, he left Hollywood and motored north to San Francisco, where he checked into a two-bedroom suite at the city's best hotel, the St. Francis. He told his friends to join him there for three days of partying and relaxation.

Just ten days later, Arbuckle was sitting in a jail cell, indicted for manslaughter in the death of a young actress, Virginia Rappe, whom he was accused of raping. Over the next seven months, he would be tried three times. The first two juries could not agree. The prosecutor's case was based on the testimony of a woman who had accompanied Rappe to the party and claimed to have seen the star drag Rappe into a bedroom and to have heard her cry out that she was being raped. However, the defense showed that the companion had been elsewhere when she claimed to have witnessed the abduction, that the autopsy revealed no evidence of an assault, and that death may well have been the result of a botched abortion. The third jury took no time in acquitting Arbuckle but paused to write a statement that the foreman received permission to read to the court. "Acquittal is not enough for Roscoe Arbuckle," the foreman said. "We feel that a great injustice has been done him. We feel also that it was only our plain duty to give him this exoneration, under the evidence, for there was not the slightest proof adduced to connect him in any way with the commission of a crime."[1] But Arbuckle's acting career was over. Criticism of the loose moral standards of the Hollywood community had been growing for a number of years. In early 1921, the country had been shocked by the suicide of Olive Thomas, a beloved star, who was rumored to have despaired over the cocaine addiction of her actor husband. Many were appalled when Mary Pickford divorced her movie star husband to marry Douglas Fairbanks.

Arbuckle's indictment spurred a demand for a ban on the exhibition of his movies. Some of the protesters were religious leaders and heads of women's groups who believed that showing the films set a bad moral example for children. Others were city officials. "Any further exhibition of such films...would tend at this time to offend public morals," the mayor of Philadelphia told the director of public safety. The mayor of Medford, Massachusetts, and the Providence, Rhode Island, Police Commission also banned the films. Further official action was unnecessary, however, as theater owners pulled the movies themselves to avoid further controversy. In New York City, the owners of more than five hundred theaters agreed to ban Arbuckle's pictures. Shortly after Arbuckle's acquittal, Will H. Hays, the president of a new movie trade association, the Motion Picture Producers and Distributors Association, announced that Paramount and the other companies who had produced his pictures were withdrawing them from circulation in deference to public outrage. Although the ban was rescinded in December, Arbuckle never worked in front of the camera again.[2]

Arbuckle's defenders have denounced the banning of the harmless films of an innocent man. But the movie industry was besieged. Since its inception around 1905, it had faced the very real possibility that it would be destroyed by censorship. Religious leaders and other members of the country's social and political elite were deeply disturbed by the advent of a business that was wildly popular. (The movies were drawing nearly 900,000 people per week to more than four hundred theaters in Manhattan alone.) The fact that the overwhelming majority of the audience were immigrants and members of the working class raised fears about social order. What were the workers learning from the movies for which they had such an insatiable appetite? As theaters spread from working-class districts to the burgeoning suburbs, middle-class parents began to worry about the social and cultural messages being given to their own children. Chicago passed the first municipal censorship ordinance in 1907. A few years later, Pennsylvania, Ohio, and Kansas created state censorship boards. The Mutual Film Corporation challenged the Ohio censorship law in a case that reached the U.S. Supreme Court in 1915. But the Court was not at all sympathetic. It ruled unanimously that movies are not constitutionally protected. "It cannot be put out of view that the exhibition of moving pictures is a business pure and simple, originated and conducted for profit, like other spectacles, not to be regarded by the Ohio Constitution, we think, as part of the press of the country or as organs of public opinion," Justice Joseph McKenna declared. The film industry faced a dire situation when New York and Florida passed film censorship laws in early 1921.[3] Its success depended on marketing films to a national audience. However, five states and over one hundred municipalities had the power to cut their product to shreds. Fatty Arbuckle was thrown to the wolves in a frantic effort to appease the industry's critics and head off further censorship.

The movie censors didn't talk about their work much, perhaps because there is little glory in telling other adults what they can see, read, and hear. But Morris Ernst, the cocounsel of the ACLU, and Pare Lorentz managed to interview Emma Viets, the chair of the Kansas City censorship board, for their 1930 book, *Censored: The Private Life of the Movie*. Viets, the former owner of a rural movie house, was proud of her work. "It is our job to help the moving picture fulfill its avowed purpose—to amuse the public in a clean and wholesome way," she said. Viets did not see herself as an enemy of the movies. On the contrary, she insisted that her cuts actually made good films better. "It is incredible how much that is questionable can be insinuated into an otherwise innocent and interesting picture. Needlessly insinuated, for in most places it destroys the continuity of the story and has no bearing on the plot," she explained. She gave an example of one picture in which she had ordered the deletion of a scene at the end in which a son gives his dying father an overdose of poison. "From a humanitarian point of view it may have been all right. But it was ethically wrong. . . . It opened up new vistas of thought and speculation," she said. "The film was long anyway and could stand cutting," she added.[4]

A woman in her fifties, Viets was a typical censor. Censors were always white, often female, and ever ready to remove scenes that would undermine the political, social, or sexual status quo. The legislation authorizing the censorship boards gave them the power to suppress a wide range of subject matter, differing mainly in their specificity. New York's definition of prohibited material included anything that was "obscene, indecent, immoral, inhuman, sacrilegious or . . . tend[s] to corrupt morals or incite to crime." Maryland's censorship board enumerated a more precise list:

> Suggestive comedy, stories built on illicit love, over-passionate love scenes, disrespect of the law and condonation of crime by officers of the law, men and women living together in adultery and without marriage, drinking and gambling made attractive, prolonged success to criminals, profanity in titles, maternity scenes, stories and incidents showing disrespect of any religion, advocacy of the doctrine of free love, and titles calculated to stir up racial hatred and antagonistic relations between labour and capital.

With a broad mandate to protect the status quo, the censors bravely tackled the enormous task of screening thousands of miles of film every year. They were more than up to the task. In 1928, they reviewed 597 feature films. Forty-four of the films were rejected outright in one or more states. The censor ordered 2,960 cuts in the rest. More than half of the cuts related to the depiction of crime, and nearly a third were aimed at sex. Only forty-two of the films were so innocuous that they escaped unscathed.[5]

The censorship boards were very precise in ordering deletions.

"Eliminate all views of party bandit holding up guest at point of gun," one censor ordered the producers of a 1933 feature, *Morton Downey*. "Eliminate all views of bandit taking jewels and money from the guests. Eliminate all views of bandit with gun still held on crowd as he prepares to leave and dialogue, 'Stick 'em up.'" Censors ordered that the scene of a child breast-feeding be cut from another 1933 movie. They came down hard on a dancing girl in *Thrown Out of the Joint* (1933). "Eliminate all views of Hilda, the dancing girl, wriggling her body in a suggestive manner during dance. Eliminate close view of girl (Hilda) shaking her breasts." The censors also disliked long kisses and frequently ordered them eliminated or shortened, specifying the exact number of film feet that should be removed. "Shorten to flash of five feet scene of Diana and Holderness on couch embracing and kissing," the Virginia film board told one producer. Sometimes, so many deletions were ordered that they destroyed the continuity of the film. After heavily cutting *The Easiest Way*, a censorship board could no longer follow the story. "We had to stop in the middle of it, because we thought we were looking at the wrong reels," one of the censors admitted.[6]

The censors' mission was to suppress ideas that challenged the morality of their time. They would turn a blind eye to the depiction of prostitution in *Old San Francisco*, a nearly nude seduction scene in *The Prodigal*, and the rampant debauchery of *The Ten Commandments* because each of these films showed the villains being punished for their sins. (In *Old San Francisco*, the heroine is saved from defilement by the earthquake of 1906—"thus explaining a catastrophe that saved many lives," Ernst observes.) But they would not stand for a story that treated an unwed mother with sympathy, even when it involved no prurient material at all. The moral failings of religious leaders had been a staple of American culture since the publication of *The Scarlet Letter*. However, when a popular play involving a villainous minister was transferred to film, the minister was transformed into a "professional reformer." The New York censors were known for being particularly strict in upholding the honesty of the police and elected officials. They were especially offended by *The Racket*, which portrayed the notorious corruption of the Chicago authorities during Prohibition, cutting all references to payoffs of judges and police officers as well as any suggestion of vote fixing. They also cut a title in this silent film that read, "Government by the professionals, of the professionals, for the professionals."[7]

Although the motion picture industry opposed government censorship and occasionally fought it, it usually responded to the threat of government action by proposing self-censorship as an alternative. The movie moguls were panic-stricken when movie censorship bills were introduced in thirty-two states in the aftermath of the Arbuckle scandal. "Hollywood front offices decided to go moral," the actor Jackie Coogan recalled. "Guys were told to cut themselves down to two or three mistresses." The studios also embraced self-censorship. The director King Vidor described a meeting called by Louis Mayer, the head of MGM, in January 1922:

> I remember that all the directors were called into the projection room. Louis Mayer was there. Suddenly he said, "Right, roll." Up on the screen came a number of clips; they were all from the latest movies that we had made that were just about to be released. When they'd all been run through, Mayer turned to us and said, "I've had all those scenes cut from your movies."... Now, believe me, they were so panicky that they had cut anything and everything that anyone could conceivably take offense to and a good deal more besides.

The movie companies also decided that they needed to create a new trade association and to put Will Hays at its head. Hays was a skilled political strategist. As the head of the Republican National Committee, Hays, at thirty-eight, had helped to engineer the landslide election of Warren G. Harding. He was also a Presbyterian from Indiana, an important asset for an industry that was run by immigrant Jews. Hays assured the country that the studios had given him the power to "clean up" the movie business.[8] He had his work cut out for him.

But it was not only movies that were under attack. The censors were targeting books as well. At times during the early 1920s, artistic freedom appeared to be in danger of disappearing entirely.

It was sex and violence that made the censors mad. Violent material had been a concern since at least 1885, when the Massachusetts legislature passed a law aimed at publications that specialized in sensational accounts of crime. It banned the sale to minors of books and magazines that featured "criminal news, police reports, or accounts of criminal deeds, or pictures and stories of lust or crimes" and also made it a crime to display this material for sale "within the view of any minor child." Seven booksellers in Boston and Lowell were convicted under the law in 1892 and hit with heavy fines. Violence was one of the primary concerns of the Chicago police officials who became the nation's first film censors. They took it on themselves to remove scenes of murder, robbery, and abduction from silent westerns like *The James Gang* and *Night Riders.* When an exhibitor appealed these cuts to the courts, the Illinois Supreme Court upheld them on the grounds that the movies were attended by large numbers of children and others whose "age, education and situation in life specially entitled them to protection against the evil influence of immoral representations." A censorship law in Toronto banned all cinematic displays of guns.[9]

There were also strong objections to the sexual content of many films. In part, this reflects the fact that movies emerged in the cities and offered images that appealed to urban audiences, including scenes of New York nightlife, details of the lives of the lower classes, and public displays of sexuality, ranging from couples kissing to prostitutes walking the streets. Sexual material did not have to be explicit to raise objections. Many films merely drew attention to the female anatomy, including Thomas Edison's 1901 film, *What Happened on Twenty-third Street,* which showed a woman's skirt being blown up by a gust of air from a street vent, revealing her underclothes. Fatty Arbuckle's films were banned not because they had any sexual content but because they drew attention to the sordid details of his case. The Good Government Club of Topeka complained "that the Arbuckle pictures caused 'unpleasant and disgusting gossip,' particularly among the youth of the State."[10]

American society in 1920 was still ruled by the social mores of the late nineteenth century. On sexual matters, it was as conservative as Victorian England. Although women had fought a long, hard battle for the vote, most Americans, including the overwhelming majority of women, believed that the proper role of women was to serve as the center of family life, raising the children on whom depended the future of their country and their race. "Home and mother and love's devotion" should constitute the themes of modern literature, Paul Elmore More, the editor of *The Nation,* wrote in 1906. Fifteen years later, a Presbyterian minister in Pittsburgh warned that the movies were threatening these cornerstones of social order. "The moving picture is poisoning the youth of America and they are slipping away from the Sunday School, the Christian endeavor and the Church." His clinching evidence was the rising rate of divorce. "There have been over one million divorce cases in the past 20 years," he said.[11]

Americans were not just reticent about discussing sex; many of them feared it. It had not always been so. In the early nineteenth century, the egalitarian social ideals that had helped fuel the American and French Revolutions had led some reformers to call for equality in the relationship between the sexes. Some attacked marriage, insisting that only when men and women could enter into sexual relationships freely would women gain true equality. In their view, sex was a healthy act so long as both parties gave their consent. At the same time, sexually explicit books, magazines, and newspapers became increasingly available as publishers and printers in the rapidly expanding cities created a "sporting press" to appeal to men. These publications ranged from sexually explicit classics like Boccaccio's *Decameron* and Petronius's *Satyricon* to publications that provided coverage of the new, overwhelmingly male entertainments, including theater, opera, and concert balls. As the number of single males grew, so did prostitution, and the sporting press covered that subject, too. Some publishers even produced guides to the city's brothels.

But the sex radicals were a bare handful of individuals, and while sporting males may have come increasingly to dominate the nation's cities, the country was still governed by the values of the rural hinterland. These values were shaped by a Christian religion that had become increasingly evangelical as revivalists called on sinners to throw off the formalities of their faith and be reborn in a personal relationship with Jesus Christ. The Christians were horrified by the attacks on the institution of marriage, and they soon received powerful reinforcement from the medical profession. In the decades before the Civil War, many doctors began to pay attention to the physiology of sex. But the more they learned about the power of the sex instinct, the more they came to fear its ability to overwhelm reason. They were convinced that masturbation could lead young men astray, causing them to lose interest in anything but sex and driving them into the arms of prostitutes. There they would find venereal disease, madness, and finally death. Obviously, marriage was not only a divinely inspired institution but an essential means of preserving society.

It was Anthony Comstock, a young Civil War veteran, who exploited the sexual anxieties of his age to create a national censorship regime for the first time in American history. He was not the first to censor material with sexual content. Twenty states and four territories had banned the publication and sale of obscene material before the Civil War. The federal government prohibited the importation of obscene material in the 1840s and made it a crime to mail obscene material in 1865. But Comstock capitalized on the growing fear of sex by targeting books. "The effect of this cursed business on our youth and society, no pen can describe," Comstock insisted. But he went on to describe the impact of a dirty book in great detail:

> It breeds lust. Lust defiles the body, debauches the imagination, corrupts the mind, deadens the will, destroys the memory, sears the conscience, hardens the heart, and damns the soul. It unnerves the arm, and steals away the elastic step. It robs the soul of many virtues, and imprints upon the mind of youth, visions that throughout life curse the man or woman. Like a panorama, the imagination seems to keep this hated thing before the mind, until it wears its way deeper and deeper, plunging the victim into practices that he loathes.

It is masturbation that starts youth down the road to ruin, and therefore even the smallest temptation could be his undoing. "The mind must not be permitted to dwell for a moment upon improper subjects," Comstock insisted. "All reading and conversation must be of the most pure and elevating character." Inevitably, books, because they could be perused privately, became the main focus of the antipornography crusade. "Bad books are worse, far worse, than bad companions," Boston's Watch and Ward Society proclaimed.[12]

In the beginning, Comstock's crusade was a one-man affair. Born in Connecticut, he shared the conviction of his Puritan ancestors that it was the duty of government to curb the behavior of naturally sinful men. He also possessed a strong sense of personal responsibility and the courage to back it up. At five feet, ten inches tall and 210 pounds, Comstock was powerfully built. At the age of eighteen, he raided a saloon in his hometown, dumping the liquor on the ground. After he moved to New York City, he began to push the police to arrest booksellers, printers, and other distributors of books and "rubber goods"—condoms, diaphragms, and mastur-batory aids. He soon came to the attention of the Young Men's Christian Association (YMCA), which had recently pushed a strengthened obscenity law through the New York legislature. In 1872, Comstock went to work as an investigator for the YMCA's Committee for the Suppression of Vice. Only a year later, using the influential connections of his organization and a display of the erot-ica that he had seized in raids, he persuaded Congress to strengthen the federal obscenity law by passing what became known as the Comstock Act. The law created a new position of special agent in the United States Post Office and gave him the power to confiscate obscene mail and arrest the senders. Comstock was only twenty-eight when he was appointed to the post. A few months later, he also became the head of the New York Society for the Suppression of Vice.[13]

For the next forty-two years, Anthony Comstock would police the American marketplace. As the years passed, he would seem in-creasingly old-fashioned with his luxuriant side whiskers and clean-shaven chin. He was ridiculed for his excesses, including his attack on playwright George Bernard Shaw as "this Irish smut dealer" and the arrest of a secretary in the Art Students' League in New York for mailing a pamphlet that included drawings of nudes. But his influence was profound. The Comstock Act made it a crime to mail a broad range of sexual material: erotica; contraceptive medications or devices; chemicals that could be used to induce abortions; sexual implements, including dildos and other masturbatory aids; contra-ceptive information; and advertisements for contraception, abortion, or sexual implements. It also gave federal judges the power to issue search warrants for "any such obscene or indecent books, papers, ar-ticles or things," which meant that investigators no longer had to witness a sale before moving against a suspected purveyor. Other cities soon followed the example of New York, and antivice societies began operating in Boston, St. Louis, Chicago, Louisville, Cincin-nati, and San Francisco. Forty-five states passed "little Comstock"

laws. Whereas the federal law banned the mailing of obscene material, these statutes made it a crime to actually sell it in a bookstore or
on a newsstand.[14]

Comstock's career was not without frustrations. The reports of
the New York Society for the Suppression of Vice repeatedly complained about New York City prosecutors who failed to vigorously
pursue obscenity cases. In addition, the ease with which obscene
material could be produced and sold meant that notwithstanding
Comstock's success in seizing hundreds of thousands of books, pictures, woodcuts, indecent playing cards, songs, and advertisements,
the goal of suppressing obscene material altogether remained elu-
sive. Ultimately, Comstock's most impressive and personally satisfy-
ing victories were not against pornographers but against men and
women who were philosophically opposed to his view of sex. Beginning with his prosecution of feminist Victoria Woodhull in 1872,
Comstock had used the obscenity laws to persecute those he condemned as "free lusters" for advocating changes in the relationship
between the sexes and the institution of marriage that he believed
would destroy society through sexual licentiousness. He accused
Woodhull of violating the law by writing about the alleged adultery
of Henry Ward Beecher, a prominent Brooklyn minister. She escaped on a technicality, but he succeeded in convicting Dr. Edward
Bliss Foote for mailing a pamphlet that contained birth control information (he was fined $3,500); Ezra Haywood for advocating the
view that sexual relations were no business of the state (he was
released by presidential pardon); and D. M. Bennett for protesting
Comstock's crusade by selling a free love tract that had already been
declared obscene (he served thirteen months in prison). Comstock's
prosecutions of the sex radicals led to the first national protest against
a censorship law in 1878 when nearly seventy thousand people
signed a petition to Congress urging the repeal of the Comstock Act.
But Congress ignored the petition, and Comstock succeeded in his
effort to suppress the discussion of sex. In 1899, the New England
Watch and Ward Society claimed to have cleaned up Boston so well
that "nothing further [was] needed but constant watchfulness."[15]

But the subject of sex was too important to be permanently suppressed. The same desire for sexual equality that had motivated the
sex radicals in the early nineteenth century helped give birth to the

campaign to grant women the vote in the early twentieth century. The leaders of the American suffrage movement avoided controversial issues like the right to equal pay and birth control. The demand for political equality was met with strong and determined resistance, and they kept their focus narrow in an effort to attract the widest possible support. Yet the fact that women were challenging their role in the American political order inevitably raised larger questions. Women, long considered the weaker sex, had taken control of their own political destiny and were demonstrating unexpected courage. In the winter of 1917, Alice Paul, who had served a prison sentence in England as a result of a suffrage protest there, began picketing the White House in an effort to win Woodrow Wilson's support for the Nineteenth Amendment. She and her supporters were ignored at first, then arrested for obstructing traffic. When fines did not deter the protesters, Paul was sentenced to seven months in prison. When she started a hunger strike, she was transferred to a mental hospital and force-fed three times a day for three weeks. Finally, newspaper coverage of the treatment of Paul and other protesters who had joined her hunger strike produced a public outcry that set her free.

Only a few months before, another woman, Margaret Sanger, had opened the nation's first birth control clinic and had been quickly arrested for distributing pamphlets telling poor women how to keep from getting pregnant. Ironically, Comstock's war against birth control was lost even before it had started. Information about a variety of birth control methods had been widely available for many years, and women in the United States and other western countries had used it to cut birth rates by nearly half at the turn of the twentieth century. Yet poor women had far less access to the information they needed than middle-class and wealthy women who could afford to consult doctors. For them, abortion was often the only available form of birth control, and Sanger described the long line of immigrant women, shawls over their heads, who waited every day outside the office of a $5 abortionist on the Lower East Side. Botched abortions and inadequate prenatal care gave the United States one of the highest maternal death rates among industrialized countries.[16]

Sanger was determined to do something to help poor women. The daughter of Irish immigrants, she had grown up in poverty herself in Corning, New York. Her father, Michael Higgins, was a stonecutter with radical political views. Although he went into business for himself, he was a talker, not a businessman. He may also have been an alcoholic. These were disastrous qualities in a man with six children, and the family struggled and was saved only by the earnings of Margaret's older brothers and sisters. From their earnings as domestics, her sisters were able to ensure that Margaret had a high school education, but college was out of the question. Margaret became a nurse and married William Sanger, an architect with Socialist views. On moving to New York in 1910, Margaret also joined the Socialist Party and became active in party activities, opening her home to Big Bill Haywood, Emma Goldman, Alexander Berkman, and the journalist John Reed, who would become famous for his 1919 book, *Ten Days That Shook the World,* an eyewitness account of the opening days of the Russian Revolution. During the day, she worked for the Visiting Nurses Association, which had been organized by Lillian Wald of the Henry Street Settlement. Sanger found her life's work as a nurse and midwife among the poor of the Lower East Side. She would lead the fight to legalize birth control for the next fifty years.[17]

Margaret Sanger first ran afoul of Anthony Comstock in 1913 when he forced a Socialist newspaper, the *New York Call,* to drop an article about venereal disease that she had written as part of a series called "What Every Girl Should Know." But the thirty-four-year-old Sanger was only getting started. The next year she published her own magazine, *The Woman Rebel,* which promised to serve as the voice of working women, including prostitutes. Sanger rejected the issues raised by middle-class feminists, including the right to work, the right to ignore fashions, and the right to keep the maiden name. These reforms did not begin to address the problem. "I believe that woman is enslaved by the world machine, by sex conventions, by motherhood and its present necessary childrearing, by wage-slavery, by middle-class morality, by customs, law and superstitions," Sanger wrote. What women needed was complete moral autonomy. To be a woman rebel is "to look the whole world in the face with a go-to-hell look in the eyes; to have an ideal; to speak and act in defiance of convention. . . .What rebel women claim is the right to be lazy. The right to be an unmarried mother. The right to destroy. The right to create. The right to live. The right to love." Sanger promised that in future issues she would advocate the principle of contraception as well as describe how to practice it. She never got the chance. The United States Post Office refused to mail *Woman Rebel* and confiscated the copies that had been submitted to it. Sanger tried to sneak copies through by mailing small bundles at scattered locations but was caught and indicted on four counts of obscenity. As her trial approached, she decided to flee the country rather than face as many as forty-five years in jail.[18]

For Comstock, there could be no compromise on the issue of birth control. Protecting against conception was simply an incitement to sexual intercourse. "Are we to have homes or brothels?" he asked in 1915 shortly after he had helped indict Sanger's husband, William, who had been caught distributing his wife's pamphlet, *Family Limitation*. "Can't everybody, whether rich or poor, control themselves?" Comstock died a few weeks after William Sanger was sentenced to thirty days in jail. But public opinion was beginning to shift. After ten months of exile in Europe, Margaret returned to the United States to stand trial. She was encouraged by growing public support for her cause. "We are done with the irresponsible stork," *The New Republic* proclaimed. "We are done with the taboo that forbids discussion of the subject." *Harper's Weekly* published a series of stories about birth control. Even the *New York Times,* which had failed to report Sanger's arrest and flight, began to cover the story, although initially it avoided using words like "prevention of conception." As her trial approached, Sanger became a celebrity. With red hair and green eyes, the slight and attractive defendant soon found the newspapers describing what she was wearing. When the prosecutors decided to drop the charges in February 1916, Sanger's star rose still higher. She immediately embarked on a speaking tour, addressing sold-out auditoriums in many of the leading cities. She would continue to encounter opposition. Efforts to deny her a platform in St. Louis led Roger Baldwin to organize his first free speech demonstration, and only a few months later she would be arrested for opening the nation's first birth control clinic in Brooklyn. But Sanger had won an important battle in the fight for birth control—and free speech.[19]

At first, American literature failed to reflect the dramatic changes symbolized by the enfranchisement of women and the demands of rebels like Margaret Sanger for equality in the bedroom as well as at the polls. In stark and self-conscious contrast with the movies, which used visceral thrills to appeal to its mass audience, the publishing community saw its mission as producing books and magazines that ennobled existence by focusing on eternal values. According to Henry Van Dyke, one of the leading American critics of the day, great literature "is that which recognizes the moral conflict as the supreme interest of life, and the message of Christianity as the only real promise of victory." Few authors before World War I were brave enough to challenge these conventions of genteel society, and the few who did found themselves in trouble with the law. In 1907, an English romance, *Three Weeks,* became a bestseller in the United States using the kind of language that is found today in TV soap operas. "Beautiful, savage Paul," the thirty-year-old married heroine whispers to her young paramour. "Do you love me?" Paul enthusiastically agrees. " 'Then,' said the lady in a voice in which all the caresses of the world seemed melted, 'then, sweet Paul, I shall teach you many things, and among them I shall teach you how—to— LIVE.' " Despite sales that quickly reached fifty thousand, the Boston antivice group, the Watch and Ward Society, had the book declared obscene. The judge rejected the publisher's claim that the words "obscene" and "indecent" were vague. "They are common words and may be assumed to be understood in their common meaning by an ordinary jury," he said.[20]

Notwithstanding this victory for good taste, the trickle of "bad" books before World War I became a torrent in the 1920s. The idealism of the Progressive movement in the early years of the century had encouraged Americans to suppress their personal desires in the interest of reform at home and the spread of democracy abroad. But the end of the war was deeply disillusioning. They had given up lives, limbs, and a large degree of personal freedom to make the world safe for democracy, but Woodrow Wilson had been unable to secure a just peace or even American participation in the League of Nations. "So much nonsense, and so many lies, were promulgated during that hysterical period in the guise of patriotic idealism, and rammed so ruthlessly into people's minds, that there has been a violent reaction," the novelist Floyd Dell explained. A new generation of authors like Dell, Sherwood Anderson, H. L. Mencken, F. Scott Fitzgerald, Sinclair Lewis, John Dos Passos, and Ben Hecht produced novels that rejected the values of self-sacrifice and social uplift. It was a literature that fitted well with younger Americans who were demanding more personal freedom and exhibiting it by dancing to a new music (jazz), drinking in defiance of Prohibition, and putting miles between themselves and their elders in the cars that were pouring off the production lines.[21]

In the desire to cast off old-fashioned values, there was also a willingness to deal more frankly with sex. Sigmund Freud had given the subject a new scientific legitimacy by demonstrating the centrality of sex in all aspects of human behavior. In literature, D. H. Lawrence proclaimed that sex had been unjustly ignored. "Let us hesitate no longer to announce that the sensual passions and mysteries are equally sacred with the spiritual mysteries and passions," he wrote in 1920. At that moment, James Joyce was in Paris finishing *Ulysses,* a novel that law enforcement authorities would find particularly troubling because it combined great artistic achievement with unprecedented sexual explicitness. In July 1920, John S. Sumner, Comstock's successor as secretary of the New York Society for the Suppression of Vice, arrested Margaret Anderson and Jane Heap, the editors of the *Little Review,* a literary magazine that had been publishing excerpts from *Ulysses.* The latest excerpt described indirectly but clearly a middle-aged man's thoughts as he secretly masturbated while observing a young girl. When a lawyer claimed that the language was too veiled to be obscene, the judge scoffed. "The man went off in his pants," he said. Anderson and Heap were fined $50, but not before Anderson tried to put the prosecutors on trial. "It was the poet, the artist, who discovered love, created the lover, made sex everything that it is beyond a function," she said. "It is the Mr. Sumners who have made obscenity."[22]

Like the publisher in the *Three Weeks* case, Margaret Anderson was arguing that the term "obscenity" should be defined in a way that would allow the publication of serious works of literature. The law had no way to distinguish between "pornographic" works, whose main purpose was sexual stimulation, and works that treated sexual subjects for other purposes. However, things were beginning to change. In 1913, Comstock had attempted to suppress the sale of *Hagar Revelly,* a novel in which a young woman is seduced by her employer and later becomes his mistress. The book was part of a growing genre of novels generated by the efforts to eliminate prostitution, which involved tens of thousands of women in New York alone. The author, Daniel Carson Goodman, a physician who was active in the antiprostitution campaign, intended his novel to be a cautionary tale, and his lawyer succeeded in convincing the jury that it was impossible to solve the problem of prostitution if you couldn't write about it. In 1920, the New York Court of Appeals, the state's highest court, ruled that only books that appealed to a "prurient" or excessive interest in sex could be banned as obscene. Two year later, it provided further protection for serious works by declaring that a book could not be condemned based on isolated passages but "must be considered broadly as a whole." It also ruled that the defense in obscenity cases could introduce testimony from experts to establish an author's reputation and a book's artistic merit.[23]

These decisions were deeply distressing to John Sumner of the New York Society for the Suppression of Vice. He was already operating under heavy handicaps. It was not easy to fill the shoes of a larger-than-life character like Anthony Comstock. Comstock had personally dragged villains to jail. At forty-five, Sumner was "a mild little man," a lawyer who tried to make the best of his averageness by presenting himself as a typical American—"a plain, ordinary, everyday, hard-working American daddy." He was also confronting something that Comstock had never faced—an avalanche of questionable books from mainstream publishers who insisted that their works had redeeming social value. Nevertheless, he fought hard to hold the line established by Comstock. "If the language of the book is lewd . . . it is a violation of the law, regardless of the literary or artistic character of the published matter," he insisted. Indeed, "the greater the artist, the more important to suppress him when he traverses the conventional standards." However, the ground that Comstock had claimed was slipping out from under the feet of his successor. In July 1922, a New York judge cited the literary qualities of the novel *Jurgen* in ordering a jury to acquit its publisher of the obscenity charge that Sumner had filed. Two months later, he lost two more cases as judges approved the sale of D. H. Lawrence's *Women in Love* and the Roman classic *Satyricon*. Sumner was particularly upset by the legalization of *Satyricon*. "The *Decameron* is a Sunday School book beside it," he said, referring to the long-standing fight to suppress Boccaccio's famous book. The decision "condemns the public ... to receive all the literary garbage of ancient and modern Europe, and some domestic decadence."[24]

Just when things looked their darkest, however, the sixteen-year-old daughter of a Manhattan judge borrowed a copy of *Women in Love* from the circulating library of her local book dealer, setting off a controversy that would carry the advocates of "clean books" as close to victory as they would ever get. Troubled by some of its passages, she took the book to her mother, who soon demanded the intervention of her husband, John Ford, a trial court judge. Ford, a bulldog of a man with a bullet-shaped head, was so outraged that he wanted to beat the bookseller, as he said later. Instead, he appealed to the district attorney, who sorrowfully informed him that the courts had only recently ruled that the Lawrence novel was not obscene under the New York statute. Ford consulted Sumner, and in February 1923 issued a call to fifty civic, fraternal, and religious organizations to meet at the Astor Hotel for the purpose of planning a campaign that would strengthen the state obscenity law. Representatives of the Catholic and Protestant Episcopal Churches, the Boy Scouts and Girl Scouts, the Colonial Dames of America, and the Daughters of 1812 heard Ford denounce the rapid spread of obscenity and approved his plan to override the protections that the courts had provided. The bill that was introduced by the new Clean Books League rejected the idea that a book should be considered as a whole and authorized a ban if any passage was found to be dirty. It also did away with the requirement that the book appeal to prurient interest, leading one critic to suggest that a passage describing a man eating corned beef and cabbage with his fingers might be banned. Finally, it excluded the use of experts to testify about the redeeming value of a book.[25]

Despite its draconian nature, the "clean books" bill made rapid progress in the New York legislature. The legislature had passed a film censorship law in 1921, and at first it seemed that the book censorship bill would face even less opposition. No one appeared to testify against it at a hearing in the assembly, and it was approved by an overwhelming margin and sent to the Senate. It was only then, as the bill stood on the verge of passage, that critics began to organize.

Alerted to the danger by an Albany reporter, publisher Horace Liveright spread the alarm. He had a lot at stake. His firm, Boni and Liveright, was one of the new publishing houses that were bringing out the avant-garde books that had been rejected by most of the established houses. He had created the Modern Library to serve as a vehicle for new writers like Eugene O'Neill, Ernest Hemingway, and Theodore Dreiser. He himself had been prosecuted for publishing *Satyricon*. Liveright found enough support among newspaper and magazine publishers to persuade the Senate to hold a hearing. "It is hardly too much to say that this is the worst censorship bill that has ever been proposed," the *New York Times* wrote in an editorial on the eve of the hearing. "If this bill is passed, Mr. Sumner will be an absolute and irresponsible censor of all modern literature."[26]

Liveright and his allies were heavily outnumbered at the hearing before the Senate Judiciary Committee. Ford and his supporters were also armed with arguments that they believed gave them the high ground. Ford thought the majority had the right to suppress books it regarded as indecent. "The question of whether a book is indecent is one to be decided by an ordinary average citizen, not by a coterie of literati," Ford had explained to the *New York Times.* "After all, such books are now allowed to enter the home of myself and other ordinary, average citizens, and it is for us to decide whether the sale of such books should be allowed." A spokesman for the Catholic Church made a less democratic argument. "We must be governed by decent laws . . . even at the risk of being denounced for seeking to impose the will of a group on the majority," he said.[27]

But the critics of the bill counterpunched effectively, using a combination of practical and principled arguments. Since any indecent passage condemned a work, the law could be used to suppress "the Bible, several dictionaries, Shakespeare, Boccaccio, Dante and other works," a lawyer argued. "There are Reds and Communists in the world and in this country who are opposed to the Bible and all religion. Are you prepared to arm them with the weapon this bill would afford?" Gertrude Atherton, a novelist, challenged the view that literature threatened children. She had not been harmed by reading the *Decameron* when she was sixteen. "I read it through and I saw nothing in it," she said. "A 16-year-old girl has to be sophisticated before she can understand sex matter if it is written in a literary manner." The arguments on the other side infuriated Ford, who jumped up shouting. "These publishers, editors and authors profess to be greatly concerned about protecting the Bible and Shakespeare," Ford said. "They don't care about the Bible. All they are interested in is the dirty profits from their own filthy books." Atherton was not intimidated by the red-faced judge. "This is perfectly absurd and it is entirely unfair," she replied. Sumner challenged her claims about the incorruptibility of sixteen-year-old girls. "Most of these books are so dull and deadly that they carry their own antidote," she replied. The critics of the clean-books bill were encouraged when the judiciary committee agreed to delay a vote on the bill. There would be more time to organize opposition.

The opponents of censorship faced a serious problem, however. Their base of support was narrow. The largest group in the coalition was the National Publishers Association, representing magazine producers. The magazine publishers had every reason to believe that they would be the first target of stronger obscenity laws. With the launch of *True Story* in 1919, publishers had learned of the tremendous appetite for confessional literature and sexual titillation. It was followed by scores of imitators. Sex quickly became a staple of men's magazines like *Captain Billy's Whiz Bang,* a collection of bawdy jokes and cartoons that sold over 425,000 copies each month. Obscenity prosecutions threatened these lucrative franchises. A representative of the Hearst magazines testified during the judiciary hearing that the suppression of a single issue of a magazine could cost the publisher as much as $1 million. Bernarr MacFadden, the publisher of *True Story,* threatened to move his company out of New York if the clean-books bill passed.[28]

But many in the book industry were not willing to fight the clean-books bill. The National Association of Book Publishers, the major publishing trade association, had refused to follow Liveright into the fight. It did not testify at the hearing and was conspicuously absent from the anticensorship coalition that was organized later. Book publishers, authors, librarians, and booksellers took pride in their role as purveyors of culture, and many considered it part of their job to protect the public from bad books. As early as 1908, Arthur Bostwick, the president of the American Library Association (ALA), warned librarians that American literature was being undermined by immigrants "whose standards of propriety are sometimes those of an earlier and grosser age." The publisher Henry Holt wrote to the *New York Times* in 1922 to condemn the growing sexual explicitness in literature. While the sex instinct is natural and necessary, "titillation through the imagination is not a process of nature at all," Holt wrote. "Its indulgence, counter to the requirements of civilization, is maleficent and destructive. It leads to more murders and suicides than all other causes put together." Holt believed that publishers who exploited sex to sell books deserved to be prosecuted. *Publishers Weekly,* the industry trade journal, wrote that publishers were convinced they were not the target of the clean-books bill. "They have taken the position that this Bill was only intended by its sponsors to meet just that type of publication and that the books of honest character had nothing to fear from the revision."[29]

Librarians and booksellers sometimes acted as censors themselves. Following Bostwick's call to arms in 1908, *Library Journal* asked librarians how they were handling requests for bad books and was flooded with suggestions from around the country for ways to thwart dirty-minded readers. One Atlanta librarian said that she had shelved one book in a place where she thought few would find it. If such a book was discovered and attained an "unprecedented popularity," it was removed from the shelves and finally discarded. The New York Public Library reported that the circulation of "immoral" classics was restricted to those who could demonstrate a scholarly interest. In 1915, Boston booksellers joined with the Watch and Ward Society to review questionable books. When a committee of three booksellers and three Watch and Ward members agreed that a book was unsuitable, they notified all Massachusetts booksellers, who had forty-eight hours to remove it or face possible prosecution. The newspapers cooperated by refusing to review or advertise the banned titles. As a result, it was almost as if the book had never been published. Richard Fuller, the owner of the Old Corner Bookstore and a member of the committee, explained: "In two weeks nobody is talking about the book at all." By 1926, the Boston Booksellers Committee had probably suppressed between 50 and 75 books, including 14 in 1923 alone. "During the last two years, we have had hell," Fuller said.[30]

However, attitudes were changing. The controversy over New

York's clean-books bill led many in the book industry to rethink their roles. Booksellers and librarians spoke out in defense of free expression at the conventions of the American Booksellers Association and the American Library Association in May 1923. Arthur Proctor, an iconoclastic young bookseller from Detroit, told his colleague that young people wanted books that portrayed life honestly:

> They are demanding these books, and so I say that the duty, the responsibility of the bookseller towards his customers, towards the general public is not just to sell books, not just to sell books that have a sweet ending, but it is their duty to get them the books in spite of the censorship, in spite of the censorship of such men as Mr. John Sumner and various older people.

Mary Rothrock, a young Knoxville librarian, delivered a similar message at the ALA convention. It is not the job of a librarian to measure a book's "possible moral effect on mature readers," she said. It is to bring "to all people the books that belong to them." Both young people touched off storms of protest. Proctor's remarks were stricken from the record.[31]

Fortunately, the fate of the clean-books bill did not depend on a unified industry response. Things had changed in Albany since the passage of the film censorship bill in 1921. The Democrats had retaken the governorship and the state senate on a platform that pledged to expand personal freedom by modifying the state Prohibition law and ending film censorship. Their leader in the senate was the debonair James J. Walker, the future mayor of New York and a man whose love of a good time made him an instinctive opponent of censorship. Tall and thin—in striped pajamas he looked like a peppermint stick, Al Smith joked—Walker took the lead in the debate on the clean-books bill. "No woman was ever ruined by a book," Walker assured his colleagues. Although some Democrats deserted him, a number of Republicans also switched sides, defeating the clean-books bill by 31-15. A few weeks later, Walker joined H. L. Mencken and others at a testimonial dinner for Horace Liveright in Greenwich Village. Liveright celebrated his victory over Judge Ford by announcing his resignation from the book publishers' association.[32]

The fight against the clean-books bill was a turning point in the attitude of the book industry toward censorship. Liveright was not the only protester within the National Association of Book Publishers. Two industry leaders, Alfred Harcourt and George Palmer Putnam, resigned committee positions in a protest over the association's failure to oppose censorship. In response, the association hired Harlan Fiske Stone to help it formulate a new position on obscenity legislation. The resulting manifesto bent over backwards to acknowledge the right to suppress obscenity, but it also attempted to shift the debate from the issue of protecting children to the First Amendment rights of adults. "Not all writing is intended for the immature, and no state ought to consider restricting book publication to such volumes as are suitable for the immature," it read. When the clean-books bill was reintroduced in 1924, the publishers sent Stone to testify against it. The American Library Association also opposed the bill, which did not even pass the reactionary assembly this time. At their convention a few months later, booksellers joined the rest of the book industry by condemning all censorship except "the censorship of intelligent public opinion." Opinion had shifted so strongly by late 1924 that H. L. Mencken declared free speech triumphant. "To be a censor today, a man must be not only an idiot; he must be also a man courageous enough in his imbecility to endure the low guffaws of his next-door neighbors." But the censors were far from finished—and Mencken was their next target.[33]

Mencken was born to be censored. Beginning his professional life as a Baltimore newspaper reporter, he developed a cynical view of average Americans, whom he dubbed "the booboisie." "No one ever went broke underestimating the intelligence of the American middle class," he famously remarked. His wit found a ready audience in a country that had grown disillusioned with democratic pieties, and Mencken developed a national reputation as a columnist and literary critic. He was particularly scathing in his attacks on fundamentalism. His coverage of the Scopes trial in July 1925 ridiculed the prosecution, William Jennings Bryan, and the state of Tennessee, helping shape the view outside the South that the case had been a national travesty. By then, Mencken had his own magazine, *American Mercury*, which included authors whose language was often as ferocious as the editor's. In a December 1925 article bemoaning the decline of Boston's cultural institutions, Charles Angoff put much of the blame on "immigrant morons." "Outside of servants, traffic cops and low politicians the Irish Catholics have given Boston nothing," he wrote. "Perhaps the old Boston culture was doomed to collapse anyhow. But one thing is certain: the invasion of these barbarians made its further growth impossible, and its renaissance will not take place until they are exterminated."[34]

As a professional incendiary, Mencken rarely worried that he might go too far. So he was unpleasantly surprised to learn in March 1926 that the April issue of *American Mercury* had been banned as obscene by the New England Watch and Ward Society. Mencken was certainly familiar with the group. He had published an article only a few months before attacking its leader, J. Franklin Chase, a former Methodist minister. But he had not hesitated a minute before publishing the article in question, "Hatrack," a piece by Herbert Asbury, a New York newspaperman. "Hatrack" was a chapter from Asbury's book *Up from Methodism,* which was critical of religion as it was practiced in his small hometown in Missouri. It was the sad story of the town's part-time prostitute who would have given up her sinful life in a minute if any of the ministers who routinely promised God's forgiveness had made the slightest gesture to reclaim her. Every Sunday, the tall and angular woman went to church hoping for rebirth only to be met with scorn. On her return, she picked up a line of waiting men and serviced them in the Masonic or Catholic graveyards, depending on their religion. Chase considered the story "filthy and degrading" and ordered the magazine withdrawn from Boston's newsstands. Felix Caragianes, a Greek immigrant who owned a newsstand in Harvard Square, refused to stop selling a magazine that was popular with his clients, who included Harvard professors and students. Caragianes was philosophical when he was arrested. "Oh well, that man from the Watch and Ward, he has his job, and I got mine," he said.[35]

Mencken decided to fight the ban. The decision "to run such a risk in defense of a principle was wildly uncharacteristic," a biographer notes. Moreover, Mencken believed that there was a legitimate role for organizations like the Watch and Ward Society in policing the reading habits of the "wowsers" in the lower classes. But he believed that this banning was clearly in retaliation for his article about Chase. He turned for advice to Arthur Garfield Hays, whom he had met when Hays was a member of the defense team in the Scopes case. The lawyer told Mencken that if he wanted to challenge the ban, he could travel to Boston and sell a copy of the magazine to create a test case. But Hays warned Mencken that he could lose. The Massachusetts law was among the strictest in the nation because it defined "obscenity" as any material "manifestly tending to corrupt the morals of youth." It also banned all books "containing obscene, indecent, or impure language," giving Chase the right to suppress a work for a single word, the power that Judge Ford had failed to win with his clean-books bill in New York. The penalty was also stiff— up to two years in prison. Mencken and Hays were soon on a train headed for Boston. "We intend to break his hold on the literature of this section, and we will fight the issue to the end," Mencken announced on his arrival.[36]

Mencken's challenge to the Watch and Ward Society generated enormous interest, both in Boston and in the rest of the nation. Having tipped the wire services to his plans, Mencken found a crowd of five thousand waiting for him at Boston Common on April 5. He had arranged to meet Chase and sell him the April issue of *American Mercury*. But the minute the crowd caught sight of Mencken and Hays, it surged toward them, intent on purchasing the magazine. As people waved money frantically, Mencken was lifted off his feet and had to tear himself free. Finally, Chase was found. After making a show of biting the coin that Chase had given him to prove that it was real, Mencken handed him the magazine. "Officer, arrest that man," Chase ordered an accompanying policeman. The large, good-natured crowd followed Mencken to the police station, where he was booked and released. In court the next day, Hays told the judge that Mencken's arrest was not a publicity stunt. "It starts to get down to fundamentals as to whether or not a small group who set themselves up as custodians of the majority's morals shall determine what the majority shall or shall not read, " Hays said. Boston wasn't the only city facing this problem. "There is a spirit throughout the country of minorities imposing their ideas upon the majorities," he added. To the surprise of many, the judge acquitted Mencken the next day. He was escorted not to jail but to Harvard, where he was hailed as a hero by six hundred cheering students. The students weren't alone. The Boston newspapers, which had been hostile to Mencken, also praised him. In his syndicated column, Will Rogers described the Watch and Ward Society as "the Ku Kluxers of Boston literature." "In thousands of newspaper and magazine articles, editorials, photographs and cartoons the issue of censorship was dramatized as never before," historian Paul Boyer observed.[37]

The Boston authorities were not impressed. After all, it had been the Watch and Ward Society that had brought the Mencken prosecution, not them, and they were determined to continue the fight for "pure" literature. A few months later, they charged two drugstore clerks with obscenity for selling a novel that featured sexual misbehavior in a college setting. In early 1927, the Boston Police superintendent Michael Crowley issued a list of eight novels that he considered obscene despite the fact that all had been issued by major publishers and were advertised and sold freely elsewhere. "I have read these books, and I think they are bad," he explained. Although some of the publishers considered challenging the chief, the ban was allowed to stand, and all of the books disappeared from the shelves of Boston retailers. In April, however, the Suffolk County district attorney William J. Foley notified Boston booksellers that Sinclair Lewis's best-selling novel *Elmer Gantry* was obscene, and the police chief hinted strongly that Dreiser's *American Tragedy* was obscene as well. Horace Liveright, the publisher of the Dreiser book, challenged the ban by having his representative, Donald Friede, sell a copy to the police. A week later, Friede was convicted of obscenity and fined despite the introduction of evidence of Dreiser's literary reputation. The next month, the police also arrested a young bookstore clerk for selling Upton Sinclair's *Oil,* a book about the Teapot Dome scandal, because it contained a reference to birth control. Frightened booksellers began pulling books from their shelves that could subject them to prosecution. Boston was facing "a sort of moral panic," a reporter for the *New York Times* wrote.[38]

The banning of acknowledged literary works that were also bestsellers led to protests. Representatives of two Boston institutions— *Atlantic Monthly* magazine and publisher Little, Brown—issued a statement denouncing police censorship as "high-handed, erratic and ill-advised." "It is difficult for men of self-respect to keep silent in the face of this violation of the historic tradition of Boston and New England," they said. The newspapers also addressed the police. "Do not make us ridiculous," the *Boston Herald* warned. "Do not imply to the world that those whom we elect to office have no comprehension . . . of intellectual freedom." Local booksellers sent the district attorney a case of fifty-seven best-selling titles, requesting an advisory opinion on whether they were obscene. At its national convention, the American Booksellers Association elected as its president John G. Kidd of Cincinnati, who had faced an obscenity prosecution for selling a work by Rabelais, and adopted a resolution condemning censorship of literature at the federal, state, and local levels. It is "unjust to accuse a publisher or bookseller of trying to pervert the public morals," it read, describing the suppression of books in Boston as "a ridiculous situation." Librarians were also being persuaded to take a stand. While many Massachusetts librarians remained cautious on the issue of censorship, most believed that elevating reading standards was not something that could be achieved by law.[39]

By the spring of 1929, Boston had become notorious for its rejection of works that circulated freely in the rest of the country. At least sixty-five books had been suppressed, including works by the philosopher Bertrand Russell and novels by H. G. Wells, Sherwood Anderson, William Faulkner, John Dos Passos, and Ben Hecht. Most of these books had been dropped by booksellers when the district attorney refused to assure them that the books could be sold legally. Booksellers received so much criticism over their timidity that they felt they had to defend themselves. "Their position as businessmen is one of neutrality," a spokesman explained. "They are not concerned either with the censorship of public morals or with the defense of art from the assault of puritanism." It is easy to assert the importance of literary freedom when you have nothing to lose, but booksellers faced the prospect of punishment. Even if they could escape the threat of a jail term, an obscenity conviction could destroy their business. "Where is the courage or the sense in taking the position that some small shopkeeper . . . who has no interest either way shall wear the crown of martyrdom?" the booksellers asked. Meanwhile, the police crackdown continued. When *Scribner's Magazine* began serializing Hemingway's *A Farewell to Arms* in the summer of 1929, the police superintendent banned it. A few months later, the mayor refused to permit a theater to mount Eugene O'Neill's *Strange Interlude.* "Banned in Boston" had become a national catchphrase, symbolizing narrowness and intolerance.[40]

But civil libertarians rallied. In April 1928, seven hundred protesters rudely challenged the city fathers during a banquet in the venerable Ford Hall. The satirical tone of the event was apparent from the beginning as young men and women paraded around the hall dressed in the costumes of characters from the books that had been banned. They circulated a petition calling on authorities to ban a new novel by banned author Percy Marks because being banned in Boston would guarantee a large sale for the book in the rest of the country. Margaret Sanger, who had been barred from speaking in Boston on four occasions since 1923, sat at a front table wearing a gag. Her speech was read by Harvard history professor Arthur Schlesinger, who had been the target of censors in other parts of the country. But the highlight of the evening was a skit, "The Suppressed Book Shop," featuring a bookseller who questions his customers closely. "But why do you want to buy a book," he asks a woman. "Because I want to be intelligent, even if I do live in Boston," she replies. The bookseller refuses to sell *Mother Goose* or *Grimm's Fairy Tales*—"Don't you know that book contains bolshevik material? Little Red Riding Hood and the Three Little Bears!" He sends his customers off with copies of the telephone book, the Democratic and Republican platforms, and other "safe" titles.[41]

Many Bostonians resented the sometimes patronizing tone of what became known as the "Ford Hall Frolic." The district attorney played on this sentiment a few days later in persuading a jury to uphold the ban on *American Tragedy.* But the protest had helped bolster the confidence of the beleaguered reformers. They soon received important new support from the ACLU. Roger Baldwin's organization had remained aloof from the fight over book censorship, both in New York and Massachusetts. At a time when the ACLU's budget was being stretched thin by the effort to defend the free speech rights of workers, its leaders did not believe they could afford to invest in the fight to amend the obscenity laws, which they judged to be less consequential. "This is a phase of free speech which we have kept clear of because of our wish to avoid complicating our main issues,"

Forrest Bailey, ACLU's codirector, explained to a Massachusetts librarian. "The issue of free speech in its larger aspects—those affecting criticism of the status quo—appears to us to be so much more important, that it would be inexpedient for us to involve ourselves in controversies where questions of morals are present." Other factors also inhibited the ACLU. Despite their commitment to sexual equality, Roger Baldwin and other Protestant ACLU leaders were puritanical about depictions of sexual activity. Perhaps equally important, they knew that many ACLU supporters shared their puritanism. "I am wholly in favor of the censorship of books, magazines, plays and movies," Richard C. Cabot, a strong ACLU supporter in Boston, wrote Baldwin.[42]

The ACLU overcame its reticence about defending sexual material in 1929. Neither Arthur Hays nor Morris Ernst, the men who would become ACLU cocounsels in that year, possessed any of the prudishness that inhibited their colleagues. Hays had defended Mencken and was then fighting the Boston ban on *American Tragedy.* Ernst was defending the New York publisher of Radclyffe Hall's *The Well of Loneliness,* a fictionalized account of Hall's struggle to accept her homosexuality. The obscenity fight that became the turning point for the ACLU, however, did not involve a novel but a sex education book. In 1928, a member of the Daughters of the American Republic ordered a copy of Mary Ware Dennett's pamphlet *The Sex Side of Life: An Explanation for Young People,* and then complained to the post office, which charged Dennett with violating the Comstock Act. The prosecution of Dennett was widely criticized. *The Sex Side of Life,* which Dennett had written for her sons ten years earlier, contained basic information about sexual organs, intercourse, and masturbation, which it discouraged. The book had been distributed privately without causing any protest, and many worried that if it were suppressed, then all sexual information would be at risk. *The New Republic,* while professing little concern about the prosecution of *American Tragedy,* was outraged when a jury took only forty minutes to conclude that the pamphlet was "pure and simple smut." "The conviction of Mrs. Dennett . . . constitutes a frightful injury not only to a principle, but to the children of this nation and to society itself," it wrote. "Towards the dirty-minded, snobbish and ignorant spy or censor we can feel only scorn and implacable hostility;

it is important to destroy in every respect whatever prestige he may enjoy." Influential members of the medical community and even conservative Republican women also voiced their concern. The case had "aroused wider interest in censorship than any case in years," the ACLU reported.[43]

The ACLU intervened strongly in the Dennett case. She was represented by Ernst, and expenses were paid by the Dennett Defense Committee, which was organized by the ACLU. Prominent people lent their name to the committee, including Mrs. Marshall Field of Chicago, the wife of the department store tycoon, and there was a $1,200 surplus in funds by the time Dennett's conviction was overturned in 1930. By then, the ACLU was deeply involved in the Boston fight. It reorganized its weak New England Committee as the Massachusetts Civil Liberties Committee (MCLC) and issued a pamphlet, *The Censorship in Boston,* that called for amending the state obscenity law to allow juries to consider a book as a whole and repealing the theater-licensing law that gave the mayor of Boston the power to ban plays. The MCLC sponsored another anticensorship rally at Ford Hall, although this one featured only local speakers in an effort to avoid offending public sentiment again. Baldwin entered the fray directly during a meeting at the Old South Church. The ACLU would fight "until all this censorship is abolished in Boston," he promised. The ACLU would demonstrate its new commitment to fighting literary censorship by giving the surplus from the Dennett defense fund to the new Committee against Stage Censorship, which was soon renamed the National Committee on Freedom from Censorship.[44]

It required one more spectacular prosecution, however, to convince the Massachusetts legislature that the state obscenity law must be changed, and it was the Watch and Ward Society that once again chose the victim. In October 1929, John Sumner of the New York Society for the Suppression of Vice learned that the Dunster House Bookshop in Cambridge had sold five copies of D. H. Lawrence's *Lady Chatterley's Lover,* which had been privately printed in Europe shortly before Lawrence's death. Sumner notified the Watch and Ward Society, which promptly set out to entrap James A. DeLacey, the owner. This wasn't easy. DeLacey, a former Yale librarian, personally disliked the new literature and had privately condemned Ernest Hemingway for his vulgarity. At first, he refused to accept an order for the book from the agent of the Watch and Ward Society. When his customer insisted, DeLacey finally agreed that he would purchase a copy for him if one was offered, since the book was not available from a publisher. Not long after, someone who said he was a Harvard student showed up at the store with a copy of the book to sell. The student was probably another Watch and Ward Society agent, for only two hours later the first agent telephoned the store to see if DeLacey had found him a copy of *Lady Chatterley's Lover.* DeLacey was arrested, convicted, fined, and sentenced to four months in jail. Although he never served any time in jail, he did not recover from the experience: his store closed, his wife divorced him, and, according to some, he died an alcoholic.[45]

The Dunster House prosecution appalled almost everyone in Massachusetts. DeLacey and his store were beloved in Cambridge, and even the prosecutor and the judge in the case joined in the denunciation of the methods of the Watch and Ward Society. The great prestige that the vice societies had formerly enjoyed had been destroyed by their inability to distinguish between hard-core pornography and high art, and many now wondered whether the censors weren't acting out their own sexual frustrations. "To read the list of books 'Banned in Boston' is to be shocked, not by the content of the books, but by the festering disease of the minds that find evil in them. Such minds have all the stigmata of the sexual invalid," wrote Bernard DeVoto, a member of the Harvard faculty. One state legislator introduced a bill requiring all censors to "submit to the state Department of Public Health satisfactory evidence of normal sexual experience." The bill was a joke, but there was a growing conviction among legislators that the law should be changed. In 1930, they finally approved amendments to the obscenity law that ended the prosecution of almost all literary works. But these changes had been relatively minor: the public no longer supported the censorship of books, and this was the change that mattered most.[46]

The censors were not just losing support at the local level. In the late 1920s, the public became increasingly aware of the role that the federal government played in determining what it could read. While postal authorities fought unsuccessfully to suppress *The Sex Side of*

Life, customs agents used their power under the tariff laws to ban the import of "obscene" books. Searching the tens of thousands of books that were imported every year was not an easy task, particularly since many of them were written in foreign languages. Yet diligence was essential because agents could be sentenced to a year in jail and a $5,000 fine if they let an obscene book slip through. As a result, they took no chances, rejecting any book that they had the slightest doubt about, including many acknowledged classics as well as the works of James Joyce and D. H. Lawrence. One customs agent, who had banned 272 books during a two-year period, rejected the very idea of classical literature. "A classic is a dirty book somebody is trying to get by me," he said. In 1928, the Customs Bureau attempted to reduce the inconsistency in the rulings by individual inspectors and issued a blacklist of over seven hundred titles. But inspectors continued to make individual judgments. In May 1929, a Boston inspector deeply embarrassed the government by banning Voltaire's *Candide.* The problem promised to grow even bigger in 1929 when the House passed a new tariff bill that expanded the obscenity ban to include works that advocated "treason, insurrection or forcible resistance to any law of the United States."[47]

The ACLU denounced the tariff bill as an attack on free speech, and this time it wasn't alone. Surprisingly, the fight over the obscenity provision of the bill, Section 305, produced a highly unusual four-day debate during which prominent members of the Senate called for the abolition of federal censorship. The leader of the free speech forces was Bronson M. Cutting, the product of an aristocratic New York family who was receiving straight As at Harvard when asthma forced him to relocate to New Mexico. A liberal Republican, he became active in politics in his adopted state and was appointed to a Senate vacancy in 1927. Cutting, a book lover and a connoisseur of classical literature, became involved in the censorship fight when a friend in Santa Fe asked him to help him with the Customs Bureau, which had seized three copies of *Lady Chatterley's Lover* that he had ordered from abroad. Unable to assist his friend, Cutting announced in July 1929 that he would attempt to eliminate Section 305. However, in light of the near universal condemnation of the Lawrence novel, Cutting chose to focus his protest on the banning of Erich Maria Remarque's *All Quiet on the Western Front,* which the government had rejected in part because of a scene in which a hospitalized soldier has sex with his wife. In a statement released by his office, Cutting denounced the ban as an example of "the danger and folly of giving customs officers the right to dictate what the American people may or may not read.... This book has been acclaimed as an outstanding masterpiece," he said. "It is an intensely moving and accurate portrayal of the lives of soldiers in the trenches." Yet, as a result of the customs ban, Americans could read only an expurgated version "that omits some of the most vigorous passages." Cutting also criticized the expansion of Section 305 to include "subversive" books. "It is doubtful whether literary censorship has at any time or place proved of benefit to public morals," he said. "On the contrary, human experience has shown that censorship usually defeats its own ends."[48]

Cutting launched the debate on October 10 by offering his amendment striking out Section 305. While much of the argument over the next two days turned on legal questions, Cutting, who was not a lawyer, directly attacked the underlying rationale of censorship, calling to his aid arguments that had been made by Tacitus, the poet John Milton, and political theorist John Stuart Mill as well as Benjamin Franklin, Ralph Waldo Emerson, and Oliver Wendell Holmes. To the defenders of censorship who argued that it was necessary to protect decency by punishing obscenity, Cutting explained that these ideas were not immutable. "The standards of decency and morality vary from generation to generation," he said. Homer, Dante, and Shakespeare had all been censored at one time or another, and only the death of a pope had prevented the painting of clothing on the naked figures in Michelangelo's *Last Judgment*.

Cutting also flatly rejected the warnings of the censors about the harmfulness of some books. "I can not think that the evil effect of works of literature is by any means as far-reaching as the proponents of this sort of legislation seem to believe," Cutting said. On the contrary, bad ideas played an important role in helping good ideas emerge. "Bad books...serve in many respects to discover, to confute, to forewarn and to illustrate," he added, quoting Milton. Cutting did not deny that there was a legitimate interest in protecting children from some books, but that responsibility lay with parents and state governments, which would continue to exercise their power under the obscenity laws. The federal government had no role to play.

The difficulty is, Mr. President, that the road to enlightenment is not a federal highway.... Each man who travels on that road has got to find the way for himself. At each turning and at each crossroad he may have to resume that age-long grapple which Milton speaks of between truth and error or between two opinions, each one of which believes itself to be the truth.[49]

For six hours on October 11, Cutting held the floor of the Senate, lecturing on the dangers of censorship and the inequities of customs restrictions. He was not alone, as liberals in both parties weighed in. "My books are my friends, my associates," William E. Borah of Idaho said. "I do not propose that anybody shall choose my friends or my associates. That is one freedom which I wish to be absolute." Cutting didn't have the votes to strike out Section 305 entirely, but he offered a second amendment that exempted books from the obscenity section, which also covered obscene photographs and contraceptive materials and information, and narrowed the ban on treasonable and insurrectionary speech to cover only material urging forcible resistance to the laws of the United States or threatening the life of the president. This amendment passed the Senate by two votes, 38-36. The debate resumed in March 1930, when the tariff bill came up for a final vote, and Cutting was forced to compromise further. Nevertheless, the final bill included important safeguards for imported books, requiring customs agents to consider a work as a whole and providing an easier appeal to the courts for banned books. The secretary of the treasury was authorized to admit "classics" and books of "literary or scientific merit." In 1935, the ACLU reported that customs was no longer blocking any books issued by established publishers.[50]

The imposition of restrictions on the Customs Bureau, the defeat of the Watch and Ward Society, and the other free speech victories of the 1920s did not convince everyone that the gains for freedom were permanent. "If an emergency should arise, a hopeful strike or a dangerous revolt or even a flaming speech, our courts could be trusted to interpret and the police to club their way through the laws to common sense and good order," journalist Lincoln Steffens observed in 1930. The federal government still had the power to choke off dissent through its stranglehold on the post office. In 1932, Cutting introduced a bill that addressed this threat, but by then no one was thinking about anything except the Depression. Still, lasting changes had occurred. The book and library community—publishers, booksellers, and librarians—had overcome their initial reluctance to defend free speech and emerged as strong advocates for the view that the American people should decide for themselves what books they would read. Under the leadership of Arthur Garfield Hays and Morris Ernst, the ACLU had also overcome its moral squeamishness and in 1931 established the National Council of Freedom from Censorship, to lead the fight to protect artistic speech. Although we cannot confirm it with data in an era before opinion polls, the average American seemed to better understand the importance of free speech. Soon, the growth of intolerance abroad would give everyone a new appreciation of the dangers of censorship.[51]

The burning of thousands of books by Nazi youth on the evening of May 10, 1933, sent a shudder through the civilized world. Coming only five months after Adolf Hitler had assumed power, it symbolized a hatred for intellectual discourse that many saw as a precursor to a new war. Propaganda Minister Joseph Goebbels, who presided over the Berlin bonfire, explained its meaning:

> Only that art which draws its inspiration from the body of the people can be good art in the last analysis and mean something to the people for whom it has been created. There must be no art in the absolute sense, such as liberal democracy acknowledges. An attempt to serve such art would end in the people's losing all internal contact therewith and the artist's becoming isolated in a vacuum of art for art's sake.[52]

The Nazi state would determine what constituted good art, consigning everything else, including the artists, to the flames. Americans were outraged. More than 100,000 people in New York and fifty thousand in Chicago marched in protests that were timed to coincide with the burnings. Seven months later, a New York judge made it clear that the United States had chosen a different path than Germany. On December 6, 1933, John M. Woolsey of the U.S. District Court in Manhattan lifted the Customs Bureau ban on James Joyce's *Ulysses*. With Ernst as his attorney, Bennett Cerf of Random

House had challenged the Customs Bureau using the new proce-
dures in the Cutting amendment. Woolsey acknowledged that many
words in *Ulysses* were commonly considered dirty but insisted that
they did not make it obscene. Joyce had been trying to re-create the
experience of lower-middle-class life in Dublin in a way that required complete honesty to the details of daily life. "When such a
real artist in words, as Joyce undoubtedly is, seeks to draw a true picture of the lower middle class in a European city, ought it to be impossible for the American legally to see the picture?" In the United
States, at least, it was the artist who made the art, not the state.[53]

CHAPTER 4

The Court Takes a Hand

Grover A. Whalen was known as "Mr. New York." As head of the mayor's reception committee from 1919 to 1953, he oversaw the ticker-tape parades that greeted the nation's heroes as they marched or were driven through the man-made canyons of lower Broadway. Perhaps it was his affability that recommended him to Mayor Jimmy Walker, New York's fun-loving mayor. In 1928, Walker chose Whalen to head the New York Police Department. Walker was a notoriously careless administrator, and it is possible that this was his worst appointment, for the new police commissioner soon demonstrated a surprising bloodthirstiness. He is alleged to have said, "There is plenty of justice at the end of a nightstick." Whether this is true or not, he soon developed a reputation as a police commissioner who gave free rein to his men in controlling strikes, which were frequent in the city's extensive garment industry. "How much civil liberty has the striker in the needle trades got under the brute rule of our Police Commissioner?" asked the Reverend John Haynes Holmes only six months after Whalen's appointment. "This man Whalen stands as a great bully to beat down with policemen's billies those who he doesn't like."[1]

If Whalen was antiunion, he was even more rabidly anti-Communist. This hadn't mattered much at the time of his appointment. Following almost a decade of prosperity, the American people made poor revolutionary fodder, and the Communist movement was small and badly divided. However, Communists around the world took heart on October 24, 1929, Black Thursday, when a sharp plunge in the New York Stock Exchange appeared to signal the capitalist crisis that Marx had predicted. After a week of devastation, the stock market began to recover and would continue to climb for several months. But in April 1930, stocks entered an uninterrupted decline that would last for two years. Unemployment was already on the rise by then, and the Communist Party began to prepare for the revolution that it believed was imminent. Spurning the requirement for a permit for meetings in New York's City Hall Park, they challenged New York police and were violently ejected on several occasions when they attempted to hold protests there. In March 1930, Mayor Walker issued a statement assuring protesters that the police would protect orderly demonstrations. "Communists, as other minority groups, should be protected in their rights of free speech," he said. But protests that threatened public peace would be suppressed, he added. Unfortunately, neither the Communists nor Whalen were interested in compromise.[2]

On March 6, a crowd estimated at between 35,000 and 100,000 gathered in Union Square in connection with International Unemployment Day. The protests had been ordered by the Third Communist International, the organization created by the Soviet government to direct the worldwide Communist movement. William Z. Foster, the American Communist Party leader who had just returned from Moscow, was determined to make the New York demonstration a success. Only a few thousand in the crowd were members of the Communist Party, however. A reporter noted that when the band struck up the Communist anthem, the "Internationale," almost no one knew the words except for the party members who surrounded the speakers' platform. Nevertheless, after hours of speeches that dealt surprisingly little with the unemployment situation, the Communist leaders electrified their supporters by announcing their intention to march to City Hall. When Foster and his aides met with Whalen, who was observing the demonstration, the police commissioner warned them that his men would block any effort to march without a parade permit. The radicals ignored him. Led by women and children holding banners, two thousand singing Communists marched into Broadway and turned south toward City Hall.

The next day newspapers would describe the "Red riot" that followed, but it was really a police riot. Instead of attempting to block the advance of the Communists by massing men across Broadway, approximately one thousand officers, many on horseback, charged the marchers. "Hundreds of policemen and detectives, swinging nightsticks, blackjacks and bare fists, rushed into the crowd, hitting out at all with whom they came in contact," the *New York Times* reported. In Union Square, a police ambulance with a blaring siren drove into the middle of the crowd, sending people fleeing toward surrounding police, who beat anyone they could catch. "A score of men were sprawled over the square, with policemen pummeling them," the *Times* wrote. "What followed is a hazy jumble in my mind," a young Communist said later—"the roar of motorcycles, the whine of sirens...shouts and screams, and the thud of police clubs against human bodies...mounted cops swinging away with their clubs as trained horses maneuvered through the crowd." The "Red riot" was over in fifteen minutes, with only one policeman hurt seriously enough to require hospitalization. As many as a hundred civilians were injured. "Most of those arrested had been severely punished before they were booked on charges of disorderly conduct," the *Times* reported.[3]

Although patriotic groups and many newspapers praised the police for refusing to permit the Communists to break the law, the battle of Union Square was Grover Whalen's Waterloo. He himself betrayed some nervousness over the level of police violence by requesting that newsreels of the riot not be shown in New York. He then made things worse for himself by revealing that police spies in the Communist Party had provoked some of the violence at the demonstration. "I thought I would crack my sides laughing at some of the under-cover men who figured in the Union Square demonstration," Whalen said a few days later. "They carried placards and banners demanding the overthrow of the government and made as much noise as the genuine Reds. But the fun started when one of the under-cover men started to razz a cop. He got a terrific punch in the eye and was knocked down before the cop was pulled off." Whalen defended the use of police spies, who he said were helping to reveal how three hundred Communists had infiltrated city agencies and private businesses. When the police commissioner began giving this information to employers so that they could fire the Communists, the outrage over police misconduct that had been growing since the riot finally forced him to resign.[4]

Despite the spectacle that they made of themselves in the Union Square riot, the New York police were far from the worst offenders against free speech among the nation's police departments. Arrests of Communists and other agitators grew in the following months to the point where many liberals began to fear a new Red Scare. In May, playwright Sherwood Anderson joined H. L. Mencken and over one hundred writers, academics, and lawyers to protest more than 1,600 arrests that had occurred around the country in the previous two months. In a statement issued by the John Reed Club, a Communist youth group, they claimed that California authorities had arrested more than 900 people "for the crime of being out of work." Another 137 had been charged with sedition in Chicago for holding an unemployment meeting in a private hall. "An Ohio court has actually sentenced two young girls to ten years in prison for distributing pamphlets," the statement read. Two men caught in the same crime in Atlanta had been charged under an archaic law against "inciting to insurrection," which carried a death sentence. "To combat this persecution for political opinion, concerted protest is necessary," it concluded. "The people of the United States must be awakened to the threatened complete destruction of their civil rights."[5]

The problem of police repression was long-standing. The police were supposed to keep the peace, creating an environment in which people could speak their minds on either side of any issue. In reality, there weren't many policemen like Sid Hatfield. Law enforcement officers almost always supported the status quo against challenges from "outsiders," including labor organizers, political radicals, and religious zealots. As a result, what Oliver Wendell Holmes called the American "marketplace of ideas" was far less open than the words of the First Amendment suggested. People were free to speak until a policeman stopped them, often with physical force.

Since 1920, the ACLU had vehemently protested against police departments that broke up radical meetings and disrupted union picketing. "Nine-tenths of all the attacks on freedom of speech and assembly are made by local police," it reported in 1929. "The police are the steady, year-in-and-year out censors and dictators." In 1928, the ACLU sent questionnaires to over two hundred police departments to discover their attitudes toward radicals and the policies governing the holding of meetings in city streets and private meeting halls. Although only forty-five departments responded, the results showed that the overwhelming majority believed that suppressing radicals was part of their job. Most reported that their cities required speakers to obtain a permit before they could hold an outdoor meeting. More than a dozen cities required permits for meeting on private property. It was also clear that the purpose of the permit system was to bar political dissidents. Few police chiefs were as forthright as the one in New Orleans, who said that permits were never issued to radicals and that his men would break up any radical meetings they discovered, whether in public parks or private halls. Nashville, Tennessee; Pasadena, California; and Fall River, Massachusetts, simply banned street meetings altogether. But almost all of the others acknowledged they stood ready to break up a meeting if they perceived a threat to public peace. Newark provided an example of how subjective the police could be in assessing threats when it barred a meeting of union members in a private hall because at the last meeting "speeches were made attacking the government."[6]

The most outrageous abuses of police power continued to occur in labor disputes. In 1929, the Communist Party and the American Federation of Labor opened a new front in the effort to unionize American industrial workers when they began to organize southern textile workers. Their efforts were almost immediately met with violence by the mill owners. The local police usually sided with the owners and often joined in assaulting union members. In Gastonia, North Carolina, the union headquarters was ransacked, and a strikers' parade was attacked by sheriff's deputies. After the city council passed an ordinance banning marches, more than one hundred strikers were arrested for picketing and parading. More violence followed, taking the lives of the police chief and a female strike leader. While suspects were indicted in both cases, only the men accused of killing the police chief were convicted. In Marion, North Carolina, police fired into a crowd of strikers, killing six and wounding twenty-four. Hundreds of people were arrested in connection with the shootings, kidnappings, and explosions in both towns, including the Marion sheriff and his deputies. But the only people convicted of crimes were strikers, who were often sent to jail for long terms on trumped-up charges. Two years later, union organizers in southeastern Kentucky encountered the same bitter resistance to their efforts to organize coal miners. By the time the union men had been defeated, eleven people had been killed and over one hundred miners had been arrested for criminal syndicalism or conspiracy. Only one man was accused of shooting a miner.[7]

The ACLU and other groups sympathetic to the workers found it difficult to assist them. In Gastonia, the ACLU offered rewards for information about the men who had ransacked the strikers' camp. It hired a private investigator to pursue the murderers of striker Ella May Wiggins, a twenty-nine-year-old mother of five, and later helped file civil suits on behalf of her children. The ACLU also filed a civil suit accusing the Gastonia police of false arrest and participated in the appeal of the men accused of killing the police chief. But with the legal system in the hands of the mill owners and their allies, the ACLU had few legal options and little success. It continued to use the weapon of publicity, producing reports on the atrocities in North Carolina and Kentucky that it hoped would lead to a public outcry and a congressional investigation. But the critics who dared to travel to the scene of the action were driven off by local authorities. When Theodore Dreiser went to Kentucky with a delegation of writers to investigate the situation for himself, he and his party were indicted for criminal syndicalism. (Dreiser was also indicted for adultery because he was foolish enough to share a room with a woman who was not his wife.) Arnold Johnson, a student from New York who was in Harlan County as an ACLU representative, was threatened with death and then jailed for criminal syndicalism for possessing an ACLU pamphlet, *What Do You Mean Free Speech?* Jessie Wakefield, a New York organizer for International Labor Defense, a Communist group, was thrown in jail by the sheriff of Harlan County, who swore to "keep her there until she rots." In her jail cell, she protested to a jailer that her group was legal everywhere in the United States. "Well, I'm the law here, and it ain't legal in Kentucky," the jailer told her.[8]

The problem that confronted dissidents everywhere was that they were at the mercy of state and local police. The First Amendment to the Constitution promised, "Congress shall make no law . . . abridging the freedom of speech, or of the press; or the right of the people peaceably to assemble, and to petition the government for a redress of grievances." But the courts had read that prohibition narrowly as a restriction on the power of the federal government. William H. King of Utah observed during a 1929 Senate debate that while Congress could not abridge the right of free speech and free assembly, there was nothing that prevented the states from imposing restrictions. "Congress may not go into a State and interfere with its domestic affairs," King said. His remarks were addressed to Alabama senator Thomas Heflin. Ironically, Heflin, an anti-Catholic bigot, was trying to get the Senate to pass a resolution condemning a violent attack on him when he had tried to speak in Massachusetts a few months earlier. King told Heflin that, regrettable as the attack was, the federal government could do nothing about it. "Some States have, as the Senator knows, passed laws that infringed upon the right of free speech.... Such laws are not subject to challenge as violations of the Federal Constitution and may be held valid if there is nothing in the State constitution that would be in derogation of such legislation."[9]

Local officials used this argument in rejecting the ACLU's protests. Local values trump the First Amendment, Walter B. Smith, a Kentucky prosecutor, wrote to Arthur Garfield Hays in May 1932:

> If a mad dog has a constitutional right to run rampant in Bell County, biting people and scattering hydrophobia, then the American Civil Liberties Union has the same right. But just as we would suppress the mad dog, we will suppress this un-American Union. [We] are little impressed ...with the cackling of your Union over "freedom of speech" and "freedom of the press" and "freedom of movement." We also believe in those fundamentals of liberty, but we believe that "freedom of speech" should be limited by a man's knowledge of what he talks about.

Yet even as Smith was writing these words, a dramatic change in the conception of civil liberties was under way. On June 1, 1931, the U.S. Supreme Court had handed down a decision that began to establish its role as the ultimate protector of free speech at all levels of government. The turning point came in a case pushed by a man who was every bit as reactionary as Walter Smith—Robert Rutherford McCormick.[10]

It wasn't hard to spot "Bertie" McCormick. He had led a division of the Illinois militia in France during 1918 and was henceforth known as "the Colonel," an honor he underscored on occasion by strolling through the newsroom in his old uniform, holding the leashes of his German shepherds in one hand and a polo mallet in the other. Sitting in his cavernous office atop the *Tribune* tower, McCormick "had his megalomaniac side, but that only made his reign one of grandeur," one of his former reporters observed. Others had harsh words for the Colonel, who saw his country surrounded by enemies. Although he had been raised in the upper class and educated in England, he was an isolationist who opposed American entry into the League of Nations and the World Court. He was also deeply concerned about the threat of communism, which he saw foreshadowed in even the mildest liberal program. He told his foreign correspondent William Shirer to steer clear of reporters for the New York newspapers. "All New York newspapermen are parlor Bolsheviks," McCormick said. McCormick was also a racist. In short, he boasted "one of the finest minds of the fourteenth century." His newspaper's reputation wasn't much better. In a 1930 survey, Washington correspondents voted the *Tribune* as among the country's "least fair and reliable" newspapers and as "a ceaseless drip of poison."[11]

Bigoted, paranoid, and grandiose, McCormick was also a determined defender of freedom of the press. He was the chairman of the American Newspaper Publishers Association's Committee on Freedom of the Press. He was also prepared to put his money where his mouth was. In 1916, the *Tribune* had blasted Henry Ford for refusing to rehire National Guardsmen who had been called to active duty and for criticizing American efforts to capture Pancho Villa, who was conducting raids on American territory. When a *Tribune* editorial called Ford an "ignorant idealist and unpatriotic American," the industrialist sued for libel, leading to three years of expensive legal maneuvering that ended in a draw. McCormick was also sued for libel by Chicago mayor William (Big Bill) Thompson, whose administration was the target of a relentless assault by the *Tribune*. Big Bill claimed that the newspaper was hurting the city's credit rating and demanded $10 million. But the Illinois Supreme Court threw the case out. "A prosecution, civil or criminal, for libel on government has no place in the American system of jurisprudence, as the people have a right to discuss their government without fear of being called for their expression of opinion," the court declared.[12]

It was McCormick's reputation for supporting First Amendment rights that led a small newspaper publisher in Minneapolis to seek his help in 1928. Jay Near was the publisher of the *Saturday Press,* a weekly newspaper that specialized in attacks on the links between organized crime and municipal authorities. Near was no white knight. He had a reputation as someone who used the threat of scandal to extort money from people who had run afoul of the law. He was also anti-Semitic, and used the fact that some of the gamblers and rumrunners in town, like Big Mose Barnett, were Jewish to make sweeping attacks on all Jews. "I am not taking orders from men of Barnett['s] faith, at least right now," Near wrote in late 1927. "There have been too many men in this city and especially those in official life, who HAVE been taking orders and suggestions from JEW GANGSTERS, therefore we HAVE Jew Gangsters, practically ruling Minneapolis." In November 1927, following a particularly vitriolic attack on city officials and Jews, District Attorney Floyd Olson (whom the *Saturday Press* had called a "Jew lover") went to court in an effort to close the newspaper under a 1925 law that authorized the suppression of "(a) an obscene, lewd and lascivious newspaper, magazine or periodical, or (b) a malicious, scandalous and defamatory newspaper." The law described such publications as "public nuisances" and denied them a chance to take their case to a jury. A month later, a judge temporarily blocked publication of the *Saturday Press* while the constitutionality of the statute was decided by the Minnesota Supreme Court. When the supreme court unanimously upheld the law in May 1928, the newspaper was ordered closed forever.[13]

McCormick hesitated before agreeing to help Near. After spending heavily to defend the *Tribune* in the Ford and Thompson libel cases, he was reluctant to underwrite the expense of an appeal to the U.S. Supreme Court, particularly since the ACLU had already agreed to take on the case. But McCormick's lawyer, Weymouth Kirkland, urged his client to intervene. "Bert, the mere statement of the case makes my blood boil," Kirkland wrote. "Whether the articles were true or not, for a judge without jury, to suppress a newspaper by writ of injunction, is unthinkable.... Any newspaper in Minnesota which starts a crusade against gambling, vice or other evils may be closed down...without a trial by jury." If the law went unchallenged, what would stop other states, including Illinois, from enacting similar laws? Kirkland also doubted the ACLU could afford to mount the vigorous defense that the issue deserved. McCormick was persuaded, but he believed that it was critical that Near also have the support of the newspaper industry. In September, he urged the directors of the ANPA to join the case. "The owners of this paper, by reason of the suppression thereof, are wrecked financially, and there is but little chance of reversal of the case unless the ANPA or some other similar public-spirited association takes over the litigation," McCormick wrote.[14]

But newspaper publishers were slow to see the First Amendment issue that seemed so obvious to Kirkland, McCormick, and the ACLU. Like the book publishers, librarians, and booksellers who had confronted the censorship controversies of the 1920s, their first response was to attempt to distinguish themselves from the people who were under attack. In fact, the mainstream press had helped to draft the Minnesota law. C. L. Butler, the publisher of the *Minneapolis Journal,* explained that the newspapers had worked closely with the legislature "to frame this law which attempted to reach the blackmailing type of publication then prevalent in Minnesota." While the law was written broadly enough to permit the prosecution of any newspaper, the major dailies were convinced that they would never be the target. When the Minnesota Supreme Court upheld the law, the *Minneapolis Evening Tribune* scoffed at the notion of "some judge who would stretch the Minnesota law to impose his will on a legitimate newspaper in legitimate conflict with his views.... The Civil Liberties Union will no doubt make a great pother about the freedom of the press, but the legitimate newspapers will be rather bored than excited about it." The distinguished *Christian Science Monitor* agreed that the real threat to journalism "is a menace which comes from the unscrupulous within the ranks of the profession." Most journalists believed that Near had got what was coming to him.[15]

ANPA president Harry Chandler, the publisher of the *Los Angeles Times,* told McCormick that the case might endanger newspapers throughout the country. As long as newspaper gag law remained on the books of a single state, the danger that it posed was contained. Appealing the case risked the possibility that the Supreme Court would declare the law constitutional, inviting the rest of the states to adopt it. His advice was to wait and see whether other states attempted to pass the law. Chandler was ignoring the fact that Near was going to appeal, with or without the support of the newspaper industry. But he was certainly right to point out that an appeal to the Supreme Court was risky.[16]

If the Minnesota gag law had not been such a glaring violation of the principle of free speech, even Bertie McCormick would probably not have chanced an appeal to the Supreme Court. For more than a generation, liberals had protested against a court that routinely sided with the owners of capital in their struggle with workers and the reformers who had attempted to regulate business practices. Yet the Court grew even more conservative. President William Howard Taft appointed five conservatives to the Court during his single term in office and then joined the Court himself as chief justice in 1921. In the following years, the Court engaged in wholesale nullification of state legislation designed to regulate business. Between 1919 and 1931, it struck down 161 laws, the overwhelming majority of which involved economic regulation. Its major weapon was the Fourteenth Amendment, which had been passed following the Civil War to guarantee that the recently freed slaves would not be denied "life, liberty or property without the due process of law" in the former Confederacy. The Court declared that businesses, too, were protected by the Fourteenth Amendment and set aside state minimum wage laws and other forms of regulation that allegedly deprived corporations of "due process."[17]

At the same time, the Supreme Court sustained almost every suppression of free speech that was presented to it. "The Court upheld virtually every conviction made under the various criminal-syndicalism and sedition laws even though in many cases the action so curtailed often constituted little more than raucous public dissent," historian Paul L. Murphy observed. For Taft and his allies, the limits on free speech were a natural corollary of the campaign to curb reform laws. Like the legislators who were attempting to extend government regulation of the workplace, the radicals and union activists who were being silenced by the police and private detectives were seeking changes that would limit the freedom of the businessmen who were the country's natural leaders. Thus, efforts to curb their speech were not violations of the liberty guaranteed by the First Amendment but attempts to safeguard the free enterprise system that was the basis of all American freedoms. In 1925, the Supreme Court upheld the conviction of Benjamin Gitlow for "criminal anarchy" for publishing a revolutionary manifesto in 1919. Gitlow was a left-wing Socialist who rejected the idea of capturing power through the electoral process. "The Left Wing Manifesto" demanded a militant and "revolutionary Socialism" that encouraged "class struggle" and mobilizing "the power of the proletariat" through mass strikes and other forms of "revolutionary mass action." At the time Gitlow was indicted, it was easy to persuade a jury that the strikes that were occurring all over the country were a prelude to Communist revolution. But the country had long since recovered its senses by the time Gitlow's case reached the Supreme Court. Nevertheless, it upheld his conviction under New York's "criminal anarchy" law, which banned statements calling for the overthrow of government by force. "A single revolutionary spark may kindle...a sweeping and destructive conflagration," Justice Edward T. Sanford wrote in his majority opinion. "It cannot be said that the State is acting arbitrarily or unreasonably when...it seeks to extinguish the spark without waiting until it has enkindled the flame."[18]

Charlotte Anita Whitney's case reached the Supreme Court two years later. A left-wing Socialist like Gitlow, she was convicted under California's criminal syndicalism law for helping organize the Communist Labor Party in 1919. The law, which was one of the worst of the state syndicalism statutes, made it a crime to teach or advocate "the commission of crime, sabotage...or unlawful acts of force and violence or unlawful methods of terrorism as a means of accomplishing a change in industrial ownership or control or effecting any political change." But Whitney was not convicted of advocating anything. The California law made it a crime even to belong to a group like the Communist Labor Party. Indeed, said Justice Sanford, who once again wrote the opinion, "such united and joint action involves even greater danger...than the isolated utterances and acts of individuals." Nor was it even necessary to advocate violence or belong to a group that advocated violence to run afoul of the Supreme Court. In 1929, Rosika Schwimmer, a Hungarian immigrant, applied for American citizenship. Her original application was rejected because she was a pacifist. A district court judge ruled that for this reason she could not take the oath of allegiance to the United States, which requires an applicant to state "that he will support and defend the Constitution and laws of the United States against all enemies." Justice Pierce Butler of the Supreme Court agreed. Schwimmer was a threat to the country. "Whatever tends to lessen the willingness of citizens to discharge their duty to bear arms in the country's defense detracts from the strength and safety of the Government," he wrote in his majority opinion.[19]

A clear majority of the justices supported all three of these decisions, but they were far from having the last word. Justices Oliver Wendell Holmes and Louis Brandeis filed dissents that contained some of the most eloquent pleas for free speech ever written. By the time of the *Gitlow* case, the eighty-four-year-old Holmes had completed his remarkable transformation from the man who had sent Eugene Debs to jail to the nation's most prominent proponent of free speech. His opinion protested against the majority's violation of the "clear and present danger" test that he had formulated in *Schenck v. U.S.* "It is manifest that there was no present danger of an attempt to overthrow the government," Holmes wrote. Nor was there any danger of the "Left Wing Manifesto" starting one. "Whatever may be thought of the redundant discourse before us it had no chance of starting a present conflagration." The more important issue was that the majority had created a false distinction between a theory, which is constitutionally protected, and an incitement, which is punishable. "Every idea is an incitement," Holmes said. "Eloquence may set fire to reason." Therefore, all ideas must be protected, even revolutionary ones. "If in the long run the beliefs expressed in proletarian dictatorship are destined to be accepted by the dominant forces of the community, the only meaning of free speech is that they should be given their chance and have their way," Holmes concluded.[20]

Brandeis came from a very different background than Holmes, the quintessential Yankee. As the child of Jewish immigrants, he had a natural sympathy for the outsider. His strong advocacy of government efforts to protect the health of workers led business groups to bitterly oppose his nomination to the Supreme Court in 1916. Yet the two men shared the view that the Supreme Court was abandoning the ideals of the Founding Fathers. "Those who won our independence by revolution were not cowards," Brandeis wrote in the *Whitney* case.

They did not fear political change. They did not exalt order at the cost of liberty. To courageous, self-reliant men, with confidence in the power of free and fearless reasoning applied through the processes of popular government, no danger flowing from speech can be deemed clear and present, unless the incidence of the evil apprehended is so imminent that it may befall before there is opportunity for full discussion. If there be time to expose through discussion the falsehood and fallacies, to avert the evil by the processes of education, the remedy to be applied is more speech, not enforced silence. Only an emergency can justify repression.

The ability to issue a political manifesto and join a political party must be protected under the First Amendment even for people whose goal is the overthrow of the existing system, Holmes and Brandeis agreed. "If there is any principle of the Constitution that more imperatively calls for attachment than any other it is the principle of free thought—not free thought for those who agree with us but freedom for the thought we hate," Holmes declared in his *Schwimmer* opinion. He could not help making fun of those who felt otherwise. "I would suggest that Quakers have done their share to make the country what it is . . . and that I had not supposed hitherto that we regretted our inability to expel them because they believe more than some of us do in the teachings of the Sermon on the Mount," he concluded.[21]

The intellectual power and the plain good sense of Holmes and Brandeis had a hard time making themselves heard during the 1920s. A long, uninterrupted period of economic growth seemed to support the view of Taft and his brethren that the economic leaders of the nation must remain free to engineer the policies that were producing a bounty shared by all. But when this fantasy of eternal economic growth was exposed by the crash of the stock market and the rapid descent into recession, the American people lost patience with the idea that the Constitution forbade government initiatives that would improve their lives. The Depression created a new tolerance for ideas that had once seemed radical and a new appreciation for those who defended free speech. In 1930, Representative Hamilton Fish of New York launched a probe that was intended to prove that Communists were behind the country's economic woes. In the process, he attacked the ACLU as "an organization whose main work is to uphold Communists in spreading revolutionary propaganda and inciting revolutionary activities to undermine our American institutions and overthrow our Federal government." Many newspapers were scathing in their response. "If the exploring committee wants to do our country a real service it will stop running down the 'agitators' and run down our national problems instead," the *Milwaukee Leader* observed. Fish was also wrong about the ACLU, the *Trenton Times* wrote: "American liberty would soon deteriorate into a weak rhetorical gesture were it not for organizations which, like the American Civil Liberties Union, battle day in and day out in opposition to reactionary restraints of whatever character."[22]

The Supreme Court remained a bulwark against the changing tide of opinion. Its judges served lifetime appointments, and Holmes, who turned eighty-nine in 1930, was proving that a lifetime could last a very long time. But unexpected deaths could change the balance on a divided court. "Damn you, if any of you die, I'll disown you," Taft told his five Supreme Court appointees shortly before leaving the White House. In the end, it was Taft himself who opened the door to change on the Supreme Court. In poor health, he resigned from the Court a month before his death in March 1930. Mercifully, he died without knowing that one of his appointees, sixty-five-year-old Edward Sanford, had collapsed and died while having a tooth extracted. But Taft would have taken comfort from the fact that the choice of the new two justices rested in the hands of another Republican president, Herbert Hoover. Hoover's choice of Charles Evans Hughes to replace Taft as chief justice and John J. Parker to replace Sanford outraged liberals. *The Nation* accused Hughes of possessing "a fixed set, intolerant mentality, closed on various issues and deadly conservative." Senate liberals were unable to block Hughes, but they did defeat Parker, who was accused of being racist and anti-union. Hoover then successfully submitted Owen J. Roberts, a moderate Republican who had made a reputation as a vigorous prosecutor in the Teapot Dome scandal.[23]

The selection of Hughes and Roberts shifted the balance of the Supreme Court, clearing the way for a profound change in philosophy. Roberts was not one of Taft's trustworthy conservatives, and throughout his career on the Court he would demonstrate an independence that partisans on the left and right would denounce as inconsistency. But the most important change had been the choice of Hughes. The new chief justice was more liberal than the criticism of his nomination suggests. Certainly, he was a good Republican. He had served two terms as governor of New York and then accepted Taft's nomination as an associate justice of the Supreme Court. He resigned his seat in 1916 to run for president and nearly defeated Woodrow Wilson. Hughes served as secretary of state in both the Harding and Coolidge administrations. In the intervening years, he had represented a number of large corporations.

But Hughes had almost always aligned himself with the liberal wing of the Republican Party. As governor, he had helped inaugurate the progressive movement through investigations of the utilities and insurance industries and then pioneered in the extension of government regulation. As an attorney in private practice, he had fought for the United Mine Workers and the Legal Aid Society. In six years as an associate justice on the Supreme Court, he had voted to uphold laws that protected women and children in the workforce by limiting their hours and paying them a minimum wage. During the Red Scare, he had been one of the first to denounce the expulsion of the Socialists from the New York Assembly and rallied the New York Bar Association against the legislature, traveling to Albany in an unsuccessful effort to present its resolution to the assembly. Hughes was just not cut out to be a popular hero. First, there were those Olympian looks. With his neatly trimmed white beard and mustache and bushy eyebrows, he "looked more like God than any man I ever knew," a lawyer who appeared before him frequently said. He also possessed a native diffidence. "It is well to be liberal, but not messy," he said.[24]

Louis Brandeis was not overly impressed by the new chief justice a few months after he had rejoined the Court in 1930. Hughes was "mundane but intelligent," he told Harvard Law professor Felix Frankfurter, who dictated a memorandum summarizing the conversation soon after they spoke. His written opinions showed "no imagination but he is a good artisan." Still, Brandeis was hopeful that Hughes and Roberts would help change the direction of the Court. "Hughes has real energy," he explained. "In the conferences, time is not much wasted." Hughes soon demonstrated that he would use his energy to expand First Amendment rights. An opening had been provided in the Supreme Court's 1925 decision in the *Gitlow* case. In a sentence that was little noticed at the time, Sanford had swept away one of the biggest obstacles to federal intervention in defense of free speech. "For present purposes we may and do assume that freedom of speech and of the press—which are protected by the First Amendment from abridgment by Congress—are among the fundamental personal rights and 'liberties' protected by the due process clause of the Fourteenth Amendment from impairment by the States," Sanford had written. Ironically, in a decision that had denied Gitlow his right to publish the "Left Wing Manifesto," the Supreme Court had declared that violations of free speech by state and local governments were subject to review by the federal courts![25]

Gitlow extended First Amendment protection in theory, but it was not until Hughes wrote the majority opinion in *Stromberg v. California* six years later that the Supreme Court exercised its authority to protect free speech for the first time. Nineteen-year-old Yetta Stromberg, a counselor in a Communist Party summer camp for children, had been sentenced to five years in prison for raising a red flag every morning, violating a state law that banned the display of a red flag "as a sign, symbol or emblem of opposition to organized government." "The maintenance of the opportunity for free political discussion to the end that government may be responsive to the will of the people . . . is a fundamental principle of our constitutional system," Hughes wrote. "A statute which upon its face, and as authoritatively construed, is so vague and indefinite as to permit the punishment of the fair use of this opportunity is repugnant to the guaranty of liberty contained in the Fourteenth Amendment."[26]

The decision in *Stromberg* was encouraging to Colonel McCormick, Roger Baldwin, and the other advocates of free speech, who were nervously awaiting the Supreme Court's decision in *Near v. Minnesota*. When the case was argued in January 1931, the Supreme Court had been asked for the first time whether a prior restraint on the press violated the First Amendment. Both Weymouth Kirkland, representing Near and the *Saturday Press,* and Minnesota's deputy attorney general, James E. Markham, agreed that prior restraints were a bad thing. Government must not have the power to approve or reject ahead of time what a newspaper or book publisher wished to publish. This had been acknowledged since the eighteenth century. "The liberty of the press is indeed essential to the nature of a free state; but this consists in laying no previous restraints upon publication," William Blackstone pronounced in his legendary *Commentaries on the Laws of England* in 1865. But Markham denied that the Minnesota public nuisance law really operated as a prior restraint. The injunction suppressing the *Saturday Press* was a punishment that had been imposed only after it had published material that unjustly damaged the reputations of public officials and other individuals. It did not prevent a newspaper from publishing what was true. Indeed, it was beneficial to legitimate newspapers because it would "have the effect of purifying the press," Markham said.[27]

Kirkland told the Court that the Minnesota legislature had failed to grasp an important fact. "Every legitimate newspaper in the country regularly and customarily publishes defamation, as it has a right to in criticizing government agencies," he said. Clearly, the *New York Times* campaign that had overthrown the corrupt administration of William Marcy Tweed involved the publication of material that trampled the good reputations of Boss Tweed and his henchmen. Kirkland argued that it is not enough to say that the First Amendment protects the right to speak only the truth. "Every person does have a constitutional right to publish malicious, scandalous and defamatory matter, though untrue and with bad motives and for unjustifiable ends," he said. Otherwise, it is government that will decide what is true or not, and one must expect that its decisions will be in defense of its own power. Had the public nuisance law been on the books in New York during the Tweed days, Tweed's handpicked judges could have quickly suppressed the *Times*. Kirkland noted that people who were the target of unjustified attacks could defend themselves by suing for libel. But libel cases could be filed only after the publication of the offending item, and the cases were decided by juries, not judges.[28]

The decision in the *Near* case was announced on June 1, two weeks after *Stromberg*. There had been speculation about whether *Stromberg* was an aberration. But Hughes left no doubt that there had been a significant shift in the Court's outlook. At the time, decisions were read when the Court was in session, with the authors of the majority and minority opinions summarizing their arguments. But Hughes read every word of his opinion in the *Near* case. He reached back to the earliest days of the American republic to demonstrate that prior restraints were anathema. He quoted James Madison's statement that it had been the practice of the individual states to treat press freedom like a flowering plant, preferring "to leave a few of its noxious branches to luxuriant growth, than, by pruning them away, to injure the vigour of those yielding the proper fruit." The importance of a free press had only grown over the years, Hughes said.

> The administration of government has become more complex, the opportunities for malfeasance and corruption have multiplied, crime has grown to most serious proportions, and the danger of its protection by unfaithful officials and the impairment of the fundamental security of life and property by criminal alliances and official neglect, emphasizes the primary need of a vigilant and courageous press, especially in the great cities.

Yet the Minnesota public nuisance law authorized public officials to haul their critics before a judge who was given the power to determine the truth of what they published and whether the criticism was published with the goal of reforming government. This was not a punishment for past misdeeds but an effort to silence voices of protest and a prior restraint. "This is of the essence of censorship," Hughes said.[29]

The 5-4 decision in *Near* was immediately hailed as a turning point in the history of the Supreme Court. Hughes had been joined by Brandeis, Holmes, Roberts, and Harlan Fisk Stone, and many journalists proclaimed the emergence of a new liberal majority. It's "just about the biggest Washington news of the decade," a reporter for the Scripps-Howard syndicate wrote. This conviction was strengthened by the fact that Hughes had gone out of his way in his opinion to make clear that he did not believe that the liberty of contract was absolute. What the Court appeared to have done was to reverse the priority that individual rights and property rights had been given. The veteran Washington correspondent Mark Sullivan observed:

> The cleavage between liberal and conservative and the dominance of
> the former appear particularly in two areas of decisions. One, speaking
> broadly, emphasizes human rights and constitutional guaranties to the
> individual, such as freedom of speech. These human rights the liberals
> of the Court tend to protect and enlarge. The other group of decisions,
> again speaking very roughly, tends to restrain property rights and to en-
> large the power of State governments in dealing with private property.

Sullivan's analysis exaggerated the liberalism of the Court. The conservatives retained enough power to seriously challenge Franklin
Roosevelt's New Deal. But the new priorities were permanent. The
Stromberg and *Near* decisions had made it the business of the federal courts to ensure that civil liberties were not violated by states
and local governments. Suddenly, it became possible to go over the
heads of the officials who had been most responsible for suppressing
speech. Lawyers who had formerly discouraged their clients from
suing in an effort to win their rights began writing the briefs that
would dramatically expand First Amendment rights over the next
seventy years.[30]

The prospects for expanding free speech improved dramatically as a
result of the economic emergency. In 1931 the American people
were unequivocal in their demand that the government do something to save them from destitution. In the 1930 elections, they
retired one hundred Republican members of the House of Representatives and ten Republican senators. Two years later, a landslide
elected Franklin Roosevelt president and gave his party control of
both the House and the Senate. More than ten million people were
unemployed, and more than 5,500 banks had closed their doors,
bringing the nation's financial system to the verge of collapse. In
these dire circumstances, people looked to Roosevelt's New Deal for
more than just a restoration of the status quo. The Depression destroyed the high esteem that businessmen had enjoyed during the
1920s and convinced many that the leaders of industry were self-
ish men who had to be curbed. In the first hundred days of his administration, Roosevelt and the Congress worked together to pass an
unprecedented number of bills to fulfill this new mandate, including the National Industrial Recovery Act, which appeared to bring

every aspect of commerce and industry under the supervision of the federal government.

This impatience with old ways provided an immediate boost for the labor movement. The public had been generally willing to accept the view of businessmen that unionism was a threat to prosperity and looked the other way as companies ran roughshod over the rights of workers. But with the collapse of business prestige, people were no longer willing to tolerate "yellow dog" contracts that forbade union membership and court injunctions that crushed strikes. Even more important, federal officials became convinced that protecting workers was not only right but necessary to rebuilding the economy. Encouraging unionism was a way of ensuring that workers would receive more of the nation's income and of creating a broader base for economic demand. As a result, Congress passed three laws in the space of three years that accomplished much of what the ACLU had been trying to achieve for workers since 1920. The Norris-LaGuardia anti-injunction law was approved by an overwhelming number of votes in both houses of Congress in March 1932, while the Republicans still controlled the Senate. It barred the federal courts from issuing injunctions that restricted a wide range of organizing activities, including "giving publicity to a labor dispute by advertising, speaking, patrolling or any other method not accompanied by force and violence" and "assembling peaceably to promote an interest in a labor dispute." A year later, the National Industrial Recovery Act formally recognized the right of workers to join unions, a right that was strengthened by New York senator Robert Wagner's National Labor Relations Act in 1935. "The Wagner Act, perhaps the single most important civil liberties statute ever passed by Congress, extended, in theory at least, the guarantees of the First Amendment to American workers who had grown accustomed to enjoying their civil liberties on the sufferance of their employers," historian Jerold S. Auerbach wrote.[31]

Civil libertarians were slow to realize that the federal government had become an ally in the fight for free speech. The rapid growth in the power of the government reminded them of what had happened during World War I, and they were alert to the danger that the government would once again abuse its power. Moreover, while they were grateful for the formal recognition of the right to organize, they were disappointed that the federal government wasn't doing more to support the workers who had been encouraged to organize. "Troops have been called out against strikers in six states. Police, gunmen, sheriffs, injunctions, all have been invoked in the effort to crush labor organizations.... [Yet] the New Deal administration has refused to interfere in this industrial strife to make good its implied support of trade unionism," the ACLU's annual report complained in 1934. The suspicion of the New Deal was so strong that the following year the ACLU passed up the opportunity to endorse the Wagner Act. Roger Baldwin's first instinct had been to oppose the bill "on the ground that no federal agency intervening in the conflicts between employers and employees can be expected to fairly determine the rights of labor." However, other ACLU leaders objected, and the organization finally took no position on the bill. Government had been the ally of business and the enemy of civil liberties for so long that Baldwin and his colleagues simply couldn't conceive of it as an enforcer of individual rights. "I did not appreciate how much further the New Dealers were prepared to go than we in federalizing the protection of civil rights," Baldwin acknowledged later.[32]

But if they were slow to recognize the New Deal as an ally, Baldwin and his colleagues lost no time in appealing to the federal courts for help. They had been thwarted repeatedly by local and state officials who proclaimed themselves the final judges in determining the limits of First Amendment freedoms. Now that the Supreme Court had committed itself to protecting free speech, the ACLU was looking forward to settling the score with local dictators. In 1937, they found a big target. Frank Hague was the mayor of Jersey City, New Jersey, the boss of the surrounding Hudson County, and one of the most powerful figures in New Jersey politics. He was used to having his way. In November, Hague instructed the police chief to disrupt efforts by organizers from the Congress of Industrial Organizations (CIO) to inform Jersey City workers of their rights under the Wagner Act. When the CIO defied Hague's order, sending dozens of men into Jersey City to distribute flyers, the police rounded them up, placing them on ferries returning to New York City or putting them in cars and driving them to the city line. Thirteen were arrested, and seven were immediately tried and sentenced to five

days in jail. In the days that followed, the CIO attempted to hold
a public meeting to protest the arrests and to demand the right to
distribute its information. But no owner of a public hall was willing to risk Hague's disapproval. The mayor did not hesitate to accept responsibility for the CIO ban. "I decide. I do," he told reporters. "Me. Right here," he said, pointing to his chest. He even
took credit for denying private meeting halls to the union men.
"A mere expression from me ... is sufficient," he said later. Hague
justified his actions as necessary "to protect our city from invasion by
the Communists and other red groups under the mask of a labor organization." Hague dismissed the issue of civil liberties. "Whenever
I hear a discussion of civil rights and the rights of free speech and the
rights of the Constitution, remember you will find him with a Russian flag under his coat; you never miss," he said. "These elements
will continue to meet a united opposition in Jersey City any time
they attempt unlawfully to create disturbing conditions here," Hague
promised.[33]

In January 1938 the CIO and the ACLU sued Hague for violating First Amendment rights. Although the trial did not occur for another six months, they soon heard news that encouraged them. In
March, the Supreme Court announced its decision in a case involving the arrest of a member of the Jehovah's Witnesses for distributing handbills without a license in Griffin, Georgia. The attorney for
the city argued that its interest in preventing littering justified this
restriction on First Amendment rights. But the Supreme Court disagreed, ruling unanimously that the Griffin ordinance was unconstitutional because it gave city officials the power to suppress handbills
they found offensive and therefore constituted a prior restraint on
free speech. If the Supreme Court would not allow local governments to license the distribution of handbills, it seemed unlikely that
it would allow Jersey City to control what was said in open-air meetings. In June 1939, the court confirmed this prediction, striking
down the ordinance that required speakers to obtain a permit from
the Jersey City authorities. The ordinance "can ... as the record discloses, be made the instrument of arbitrary suppression of free expression of views on national affairs," Justice Owen Roberts declared
in his majority opinion. Public officials have a responsibility to the
First Amendment as well as to the maintenance of public order.

"Uncontrolled official suppression of the privilege cannot be made a substitute for the duty to maintain order in connection with the exercise of the right," Roberts said. City officials could no longer act as if their power to regulate speech was absolute. They had a new master. "The court undertook . . . to direct cities in the management of parks and streets," Zechariah Chafee Jr. observed.[34]

A revolution had occurred in the way that individual rights were conceived and enforced. In many ways, Frank Murphy, who joined the Supreme Court in 1940, symbolized this change. Born in Michigan, Murphy was a strong defender of civil liberties, first as mayor of Detroit during the early years of the Depression and then as governor. In 1937, he refused to send in troops to evict the sit-down strikers at the General Motor plants in Flint, Michigan, forcing the company to negotiate with the fledgling United Auto Workers union. Murphy carried his commitment to civil liberties into the federal government in 1939 when he was appointed attorney general. He created the Civil Liberties Unit in the Justice Department to "direct, supervise and conduct prosecutions of violations of the Constitution or Acts of Congress guaranteeing civil rights to individuals." In a letter to Baldwin, Murphy explained, "I am anxious that the weight and influence of the Department of Justice should be a force for the preservation of the people's liberties." [35]

It was no surprise that Murphy's first majority opinion for the Supreme Court upheld the right to picket as an expression of First Amendment rights. "In the circumstance of our times the dissemination of information concerning the facts of a labor dispute must be regarded as within the area of free discussion that is guaranteed by the Constitution," he declared in *Thornhill v. Alabama*. Murphy did not question the right of the authorities to intervene when strikers turned violent. But peaceful picketing could not be suppressed under the test that Oliver Wendell Holmes had set forth twenty years earlier in the *Schenck* case. "No clear and present danger of destruction of life or property, or invasion of the right of privacy, or breach of the peace . . . [is] inherent in the activities of every person who approaches the premises of an employer and publicizes the facts of a labor dispute involving the latter," Murphy concluded.[36]

When the ACLU had looked forward to the day that the right to picket would be finally established, it had never expected that its hero would be a former mayor, much less a former official of the Department of Justice or a member of the Supreme Court. Even more thrilling was the prospect that Holmes's clear and present danger standard would become the foundation for a rapid expansion of the right of free speech.

CHAPTER 5

The Second Red Scare

A few minutes after he had been sworn in as attorney general at a White House ceremony on January 2, 1939, William Francis Murphy held his first press conference in the office of one of Franklin D. Roosevelt's assistants. There he allowed the reporters to examine the worn family Bible on which he had sworn his official oath. His mother had given him the book when he was in grammar school, and many of the pages had broken free of the binding. Murphy told the reporters that he read the Bible for an hour every day, and then he recited for them his favorite text—the fourth and fifth verses of Isaiah 9. Such a deep, personal faith in the nation's top law enforcement officer might have caused qualms among civil libertarians. The fact that Frank Murphy was a Catholic with blue eyes and curly red hair could have raised questions about his commitment to the separation of church and state. But the words of Isaiah revealed a lot about Murphy: "But He shall judge the poor with justice and shall approve equity for the meek of the earth. And justice shall be the girdle of his loins; faith the girdle of his reins."[1]

Murphy had already demonstrated a strong commitment to protecting the weak from abuses of power by both government and business. Roger Baldwin had admired Murphy since 1925, when he had presided over the trial of an African American family, the Sweets, and several of their friends, who were charged with firing on a mob that was attacking a home that the Sweets had just purchased in a white neighborhood of Detroit. A member of the mob died of gunshot wounds, and the conviction of the Sweets for murder appeared inevitable. When the jury deadlocked and the Sweets were eventually freed, the NAACP described the case as "one of the most important steps ever taken in the struggle for justice to the Negro in the United States." The Sweets' attorney, Clarence Darrow, gave much of the credit to Murphy. It was "the first time in all my career where a judge really tried to help, and displayed a sympathetic interest in saving poor devils from the extreme forces of law, rather than otherwise," he said. Murphy's reputation grew during his service as mayor of Detroit, governor of Michigan, and governor-general of the Philippines. Murphy is "a man of high integrity... and rare courage for... [one] so long in public life," Baldwin wrote in 1934.[2]

In the oral reminiscences that he recorded at Columbia University many years later, Baldwin recalled that the ACLU had depended on the volunteer work of a wide range of attorneys, including "scores of conservative and therefore more respectable lawyers who risked association with us on briefs in special cases." But most of the work was done by less distinguished men who were themselves members of minorities. "The ordinary run of our more faithful attorneys were among the less influential," Baldwin recalled. "[They were] lawyers whose natural sympathies inclined them our way— the Jewish lawyers, the Socialists, the labor attorneys, the Irish, a few Negroes and those liberals genuinely devoted to principles." Frank Murphy was one of those who were naturally inclined to see things from the point of view of the oppressed. Murphy's grandparents on both sides were Irish immigrants who carried to their new home a deep resentment of English rule. Later, it would be falsely claimed that one of his ancestors had been hanged as an Irish rebel, but his father was an Irish nationalist at an early age, and Frank shared a passion for Irish freedom. When still a small boy, he was asked on Election Day whether he was a Republican or a Democrat. "I am an Irishman," he replied. Yet Murphy's outlook was not the product of any personal experience with oppression. Although he grew up in Harbor Beach, Michigan, a rural town with few Catholics, Murphy's father was a moderately prosperous attorney and a leader of the local Democratic Party. His sensitivity to the plight of the poor and the powerless grew out of his mother's deep religious faith and his father's insistence that he not forget his immigrant roots. When

Murphy's father enrolled him in his alma mater, the University of Michigan, in 1908, he showed his son a campus building that he had helped to construct by carrying bricks and mortar to help pay his way through college. Like many immigrant parents, the Murphys put heavy pressure on their son to succeed. They produced a young man who was both ambitious and principled. Many years later, Murphy told Louis Brandeis that he had decided at an early age that "I would thrust my lance at intolerance."[3]

Murphy's determination to fight injustice got off on the wrong foot in 1919. He had been practicing law for several years when the United States declared war in 1917. After serving in the army, he won a job in the office of the U.S. attorney in Detroit just weeks before the federal government began rounding up foreign radicals. He defended the Red Scare at the time, but in the long public career that followed, Murphy demonstrated his belief that "the appetite for tyranny always grows." In 1930, he was elected mayor of Detroit. Although unemployment was high and unrest was growing, Murphy defended free speech as important for "not only our democratic form of government, but the peace and safety of society." He reversed the repressive policies of the former administration, urging the city council to allow the city's public places to become open forums, and overturned a police decision that denied a parade permit to Communist organizers of an unemployment protest. When Murphy became governor-general of the Philippines a few years later, he instructed the police to protect meetings even when they might provoke violent opposition. As governor of Michigan in 1937, Murphy demonstrated that he was prepared to carry his defense of the rights of workers to the very brink of illegality when he refused to enforce a judge's order to arrest members of the fledgling United Auto Workers union who were conducting a sit-down strike in General Motors plants.[4]

So it was not surprising that the new attorney general almost immediately turned to civil libertarians for advice on how the Justice Department could "help stimulate in our people a disposition to rediscover and embrace the civil liberties." He ordered research into a suggestion made by Lee Pressman, the general counsel of the CIO, that the civil rights statutes passed to protect African American voters after the Civil War might provide the federal government the authority to intervene in places like Harlan County, where local authorities were failing to protect free speech. The initial results seemed promising enough to justify a full-scale inquiry, and on February 3, 1939, just a month after taking office, Murphy announced the formation of the Civil Liberties Unit (CLU) in the department's criminal division. "In a democracy, an important function of the law enforcement branch of government is the aggressive protection of the fundamental rights inherent in a free people," Murphy explained. "It is the purpose of the Department of Justice to pursue a program of vigilant action in the prosecution of infringement of these rights." Murphy was well aware of the historical significance of what he was doing. In July, he reported to Franklin Roosevelt:

> Through this unit for the first time in our history the full weight of the Department will be thrown behind the effort to preserve in this country the blessings of liberty, the spirit of tolerance, and the fundamental principles of democracy.... It is my personal opinion that the creation of this unit at your order, with all the emphasis it places upon protection of the civil liberties of the individual citizen and of minority groups, is one of the most significant happenings in American history.

The ACLU and its supporters rejoiced. "These are great days for civil liberties," *Unity Magazine* declared. "When the government itself actually undertakes the job of protecting the rights of the people, something is happening."[5]

The American people responded to the government's new initiative on civil liberties. The twelve lawyers in the Civil Liberties Unit were deluged with hundreds of complaints from around the country, and a new flood came in whenever the attorney general spoke about civil liberties, which he did frequently. Unfortunately, Murphy could offer little more than words. Only two sections of federal law appeared to give the department the ability to act, and these were vaguely written and even contradictory. As a result, the CLU filed only a few cases in its early years. However, it conducted a number of investigations that put local and state officials on notice that it was prepared to intervene if they violated civil liberties. Perhaps even more important, Murphy's speeches educated both the public and its officials about the importance of protecting free speech. Roger Baldwin commended the attorney general following a speech about the responsibilities of city officials to defend civil liberties. "That does more good than anything we do in months," Baldwin said. "I almost believe we should begin to feel that we could go out of business." There was more than flattery in his words. Baldwin had been leading the fight for civil liberties for twenty years. Now fifty-five, he was overjoyed to be receiving the assistance of the American government.[6]

Murphy's speeches about civil liberties became increasingly important as the year progressed, and the world moved once again to the brink of war. When war was finally declared in Europe in September 1939, it inevitably increased the likelihood that the United States would be forced into the conflict, raising the prospect of another onslaught on civil liberties. Murphy insisted that there was no conflict between security and freedom:

> I do not believe that a democracy must necessarily become something other than a democracy to protect its national interests. I am convinced that if the job is done right—if the defense against internal aggression is carefully prepared—our people need not suffer the tragic things that have happened elsewhere in the world and that we have seen, in less degrees, even in this land of freedom. We *can* prevent and punish the abuse of liberty by sabotage, disorder and violence without destroying liberty itself.

Murphy urged a strict application of the clear and present danger test propounded by "the immortal Holmes." Let the enemies of democracy speak. "We have no reason to fear their competition," Murphy said. "We have a better article to sell." Murphy also urged "responsible" administration to avoid the "inhuman and cruel things" that occurred during World War I. This meant putting the Justice Department fully in control of laws punishing subversive activity and discouraging sedition hunting by private groups and local officials. Finally, the American people must play their part. "We need, and we earnestly ask, from every citizen and every government an unswerving resolve that for as long as this crisis endures, we will keep our heads—that we will not abandon the Bill of Rights," Murphy said. Americans must prove "for all time that ours is a two-fold strength—the physical strength of self-defense and the moral strength of unflinching devotion to our ideals," he concluded.[7]

Murphy was asking a lot of the American people. The danger of abuses of civil liberties was always the greatest when people were frightened, and the fear of subversion was growing daily. The American Communist Party was small, but its membership more than doubled, to eighty thousand, between 1936 and 1938. Admirers of Adolf Hitler and Benito Mussolini were also busy organizing groups. Although the number of domestic Fascists was small, members of organizations like the Silver Shirts and the German-American Bund attracted a lot of attention by dressing like Nazis and staging big demonstrations in New York, Cleveland, and Chicago. More than eighteen thousand Bundists gathered at the group's camp in New Jersey in 1937. In response to growing apprehension, the House of Representatives created a special Committee on Un-American Activities in 1938 to investigate "the extent, character and objects of un-American propaganda activities in the United States." The committee soon became a thorn in the side of the Roosevelt administration, as it accused prominent New Dealers of Communist sympathies. But conservatives weren't the only ones worried that a "Fifth Column" of disloyal Americans would engage in espionage and sabotage on behalf of Germany and the Soviet Union. In May 1940, Roosevelt himself asserted the existence of a Fifth Column and warned that the nation's "strength can be destroyed" unless steps were taken to unmask it. The following month, Congress gave the president the nation's first peacetime antisedition act. The Smith Act made it a crime to "advocate, abet, advise, or teach the duty, necessity, desirability or propriety of overthrowing or destroying any government in the United States by force or violence."[8]

Murphy was also expecting a lot of the U.S. Supreme Court, considering its failure to protect free speech during World War I. The prospects appeared to improve when Roosevelt appointed Murphy to the Court at the beginning of 1940. But that did not prevent the Supreme Court from handing down a decision in June that suggested that free speech might once again become a casualty of war. Just three weeks before the Smith Act was passed, the Court ruled that government could require its citizens to salute the American flag even when the act violated their religious beliefs. The case involved two Jehovah's Witnesses, Lillian Gobitas, twelve, and her brother William, ten. Lillian and William lived with their parents and three siblings in Minersville, a small town in the coal fields of eastern

Pennsylvania. The family was well liked; Walter Gobitas, the town grocer, was known for his generosity, which included extending credit to families that had been hit hard by the Depression. However, the Jehovah's Witnesses were not popular in eastern Pennsylvania or anywhere else. Their faith was based on a belief in the imminent arrival of Armageddon, and they pushed it hard in door-to-door proselytizing that many people found offensive. It didn't help that the Witnesses arrogantly dismissed other religions as "rackets." They were particularly hard on the Catholic Church, which they condemned as "the wickedest organization of liars, murderers and gangsters that has ever cursed the planet." Lillian began "witnessing" at the age of eight, handing "testimony cards" to people whom she had caught at home on a Sunday. "I have an important message," she told them. "Would you please read this?" Sometimes people were more than annoyed by the presence of the Witnesses. Lillian was eleven when she and her coreligionists were attacked by a mob in New Philadelphia, Pennsylvania. The police rounded up the Witnesses and held them until the crisis had passed. The women and children were then released, but the men were held, probably for creating a breach of the peace.[9]

Although religious, Lillian had no desire for martyrdom. But in 1935 Joseph Rutherford, the leader of the Witnesses, made a speech in which he praised Witnesses in Germany who were being persecuted for refusing to give the Nazi salute, which they considered a form of idol worship. (No less than a third of German Witnesses would die in concentration camps.) Inevitably, many Witness children in the United States drew a parallel between the Nazi salute and the salute that they were required to give while reciting the Pledge of Allegiance in school every morning. The comparison was strengthened by the fact that the form of the American salute at the time was disturbingly similar: after giving a military salute with their right hand, the children slowly extended their arms forward at eye level. Lillian and her brother decided that they would refuse to participate in either the salute or the recitation of the pledge. But Lillian's resolve deserted her. "I was very chicken," she said later. She was a straight-A student who had just been elected president of her seventh-grade class. Lillian worried that she was about to lose her popularity. "Oh, if I stop saluting the flag I will blow all this," she said to herself. It was William who acted first, keeping his hand jammed into the pocket of his pants despite his teacher's best effort to pry it loose and force it into a salute. Lillian joined the boycott the next day. Both children were expelled from school.[10]

Although the lower courts ruled that school officials had violated First Amendment rights, the Supreme Court upheld the expulsion in a decision that was heavily influenced by the now nearly hysterical concern over national security. In his majority opinion, Justice Felix Frankfurter declared that the issue was not the right to religious freedom but whether legislatures may act to encourage national unity "without which there can ultimately be no civil liberties." The effect of world events on Frankfurter's thinking was reflected in a letter he wrote to Justice Harlan Fiske Stone, the only dissenter. (Murphy had also drafted a dissent but had been persuaded to go along with the majority.) "Time and circumstances are surely not irrelevant considerations," Frankfurter wrote.[11]

This wasn't the first case involving Jehovah's Witnesses to reach the high court. The Witnesses had challenged ordinances restricting their right to propagate their faith, and the Supreme Court had already struck down several ordinances by June 1940 without any notable outcry. But the *Minersville School District v. Gobitis* case tainted the loyalty of the Witnesses at a dangerous time, and the reaction was immediate and terrifying. (The spelling of the case differs from the spelling of the family name.) Mob violence swept the nation as Witnesses were "beaten, kidnapped, tarred and feathered, throttled in castor oil, tied together and chased through the streets, castrated, maimed, hanged, shot, and otherwise consigned to mayhem." Appeals to the police for protection were unavailing. In one southern community, the sheriff watched as a mob assaulted seven Witnesses and hit a woman in the back with a brick. When an observer urged the sheriff to intervene, he refused. "They're traitors—the Supreme Court says so," he explained. In the three months following the *Gobitis* decision, the ACLU counted 236 attacks involving more than one thousand Witnesses in forty-four states.[12]

When the United States finally entered the war following the Japanese attack on Pearl Harbor on December 7, 1941, civil libertarians hoped for the best but feared the worst. They knew they had the support of Attorney General Francis Biddle, who was an ACLU member. A week after Pearl Harbor, Biddle warned that "although we had fought wars before, and our personal freedoms had survived, there had been periods of gross abuse, when hysteria and fear and hate ran high, and minorities were unlawfully and cruelly abused. . . . Every man . . . who cares about freedom must fight for the *other* man with whom he disagrees." Two months later, however, Roosevelt signed an executive order authorizing the secretary of war to exclude "any or all persons" from military zones he designated within the United States. In March, the military issued the first of more than one hundred orders that forcibly removed 120,000 Japanese American citizens from their homes on the West Coast and sent them to ten hastily assembled prison camps in remote locations throughout the West. The imprisonment of almost all of this country's citizens of Japanese ancestry, which occurred without a single documented case of treasonable conduct by a Japanese American, is one of the worst civil liberties abuses in American history.[13]

While the internment of Japanese Americans was certainly the most glaring injustice during the war, the government undertook more than two hundred prosecutions that sought to suppress individuals or groups based more on what they said than what they did. William Dudley Pelley had been a thorn in the side of the Roosevelt administration from the day he founded the Silver Legion of America in 1933. The son of an itinerant New England preacher, he became convinced that it was his mission to save America from a Jewish conspiracy. Pelley called himself "the American Hitler," and the uniform that he designed for the Silver Legion clearly resembled the one worn by the Nazis, although the shirt worn by his followers was silver and not brown. But his Silver Shirts never enrolled more than fifteen thousand men and were engaged in only isolated acts of violence. Roosevelt had been forced to put up with Pelley's harsh attacks on him as the "Dutch Jew" who headed the "Great Kosher Administration." But once war was declared, he demanded action. In March 1942, when Pelley accused Roosevelt of lying to the American people by playing down the extent of the damage that the Japanese had inflicted on Pearl Harbor, Roosevelt wrote to Francis Biddle. Biddle had managed to deflect earlier suggestions by the president that he do something to suppress the extreme critics of the administration. But this time Roosevelt gave the attorney general his marching orders. "When are you going to indict the seditionists?" he asked. Pelley was indicted, convicted, and sentenced to fifteen years in prison for violating the Espionage Act of 1917 by "making statements with intent to interfere with the operation or success of the military." Later in the year, the government launched the biggest sedition trial of the war by indicting twenty-six Fascist leaders for conspiring to undermine the morale of the armed forces. Zechariah Chafee condemned the prosecution as "indefensible." Roger Baldwin called it "monstrous."[14]

Despite the shameful treatment of Japanese Americans, there were fewer abuses of civil liberties during World War II than there had been during World War I. In part, this was because after the Japanese attack there was no significant antiwar movement to generate the kind of dissent that had occurred in 1917. Yet the federal government, particularly Biddle and his predecessors, Murphy and Robert Jackson, could take much of the credit. All three spoke passionately about the importance of civil liberties, and Jackson and Biddle worked actively to prevent state and local governments from embarking on another loyalty campaign. No state passed sedition legislation during the war. The attorneys general also warned against the dangers of vigilantism and repeatedly rejected proposals to create private groups to play the role that the American Protective League had played during World War I. "Mob groups almost invariably seize upon people who are merely queer or who hold opinions of an unpopular tinge," Jackson explained in 1940.[15]

There was also a remarkable change in the attitude of the Supreme Court. In June 1942, three justices shocked the country by announcing that they had changed their minds and now believed that the First Amendment protected the right of Jehovah's Witnesses to refuse to salute the flag. Just two years after the decision in the *Gobitis* case, Frank Murphy, Hugo Black, and William O. Douglas acknowledged that "we now believe that it was wrongly decided." A year later, they joined Chief Justice Harlan Fiske Stone, the original dissenter in *Gobitis,* and Robert Jackson, who had joined the Court after the decision, in overturning a regulation issued by the West Virginia Board of Education requiring students to salute the flag. The opinion, written by Jackson, was eloquent:

> If there is any fixed star in our constitutional constellation, it is that no
> official, high or petty, can prescribe what shall be orthodox in politics,
> nationalism, religion or other matters of opinion or force citizens to
> confess by word or act their faith therein. If there are any circumstances
> which permit an exception, they do not now occur to us.

In later cases, the Court prevented the government from revoking
the citizenship of immigrants who had "indicated by disloyal conduct that they were not at the time of naturalization 'attached to the
principles of the Constitution.'" As a result, it voided "orders of cancellation" that had been issued to more than one hundred people because of their extremist views. It also overturned the convictions of
several people who had been found guilty of "subversive advocacy,"
including an anti-Semite who had denounced both the war and the
president. "An American citizen has the right to discuss these matters either by temperate reasoning or by immoderate and vicious in-
vective," the Court declared. There is little question that the same
remarks would have landed the man in jail during World War I,
Geoffrey Stone, a legal scholar, has observed. Taken together, these
decisions marked an important change. "The Supreme Court for
the *first time* played a significant role in cabining the tendency of a
government to punish those who dissent or otherwise voice 'anti-
American values in wartime,'" Stone said.[16]

Civil libertarians emerged from World War II confident that
they were winning their fight for individual rights. As the ACLU
marked its twenty-fifth anniversary at a "lavish" conference and dinner in New York, telegrams of congratulations arrived from President Harry S. Truman and the governor of New York. Counsel
Arthur Hays observed that ACLU meetings were now "addressed by
the Attorney General, with district attorneys, Senators, mayors, and
other important dignitaries at the speaker's table." The organization's
eyes were clearly on the future as it announced that five of its eight
"immediate tasks" involved an attack on racial discrimination. Yet
the base of support for civil liberties was dangerously narrow. With
only seven thousand members, the ACLU remained an organization
that drew its support from a small segment of the upper middle class.
What would happen if suddenly the government turned against it
and some of its strongest supporters feared being identified as mem-

bers? Nobody was asking this question in 1945. "Not a single session was devoted to the issue of loyalty and security questions or the rights of unpopular groups," a historian of the ACLU has noted. Yet the organization was about to face a new Red Scare, which would last for nearly a decade, wiping away many of the gains that had been made since 1920.[17]

It was natural for the civil libertarians to feel confident. After all, the Fascists had been defeated, and the world had once again been made safe for democracy. But there was another way to look at foreign affairs that produced a far more pessimistic outlook, for the defeat of Germany had been made possible only by the Soviet Union, which had absorbed an invasion that cost the lives of millions and then launched a counterattack that carried it to the doors of Hitler's bunker in Berlin. As a result of their relentless military advance, the Soviets gained vast new territories in the heart of Europe that it had no intention of relinquishing, including Poland, Hungary, and Czechoslovakia. In March 1946, Winston Churchill warned that "an Iron Curtain had descended across the continent." Communism seemed to be spreading in other parts of the world as well. In Greece, a Communist-led insurgency was making progress against the right-wing government. In 1947, President Harry Truman announced that the United States would provide military assistance to Greece, Turkey, and any other country threatened by communism. "I believe that it must be the policy of the United States to support free peoples who are resisting attempted subjugation by armed minorities or by outside pressures," he explained. But American threats did not impress the Communists who took control of China in the summer of 1949. A month later, the Soviets delivered another blow by testing their first atomic weapon, destroying in a flash the sense of security that Americans had enjoyed by virtue of their nuclear monopoly. Less than a year later, in June 1950, North Korean troops poured across the border of South Korea in an effort to unify the country under Communist rule. When the United Nations called on its members to support South Korea, Truman ordered U.S. troops to intervene. With stunning speed, America found itself once again at war. This time, Communists were the enemy.[18]

The threats from abroad soon focused attention on the danger of subversion at home. Although the United States and the Soviet Union had been allies during the war, both had spied on each other. Evidence of Soviet spying began to appear soon after the war ended. In 1945, Elizabeth Bentley, a thirty-seven-year-old Vassar graduate, told the FBI that dozens of federal employees in Washington had given her documents that she had passed to the Soviets. Bentley lacked any proof of her charges, but this did not stop her from creating a national sensation as "the Red Spy Queen" when she testified before the House Un-American Activities Committee (HUAC) in 1948. HUAC's next witness, Whittaker Chambers, proved even more frightening. Chambers claimed that he, too, had been a Soviet courier and named Alger Hiss, a former State Department official, as one of the spies in his network. When Hiss denied the charge, Chambers led investigators to a pumpkin patch where he retrieved microfilm containing documents in Hiss's handwriting as well as typewritten pages that were later traced to Hiss's typewriter.

There was nothing new about the charge that the New Deal had been full of Communists. Republicans and conservative Democrats had been complaining about radical New Dealers for years. However, the evidence of spying by Communists was alarming. It suggested that there were American citizens who would betray their country's deepest secrets. Nor was the danger confined to espionage. In February 1950, Wisconsin senator Joseph McCarthy charged in a speech in Wheeling, West Virginia, that the State Department was full of Communists and Communist sympathizers who were shaping American policy in ways that aided an international Communist conspiracy. McCarthy singled out John S. Service, a foreign service officer, whom he blamed for helping "lose" China by sending home reports that were critical of the Chiang Kai-shek, the leader of the Chinese Nationalists. McCarthy insisted that Service was hardly alone in his betrayal. "I have in my hand 57 cases of individuals who would appear to be either card-carrying members or certainly loyal to the Communist Party but who are nevertheless still helping to shape our foreign policy," McCarthy said. The idea that one individual or even a small group of people were responsible for the triumph of communism in China seems ludicrous today. But McCarthy's warning against betrayal was powerfully reinforced only a few months later when Julius Rosenberg was arrested and accused of transmitting information to the Russians that helped them produce the atomic bomb.[19]

The belief that all Communists were spies or traitors was rooting itself deeply in the American psyche. It had not always been so. While the Communists had never been popular, they had established a reputation for taking on some of the toughest fights for the rights of working-class Americans. They had joined the miners of West Virginia and the textile workers of North Carolina in attempting to build unions that could secure a living wage. When the Congress of Industrial Organizations launched a national campaign to organize unskilled workers, Communists played a prominent role in recruiting workers in the steel and auto industries. They were among the leaders of the fledgling United Auto Workers and helped win the 1937 sit-down strike against General Motors, a turning point in the fight to build industrial unions. They had also demonstrated a deep commitment to fighting racial discrimination by defending the nine African American teenagers who had been falsely accused of raping two white women in Scottsboro, Alabama. In foreign affairs, they stood out for the militancy of their opposition to the growth of fascism and sent thousands of their members to fight in the Spanish Civil War against Francisco Franco, who was supported by both Germany and Italy. The popularity of the Communist Party grew rapidly during the 1930s, particularly after it decided in 1935 to moderate its revolutionary rhetoric in an effort to build a popular front to oppose fascism. Its membership doubled to eighty-two thousand between 1936 and 1938. The party seemed to be on the verge of entering the mainstream. "It served as the unofficial left wing of the New Deal, its cadres and rank and file supplying manpower and leadership for a wide array of social reform movements and progressive groups," one historian has written.[20]

The Communist Party faced enormous hurdles in its quest for respectability. It was never able to entirely abandon its habit of secretiveness. Party members rarely identified themselves as such, preferring to work through dozens of "front" organizations whose officers were generally not Communists, although they made no effort to disguise their support for the positions of the Communist Party. This desire for anonymity was understandable in a party that had been a victim of government repression since its founding. But it also reflected the ideology of a revolutionary party. The Communists believed in the inevitability of a revolution in which the working class would seize power from the bourgeoisie and establish a Socialist state. As the vanguard of the revolution, Communists felt they must be ready at a moment's notice to elude capture. The Communist Party was also hurt by its close ties to the Soviet Union. Ardent admirers of the Russian Revolution, American Communists followed the party line even when it was political suicide. In 1939, when the Soviet Union signed a nonaggression pact with Hitler, Communists in the United States hid their deep shock and abandoned the Popular Front, embracing a new isolationism that permanently alienated many of their liberal admirers. Liberals were also angered by the Communists' sectarianism. Communists were capable of sacrificing any principle in their desire to strike out at other left-wing groups. Though they defended free speech for themselves and their allies, they applauded the sedition prosecution of members of the Socialist Workers Party in 1941. In the end, despite their secretiveness and efforts to blend in, members of the Communist Party were easy to spot because of the organizations they joined, the political positions they took, and the fanaticism that often characterized their acts. This would become very important during the new Red Scare. "We were sitting ducks," a Communist organizer said later.[21]

The federal government began its campaign against the Communists in March 1947. Under pressure from Republicans to oust Communists from government service, President Truman launched a loyalty program that was quickly copied by state and local governments as well as private employers. The scope of the federal program was sweeping. It applied to all government employees, not just to those whose jobs could affect national security. It also involved investigating people who had done nothing to indicate disloyalty. Investigators were ordered to ferret out anyone found to belong to or have any "sympathetic association" with any "fascist, communist or subversive" group. In practice, this meant that any evidence of radical views—from the books they read to the paintings that hung on the walls of their homes—could be used against them. In addition, people were fired merely for associating with anyone who had radical ties. One man lost his job because his parents had an insurance policy issued by a Communist "front" group. The most damning evidence often came from the files of the FBI. Although the FBI acknowledged that its files contained unverified information, it refused to identify the people who had supplied it. As a result, although government employees had a right to a hearing, they were unable to confront their accusers. The chance of prevailing in such an unfair proceeding seemed hopeless to many. Although the government dismissed a relatively small number of men and women—2,700—at least 12,000 and probably many more resigned when they learned that they had failed their initial screening.[22]

The federal government began planning a direct assault on the Communist Party within weeks of the launch of the loyalty program. When Congress enacted the Smith Act, in 1940, Zechariah Chafee had warned that the statute was "a loaded revolver." The government pulled the trigger in July 1948, indicting eleven leaders of the Communist Party in New York City. The Communists were not charged with buying guns or taking any overt steps to overthrow the government or even conspiring to take such steps. Under the broad wording of the Smith Act, they were accused of a conspiracy to "advocate, abet, advise or teach the duty...of overthrowing or destroying any government in the United States by force." Prosecutor John F. X. McGohey delineated the charges further in his opening statement:

> That they would recruit new members of their party; and that they...
> would publish books, magazines and newspapers; that they would organize schools and classes, in all of which it was planned that there would be taught and advocated the Marxist-Leninist principles of the duty and necessity of overthrowing and destroying the Government of the United States.

The government's case, like the Smith Act itself, was a direct attack on free speech. It provided an opportunity to shift the focus of the trial from allegations of subversion to fundamental violations of civil liberties. However, the Communists rejected their best line of defense.[23]

The Communists saw their trial as an opportunity to vindicate the principles of Marxism–Leninism. Since 1945, they had been led by Eugene Dennis, the forty-year-old party secretary who had risen to prominence based largely on his zeal in promoting the policies promulgated in Moscow. He had shown his commitment to the party on more than one occasion. In 1939, when the Soviet Union had signed a nonaggression treaty with Hitler, Dennis had been ordered to go underground to avoid possible arrest. He spent seventeen months hiding out in summer cottages in upstate New York. He and his wife had also agreed to leave the Soviet Union without their five-year-old son because the child spoke only Russian and the party feared that he would be used to confirm charges of Moscow domination of the American party. Dennis refused to base his defense on the First Amendment or even to allow an attorney to represent him during the trial. Instead, he and his codefendants lectured the court on the sins of capitalism and the inevitability of the workers' triumph. Unfortunately, this played directly into the hands of the prosecution, which presented the American Communists as agents of international revolution. Following one of the longest and bitterest trials in American history, Dennis and his colleagues were convicted and sentenced to ten-year prison terms. Not surprisingly, the trial and the rapidly growing Red Scare had a dampening effect on May Day celebrations in 1949. Although the Communists called it "a despicable, contemptible falsehood," the police estimated that there were both fewer marchers and smaller crowds than the year before.[24]

The executive was not the only branch of the federal government that was intent on suppressing the Communist Party. Ever since its founding in 1938, the House Un-American Activities Committee (HUAC) had been under the control of conservative legislators who were more concerned about the threat of communism than of fascism. It was primed and ready to play a key role in the Communist witch hunt. HUAC made this clear in 1947 when it opened hearings on the alleged Communist subversion of the motion picture industry. An investigation of Hollywood was an obvious choice because it guaranteed headlines and because a number of people in the film industry, particularly writers, had joined the Communist Party during the 1930s. "Scores of screen writers who are Communists have infiltrated into the various studios . . . [and] have employed subtle techniques in pictures, in glorifying the Communist system," HUAC charged. Ten film workers tried to stand up to the committee. When they were asked if they had ever been members of the Communist Party, they cited their rights under the First Amendment to refuse to answer questions about their political affiliations. However, they were refused permission to read statements, and when they tried to read them anyway several were dragged from the room by U.S. marshals. All ten were later cited for contempt of Congress and sentenced to one-year jail terms. In the future, "unfriendly witnesses" would be given only two choices: either answering questions about membership in the Communist Party and identifying other party members or refusing to testify, citing the Fifth Amendment guarantee against self-incrimination. "Taking the Fifth" allowed unfriendly witnesses to escape prosecution for contempt, but it also silenced people like playwright Arthur Miller and novelist Lillian Hellman, who were willing to testify about their own political activities but refused to identify other party members. As a result, there was no one to challenge the HUAC and the other congressional investigating committees, as they portrayed all Communists as traitors.[25]

State and local officials joined in the hunt for Communists. Almost every state and many local governments passed legislation that sought to weed out Communists that were on the public payroll. Some states followed the federal government in establishing loyalty reviews; others required their employees to swear that they were not Communists. Those who refused to take the loyalty oath were discharged. Several state legislatures had their own investigating committees. The Washington Fact-finding Committee on Un-American Activities launched a probe of the University of Washington in 1948, which revealed that several professors had been Communists. Three of the professors refused to cooperate with the investigation and were fired by the university president, who argued that Communists were not entitled to the protections of academic freedom because they hid their party membership and were committed to "dogmas that are held to be superior to scientific examination." Pressure from the California State Committee on Un-American Activities persuaded the University of California to impose a loyalty oath on its faculty and staff. Thirty professors who were not Communists refused to sign the oath and were fired. At least one hundred professors were fired for their political views during the McCarthy era. Most of them held tenure and received formal hearings prior to their firing. There were probably many more who were dismissed without fanfare because they were untenured and were simply not rehired. Hundreds of secondary and elementary school teachers were also dismissed. More than fifty public college and high school teachers were fired in New York City.[26]

Private employers were no more willing to employ people who had been identified as traitors than the government. For a moment during 1947, it appeared that this might not be so. The heads of the Hollywood studios did not welcome the disruption caused by the HUAC hearings. They resented the demands of a bunch of unknown congressmen and worried that they would lose the talents of the "Red" screenwriters, directors, and actors. But the Red Scare was bigger even than Hollywood, and in December the studios fired the Hollywood Ten and issued a statement promising that they would not knowingly employ Communists or anyone else who advocated the violent overthrow of the government. The Hollywood Ten were the first names on the Hollywood blacklist, but they were soon joined by other writers, actors, and directors who had once belonged to radical groups. Two hundred men and women who refused to cooperate with HUAC were blacklisted and became unemployable under their own names during the 1950s; the American Legion consigned another three hundred to an unofficial "graylist," which made it difficult for them to find work. Radio and the nascent TV industry also bent to the demands of the Red baiters who published *Red Channels,* a publication that accused more than 150 performers of radical connections. The TV producer David Susskind would later testify that the networks and sponsors had forced him to obtain clearance for any entertainer he wanted to hire. For one program, he submitted over five thousand names during a two-year period. He estimated that a third of the performers were rejected. Susskind said that they had even blocked the hiring of an eight-year-old actress because her father was suspect.[27]

The Red Scare would not have been as damaging if liberals had taken a strong stand against it. At first, it seemed that they would. In 1947, supporters of the Hollywood Ten created the Committee for the First Amendment to build opposition to HUAC in the weeks before its hearings on Communist subversion in the film industry. Some of the most prominent names in Hollywood joined the committee, including Humphrey Bogart, Lauren Bacall, Lucille Ball, Judy Garland, Danny Kaye, Gene Kelly, Burt Lancaster, and Frank Sinatra. But the hearings deteriorated into a shouting match, and many of the stars were shocked to learn that eight of the ten had been Communists. They had signed on to protect free speech, not to defend Communists. Many of them shared the fear of communism that was beginning to infect other Americans. Bogart said he had been a "dope" to let himself be used. In addition, as big as they were, the stars could not help but worry over the damage they might be doing to their careers. As the Red Scare grew, the anti-Communists began to expand the blacklist to include not only party members but anyone who opposed the measures taken to curb them. More than eighty people who signed a petition urging the Supreme Court to overturn the contempt convictions of the Hollywood Ten later found themselves blacklisted as well. John Henry Faulk, the host of a radio program in New York, lost his job because he had opposed the blacklist as a candidate for office in his union, the American Federation of Television and Radio Artists.[28]

Elected officials who had once been strong defenders of civil liberties soon learned to fear the power of the anti-Communists. In 1950, Maryland senator Millard Tydings conducted hearings on McCarthy's claim to have discovered evidence of Communist subversion in the State Department. Several months later, the Tydings Committee issued a report rejecting the "proof" of these charges as "gossip, distortion, hearsay and deliberate untruths." McCarthy responded with fury, labeling Tydings, a conservative Democrat, "a Commiecrat" who was "protecting Communists for political reasons." When the Korean War broke out in June, McCarthy and his supporters took advantage of war fever to heap even more abuse on their enemies, denouncing them as "egg-sucking liberals" who defended "Communists and queers." ("Egg-sucking liberals" is probably a reference to dogs on farms that traitorously sneak into the henhouse and eat newly laid eggs, gobbling down their masters' profits. As for "Communists and queers," McCarthy often suggested that there was something effeminate about communism and that his opponents were not quite manly.) Tydings and several other candidates who had been smeared as soft on communism were defeated, leading many Democrats to believe that it was impossible to challenge McCarthy. At one point, he taunted his liberal opponents on the Senate floor, daring them to examine the "evidence" that he had piled high on his desk. Seventy-three-year-old Herbert H. Lehman, a former governor of New York, crossed the aisle and held out his hand for the documents, but no other senator supported him. "Go back to your desk, old man," McCarthy growled.[29]

Congressional courage was at its lowest ebb in the fall of 1950, when Congress considered the Internal Security Act, one of the most dangerous bills ever introduced in the United States. Like the anti–Ku Klux Klan law passed by the New York legislature in 1923, its goal was to eliminate an organization by exposing its membership. Later known by the name of its Senate sponsor, Pat McCarran of Nevada, the McCarran Act required the Communist Party to register with the Subversive Activities Control Board (SACB) and to disclose the names of its members. Communists were declared ineligible for government employment, but the more fearful prospect to a party member was the threat of being identified publicly as a Communist and becoming a target for retaliation by private employers and patriotic groups. Communist "front" organizations were also required to register with the SACB, and the attorney general was authorized to add to the SACB list the name of any group that he believed had been guilty of advocating "Communist" policies. President Harry S. Truman spelled out the danger of this provision in vetoing the McCarran Act in 1950:

> This provision could easily be used to classify as a Communist-front organization any organization which is advocating a single policy or objective which is also being urged by the Communist Party.... Thus, an organization which advocates low-cost housing for sincere humanitarian reasons might be classified as a Communist-front organization because the Communists regularly exploit slum conditions as one of their fifth-column techniques.

Truman drew the ominous implications of the legislation for free speech. "Obviously, if this law were on the statute books, the part of prudence would be to avoid saying anything that might be construed by someone as not deviating sufficiently from the current Communist propaganda line," Truman wrote. "And since no one could be sure in advance what views were safe to express, the inevitable tendency would be to express no view on controversial subjects."[30]

Although the McCarran Act clearly violated the First Amendment, congressional opponents had been unwilling to confront the anti-Communists directly during the debate over the bill. Instead, they attempted to torpedo it by offering a substitute measure giving the president the power to declare an internal security emergency in case of invasion, declaration of war, or domestic insurrection. The attorney general was then authorized to detain any person for whom there was "reasonable ground to believe that such person probably will engage in, or probably will conspire with others to engage in, acts of espionage or sabotage." That some of the Senate's leading liberals, including Hubert Humphrey of Minnesota, Paul Douglas of Illinois, and Estes Kefauver of Tennessee, could support a bill that envisioned the creation of American concentration camps gives a good idea of the state of American politics in 1950. The irony is that not only did their bill not draw off any votes from the McCarran Act, the anti-Communists embraced the idea and added it to their own bill as an amendment. In the end, liberals and conservatives joined to pass the McCarran Act. It was then repassed over Truman's veto by a vote of 286 to 48 in the House and 57 to 10 in the Senate.[31]

As their world collapsed around them, many of the victims of the Red Scare naturally turned to their professional associations to defend them. The college professors who were pursued by investigating committees and then fired had every reason to hope that they would receive the support of the American Association of University Professors (AAUP). It had been defending academic freedom since its founding in 1915, and in 1947 it had publicly rejected the principle underlying the federal loyalty program. "So long as the Communist Party in the United States is a legal political party, affiliation with that party in and of itself should not be regarded as a justifiable reason for exclusion from the academic profession," it declared. Yet, over the course of the next seven years, as more than one hundred professors were fired for their political views, the AAUP conducted only one investigation and failed to issue any reports condemning the firings. When the American Bar Association (ABA) created the

Committee on the Bill of Rights in 1938, civil libertarians hoped that this was a sign that the association was beginning to abandon its reactionary views. But the conservatives in the association reasserted themselves during the cold war, creating the Special Committee on Communist Tactics, Strategy and Objectives, and passing resolutions that called for excluding Communists and anyone who had taken the Fifth Amendment from the practice of law. Lawyers had not been eager to represent people who were accused of being Communists anyway, knowing that they would lose well-paying clients. With the ABA supporting the anti–Communists, the vast majority felt no obligation to defend them. Some Communists were rejected by over two hundred lawyers.[32]

The second Red Scare should have been the ACLU's shining hour. After all, it had been born during the first Red Scare, and its leaders knew what it was like to stand alone when everyone around them was either infected with anticommunism or fear of the anti-Communists. At times, it fought brilliantly. In 1950, the public learned that the blacklist that had ruled the movie industry since the firing of the Hollywood Ten in 1947 was operating in the television and radio industry as well. Jean Muir, an actress on a popular television series, was fired after her name appeared in *Red Channels,* a publication that listed the names of 151 writers, directors, and performers who were alleged to have Communist sympathies, including Leonard Bernstein, Lee J. Cobb, Dashiell Hammett, Lillian Hellman, Lena Horne, Gypsy Rose Lee, Arthur Miller, Zero Mostel, Edward G. Robinson, Artie Shaw, Howard K. Smith, William L. Shirer, and Orson Welles. The entries in *Red Channels* consisted of a listing of the occasions on which a particular person had participated in suspicious activity like signing a petition, speaking at a rally, or even attending a fund-raiser. While the list included allegedly Communist groups like Consumers Union, the publisher of *Consumer Reports,* most of the organizations listed in *Red Channels* were Communist "front" groups that were on the list compiled by the attorney general to ensure that the government didn't hire subversives. The firing of Muir propelled the ACLU into action. It commissioned author Merle Miller to write an exposé of the blacklist. Published as a trade book by Doubleday, Miller's study, *The Judges and the Judged,* honed in on the arbitrariness of the blacklist:

> Does a man have "leftist leanings" if . . . he attended a "spring ball" for
> the *New Masses* in March 1938? . . . Does one affiliation suffice? Will a
> dozen do? Are 41 necessary? Who can say? . . . Those who would do the
> suppressing are a greater threat to the democratic idea than those who
> would be suppressed.

The Judges and the Judged was both a commercial and a critical success.[33]

But the leaders of the ACLU were usually divided in their views of how to respond to the Red Scare. Even before the war, anti-Communists on the ACLU board had demanded that the organization declare its opposition to the Communist Party. While the Communists and the civil libertarians had often worked together, there had always been considerable distrust between them. Communist Party attacks on other leftist groups alienated ACLU board members like Norman Thomas, the leader of the Socialist Party. The Communists had also demonstrated intolerance toward the First Amendment rights of their enemies. The hostility toward the Communists came to a boil in 1940. Pressured by the newly formed HUAC, the ACLU passed a resolution barring Communists and other members of "totalitarian" groups from serving on its board and then expelled one of its founders, Elizabeth Gurley Flynn, a member of the Communist Party's national committee. The expulsion of Flynn was a "disaster," according to Samuel Walker, an ACLU historian. "A breach of principle, it both failed to placate right-wing critics, who continued to vilify the ACLU as a Communist front, and outraged the left, many of whom would never let the ACLU live down the 'trial,'" he wrote. Once the war began, further compromises were urged on the group by conservatives on the ACLU board who believed that civil liberties must be curtailed during times of national emergency. They prevented the ACLU from challenging the government's right to intern American citizens during wartime and passed a resolution stating that the ACLU would not automatically defend everyone charged with sedition.[34]

As a result, as the ACLU faced the Red Scare, nearly half of its board was prepared to limit the civil liberties of Communists, based either on their personal hostility to the Communists or on their support for national security during the cold war. The ACLU never challenged the right of the government to impose a loyalty test on all of its employees. It did protest the creation by the attorney general of a list of "subversive" organizations, correctly predicting that this would become the basis for a blacklist that would spread far beyond the federal government. But the ACLU board split down the middle over whether to challenge the list in court and finally approved a proposal to file an amicus brief by a one-vote margin. The board voted to oppose the emergency detention provision of the McCarran Act but only after another close vote—11-9.

On several issues, the ACLU supported greater restrictions on free speech. It endorsed a bill in Congress to limit the picketing of federal courthouses, which its sponsors said was necessary to prevent Communists from intimidating the courts through mass demonstrations. It also refused to support the singer Paul Robeson when the State Department revoked his passport in 1950. Robeson was a towering figure in the African American community. Born in Princeton, New Jersey, Robeson had originally hoped to be a lawyer and graduated from the Columbia University Law School in the same class as future Supreme Court justice William O. Douglas. But Robeson's father was a former slave, and he was passionately committed to the fight for racial justice. He quit his first job in a law firm when a white secretary refused to take dictation from him because of his color. He then abandoned law and pursued an acting and singing career, which brought him world renown. At the same time, he became a strong critic of America's racial policies and a defender of the Soviet Union. These qualities made him anathema to many Americans and even provoked a riot when he attempted to perform in Peekskill, New York, in 1949. Robeson became such a polarizing figure that some loyalty boards asked potential government employees whether they owned any Robeson records. Robeson's passport was revoked not because he had committed illegal acts but because he refused to sign an affidavit denying that he was a Communist. The revocation made it virtually impossible for him to make a living, since he was blacklisted in the United States. Nevertheless, the ACLU did not challenge the government's claim that the First Amendment does not guarantee an unrestricted right to travel.

The ACLU's compromises with principle weakened it in the eyes of its enemies. When ACLU counsel Arthur Hays testified against legislation that later became part of the McCarran Act, he declared that outlawing the Communist Party was "indefensible." Congressman Richard Nixon interrupted him. The thirty-five-year-old congressman from California had been elected to Congress only a few years earlier, but he had enjoyed a meteoric rise by becoming one of the leading anti-Communists in the House. It had been Nixon who had forced Alger Hiss to acknowledge that he knew Whittaker Chambers, giving new credibility to Chambers's claim that the government was riddled with spies. With his HUAC colleague Karl Mundt of South Dakota, Nixon had also authored the registration provision that would become the heart of the McCarran Act. Hays had plenty to say, but Nixon didn't give him a chance. Wasn't it true that the ACLU had barred Communists from its leadership positions? he asked. Hays was forced to agree. "In other words, you did not feel that the American Civil Liberties Union could do a proper job with the Communists, so you passed a rule against them, but you wouldn't want us to do that on a national level?" Nixon asked. The hearing room filled with laughter.[35]

When even the ACLU was afraid to take an uncompromising stand in defense of civil liberties, it is not surprising that support for free speech among the general public sank to a new low in the early 1950s. Even a decade later, social scientists measured a shocking loss of faith in the First Amendment. A 1963 study found that 91 percent of the public opposed permitting a Communist to teach in a public high school, and more than 50 percent would have barred a Socialist teacher as well. Nor was the country concerned only about the exposure of young minds to radical ideas: 77 percent favored stripping Communists of their American citizenship, and 68 percent believed a Communist should not even be allowed to work as a store clerk. By 1951, the fear of unorthodox ideas had grown to the point where it became impossible for many Americans to determine what was radical and what was basic Americanism. A reporter for a Wisconsin newspaper proved this by creating a petition that included nothing but the preamble to the Declaration of Independence. Only 1 percent of those who were asked agreed to sign.[36]

Such experiments convinced thoughtful Americans that their compatriots were paralyzed by a fear that was threatening to undermine the country's traditions. Increasingly, they began to speak up. In January 1952, Supreme Court justice William O. Douglas published an influential article, "The Black Silence of Fear," in the *New York Times Magazine*. "Fear has driven more and more men and women in all walks of life either to silence or to the folds of the orthodox," Douglas wrote. People no longer felt free to explore ideas, and the consequences for the nation could be disastrous:

> The great danger of this period is not inflation, nor the national debt, nor atomic warfare. The great, the critical danger, is that we will so limit or narrow the range of permissible discussion and permissible thought that we will become victims of the orthodox school. If we do, we will lose flexibility. We will lose the capacity for expert management. We will then become wedded to a few techniques, to a few devices. They will define our policy and at the same time limit our ability to alter or modify it.

Douglas was particularly worried because anti-Communist orthodoxy was causing the United States to align itself against rebels in Asian countries who were fighting for independence against colonial powers.[37]

Douglas's words did not sway many minds at the time. The country was still at war, and Joseph McCarthy continued to dominate American politics. Since the time of his 1950 Wheeling, West Virginia, speech, McCarthy had been the biggest story in the country, dominating newspapers, radio, and the fledgling television industry. But the political tide had begun to turn by early 1954. The end of the Korean War made this possible, but McCarthy played a role in his own downfall. Being the center of attention required him to continue to manufacture the spectacular revelations that had the reporters hanging on his every word. After he had finished with the State Department, he identified a number of new targets, including the Government Printing Office, the American delegation to the United Nations, the Central Intelligence Agency, and the army. McCarthy's attack on the army brought him into direct conflict with the administration of President Dwight Eisenhower. In February 1954, Secretary of the Army Robert T. Stevens forbade his officers to testify before McCarthy's committee after he had humiliated a general during a hearing, declaring him "unfit to wear that uniform." McCarthy was still a formidable opponent. "Just go ahead and try it," McCarthy warned Stevens. "I am going to kick the brains out of anyone who protects Communism." Yet, for the first time in four years, it appeared that McCarthy was misreading the mood of the country.[38]

The resistance to McCarthy soon received powerful reinforcement from the country's leading journalist, Edward R. Murrow. Murrow had first come to the attention of the American public during 1940, when he was serving as the London bureau chief of the CBS radio network. It was Murrow who brought the European war home to his countrymen through his program *This Is London*. When Germany began the bombing blitz of London, which was intended to break the spirit of the English people, Murrow stood atop the BBC's Broadcast House, describing the effect of the falling bombs on the darkened city. He went on to become one of the country's best-known war correspondents. When he returned home after the war, his dark, handsome looks, ubiquitous cigarette, and tough, staccato delivery made him a natural for the new world of television, and he quickly became a star on CBS, where he hosted a half-hour news magazine, *See It Now,* which he coproduced with Fred Friendly. Murrow and Friendly were appalled by the excesses of the Red Scare, but they felt constrained by their professional commitment to tell both sides of every story.

In the fall of 1953, however, Murrow and Friendly learned that a twenty-seven-year-old air force officer, Milo Radulovich, had been ordered discharged after a loyalty review turned up evidence that his father and sister held radical political views. The board was not required to reveal the evidence against the officer, but his lawyer was shown a report that claimed that Radulovich's father subscribed to a Socialist newspaper. In addition, there were rumors that his sister had participated in a civil rights demonstration and had marched on a Communist picket line. The unfairness of visiting the "sin" of a father on a son promised great television. Radulovich was also appealing. He was not an active duty officer but a member of the air force reserve who was working two jobs to put himself through the University of Michigan. Appearing on camera with his wife and baby, he criticized the loyalty board for asking him to break with his father and sister. "If I am being judged on my relatives, are my children going to be asked to denounce me?" he asked. Radulovich's neighbors in the small town of Dexter, Michigan, supported him strongly, petitioning the air force on his behalf. The *See It Now* program on the case stirred a storm of protest across the country, and a month later the air force announced that Radulovich could stay.[39]

On November 24, 1953, *See It Now* opened its broadcast with a three-minute tape of the secretary of the air force reinstating Radulovich. The rest of the program was devoted to a report on the difficulties that ACLU organizers had faced in finding a place in Indianapolis where they could hold a meeting to organize an Indiana affiliate. It was another program about the violation of traditional American freedoms by a country that was panicked over the Communist threat that nevertheless carefully counterposed the points of view of spokesmen for the ACLU and the American Legion. But Murrow was about to abandon any pretense of objectivity. Earlier in the week, one of his reporters told him that McCarthy's chief investigator, Donald A. Surine, had threatened to reveal evidence that "Murrow was on the Soviet payroll in [1935]" unless he laid off "this Radwich stuff." "Mind you, Joe, I'm not saying Murrow is a Commie himself, but he's one of those goddamn anti-anti-Communists, and they're just as dangerous," Surine said. Murrow was furious, and as he left the studio on the evening of November 24, he asked Friendly how much film of McCarthy there was in the CBS archives. Friendly estimated fifty thousand feet but wasn't sure whether it included McCarthy's Wheeling speech. Murrow asked him to try to find it.[40]

Four months later, on March 8, 1954, *See It Now* broadcast "Report on Senator Joseph R. McCarthy." The program consisted mainly of a montage of statements made by McCarthy that Murrow dissected to reveal his dishonesty. There was film of McCarthy promising not to turn his anti-Communist campaign to partisan purposes and then another clip of him accusing the Democrats of bearing "the stain of a historic betrayal." McCarthy was shown portraying the ACLU as a "subversive" group. Then, Murrow reappeared and stated, "The Attorney General's list does not and never has listed the ACLU as subversive." Murrow agreed that congressional investigations served an important purpose. "But the line between investigating and persecuting is a fine one, and the junior

Senator from Wisconsin has stepped over it repeatedly," he said. As the program wrapped up, Murrow made it clear that he had a larger purpose than criticizing McCarthy. He was attacking the fear at the heart of the Red Scare:

> We will not walk in fear, one of another. We will not be driven by fear into an age of unreason if we dig deep in our history and our doctrine and remember that we are not descended from fearful men, not from men who feared to write, to speak, to associate and to defend the causes that were for the moment unpopular. This is no time for men who oppose Senator McCarthy's methods to keep silent—or for those who approve. We can deny our heritage and our history but we cannot escape responsibility for the result.

Whose fault was McCarthyism? "Not really his," Murrow concluded, looking up from his notes. "He didn't create this situation of fear: he merely exploited it—and rather successfully. Cassius was right. The fault, dear Brutus, is not in our stars, but in ourselves."[41]

Although no one would have believed it at the time, McCarthy's career was almost over. Certainly, Murrow's broadcast played an important role. The response from the *See It Now* audience was unprecedented. CBS received more than one thousand telegrams in the first few hours after the broadcast and more than 100,000 congratulatory messages over the next several days. But, ultimately, McCarthy was a victim of his own recklessness. His attack on the army led to a motion in the Senate to censure him, and his staff was accused of pressuring the army to secure special treatment for a former staff member. McCarthy attempted to defend himself during two months of nationally televised hearings, but daily exposure to the blustering of their former hero only disillusioned the public. In December, he was censured by the Senate by a vote of 67-22. McCarthy continued to make charges, but his heavy drinking worsened, and he died in May 1957.

It took great courage to challenge the Red Scare because protesters were inevitably attacked themselves. Yet despite what novelist Norman Mailer described as a "collective failure of nerve" on the part of people, organizations, and institutions that should have defended civil liberties, Murrow was by no means alone. Some of the nation's most prominent newspapers and columnists helped strip McCarthy of his aura of invincibility. One of the boldest challenges to the anti-Communist crusade, however, was mounted by a man who owned neither a printing press nor a national reputation. In 1956, the radio commentator John Henry Faulk filed a libel suit against two of the men who were largely responsible for blacklisting radio and television personalities. Faulk was furious over the effort to portray him as a Communist because he had spoken out against the blacklist. He didn't listen to his wife, his business manager, or the many friends who warned him that he was risking his blossoming career. Nor was he deterred when Louis Nizer, the attorney who had agreed to represent him, warned that it would be years before the case would finally come to trial. Faulk lost his job at WCBS radio the following year. The radio station denied that Faulk's firing had anything to do with his controversial lawsuit, but it clearly worried other prospective employers because Faulk was unable to find another job for the next five years. He finally got his day in court in 1962.[42]

Lasting over two months, the trial reached its climax on an unusually warm day in June when the defendant Vincent Hartnett took the stand. Hartnett was a professional anti-Communist who had helped prepare *Red Channels* before he went to work for AWARE, Incorporated, which described itself as "an organization to combat the Communist conspiracy in entertainment-communications." AWARE's main job was to check the backgrounds of the entertainers who were seeking jobs in television and radio. Advertisers and network executives paid $5 per name to ensure that they would never hire someone who might be accused of being a Communist. While even Faulk believed that Hartnett was probably sincere, sincerity was no defense against a charge of libel. He was also facing Nizer, a great trial lawyer at the peak of his career. Nizer's relentless examination forced Hartnett to concede that AWARE had had no interest in Faulk until he came out in opposition to blacklisting as a candidate for office in the New York chapter of the American Federation of Television and Radio Artists; that the evidence he had cited in an AWARE publication did not prove that Faulk was a subversive ("I had no knowledge, I had no evidence to back up a charge that he was a pro-Communist," Hartnett said); and finally that Hartnett had nevertheless written to the advertising agency Young and Rubicam that Faulk "has a significant Communist-front record"— a move that made unemployable a forty-four-year-old entertainer who appeared to be on the cusp of national success.[43]

Things were not going well for Hartnett even before Faulk noticed that he was taking notes in the witness box. Even as he fended off Nizer's question, he was noting the time that certain people were entering and leaving the room. Faulk mentioned this to Nizer during a lunch break. When Nizer asked Hartnett what he was doing, he acknowledged that he was keeping track of who was attending the trial. According to Faulk, this admission "brought a gasp from the judge and the jury, who leaned forward and peered at Hartnett as though he had admitted to a monstrous crime." Apparently, they believed that Hartnett intended to use this information against Faulk's friends and supporters in the entertainment business. Several days later, Hartnett's attorney tried to repair this damaging assumption. He asked Hartnett whose names he was writing down. Hartnett replied that they were actors—"like Eliot Sullivan, who was sitting next to Mrs. Faulk." Some of them had been unfriendly witnesses when they appeared at HUAC hearings. Hartnett's lawyer had hoped to hurt Faulk by linking him to leftists, but the tactic backfired. Moving toward the spectators, Nizer asked Hartnett to identify "Mrs. Faulk." "I believe she is the lady over here," Hartnett said, pointing. Faulk described the denouement:

> Nizer turned dramatically to the woman spectator and asked her name. The woman stood and said, "My name is Helen Soffer. S-O-F-F-E-R." Pandemonium broke out. Even Judge Geller could not escape the emotional impact of Hartnett's blunder. Lou waited for a lull and then in a searing voice addressed the defendant. "Sir, is that an example of the accuracy with which you have identified your victims for the past ten years?"

Shortly after the jury was charged, it returned with a question. "Can the jury award more damages than the plaintiff's attorney asked?" the foreman asked. It subsequently ordered Hartnett and his co-defendant, Laurence Johnson, a Syracuse, New York, supermarket owner who had pressured advertisers to enforce the AWARE blacklist, to pay Faulk $3.5 million, a sum that was seven times larger than the biggest libel verdict that had ever been awarded.⁴⁴

The courage of men and women like Murrow and Faulk played an important role in ending the Red Scare because it encouraged others to speak up. But for the first time, the Supreme Court also helped end a national witch hunt. This was surprising because it had added fuel to the fire at first. In 1951, the Supreme Court upheld the convictions of Eugene Dennis and the other Communist leaders who had been prosecuted under the Smith Act. The membership of the Court had shifted significantly since the war. Frank Murphy died in 1949 at the age of fifty-nine, and Wiley Rutledge, another civil libertarian, died just a few months later. As a result of two retirements, Harry Truman was able to appoint four justices who supported his anti-Communist policies.

In 1956, however, the Supreme Court began to reverse itself. Once again, a significant change in the membership of the Court played a role as four new justices took the place of men who had been sympathetic to anti-Communist policies and programs. The new justices included Earl Warren, a former governor of California who replaced Vinson as chief justice, and William Brennan, a member of the New Jersey Supreme Court who had publicly compared McCarthyism to the Salem witch trials. (McCarthy, a fellow Irish Catholic, had cast the only vote against him during the Senate vote confirming his appointment in March 1957.) The shift in the Supreme Court's attitude became apparent on June 17, 1957, which became known as Red Monday because of the four decisions issued on the day that struck at different aspects of the assault on free speech that had begun a decade earlier. In one of the most important cases, *Yates v. United States,* the Court effectively gutted the Smith Act by overturning the convictions of a number of Communist leaders who were found guilty on essentially the same evidence used in the *Dennis* case. Although the Smith Act remained on the books, Justice John M. Harlan made it clear that the government must prove something more than the fact that the defendants had taught the inevitability of proletarian revolution. The "essential distinction is that those to whom the advocacy is addressed must be urged to *do* something, now or in the future, rather than merely to *believe* in something," he wrote in his majority opinion. In another decision delivered on Red Monday, the Court overturned the conviction of John T. Watkins, a United Auto Workers official, who had refused to tell HUAC the names of former Communists. The Court's decision was based on a technicality, but the language of its ruling made it clear that a majority of its members now doubted the legitimacy of HUAC. "Who can define the meaning of 'Un-American?'" it asked.[45]

Yet even the Supreme Court could not undo the damage that had been inflicted on American society during the second Red Scare. The anti-Communists had legitimized the attack on radical ideas, and the result had been to create a chilling effect that spread through every facet of intellectual life. The 1950s have been portrayed as a decade peopled by a "Silent Generation" whose guiding principle was conformity. While this is an exaggerated picture of a period that saw the emergence of the civil rights movement, it accurately portrays life on the college campuses that had been badly frightened by purges of faculty members based on their political beliefs. "The vast majority of teachers have learned that promotion and security depend upon conformity," a college administrator reported. As a result, there was "a subtle, creeping paralysis of thought and speech" in higher education, the *Christian Science Monitor* observed in March 1954. The impact of McCarthyism on the government was even more devastating. The purge of the State Department over the "loss" of China eliminated the experienced foreign service officers who might have warned the nation of the danger of a war in Vietnam, and instead filled the country's leaders with dread over the possibility that they might be held responsible for the loss of another country to communism. The personal losses sustained by the victims of McCarthyism could also be catastrophic. Red Monday did not end the ordeal of Americans who refused to cooperate with the investigating committees or otherwise had politically suspect views. They continued to go to jail, and although the blacklist in the entertainment industry had begun to lose some of its effectiveness, it continued to operate until the mid-1960s.

Even the 1962 Court victory of John Henry Faulk did not succeed in rehabilitating his career or even begin to compensate him for the destruction of his prospects. (His opponents ultimately settled the case for $175,000, most of which went to pay for legal costs.) Yet

Faulk denied any bitterness. "I consider that it was a rare, and indeed, a great privilege to have had the opportunity to stake my convictions against those who shared AWARE's attitudes about our constitutional freedoms," he explained.

> My fight against AWARE was neither heroic nor courageous. It was nothing more than any American citizen should do, when forces of repression and fear threaten to undermine our character of government, constitution, and the heritage of freedom that has served us so well in the past two centuries.

In the end, the best thing that can be said of the Second Red Scare is that, like its predecessor, it demonstrated how far the country still had to go to protect the civil liberties of its citizens.[46]

CHAPTER 6

The Fight for Artistic Freedom, 1945–1966

Though the movie censors tried the facts to hide,
The movie goers up and multiplied.
E. Y. Harburg, Finian's Rainbow

The smell of burning comic books was almost as strong as the smell of burning leaves in the fall of 1948. In Spencer, West Virginia, six hundred grade-school children gathered around a small pyre of two thousand comic books that they had spent several weeks collecting. "We are met here today to take a step which we believe will benefit ourselves, our community and our country," thirteen-year-old David Mace explained. "We also pledge ourselves to try not to read anymore," he added, injecting a note of realism. In Binghamton, New York, Catholic students responded to a message from their bishop denouncing "the pictorial magazine and comic book which portray indecent pictures and sensational details of crime." John Farrell, the president of the junior class, and a delegation of students visited thirty-five retailers and persuaded them to discontinue the sale of "indecent and objectionable literature," then joined the other students at St. Patrick's School in burning a pile of comics behind the school. In Rumson, New Jersey, the adult leaders of the Cub Scouts put their children on one of the town's fire engines and toured the city with siren blaring, stopping occasionally to allow the scouts to hop down and ring the doorbells of private homes in search of comics books for burning. In the end, they decided against a bonfire, but the perverse idea of using a fire engine to burn books would appear again a few years later in a short story by Ray Bradbury, which became the novel *Fahrenheit 451*.[1]

Comic books were not the only target of censorship in the postwar period. Despite the liberalization that had occurred in the 1920s, books, magazines, movies, and radio were still controlled either directly, by government, or indirectly, through "voluntary" codes of conduct like the Production Code Authority, which regulated the content of movies, and the code of standards adopted by radio and TV broadcasters. Private organizations were also active in forcing the removal of magazines and books that they found offensive. When they teamed up with government, they could have a devastating effect. In 1954, they would force comic-book publishers to fold their very lucrative horror titles, squelching efforts to broaden the content of comic art to appeal to adults. But the censors were beginning to lose their grip. Although they claimed to speak for the public, they were far more conservative than their neighbors, who were increasingly resentful of efforts to limit their choices in books, magazines, and movies. In addition, the censors found themselves confronting organized resistance on the national level. Librarians became increasingly aggressive defenders of free speech, and they received support from publishers, booksellers, and the press. A decisive blow would be struck by the U.S. Supreme Court in 1957 when, in the course of upholding a ban on "obscene" books, it legalized the sale of any sexually explicit work that was not "utterly without redeeming social importance." By the mid-1960s, the censors were bemoaning their loss of influence.

The federal government's power to censor had suffered a setback in 1930. Senator Bronson Cutting had clipped its wings when he won his fight against the customs bureau, and customs inspectors lost the freedom to suppress the importation of literary classics from abroad. Henceforth, they were forced to consider a book as a whole before deciding whether it was obscene. If they still refused to admit it, the decision could be challenged in federal court. This was what Random House did with *Ulysses.* Following Judge Woolsey's ruling that it was not obscene and could be legally imported, Random House published the first American edition of Joyce's book. But the federal government still possessed a potential stranglehold on artistic speech. Since the passage of the Comstock law in 1873, the post office had been charged with the responsibility of suppressing "any obscene or indecent book, pamphlet, paper, advertisement, drawing, lithograph, engraving, wood cut, daguerreotype, photograph, stereoscopic picture, model, cast instrument or other article for indecent or immoral nature." Postal authorities pursued a fairly tolerant policy in the 1930s, after their disastrous effort to prosecute Mary Ware Dennett for mailing her sex education pamphlet, *The Sex Side of Life*. But in the 1940s, the post office once again sought to exercise sweeping censorship powers in the name of fighting obscenity.[2]

Postal authorities banned many novels because of their sexual content. A post office attorney acknowledged that Lillian Smith's *Strange Fruit* was "a plea for social equality" for African Americans. "The book aspires to fill the role of *Uncle Tom's Cabin* in the life of the modern negro problem," he said. But that wasn't enough to save it because it portrayed a sexual relationship between a white man and a mulatto woman in too much detail. "The worst part is the filthy language," the lawyer explained. "It is obscene in that it is disgusting, repulsive, nauseating." Erskine Caldwell's *Tobacco Road* was declared unmailable, as were John O'Hara's *Appointment in Samarra* and Ernest Hemingway's *For Whom the Bell Tolls*. John Steinbeck's *The Grapes of Wrath* was spared despite "numerous passages . . . which, taken by themselves, must be regarded as obscene."[3]

Post office censorship had little impact on books because they were delivered to booksellers by freight companies and therefore did not travel through the mail. Many of the condemned titles had become bestsellers long before. But the post office had the magazine industry by the throat. Most magazines were delivered through the mail under a second-class permit that saved the publishers hundreds of thousands of dollars over what they would have to pay for first-class delivery. Because second-class mail was subject to inspection, postal authorities could also easily determine the content of what was being mailed, and in the late 1930s they became increasingly alarmed by the profusion of new magazines that featured pictures of women wearing skimpy costumes, including *Spark, Stocking Parade,* and *Peek*. In 1940, a new postmaster general, Frank Walker, began a crackdown on the "cheesecake" magazines as well as romance and detective magazines that he deemed too sexual. He threatened to revoke the second-class permits of more than sixty publications, including some that were issued by leading magazine publishers.

Walker was so confident of his role as a national censor that he attempted to ban one of the country's most popular magazines, *Esquire*. *Esquire* premiered in December 1933, the depths of the Depression, but it was an instant hit and was selling over 700,000 copies monthly by 1937. The magazine had found its niche by catering to the burgeoning class of white-collar men who were looking for advice on how to dress and behave in an urban society. There had never been a fashion magazine for men before, and editor Arnold Gingrich realized that he would have to do something to overcome men's fear of being regarded as sissies for concerning themselves with their dress. Advertising itself as "the magazine for men," *Esquire* presented itself as a three-ring circus. "Gingrich's three rings were fashion, offbeat masculine writing, and sex. And all three rings were to be hairy chested," a historian of the magazine has written. Gingrich published journalism and short fiction by many of the leading male writers, including Ernest Hemingway, John Dos Passos, and F. Scott Fitzgerald. But the magazine was best known for its risqué cartoons and the sexy pinups that began to appear as centerfolds in 1939. Postal authorities objected to *Esquire's* strong sexual content, forcing Gingrich to travel to Washington every month to show them the upcoming issue. When they objected to something, "I would make all the required changes on the spot," Gingrich said. The editor could not afford to be resentful. The loss of the magazine's second-class permit would cost $500,000 in additional postage annually, destroying its profitability.

Even Gingrich's monthly visits to Washington, however, were not enough to placate the postmaster general. In 1943, he revoked *Esquire's* mailing privileges, citing more than ninety "obscene" items in the magazine, including twenty-two pinups by artist Alberto Varga and numerous cartoons, photographs, and illustrations. One of the cartoons showed a group of soldiers surrounded by women with spears. "It's no use, Sarge. We're surrounded," says one of the soldiers. "Yippee!" The post office also objected to the use of the words "bottom, juke, diddle, bawdy house, prostitute, street-walker, syphilis, sunny south (referring to a woman's posterior), fanny and sonofabitch." Postmaster Walker did not succeed in banning *Esquire*. The magazine went to court to challenge his authority to deny second-class privileges and was vindicated in 1945 by an appeals court ruling that urged the post office to stick to the "more prosaic" task of delivering the mail. A year later, the Supreme Court unanimously upheld this decision.[4]

Author and critic Edmund Wilson was not so fortunate. In the same month as the Supreme Court decision in the *Esquire* case, the nation's largest publisher, Doubleday, issued Wilson's novel *Memoirs of Hecate County*, which included some unusually explicit descriptions of sexual intercourse between unmarried adults. Wilson was a highly respected critic who had worked at *The New Republic* and *The New Yorker*. He was also the author of thirteen nonfiction works and a previous novel. But he had little popular success until *Memoirs of Hecate County*, which was leaping off the shelves despite mixed reviews. "Well, Edmund, I'm glad to see that you've written a book that will sell," Wilson's mother told her boy. Wilson's success was short-lived. In July, John Sumner of the New York Society for the Suppression of Vice raided several Doubleday bookstores in Manhattan and seized 130 copies of the book. New York District Attorney Frank Hogan charged Doubleday with selling obscene material. Hogan detailed his objections in a trial brief:

> There are 20 separate acts of sexual intercourse [pages 109, 113, 114, 119, 120, 122, 153, 155, 159, 160, 161, 168, 180, 181, 189, 190, 191, 192, 194, 196, 197, 198, 207 and 231]. These take place between the protagonist and four different women. Eighteen of the acts occur in the space of an hour or two with two different women. Three of the acts occur with two married women.

While explicit, Wilson's descriptions of sex were clearly artistic:

> She became, in fact, so smooth and open that after a moment I could hardly feel her. Her little bud was so deeply embedded that it was hardly involved in the play, and she made me arrest my movement while she did something special and gentle that did not, however, press on this point, rubbing herself somehow against me—and then came, with a self-excited tremor that appeared to me curiously mild for a woman of her positive energy. I went on and had a certain disappointment, for, with the brimming of female fluid, I felt even less sensation; but—gently enough—I came, too.

One of the three judges who presided at the trial believed that Wilson "obviously had serious intentions" in writing the book that prevented it from being obscene. Nevertheless, Doubleday was convicted, and the Supreme Court later divided 4-4 on the case, which allowed the conviction to stand. Once *Memoirs of Hecate County* had been declared obscene in New York, its publisher withdrew it from circulation in the rest of the country to avoid the risk of another prosecution. Booksellers and librarians removed it from their inventories. Wilson's book had been banned.[5]

Much of the censorship that occurred during the 1940s and 1950s was exercised not by government but by industries that were anxious to forestall direct government censorship. To avoid transmitting any show that might cause them to lose their government licenses, radio broadcasters banned speakers with radical views and refused to permit the use of the words "sexual," "syphilis," "damn," and "hell." In 1939, the National Association of Broadcasters adopted a "voluntary" code of standards intended to guarantee that all programming would be in "good taste." Self-censorship was extended to television when the new industry was born in the late 1940s.

It was the movie industry that set the example for other media industries in self-censorship. Will Hays's rescue of the movie industry in the wake of the Fatty Arbuckle scandal had not ended the threat of censorship. As the Depression took hold, there was a dramatic decline in attendance at movie theaters. Desperate producers tried to save themselves by releasing pictures that heavily exploited sex and violence, outraging the industry's many critics. In early 1934, a Catholic organization, the Legion of Decency, collected pledges from over eleven million people that they would boycott the movies unless the industry immediately took steps to eliminate the new explicitness. Already facing financial disaster, the movie moguls surrendered, adopting detailed restrictions on content and creating the Production Code Administration (PCA) to ensure that they were enforced.[6]

The PCA was powerful. Censors reviewed film scripts in advance to ensure that nothing violated the code. Recognizing that audiences demanded sex and violence, the code did not ban them altogether but required that any display of bad behavior had to be balanced by "compensating moral value." An evildoer had to either reform or be punished. While the code was flexible in places, it banned outright "a vast range of human expression and experience," film historian Robert Sklar observed. Prohibited subjects included homosexuality ("sex perversion"), interracial sex, abortion, and incest. Profanity and many "vulgar" words, including "sex," were also banned. There was no law that required a producer to submit a script to the PCA, but theater owners refused to exhibit any film that did not bear the PCA's seal of approval. As a result, the review process usually became a negotiation. In 1950, director Elia Kazan knew that he would have to fight hard to get the censors to approve a script based on Tennessee Williams's play *A Streetcar Named Desire.* In the play, Blanche DuBois visits her sister, Stella, who is married to Stanley Kowalski. Blanche's husband, a homosexual, has killed himself, and Blanche has been fired as a teacher after seducing one of her students. At the climax, she is raped by Stanley and suffers a mental breakdown. Nevertheless, Stella remains with Stanley at the end of the play. The PCA demanded a series of cuts, but Kazan drew the line at eliminating the rape. He was allowed to keep it if it was done "by suggestion and delicacy" and if he was willing to supply "compensating moral values." In the movie, Stella leaves Stanley, ironically creating one of the iconic denouements in the history of film as Marlon Brando, playing Kowalski, stands in the courtyard of his seedy New Orleans apartment house, screaming Stella's name. Yet even the approval of the PCA was sometimes not enough to satisfy the censors. Over Kazan's strenuous objections, Warner Brothers, which owned the picture, cut four more minutes in order to win the approval of the Legion of Decency.[7]

The censorship practiced by government and industry did not go far enough for some people. They joined private groups that sought to suppress objectionable works. The most prominent was the National Organization for Decent Literature (NODL), a Catholic group that had been organized in the 1930s as an adjunct to the Legion of Decency. The NODL's original target was indecent magazines, but in 1947 it urged Catholic parishes to launch campaigns to remove objectionable comic books and paperbacks from their local newsstands. It recommended that a committee of church members visit retailers every two weeks armed with a list of titles that had been declared harmful by a NODL reviewing panel made up of 150 mothers. If they found any of the publications, they were to inform the manager. The NODL officially opposed the use of boycotts and other coercive measures against stores that refused to remove offending works. However, it applied pressure by encouraging the creation of a "white list" of stores that had agreed to cleanse themselves; the list was read in the local Catholic church and printed in parish publications. Approximately 25 percent of the population was Catholic in the 1950s. So, although a large group, Catholics were still a minority. Thus, the NODL urged Catholics to reach out to Protestants for support, joining citizens' committees with members of the American Legion, church groups, women's clubs, and parent-teacher groups.

One of the NODL's main targets was paperbacks. The invention of paperback books had created a revolution in publishing by making it possible to sell compact and inexpensive editions of books at a much wider variety of outlets, including newsstands, drugstores, and groceries. From the NODL's perspective, however, the publication of paperbacks encouraged the spread of salacious titles. As the sale of paperback books grew, so did the size of the NODL list. By 1954, it included over three hundred books. While many of these were not great works of literature, many were. Nobody would ever publicly protest the censorship of *Hot Dames on Cold Slabs,* but the list also contained works by William Faulkner, James M. Cain, Erskine Caldwell, James T. Farrell, W. Somerset Maugham, John O'Hara, and Emile Zola. The NODL condemned Ernest Hemingway's *Farewell to Arms,* James Michener's *Tales of the South Pacific,* and John Dos Passos's *The Forty-Second Parallel.* Nor did it confine itself to fiction. It also targeted sex education books like *The Sexual Side of Marriage* and *How Shall I Tell My Child.* The proscriptions of the NODL were not only sweeping; they were effective. Most retailers could not afford to court the disapproval of the local censors, so they pulled the books off the shelves when they were told to do so. The problem became so pronounced by May 1957 that the ACLU issued a statement signed by 150 people prominent in literature and the arts blasting the NODL's methods of operation.[8]

The activities of the NODL inspired local police and prosecutors, who joined in the pressure campaign by warning retailers and distributors not to sell the works on the NODL list. The Georgia legislature and at least eight cities, including Miami and Milwaukee, established censorship boards to draw up their own lists of forbidden works. The most effective local censorship regime was established in Detroit, where the police department created a "license and censor bureau" that reviewed all paperback books that were submitted to it by distributors prior to their circulation in the city's limits. More than one hundred titles were banned outright between 1950 and 1952. However, the police kept a second, longer list, consisting of titles that were "partially objectionable." Retailers were told that they could sell these books unless someone complained. Since the NODL was active in Detroit, the overwhelming majority of retailers were unwilling to sell any books on the second list either. If the police were in any doubt about the legality of a particular work, they could submit it to an assistant prosecutor for a ruling. This didn't often result in clearance, however. "The assistant prosecutor . . . applied a simple test in arriving at his official opinion: if he didn't want his young daughter to read the book, he decided it was illegal." It was only when publishers began to seek injunctions to block the use of blacklists that police departments became more cautious about their censorship efforts.[9]

Efforts to censor comic books did not arouse the same degree of opposition as the attack on paperback books. If there was one thing almost everyone could agree on during the late 1940s and early 1950s, it was that juvenile delinquency was a growing problem and that comics books were a contributing factor. Americans had been hearing predictions of an epidemic of juvenile crime since the early years of World War II. It seemed logical to assume that the traumatic social upheaval that was required to put the country on a war footing would inevitably undermine social stability. Millions of men, the husbands and fathers who had helped preserve order, suddenly disappeared overseas, and millions of women, including the mothers who had provided a stable environment for their children, were now working outside the home. Many Americans saw the "zoot-suit riots" that erupted in Los Angeles during 1943, when servicemen attacked teenagers wearing bizarre-looking costumes, as a harbinger of the trouble ahead. The predictions of juvenile mayhem did not end when the soldiers began returning home in 1945. The next year, Attorney General Tom Clark created the Attorney General's Panel on Juvenile Problems and sponsored a national conference to develop strategies for dealing with an anticipated crime wave.

In retrospect, much of the concern over juvenile delinquency appears to have been misplaced. There is no clear evidence that the "epidemic" of juvenile crime actually occurred. Yet parents were not wrong in sensing that dramatic social changes were under way and that these changes were undermining traditional sources of control. An independent youth culture was developing, fueled by an expansion of the teenage workforce that could buy more of what it wanted, including the cars that were both a symbol and a source of its new independence. At the same time, many more kids were attending high school, where they encountered a peer group that exercised a far greater control over their tastes than their parents did. The growth of television created still more competition for parents. An industry that had barely existed in 1948 put fifteen million television sets into American homes by 1952 and more than doubled the number just three years later.

A few skeptics questioned the widespread conviction that kids today are just no damn good. "This wave of popularizing crime has emanated measurably from the Department of Justice," Elisha Hanson, the counsel for the Newspaper Publishers Association, said in 1948. But concern about children deepened with the advent of the cold war. "Throughout the United States today, indeed throughout the free world, a deadly war is being waged," Lois Higgins of the Chicago Crime Prevention Bureau told Congress in 1954. Higgins believed that there was a Communist plot to use drugs and dirty books to encourage juvenile delinquency. "Let us tell them [our children] about the secret weapons of our enemy," Higgins urged. "Let us tell them, too, that obscene material that is flooding the Nation today is another cunning device of our enemies, deliberately calculated to destroy the decency and morality which are the bulwarks of society." Even during the cold war, not everyone blamed juvenile delinquency on a Communist plot. But almost everyone seemed willing to believe the worst about comic books.[10]

The man who lit the fuse of the comic-book controversy was Fredric Wertham, a German immigrant. Wertham was no book burner. He was a psychiatrist who had emigrated to the United States in the 1920s to take a job as the chief resident of the psychiatric clinic at Johns Hopkins Hospital. During the decade he lived in Baltimore, Wertham became well known in the city's intellectual community and a friend of its leading light, H. L. Mencken. He also developed a reputation as someone who cared about the poor and was one of the few psychiatrists in the city who had African American patients. In 1932, Wertham moved to New York City, where he served as the senior psychiatrist at Bellevue Hospital and launched a campaign to open a municipal psychiatric clinic in Harlem. Failing to secure the city's support, Wertham opened his own clinic in the basement of a Harlem church and provided counseling for twenty-five cents per visit. His experience in Harlem convinced him that racial discrimination played an important role in creating psychological problems, a view that he presented during testimony in the Delaware case that later became part of *Brown v. Board of Education* and helped persuade the Supreme Court to outlaw segregation in education in 1954. Nor was Wertham a prude. In 1948, he testified that a nudist magazine, *Sunshine and Health,* was not pornographic and should not be excluded from the mail.[11]

Nevertheless, Wertham hated comic books. Like many liberals, he believed they undermined reading skills and threatened the nation's intellectual life. But this was not the main thrust of the campaign against comics that he launched with an article in *Saturday Review of Literature* in May 1948. The article, "The Comics...Very Funny!" warned Americans that comics were making their children more violent and sexual. It offered no scientific evidence. Wertham acknowledged that many sociologists, educators, psychiatrists, and psychologists did not believe that comic books were harmful. But he denounced them as "apologists" and accused them of ignoring the obvious fact that children were imitating the violence they saw in comic books. The crime comics were obviously the worst, but Wertham believed that Superman and Batman were part of the problem of "this enormous overstimulation of fantasy with scenes of sex and violence." (In a later analysis, Wertham, who criticized the comics for overemphasizing the sexual organs, would also charge that there was a clear suggestion that Batman's relationship with Robin was homosexual.) Wertham was not reluctant to name the villain of his morality play. Comic-book publishers were using their product—the "marijuana of the nursery"—to "seduce the children and mislead the parents." He could cite impressive statistics to prove that comic books were a growing problem. The sale of comics was growing at a rate that rivaled only television. The average monthly circulation of comic books jumped from seventeen million in 1940 to nearly seventy million by 1953 as the number of publishers rose to over 650, more than doubling between 1950 and 1953. Wertham may not have been exaggerating when he estimated that a child sat down with a comic book one billion times a year.[12]

Unlike the NODL, which claimed that almost all retailers agreed to remove comic books when asked, Wertham believed that government censorship was necessary. The police were already acting as censors in some places, although they lacked statutory authority and guidelines that could help them identify the offending material. (They sometimes ordered a store to remove everything on the NODL list.) Wertham wanted to ban the sale or display to children under fifteen of any "crime comic books" that suggested "criminal or sexually abnormal ideas" or created an "atmosphere of deceit, trickery, and cruelty." The National Congress of Parents and Teachers and the National Education Association (NEA) strongly supported censorship of comic books. This was not a free speech issue, the NEA *Journal* explained: "Press freedom . . . was never intended to protect indecency or perversion of the child mind." In September 1948, the Los Angeles Board of Supervisors passed the first comics ban, prohibiting the sale of crime comics to anyone under eighteen. Within weeks, Chicago, Hartford, Topeka, Des Moines, and Birmingham adopted the Los Angeles law. By the end of the year, fifty cities had approved comics legislation.[13]

The publishers of comic books responded to the threat of censorship by creating a system of self-regulation that was intended to purge the comics of material that was inappropriate for children. But in 1950 the content of comic books became more controversial than ever when one of the industry's most creative men, William Gaines, the publisher of Entertaining Comics, launched a number of new titles that emphasized the macabre and shocking, including *Tales from the Crypt, The Vault of Horror,* and *The Haunt of Fear.* Gaines believed that comics were not just for kids. Some of his titles reached for an adult audience through story lines that dealt with contemporary social problems, including racial discrimination, mob violence, and small-town parochialism. His horror comic books were an instant hit, and other publishers were soon introducing their own horror comics, which grew to include nearly one hundred titles.

Already angry about the popularity of crime comics, the critics of the comics industry pointed to the new horror comics as proof that government must take further steps to protect the nation's children. The pressure on the industry grew in the spring of 1954 when a Senate committee chaired by Estes Kefauver, a New Deal liberal from Tennessee, held hearings on the comic-book industry in New York. Wertham, a star witness, was the author of a new jeremiad against comic books, *Seduction of the Innocent,* which would become one of the most talked about books of the year. Wertham and other witnesses shocked the committee with examples from recent comic books. The cover of one of Gaines's comics showed an ax murderer holding the severed head of a woman in one hand and a dripping ax in the other. Another book, *Foul Play,* featured a drawing of men playing baseball with severed body parts. "They play baseball with a dead man's head," Wertham told the committee. "Why do they do that?" The witnesses also summarized some of the latest plotlines. In one story from the comic *The Haunt of Fear,* a child discovers that his new foster parents are vampires. When they try to kill him, however, he turns into a werewolf and eats them. Another story summarized for the committee, "Stick in the Mud," portrayed the comeuppance received by a teacher who marries and murders the wealthy father of one of her students. (She drowns in quicksand as the gleeful son looks on.)[14]

In September 1954, the comic-book publishers responded to the threat of government censorship by creating a new trade association, the Comic Magazine Association of America (CMAA). A month later, the CMAA issued a new comics code that was far more restrictive than the original. The new code banned any comic that showed sympathy for criminals as well as "all of the visual elements and subject matter that defined horror comic books," including the use of the words "horror" and "terror" in the title. There were new rules for sexual content as well:

> Women were not to be drawn in "salacious" or "suggestive" dress and postures, and "passion or romantic interest" would "never be treated in such a way as to stimulate the lower and baser emotions." Respect for parents, "the moral code," and "honorable behavior" was to be fostered at all times. Romantic stories should always "emphasize the value of the home and the sanctity of marriage."

The code was also more effectively enforced. Almost all of the publishers, wholesalers, engravers, and printers joined the CMAA, making it very difficult to produce a comic that did not carry its seal of approval. The new "comics czar," Charles F. Murphy, a former New York City judge, described exactly how difficult it was to obtain the seal at a press conference in December. In the first 285 comics the CMAA examined, it had rejected 126 stories and 5,656 drawings, he said.[15]

The CMAA's new code did not forestall direct government censorship. In 1955, thirteen states passed laws to restrict the sale of crime and horror comic books, either banning their sale to minors or outlawing them altogether. But there was nothing left to ban. Even Gaines had given up. In the wake of the Kefauver hearings, nervous distributors had been returning his comics. He tried to rally his customers. "Due to the efforts of various 'do-gooders' and 'do-gooder' groups, a large segment of the public is being led to believe that certain comic magazines cause juvenile delinquency," Gaines wrote in an editorial that appeared in his comics. He urged them to write to their representatives in Congress, but it was too late. A short time later, Gaines called a press conference and announced that he was closing his crime and horror comics titles to create a "clean, clean line" because that, apparently, was "what the American parents want." Only one of Gaines's titles continued to satirize American life—*Mad* magazine. Nothing else on the newsstand could interest any but the youngest child, according to Bradford W. Wright, a comics historian. "Reflecting a bland consensus vision of America, comic books now championed without criticism American institutions, authority figures, and middle-class mores," he concluded.[16]

But the censors were trying to stifle a powerful force. While they presumed to speak for the country as a whole, Americans had long demonstrated a strong interest in sex and violence in literature and film. In 1922, in the wake of the Fatty Arbuckle scandal, Massachusetts had held a referendum on a plan to create a film censorship board. Motion picture producers and theater owners campaigned aggressively against the idea and even inserted appeals directly into the movies exhibited around the state. The voters rejected censorship by a better than 2-to-1 margin. The censors had held the upper hand by claiming that they were preventing the spread of books, magazines, and movies that undermined the values that preserved the social order. But another ideology was already on the march. Proclaimed initially by the ACLU, it argued that free speech was an essential element of democracy. At first, the ACLU had focused on political speech—the rights of Socialists, union organizers, and other minority groups to meet and make themselves heard. By the end of the 1920s, however, the fight for free speech had broadened into a battle for artistic freedom as well. The struggle to defeat the New York "clean books" bill and to liberalize the Massachusetts obscenity law saw authors, publishers, librarians, and booksellers uniting for the first time in support of the idea that people must be free to make their own decisions about what books they would read. This idea would grow stronger in the years following World War II in part because the American Library Association and book publishers espoused it with growing fervor and because the public's appetite for material about sex, both titillating and scientific, was insatiable.

It is surprising that librarians emerged as leading defenders of free expression in the postwar period. Early in the century, librarians had believed that it was their role to protect their patrons from objectionable books. This had begun to change in the 1920s, when librarians played an important role in amending the Massachusetts obscenity law. Still, librarians seemed an unlikely group to lead the fight against the censors. The status of the library profession was low compared with that of other careers. In 1952, only 58 percent of librarians had graduated from college and only 40 percent had studied library science in graduate school. The typical male librarian was "rather submissive in social situations and less likely [than the average college student] to show qualities of leadership," a 1952 study reported. The fact that most of the country's more than thirty thousand librarians worked for public institutions and were therefore accountable at some point to elected politicians who did not share a deep commitment to intellectual freedom encouraged them to censor controversial books. "I have never met a public librarian who approved of censorship or one who failed to practice it in some measure," Leon Carnofsky, a library school professor, observed in 1950. Yet a handful of people were strong advocates for the view that protecting free speech was a critical part of the librarian's professional responsibilities. In 1939, they persuaded the American Library Association (ALA) to adopt the Library Bill of Rights. Pointing to the "growing intolerance, suppression of free speech and censorship" abroad, the ALA declared that librarians should purchase books based on their "value and interest" and should ignore "the race or nationality or the political or religious views of the writers." In addition, libraries should try to present all sides of controversial issues and make their meeting rooms available "to all groups in the community regardless of their beliefs or affiliations."[17]

The ALA soon realized that declaring the principle of intellectual freedom was not enough. Even before the ink was dry on the Library Bill of Rights, controversy erupted over John Steinbeck's new novel, *The Grapes of Wrath*. The magazine *Collier's* condemned its portrait of the mistreatment of migrant workers as "propaganda for the idea that we ought to change our system for the Russian system." Other critics declared it vulgar and immoral for presenting the lives of migrants as "bestial." In response to this outcry, the Kansas City, Missouri, Board of Education banned *The Grapes of Wrath* from the public library shelves. Libraries around the country joined in the ban, although at least one librarian attempted to salve his conscience by denying that he had censored the book—he had merely refused to buy it. The ALA created the Special Committee on Censorship to determine what steps it could take to help librarians live up to their Bill of Rights. Educating librarians was obviously a priority. The committee would have to "awaken" librarians to "the principle of freedom," Jens Nyholm, a librarian at the University of California at Berkeley, observed. It might even have to confront those who were intent on censorship. "The committee may have to fight with and for the readers against their own librarians," Nyholm said. In 1940, the special committee was made permanent and renamed the Committee on Intellectual Freedom to Safeguard the Rights of Library Users to Freedom of Inquiry. A few years later, the name was shortened to Intellectual Freedom Committee (IFC).[18]

The IFC pushed the ALA into the forefront of the censorship fight. With the advent of the cold war, the American Legion, the Daughters of the American Revolution, and other patriotic groups urged libraries to purge their collections of "un-American" materials. In California, they led a campaign against a social studies series called Building America and attempted to ban Marguerite Stewart's *Land of the Soviets.* The superpatriots also condemned Howard Fast's novel *Citizen Tom Paine* and the distinguished liberal magazine *The Nation,* and both were removed from school libraries in New York City. These attacks prompted the IFC to call for a strengthening of the Library's Bill of Rights, which did not explicitly state that fighting censorship was a duty of all librarians. The new statement, adopted in February 1948, stated the new imperative plainly. "Censorship of books, urged or practiced by volunteer arbiters of morals or political opinion or by organizations that would establish a coercive concept of Americans, must be challenged by libraries," it read. Just a few months later, the ALA demonstrated its new militancy by intervening in the controversy over the banning of *The Nation* by the New York City Board of Education. Intellectual Freedom Committee chairman David K. Berninghausen was the first ALA official to ever testify at a hearing opposing censorship when he appeared at the school superintendent's office and condemned the ban as a violation of the Library's Bill of Rights. Later in the year, the ALA also helped defeat a plan to appoint a censorship board in Los Angeles County, where a member of the board of supervisors had accused the chief librarian of possessing "those liberal thoughts that we don't like in the mind of the head of our library."[19]

Many librarians remained skeptical of the ALA's aggressive new policy on censorship. By February 1949, twenty-five state library associations had answered the ALA's call to form their own intellectual freedom committees, but many hung back, preferring to "let sleeping dogs lie." Berlinghausen bemoaned the fact that librarians were reluctant to bring cases to the attention of his committee. In many instances, the IFC was learning about library attacks from other people in the community. This complacency received a severe shock in July 1950 when Ruth Brown, an employee with thirty years of service, was fired by the Bartlesville, Oklahoma, library board after it received complaints that she had subscribed to five "subversive" publications—*The Nation, The New Republic, Soviet Russia Today, Negro Digest,* and *Consumer Reports.* In fact, the magazines were a mere pretext for firing Brown, whose real crime was that she had challenged racial segregation by accompanying two African American friends to a whites-only restaurant and requesting service. However, the board chose to make an issue of her choice of magazines. "What do you think of buying such trash from your very inadequate book fund?" one commissioner asked during a hearing, referring to *The Nation* and *The New Republic.* "Considering that they were our only two liberal magazines and we subscribed to about 75 other magazines, I felt perfectly justified," Brown replied. At the request of the ALA, the Oklahoma Library Association's Intellectual Freedom Committee conducted an investigation of the Bartlesville case and issued a widely quoted report that condemned the firing as a violation of intellectual freedom. "Miss Brown was unjustly and cavalierly discharged because of her private beliefs and her professional belief in free libraries," the report concluded. Ruth Brown's case riveted the attention of other librarians. If she could be fired for subscribing to mainstream magazines, then no librarian's job was safe. Ten years later, an article in the *American Library Association Bulletin* would argue that the Ruth Brown case did more "than any other in our time to shock librarians into examining their beliefs in intellectual freedom."[20]

The support for free speech among librarians would also grow as a result of the attacks of Joseph McCarthy and his supporters. Brown took her brave stand against segregation just one week before McCarthy's Wheeling, West Virginia, speech launched his career as the nation's chief inquisitor. After the outbreak of the Korean War in June, the American Legion in Peoria, Illinois, demanded that the local library withdraw from circulation several films that it said contained Communist propaganda. The next year, the Sons of the American Revolution demanded that the Montclair, New Jersey, library label and restrict the circulation of all "Communistic or subversive" books and magazines. The superpatriots also wanted the librarian to keep a record of everyone who used the labeled material. In June 1951, the ALA took a strong stand against labeling as "an attempt to prejudice the reader, and as such, it is a censor's tool." However, the ALA was powerless when McCarthy himself led the campaign to censor government libraries abroad. In February 1953, McCarthy subpoenaed author Howard Fast to appear before his committee as a way of demonstrating the kind of un-American writers whose books were available in the libraries operated in foreign countries by the State Department's International Information Administration. The State Department caved in the next day, banning material by "any controversial persons, Communists, fellow travelers, 'et cetera.'" Over the next five months, it issued a blizzard of directives, requiring the removal of specific issues of periodicals that contained material deemed harmful to American interests as well as all books by individuals who had taken the Fifth Amendment before congressional committees. The department even ordered the removal of an issue of the *Annals of the American Academy of Political and Social Science,* which contained an article about the United Nations. To ensure that the books of "75 communist authors" were being removed as promised, McCarthy dispatched two aides, Roy Cohn and David Schine, to tour Europe and visit the libraries operated by the State Department.[21]

The threat of McCarthyism persuaded the leaders of the ALA to seek support from outside the library community. Over a weekend in early May 1953, twenty-five librarians, book publishers, and citizens "representing the public interest" met at the Westchester Country Club in Rye, New York, to discuss what could be done to halt what IFC chairman William S. Dix called the "national trend toward the restriction of the free trade in ideas." The result was a draft statement, "The Freedom to Read," that would be issued by the ALA and the American Book Publishers Council. "The freedom to read is essential to our democracy. It is under attack," the statement began. "We, as citizens devoted to the use of books and as librarians and publishers responsible for disseminating them, wish to assert the public interest in the preservation of the freedom to read." Following a preamble that eloquently expressed the theory of free speech, the statement identified seven specific propositions defining the freedom to read: that it was in the public interest for publishers and librarians to make available the widest diversity of views and expressions; that publishers and librarians do not need to endorse every idea or presentation contained in the books they make available; that a book should be judged by its content, not the political views of its author; that while obscenity laws must be enforced, it is wrong to limit the efforts of writers to achieve their artistic goals and to deny to adults books that may be unsuitable for adolescents. The statement concluded with an appeal to the book industry and the public: "Books are the major channel by which the intellectual inheritance is handed down, and the principal means of its testing and growth. The defense of their freedom and integrity, and the enlargement of their service to society, requires of all bookmen the utmost of their faculties, and deserves of all citizens the fullest of their support."[22]

The drafters of "The Freedom to Read" could not be sure how their statement would be received. The country was at war, and McCarthy's power was at its peak. Edward R. Murrow's program profiling the case of Milo Radulovich would not air until October. The librarians who had participated in the drafting of the statement took careful steps to make sure that it would be adopted at the ALA's annual conference in June. Then, just a week before the ALA meeting, President Eisenhower, who had assiduously avoided criticizing McCarthy, shocked many by condemning censorship in a speech at a Dartmouth College commencement. "Don't join the book burners," Eisenhower said.

> Don't be afraid to go in your library and read every book as long as any document does not offend our own ideas of decency. That should be the only censorship. How will we defeat communism unless we know what it is? . . . Now we have to fight it with something better. Not try to conceal the thinking of our own people. They are part of America and even if they think ideas that are contrary to ours they have a right to them, a right to record them and a right to have them in places where they are accessible to others. It is unquestioned or it is not America.

The president's words electrified the librarians, and they arrived at their annual conference eager to approve "The Freedom to Read." When it was offered at a session on June 25, it was approved "overwhelmingly by a shouting and enthusiastic vote." It was hailed by a large section of the press as well. The *New York Times* ranked the statement with "America's outstanding state papers" and joined the *Washington Post,* the *Christian Science Monitor,* and the *Baltimore Sun* in reprinting it in full. Two dozen newspapers would comment favorably on the statement over the next two weeks. Meanwhile, other organizations rapidly endorsed the statement, including the American Booksellers Association, the American Newspaper Guild, and the American Bar Association. By adopting "The Freedom to Read," librarians and publishers had committed themselves to a formidable task—opposing censorship. But the cold war was coming to an end, and political censorship would soon begin to wane. The next free speech battle would involve books that would hardly meet with the approval of President Eisenhower—*Lady Chatterley's Lover* and *Tropic of Cancer.*[23]

By the end of World War II, everybody was talking about sex. The war itself had played an important role in drawing attention to it. The country's leaders noted with alarm the rapid rise in illegitimacy and venereal disease. "We must accept the fact that total war relaxes moral standards on the home front," former president Herbert Hoover acknowledged in 1944. The social strain increased in the immediate aftermath of the war as husbands and wives reunited only to discover that they were no longer compatible. There was a record number of divorces in 1946—over 500,000. People were tired of hearing ministers, moralists, and ex-presidents urging them to return to traditional moral values. They wanted information about how their fellow Americans actually behaved, particularly in the bedroom. On January 5, 1948, Alfred Kinsey, an entomologist who was noted for his classification of the gall wasp, told them about the secret lives of men in an eight-hundred-page scientific study, *Sexual Behavior in the Human Male.* Based on interviews with over seventeen thousand men, Kinsey estimated that 85 percent of white males had engaged in sexual intercourse before marriage (mostly with prostitutes) and that 50 percent of them had engaged in adulterous sex. Even more shocking, Kinsey reported that 37 percent had reached orgasm at least once through homosexual contact. In the following months, Kinsey's findings would become the target of withering scientific criticism. But his book became a bestseller. His publisher, who specialized in academic books, had originally planned to print only 10,000 copies. By the middle of January, the publisher had already gone back to the printer six times, and more than 185,000 copies were in print. Kinsey did not like all of the enormous publicity that came to him as a result, but he estimated that 95 percent of the press coverage had been favorable. "I think we have under-estimated the public's capacity to look facts in the face," Kinsey said. He caused even more controversy five years later when he published *Sexual Behavior in the Human Female.* However, once again, the public was receptive. Carl E. Lindstrom, the executive editor of the *Hartford Times,* was surprised by the reaction when he published a summary of the latest Kinsey report. "Having braced for a tumult of criticism and outraged sensibilities, the silence that followed was deafening," he said. "Not a single phone call disturbed the tranquility of my hours at home; not a letter nor a personal visitation." The American people were ready for a more sophisticated approach to the subject of sex.[24]

And plenty of people were ready to challenge the censors to give it to them. By 1953, the censorship of motion pictures was looking particularly wobbly. In 1946, industrialist Howard Hughes had launched "one of the most vulgar advertising campaigns in motion picture history" to promote his film *The Outlaw* and its large-breasted star, Jane Russell. "What Are the Two Great Reasons for Jane Russell's Rise to Stardom?" asked the ads that saturated all media. Over Los Angeles, a skywriter spelled out the name of the film and then punctuated it with two large circles that he then dotted in the middle. Protests over the vulgarity of the advertising led the Production Code Administration (PCA) to remove its seal of approval from the film. Ten years earlier, this would have killed the movie, but Hughes pressed on, getting bookings at independent theaters even in conservative cities like Atlanta, Louisville, and St. Louis, where the public poured in to see the film that so many wanted to censor. In Atlanta, *The Outlaw* even outdrew *Gone with the Wind*. A heavier blow fell on the film censorship regime in 1948 when a government antitrust suit forced the movie studios to sell their theater chains, which controlled most of the movie houses in the country. The fact that the newly independent theaters were more concerned about profits than upholding morality became clear in 1953 when Otto Preminger released *The Moon Is Blue,* a mild sex comedy that the PCA refused to sanction because it made an attempted seduction a subject of comedy. Despite the absence of the seal, three of the five major theater chains booked the movie into over 2,400 theaters. Even widespread picketing by supporters of the Legion of Decency and the arrest of a theater manager in Jersey City could not prevent the success of the movie. By the end of the year, it had grossed $3.5 million, a figure that placed it among the top fifteen films of the year.[25]

One of the pioneers in the new movement toward sexual candor was a GI who had recently returned to his hometown of Chicago to finish his education. "Why does tolerance turn into intolerance, rationality into irrationality, when man contemplates the problem of sex?" Hugh Hefner wrote in a term paper, "Sex Behavior and the U.S. Law."

> Why does Webster's Collegiate Dictionary define masturbation as "self-pollution," why do the lawmakers become so emotional in their legislation against sodomy, why are excellent literary works sometimes banned as obscene, why is it still against the law in some states to circulate information regarding birth control and venereal disease?

The child of fundamentalist Methodists, Hefner was in the process of shedding the sexual mores that had kept him a virgin until his marriage at the age of twenty-three. He was also a young man looking for his niche in life. His literary talents did not carry him far, but he believed that a new magazine that treated sex as a healthy part of the life of urban, upwardly mobile young men might find a market. In early 1953, using his apartment furniture as collateral, Hefner obtained a bank loan for $600 and spent almost all of it for a nude picture of Marilyn Monroe, a rising star who had posed for the photographs when she was still unknown. He used the photograph to attract enough investors to put together a magazine that he called *Playboy*. In the summer, as salesmen attempted to book advance orders, there was a strong chance that Hefner would fail. American men were used to *Esquire*'s pinups, the scantily clad women in the cheesecake magazines and the tastefully presented nudes in art and photography publications. Most had never seen a color photograph of a nude woman before. It wasn't certain whether they would buy a magazine that contained one or whether the censors would stop them if they tried. The experiment was launched in the fall when the December issue of *Playboy* went on sale. By the end of the first month, more than 50,000 copies had been sold, and both *Time* and *Newsweek* had complimented the new publication. *Playboy* "makes old issues of *Esquire* . . . look like trade bulletins from the W.C.T.U. [Women's Christian Temperance Union]," the *Saturday Review* wrote. A year later, *Playboy* was selling 175,000 copies per month; sales reached 900,000 in 1957.[26]

Hugh Hefner's *Playboy* was a protest against the repressed sexuality of his age, albeit a highly commercial one. However, other protests were also being heard in the "conformist" fifties. On October 6, 1955, a twenty-nine-year-old poet, the balding, bearded Allen Ginsberg, stepped on the stage of the Six Gallery in San Francisco and read for the first time his poem *Howl,* a jeremiad against modern life. "I saw the best minds of my generation destroyed by madness, starving hysterical naked," he began. Packed tightly into the small studio, the audience of one hundred people was soon shouting encouragement at the end of every line. Michael McClure, another poet who read that night, recalled:

> Ginsberg read on to the end of the poem, which left us standing in wonder, or cheering and wondering, but knowing at the deepest level that a barrier had been broken, that a human voice and body had been hurled against the harsh wall of America and its supporting armies and navies and academies and institutions and ownership systems and power support bases.

Ginsberg, Jack Kerouac, Lawrence Ferlinghetti, and the other writers who became known as the Beat Generation expressed a deep dissatisfaction with American life. Many Americans returned their contempt, and some looked for ways to punish the long-haired and sexually libidinous beatniks. In 1957, customs agents decided that *Howl* was obscene and seized five hundred copies that had been printed abroad. Later, San Francisco police purchased a copy of the book from a clerk at the City Lights Bookstore, which was owned by Ferlinghetti. Both the clerk, Shigeyoshi Murao, and Ferlinghetti, who was also the owner of City Lights Publishers, which had published *Howl,* were arrested for selling an obscene book. Fortunately, at that very moment, the U.S. Supreme Court was struggling to reconcile the law of obscenity with the public's demand for greater freedom in the discussion of sex. Within weeks of the San Francisco arrests, it would issue a decision that would make it impossible to ever again successfully prosecute a book that dealt seriously with what the Court described as "a great and mysterious motive force in human life."[27]

The showdown over obscenity had been coming for some time. After all, the Supreme Court had faced the issue eight years earlier when the *Memoirs of Hecate County* had been presented to it for a decision. The justices had evenly divided over the question of whether the book was obscene. Had Felix Frankfurter cast his vote, the Court would have been forced to issue a decision clarifying the status of books, magazines, and movies with sexual content. But Frankfurter and author Edmund Wilson had been friends, so the justice abstained; the lower-court decisions condemning the book were allowed to stand, and Wilson's bestseller was banned. Civil libertarians took comfort from the fact that four justices apparently believed that the book was not obscene. It appeared that it was only a matter of time before the Supreme Court would decide whether laws passed in the middle of the nineteenth century would continue to restrict the kind of reading material that people could purchase a hundred years later.

Fortunately, as the question of defining obscenity became more urgent, the Supreme Court was growing increasingly receptive to cases involving individual rights. New social forces were pressing for the solution of old problems. The fight for racial justice resumed in 1941, when A. Phillip Randolph, the president of the Brotherhood of Sleeping Car Porters, threatened to stage a march on Washington to protest the exclusion of African Americans from jobs in the defense industries. The National Association for the Advancement of Colored People began filing lawsuits challenging racial discrimination in schools. The demand for racial equality finally reached the Supreme Court in 1952, when the case of *Brown v. Board of Education* was argued for the first time. The Court hesitated, ordering the case reargued the following year. In October 1953, however, the Court got a new chief justice who showed no reluctance to act. Earl Warren, a Republican who had served three terms as governor of California, believed that the Supreme Court should play an active role in the political process, correcting injustices that the legislative and executive branches refused to address. Under his leadership, the Court unanimously repudiated its 1897 decision in *Plessy v. Ferguson* upholding the constitutionality of segregation and ordered the integration of the nation's schools with "all deliberate speed."

Booksellers, publishers, and even movie distributors were also turning to the courts and beginning to find some relief there. In 1948, the year before the *Memoirs of Hecate County* reached the Supreme Court, the Court had decided the case of a New York City bookseller who had been convicted of violating a state law banning the sale of any book or magazine "principally made up of criminal news, police reports, or accounts of criminal deeds." In a 6-3 ruling, the Court declared that the law violated the First Amendment because its definition of a prohibited publication was "too uncertain and indefinite" to allow a bookseller to determine when he was violating the law. Four years later, the Court finally agreed that movies are protected by the First Amendment. It ruled that New York's film censors had violated the First Amendment by denying a license to exhibit Roberto Rossellini's film *The Miracle* because Francis Cardinal Spellman thought it was "sacrilegious." Even Felix Frankfurter, the Court's strongest advocate of giving broad discretion to the legislative branch, could not stomach a Michigan law that came before the Court in late 1956. The law made it a crime to publish, print, or sell any work containing "obscene, immoral, lewd or lascivious language ... tending to incite minors to violent or depraved or immoral acts." Lawyers for Michigan argued that the state must have the power to ban works that were harmful to children, even if the law violated the First Amendment rights of adults. On behalf of a unanimous court, Frankfurter disagreed:

> Surely, this is to burn the house to roast the pig. . . . The incidence of this enactment is to reduce the adult population of Michigan to reading only what is fit for children. It thereby arbitrarily curtails one of those liberties of the individual . . . that history has attested as the indispensable conditions for the maintenance and progress of a free society.

There had been a new justice sitting on the bench when *Butler v. Michigan* was argued in October. A talented legal scholar, fifty-year-old William J. Brennan Jr. would become Earl Warren's closest collaborator on the Court. It was to Brennan that Warren turned in the spring of 1957 to undertake the difficult task of finally defining "obscenity."[28]

"I made two mistakes as President, and they are both sitting on the Supreme Court," former president Dwight Eisenhower acknowledged ruefully. One of the "mistakes" was Earl Warren; the other was William J. Brennan Jr. In the case of Brennan at least, he had no-body but himself to blame. Brennan was a distinguished judge on the New Jersey Supreme Court at the time of his appointment, but his liberal political philosophy was no secret. Like Frank Murphy, Bren-nan was the son of Irish immigrants who had struggled to establish themselves in their new country. Brennan's father had started out by shoveling coal at a brewery in Newark but soon showed a talent for organizing workers. He became an official in the International Brotherhood of Firemen and Oilers and was eventually elected to head the county labor coalition. Brennan Sr. was beaten by police in a bloody strike in 1916. "What got me interested in people's rights and liberties was the kind of neighborhood I was brought up in," Jus-tice Brennan explained later. "I saw all kinds of suffering—people had to struggle."

Brennan went to Harvard Law School because his father wanted him to be a lawyer. But he remained close to his roots, returning to Newark in 1931 and becoming a specialist in labor law at a time when the field was growing rapidly as a result of the reforms of the New Deal. Nor did the young lawyer lose his concern for liberty as he rose to become a prosperous attorney. In 1954, barely a week af-ter the broadcast of Edward R. Murrow's "Report on McCarthy," Brennan, at a St. Patrick's Day dinner in Boston, said that the fight against communism must not be allowed to jeopardize individual rights. "We cannot and must not doubt our strength to conserve, without sacrifice of any, all of the guarantees of justice and fair play and simple human dignity which have made our land what it is," he said. Fortunately, he added, "some practices of the contemporary scene reminiscent of the Salem witch hunts" are "but passing aber-rations even now undergoing systematic deflation." Although Bren-nan didn't mention McCarthy by name, the senator was stung by his remarks. During Brennan's confirmation hearings, he would throw the nominee's words back in his face, accusing him of being soft on communism.[29]

Brennan was far from being a free speech absolutist, however. The Supreme Court already had two of those. Hugo Black and Wil-liam O. Douglas opposed all government restrictions on free speech. But as he sat listening to the arguments in the case of *Roth v. United States* on April 22, 1957, Brennan was reminded that his libertarian-ism had limits. He was handed a box that contained a variety of "hard-core" pornography that had been seized by the post office. A government attorney summarized the contents:

> Photographs of all sorts of persons—people without any clothes on, in all postures, groups and individuals. They are engaged in activity, perversion of every kind. . . . A second category of material is little booklets, a series of sex episodes, one after the other, usually illustrated with these photographs or drawings. The third category is comic books.

The introduction of evidence in the Supreme Court was highly improper, particularly because none of the material was actually at issue in the case. Samuel Roth was a well-known publisher of what legal scholars William B. Lockhart and Robert S. McClure have described as "not-very-erotic erotica." He had been indicted for mailing a magazine, *American Aphrodite,* that contained a risqué story by Aubrey Beardsley, a prominent English author and artist. But the government was trying to drive home the point that if the Comstock Act was declared unconstitutional, the country would be inundated with filth. The point was taken. Brennan, the first justice to be handed the box, took a look at one of the items in the box and quickly returned it. "I didn't want to look at it," he recalled many years later. Then, either Douglas or Justice Tom Clark "took a bunch of the stuff and passed it down the bench," Brennan said. (Apparently, not everyone found the material shocking because when the box was returned to the government, the solicitor general complained to Brennan that "half the stuff was gone.")[30]

Two months later, the memory of the material that the justices had perused was probably still fresh in their minds when they voted 6-3 to uphold the conviction of Samuel Roth. Justice John Marshall Harlan joined Black and Douglas in dissent because he had actually reviewed *American Aphrodite* and did not believe that it was obscene. But the rest believed that they must support the right of the government to protect its citizens from obscenity. Brennan had no trouble in finding justification for this position. "Expressions found in numerous opinions indicate that this Court has always assumed that obscenity is not protected by the freedoms of speech and of the press," he wrote. The First Amendment was written "to assure unfettered interchange of ideas for bringing about political and social changes desired by the people." But obscenity played no role in the exposition of ideas. It was "utterly without redeeming social importance" and could therefore be banned. While upholding the concept of obscenity, however, Brennan explicitly rejected the definition that had been used in American law since it was enunciated in 1868 in an English legal case, *Regina v. Hicklin*. Under the so-called *Hicklin* rule, a publication was obscene if "the tendency of the matter...is to deprave and corrupt those whose minds are open to such immoral influence." This definition had been used to ban works based on a single passage that might be considered inappropriate for a minor. But Brennan endorsed a more liberal formulation that had recently been advanced by the American Law Institute. In the future, the test would be "whether, to the average person, applying contemporary community standards, the dominant theme of the material, taken as a whole appeals to prurient interest."[31]

Brennan hoped that the new definition of "obscenity" would give the courts the tools they needed to distinguish obscenity from sex. "Sex and obscenity are not synonymous," he wrote.

> Obscene material is material which deals with sex in a manner appealing to prurient interest. The portrayal of sex, e.g. in art, literature and scientific works, is not itself sufficient reason to deny material the constitutional protection of freedom of speech and press. Sex, a great and mysterious motive force in human life, has indisputably been a subject of absorbing interest to mankind through the ages; it is one of the vital problems of human interest and public concern.

Works that dealt with sex that were not "utterly without redeeming social importance" must be protected. "The fundamental freedoms of speech and press have contributed greatly to the development and well-being of our free society," Brennan wrote. "Ceaseless vigilance is the watchword to prevent their erosion by Congress and by the States. The door barring federal and state intrusion into this area cannot be left ajar; it must be kept tightly closed, and opened only the slightest crack necessary to prevent encroachment upon more important interests." While Brennan was undoubtedly sincere, Samuel Roth could not be blamed for thinking that the only door that was being shut tight was the door to his cell as he began his five-year prison term. (Roth, who was sixty-two at the time of his imprisonment, was released in 1961. He returned to publishing for several years before retiring and died in 1974.)[32]

Roth was not the only person who viewed the Supreme Court's decision as a victory for the censors. The censors themselves were delighted. "The cause of decency has been strengthened," Monsignor Thomas E. Fitzgerald, the executive secretary of the National Organization for Decent Literature, proclaimed. Postmaster General Arthur Summerfield was particularly pleased. He could take pride in the fact that the exhibits the Supreme Court had examined during oral argument had come from his collection of confiscated pornography. "The Post Office Department welcomes the decision of the Supreme Court as a forward step in the drive to keep obscene materials out of the mails," he said. Civil libertarians confessed their disappointment. Harry J. Kalven Jr., a law professor, scoffed at Brennan's effort "to add a good word on behalf of sex," dismissing the description of sex as "a great and mysterious motive force" as "the least controversial utterance in the Court's history." A *Washington Post* editorial concluded that the decision left the issue as muddled as before. "It is to be hoped that, in subsequent opinions, the Supreme Court will define more clearly the point beyond which the wish to protect the weak from bad literature may not trespass upon the normal citizen's right to read what he pleases," it declared.[33]

Within months, however, the Supreme Court demonstrated that its new definition of obscenity was narrower than both the critics and the defenders of the *Roth* decision imagined. Following Harlan's example, the Court began to review the material that lower courts had declared obscene, including a film, *The Game of Love,* a collection of imported nudist and art-student publications containing nude photographs, and a magazine for homosexuals. No longer dealing with obscenity in the abstract, the Court reversed the convictions in three cases and sent the fourth back to the lower courts for further review. In 1959, the Court issued two decisions that were even more upsetting to the nation's moral guardians. The first case concerned a movie adaptation of D. H. Lawrence's *Lady Chatterley's Lover.* New York's movie censors had refused to license the film because "the whole theme of this motion picture is immoral . . . for that theme is the presentation of adultery as desirable, acceptable and proper pattern of behavior." The Supreme Court overruled the censors, declaring that their action violated "the First Amendment's basic guarantee . . . of freedom to advocate ideas . . . [and] thus struck at the very heart of constitutionally protected liberty." In the second case, it reversed the obscenity conviction of Eleazar Smith, a Los Angeles magazine dealer, because there was no proof that he knew he was selling an illegal work. Now it was the censors' turn to complain. A Michigan congressman charged that the Court had "endorsed adultery," and Senator James O. Eastland of Mississippi introduced a constitutional amendment that protected the right of every state "to decide on the basis of its own public policy questions of decency and morality." Others worried that the decision in *Smith v. California* had "crippled municipal efforts to curb obscenity."[34]

Publishers were soon testing the limits of the Supreme Court's new tolerance for works with sexual content. Edmund Wilson had been pressing his publisher, Roger Straus, to reissue *Memoirs of Hecate County,* but Straus and his lawyers were reluctant to challenge the New York officials who had banned the book. Following the *Roth* decision, Straus decided to take a chance, although he took the precaution of publishing the book in Philadelphia under the imprint of a Pennsylvania publisher that he had acquired. In the same year, 1958, G. P. Putnam published another controversial novel, Vladimir Nabokov's *Lolita,* the story of a man's sexual relationship with a twelve-year-old girl. The fact that neither book was prosecuted was not lost on Barney Rosset.

As the publisher of Grove Press, Rosset had established a reputation as a man who was willing to take a chance. He had published many of the leading avant-garde writers in Europe, including Samuel Beckett, Eugène Ionesco, and Jean Genet. But he took his risk taking to a new level in 1959 by issuing an unexpurgated paperback edition of *Lady Chatterley's Lover.* By that time, the Supreme Court had already blocked the effort to ban the film version of the book. But the movie was not as sexually explicit, nor had it used the words "shit" and "fuck." Postal authorities could not tolerate the publication of one of the most notorious books in the English language and went to court in an effort to have it declared obscene. A district court judge rejected the government's argument, citing the *Roth* decision.

He was upheld on appeal in an opinion written by the judge who had helped send Samuel Roth to jail just a few years earlier.

Rosset was not the kind of man to quit when he was ahead. If *Lady Chatterley's Lover* was not obscene, Rosset reasoned, it might finally be possible to publish Henry Miller's *Tropic of Cancer*, a novel that had become an underground classic since its publication in Paris in 1934. *Tropic of Cancer* had never been published in the United States, and customs officials had done their best to keep it out of the country. Rosset had purchased his copy in 1941 at the Gotham Book Mart, a Manhattan bookstore that was a meeting place for writers from around the world. Rosset was a college student at the time, and the store owner, Frances Steloff, asked him why he wanted it. When he said that he needed it for a college assignment, Steloff reached under the counter for the book and handed him a copy that had been printed in Mexico. *Tropic* lives up to Miller's promise to record "all that which is omitted in books." "Nobody, so far as I can see, is making use of those elements in the air which give direction and motivation to our lives," he writes in its opening pages. The book is the story of Miller's hand-to-mouth existence in Paris as he struggled to establish himself as a writer, and much of it describes his search for food and sex among the other lice-ridden inhabitants of the urban underworld. Miller describes his encounters with prostitutes with relish:

> After me, you can take on stallions, bulls, rams, drakes, St. Bernards. You can stuff toads, bats, lizards up your rectum. You can shit arpeggios if you like, or string a zither across your navel. I am fucking you, Tania, so that you'll stay fucked.... I will bite into your clitoris and spit out two franc pieces.

Miller's graphic descriptions of sex did not prevent him from winning either critical acclaim or commercial success. The English writers George Orwell and Lawrence Durrell were only two of his many admirers. "If you have read Balzac, or Baudelaire, or Goethe, you are expected to have read Miller," poet and critic Kenneth Rexroth observed in an article about Miller's influence abroad. "Miners in the Pyrenees, gondoliers in Venice, and certainly every *poule* in Paris, when they hear you're from California, ask, first thing, 'Do you know M'sier Miller?' " By 1956, Miller was one of the most popular authors in Japan, ranked just below Ernest Hemingway and John Steinbeck. Yet most of the copies of *Tropic of Cancer* that were circulating in the United States had been smuggled home in the duffel bags of returning GIs. Knowing there was a potentially huge market for the sale of the book, Rosset finally persuaded Miller to allow *Tropic* to be published in the United States, and it was released in June 1961.[35]

At first, things went better than even Rosset could have hoped. As expected, the post office seized copies of *Tropic* and scheduled a hearing at which it intended to have them declared obscene. However, the hearing was canceled and the books were returned after the Justice Department advised postal officials that the novel was not obscene under *Roth*. Customs officials would later follow suit, dropping their twenty-seven-year-old ban on the book. Rosset was ecstatic as orders poured in from around the country. Grove Press had to go back to press five times before the book had even been published; more than sixty-eight thousand copies were sold in the first week.

But state and local officials were not required to listen to the Justice Department. There were obscenity laws on the books of almost all of the states and many cities, and there was growing pressure on local authorities to enforce them. In 1957, a Cincinnati attorney, Charles H. Keating Jr., had organized Citizens for Decent Literature (CDL) to clean up the town. CDL eschewed the use of blacklists that had helped make the NODL notorious and focused instead on giving the police legal advice on how to prosecute obscenity cases, which were relatively rare. As the CDL grew into a national organization with more than two hundred affiliated groups by 1960, the number of obscenity arrests also grew. But nothing that had gone before could prepare the country for the assault on booksellers, wholesalers, and magazine distributors who handled *Tropic,* particularly after Grove was forced to release its paperback edition in October to forestall the threat that competitors would release a pirated version. Police officials throughout the country began by issuing "unofficial" warnings that the book was obscene. This was sufficient to suppress *Tropic* in many places. Six hundred thousand books were returned to Grove by frightened wholesalers and retailers. But officials in more than sixty communities followed through on their implied threats by making arrests. " 'Tropic of Cancer' has run into more massive opposition from censors across the United

States than any other serious publishing venture in memory," Anthony Lewis, a *New York Times* reporter, wrote in January 1962. "Though 2.5 million copies are in print, it is impossible to buy the book in most parts of the country."[36]

For three years, Barney Rosset fought the national campaign to ban *Tropic of Cancer.* As part of his effort to encourage retailers to handle *Tropic,* he had promised to pay the legal expenses of anyone who was arrested for selling the book. Even with the help of volunteer attorneys provided by the ACLU, his legal costs mounted quickly. Paying the bills would have been easier if he had been winning all the cases, but the legal record was mixed. Five state supreme courts would eventually consider whether *Tropic* was obscene under state laws, and two of them upheld lower-court decisions banning the book. Some hoped that the Supreme Court would allow the lower court decisions to stand. But once again it disappointed the censors. "It has been suggested that this is a task in which our Court need not involve itself," William Brennan wrote in June 1964 in a case involving Nico Jacobellis, a theater owner who had been charged with obscenity. "The suggestion is appealing, since it would lift from our shoulders a difficult, recurring, and unpleasant task." But Brennan firmly rejected this view:

> Such an abnegation of judicial supervision in this field would be inconsistent with our duty to uphold constitutional guarantees.... Jacobellis has been subjected to a criminal conviction for disseminating a work of expression and is challenging that conviction as a deprivation of rights guaranteed by the First and Fourteenth Amendments.... This Court cannot avoid making an independent constitutional judgment on the facts of the case as to whether the material involved is constitutionally protected.

The *Jacobellis* case concerned the alleged obscenity of a film, *The Lovers,* by French director Louis Malle. Brennan joined five members of the Court in declaring the film to be constitutionally protected, including Potter Stewart, who issued his own opinion. Stewart noted that the *Roth* decision had narrowed the definition of "obscenity" to cover only "hard-core pornography." "I shall not attempt further to define the kinds of material I understand to be embraced within that shorthand description.... But I know it when I see it, and the motion picture involved in this case is not that," Stewart said.[37]

The *Jacobellis* case reaffirmed the Supreme Court's determination to protect nonobscene sexual expression. Although Brennan's opinion broke no new ground, it directly addressed efforts by policemen and judges around the country to undermine the *Roth* decision. Some courts had declared that juries could ban a work as obscene if its prurience outweighed its social importance. But "a work cannot be proscribed unless it is 'utterly without social importance,'" Brennan declared. Other law enforcement officials had decided to treat the concept of "contemporary community standards" in *Roth* as an invitation to apply local standards in determining obscenity. "This is an incorrect reading of *Roth*," Brennan said. To allow local communities to apply their own definitions of "obscenity" would inevitably have a chilling effect on producers and distributors of books and magazines, who would be unwilling to take the risk of distributing material that had been declared illegal anywhere in the country, even in communities where it would not be judged illegal under local standards. "The Court has explicitly refused to tolerate a result whereby 'the constitutional limits of free expression in the Nation would vary with state lines,'" Brennan said. "It is, after all, a national Constitution we are expounding."[38]

The Court underlined its message in another decision issued on the same day as *Jacobellis*. Without comment, it reversed the decision of the Florida Supreme Court that had declared *Tropic of Cancer* obscene. Following the *Roth* decision, it had been civil libertarians who complained. This time it was the censors who expressed their outrage. "These decisions cannot be accepted quietly by the American people if the nation is to survive," a group of Catholic, Protestant, and Jewish religious leaders declared. "Giving free rein to the vile depiction of violence, perversion, illicit sex and, in consequence, to their performance, is an unerring sign of progressive decay and decline." But the Supreme Court's position held firm. In 1966, it eliminated the last vestige of book censorship by legalizing the sale of the notorious *Fanny Hill,* which had been banned for the first time in 1820. Over the next four years, it reversed thirty-one obscenity convictions. Although "hard-core pornography" remained illegal, the Supreme Court had finally set literature free.[39]

CHAPTER 7

Let the Sunshine In

In 1955, the police in Montgomery, Alabama, were not inclined to exaggerate the size of Negro protest meetings. They estimated that 5,000 people had gathered inside and around the Hope Road Baptist Church on the evening of December 5, but the organizers of the event said that 10,000 to 15,000 were there to express their anger at the arrest of Rosa Parks, a forty-two-year-old seamstress who had refused to give up her bus seat to a white man. The streets around the church were so crowded that the main speaker, Martin Luther King Jr., had to climb out of his car and walk the last few blocks. King was only twenty-six years old, and he was a newcomer to Montgomery. Over the objections of his wife, Coretta, a native of Alabama, who had no desire to return to her segregated homeland, King had accepted the job of pastor at the Dexter Avenue Baptist Church only the year before. He was eager to join the civil rights movement, which had been given new life in May 1954 when the U.S. Supreme Court declared segregation of the public schools unconstitutional. Coretta had persuaded him not to run for president of the local chapter of the National Association for the Advancement of Colored People (NAACP), arguing that his duties as pastor and a new father did not give him enough time. However, he could not reject the leadership of the Montgomery Improvement Association, the organization that had just been formed to protest Parks's arrest. "You know something Finley," King said to the friend who had driven him to the church. "This could turn into something big." It took

King fifteen minutes to make his way through the crowd. As he entered the church, he passed loudspeakers that had been hung to carry his words to the people outside.[1]

The young man standing in the pulpit was unknown to almost everyone in the Holt Street church. At first, they followed him politely—from a distance. "We are here this evening—for serious business," he began in a deep voice. "Yes!" one or two people answered in quiet voices. "We are here in a general sense, because first and foremost—we are American citizens—and we are determined to apply our citizenship to the fullness of its means," King said. "But we are here in a specific sense—because of the bus situation in Montgomery."

> The situation is not at all new. The problem has existed over endless years. Just the other day—just last Thursday to be exact—one of the finest citizens in Montgomery—not one of the finest Negro citizens— but one of the finest citizens in Montgomery—was taken from a bus— and carried to jail and arrested—because she refused to give up—to give up her seat to a white person.

More "yeses" and "amens" punctuated King's speech. But the crowd was holding back, waiting to see where this new pastor would lead them, until he praised Parks for "the boundless outreach of her integrity." "Nobody can doubt the height of her character," King said. "Nobody can doubt the depth of her Christian commitment. And just because she refused to get up she was arrested." He paused and then raised his voice for the first time. "And you know my friends, there comes a time when people get tired of being trampled over by the feet of oppression," he said. Suddenly, the church was engulfed in pandemonium. Taylor Branch, King's biographer, wrote:

> A flock of "Yeses" was coming back at him when suddenly the individual responses dissolved into a rising cheer and applause exploded beneath the cheer—all within the space of a second. The startling noise rolled on and on, like a wave that refused to break, and just when it seemed that the roar must finally weaken, a wall of sound came in from the enormous crowd outdoors to push the volume still higher.

The room thundered from the sound of feet stomping on a wooden floor as King raised his voice again. "There comes a time, my friends,

when people get tired of being thrown across the abyss of humiliation, where they face the bleakness of nagging despair.... We are
here—we are here because we are tired now."[2]

> Now let us say that we are not here advocating violence.... We have
> overcome that. I want it to be known throughout Montgomery and
> throughout this nation that we are Christian people. The only weapon
> that we have in our hands this evening is the weapon of protest. If we
> were incarcerated behind the iron curtains of a communistic nation—
> we couldn't do this. If we were trapped in the dungeon of a totalitarian
> regime—we couldn't do this. But the great glory of American democ-
> racy is the right to protest for the right.

While forswearing violence, King was emphatic about the need
to use force to win equal rights. "I want to tell you that it is not
enough for us to talk about love," he said. "Love is one of the pinna-
cle parts of the Christian faith. There is another side called justice....
Justice is love correcting that which would work against love." King
knew that many would criticize the bus boycott that had begun that
morning as a form of coercion. But he insisted that the use of non-
violent force was a legitimate form of protest. "Not only are we using the tools of persuasion—but we've got to use the tools of
coercion," he said.

The Montgomery bus boycott propelled Martin Luther King
onto the national stage. For the next twelve years, he would lead one
of the largest and most militant protests the United States has ever
known. Yet the civil rights movement was only the starting point for
a decade of protests. It soon inspired young Americans to attack restrictions on their free speech that had been imposed by colleges
and universities. Then the war in Vietnam brought dissent in America to the brink of violent rebellion. There were efforts to suppress
both the civil rights and the antiwar movement. Protesters were
beaten and thrown in jail. King was assassinated in 1968. Many believed the United States was becoming a Fascist state. Instead, the
1960s produced important new safeguards for First Amendment
rights. These years of protest may not have produced the dawning
of the age of Aquarius—when, according to the 1968 rock musi-
cal *Hair*, "Peace will guide the planets and love will steer the stars."

But decisions by the Supreme Court and reforms intended to open government to greater public scrutiny did at least begin to "let the sunshine in."[3]

The battle began in the South. Many white southerners were so stunned by the Supreme Court's decision in *Brown v. Board of Education* in May 1954 that for a moment it seemed that they might peacefully accept the end of segregation. But that moment passed quickly. Opponents of the decision began to organize at the local level in the summer of 1954 when the first White Citizens' Council was formed in Indianola, Mississippi, in the heart of the "black belt," the state's cotton-producing region. Dedicated to "states' rights and racial integrity," White Citizens' Councils enrolled 250,000 members in hundreds of communities throughout the South by early 1957. By that time, southern members of Congress had found their voice. "We regard the decision of the Supreme Court in the school cases as a clear abuse of federal power," 101 of the 128 southern members of the House and Senate declared in the "Southern Manifesto." "We pledge ourselves to use all lawful means to reverse [it]." Virginia senator Harry F. Byrd's promise of "massive resistance" to *Brown* was quickly fulfilled as the White Citizens' Councils targeted any southerner who seemed willing to compromise on the issue of race. In Little Rock, Arkansas, where federal troops had to protect the nine black students who desegregated Central High School, the Capitol Citizens' Council organized economic boycotts against defenders of integration, including the *Arkansas Gazette,* which lost 10 percent of its circulation. A baker was targeted because his teenage daughter was known to oppose segregation and one of his employees was a member of the school board that approved the integration of the high school. Once again, the Ku Klux Klan made its appearance and attempted to terrorize those who could not be persuaded by "lawful means."[4]

Despite their anger at the Supreme Court, the segregationists' main nemesis was not the federal government but a private organization—the National Association for the Advancement of Colored People. At a time when the federal government remained unwilling to play an active role in securing equal rights for African Americans, the NAACP had taken the lead in forcing the issue of race onto the national agenda. It was the NAACP that had brought the school segregation issue to the Supreme Court. Only a small fraction of the NAACP's 300,000 members lived in the South—there were only 14,000 NAACP members in the entire state of Alabama—and almost all of them were African American. However, southern members of the NAACP—people like Rosa Parks, who had been the recording secretary of the Montgomery branch for many years—possessed great courage. In the wake of the *Brown* decision, they heeded the call of the national NAACP and began to file petitions urging their local school boards to comply with the Supreme Court's order that they plan for the desegregation of the schools "with all deliberate speed." Some sixty petitions were filed in the summer of 1955 alone.[5]

The segregationists did not have to depend on terror to turn back these challenges to the racial status quo. As the "Southern Manifesto" demonstrated, they had the support of the region's political leaders, and they used their control of the South's political institutions to conduct a systematic campaign to suppress the protest—legally. On February 25, 1956, Martin Luther King and a hundred others were arrested on a charge of conducting an illegal conspiracy in connection with the three-month-old Montgomery bus boycott. A month later, King was convicted and sentenced to 386 days in jail in lieu of a $500 fine that he refused to pay.

The main thrust of the legal attack was directed at the NAACP. Soon after King's conviction, the Alabama attorney general sued the NAACP, accusing it of engaging in injurious activities by supporting the bus boycott and furnishing legal assistance to African American students who were trying to enroll in the state university. Reviving the tactic of exposure that had been used against the Klan in New York in 1923 and against the Communists in 1950, he obtained an injunction barring further NAACP activity in Alabama until the organization provided a number of records, including a list of the names of all of its members in the state. The NAACP refused to turn over the list because it feared that it would be used by segregationists to threaten its members with economic reprisals and "the use of actual force." Unmoved, the judge hit the organization with a $100,000 fine for contempt.[6]

Southern legislators greeted the idea of exposing the NAACP's membership enthusiastically. They were convinced that the racial unrest that was sweeping the South was the result of outside agitators who were "stirring up" trouble among otherwise contented folk. When Virginia delegate Harrison Mann introduced a bill requiring the filing of a membership list by any group engaged "in promoting or opposing in any manner the passage of legislation by the General Assembly on behalf of any race or color," he insisted that it would promote "harmonious relations between the races." Four other southern states joined Virginia in its quest to restore racial harmony by targeting the NAACP's membership lists.

But exposing its members was only one of the tactics used against the NAACP. The Virginia legislature attacked the main weapon in the group's arsenal by attempting to curb its ability to represent clients in legal challenges to racial discrimination. The NAACP had developed a highly trained cadre of lawyers who filed lawsuits on behalf of its members throughout the South. The organization paid the lawyers a modest salary and supervised the conduct of the plaintiffs' cases. The legislature attempted to undermine this system by making it illegal for the NAACP and other groups to seek clients. Other states tried different approaches. The Arkansas legislature banned the hiring of NAACP members by any state or local government agency, including school boards. The purpose of the law couldn't be clearer, its author, Arkansas attorney general Bruce Bennett, proclaimed. It "was meant to harass and cripple the NAACP and as such has accomplished its purpose," he said.[7]

But it was the Supreme Court, not a state attorney general, that would have the final say on the constitutionality of the anti-NAACP legislation. No fewer than six cases came before the Court between 1957 and 1963, and the justices made their position very clear. "There is . . . little suspense in the story we are about to tell," law professor Harry Kalven Jr. said in The Negro and the First Amendment, a series of lectures published in 1965. "The Court will protect the NAACP." The first important case that came before the Court involved Alabama's effort to force the NAACP to turn over its membership list. Writing for a unanimous court, Justice John M. Harlan reversed the judgment against the NAACP, voiding the $100,000 fine for contempt. Rejecting the Supreme Court decision that had upheld the New York anti-Klan statute in 1928, Harlan wrote that the right to associate with others to advocate political views is obviously compromised if disclosing participation in a group threatens its members and discourages them from participating in the group. The Supreme Court also swept aside Virginia's effort to curb NAACP litigation. In his majority opinion, Justice Brennan declared that public-interest lawsuits like those filed by the NAACP could not be judged according to the same rules that applied to suits filed by individuals and commercial corporations:

> In the context of NAACP objectives, litigation is not a technique of resolving private differences; it is a means for achieving the lawful objectives of equality of treatment by all government, federal, state and local, for the members of the Negro community in this country. It is thus a form of political expression. Groups which find themselves unable to achieve their objectives through the ballot frequently turn to the courts.

This opinion by Brennan in *NAACP v. Button,* a 1963 case, broke new constitutional ground by declaring for the first time that litigation is a form of speech and, therefore, protected by the First Amendment. But free speech activists longed for a still more affirmative statement of First Amendment protections. It would come the following year, and once again the case would arise from the ferment in Alabama.[8]

The case of *New York Times v. Sullivan* reached the Supreme Court four years after it had been filed in Montgomery. In April 1960, Montgomery city commissioner L. B. Sullivan had sued the *Times* for libel, claiming he had been defamed by an advertisement placed by the Committee to Defend Martin Luther King and the Struggle for Freedom in the South. Titled "Heed Their Rising Voices," the full-page ad described the efforts being made to suppress a civil rights movement that was spreading rapidly and growing increasingly militant. In February, four African American students sat down at a whites-only lunch counter in Greensboro, North Carolina, and refused to move when they were denied service. Students were soon staging sit-ins throughout the South. They were being arrested, physically abused, and in some cases expelled by their state-run colleges. "In Montgomery, Alabama," the ad read, after students sang "My Country, 'Tis of Thee" on the State Capitol steps, their leaders were expelled from school, and truckloads of police armed with shotguns and tear-gas ringed the Alabama State College Campus. When the entire student body protested to state authorities by refusing to re-register, their dining hall was padlocked in an attempt to starve them into submission.

The *Times* ad urged people to contribute to the fight against "the Southern violators of the Constitution" and to help pay for the legal fight that had been forced on Martin Luther King when an Alabama grand jury indicted him for perjury in connection with the filing of two state income tax returns. The ad was signed by Eleanor Roosevelt, leading figures in the civil rights movement, and show business celebrities. The names of twenty African American ministers from the South appeared at the bottom.[9]

There was only one problem with the ad—it didn't have all of its facts straight. The students in Montgomery sang "The Star-Spangled Banner," not "My Country, 'Tis of Thee"; they were expelled for participating in a sit-in, not for singing; police had not ringed the campus; and the dining hall had never been padlocked. The errors both outraged and delighted Sullivan. Since the beginning of the civil rights movement, southern defenders of segregation had accused northern newspapers and the television networks of distorting their viewpoint and encouraging the protesters. The most recent examples were two stories filed by *Times* reporter Harrison Salisbury that presented a scathing portrait of race relations in Birmingham. Now, as a result of these relatively minor errors, Sullivan believed he had found a way to strike back at the northern media. His lawsuit sought $500,000 in damages, a sum that was daunting even for a newspaper as large as the *New York Times*. Other politicians quickly piled on. Soon, eleven Alabama officials were suing the *Times* for over $5 million. Many of them also sued the four Alabama ministers whose names had appeared in the ad, including the Reverend Ralph Abernathy, who worked closely with King. Libel suits might do more than curb the powerful *New York Times*; they might help snuff out the civil rights movement itself.

The editors of the *Times* did not know how seriously to take the *Sullivan* case at first. Libel suits were relatively rare at the time, and the errors in the ad did not seem very important. They also took comfort in the fact that Sullivan had not even been mentioned in the ad. He would have to prove that the charges against the Montgomery police could reasonably be regarded as charges against him because it was his job to supervise them. But the *Times* lawyers were not smiling. They knew that libel laws favored the plaintiff. Sullivan did not have to show any evidence that his reputation had been damaged. If the statements in the ad could be imputed to be criticism of him, the newspaper would have only one defense—truth—and the lawyers knew that the statements had been false. The *Times* badly needed a friendly judge. But the case had been filed in the Circuit Court of Montgomery County, an Alabama state court, and the judge would be Walter Burgwyn Jones, the proud son of a Confederate soldier who had issued decisions restricting the NAACP, enjoining civil rights demonstrations, and blocking the Justice Department from examining voting records. They expected no mercy, and they received none. At the end of a three-day trial, the *Times* was ordered to pay Sullivan $500,000.[10]

The *Times* was in trouble. Although it was the country's premier newspaper, it was not highly profitable, and the Alabama lawsuits threatened its survival. The *Times* could appeal the decision in the *Sullivan* case, but there was little reason to hope that the Alabama Supreme Court or even the U.S. Supreme Court would take its side. The U.S. Supreme Court had repeatedly declared that libel was not protected by the First Amendment. The right to sue for libel had existed for centuries in both English and American law. The ability to punish people who tell lies about you was recognized as indispensable to a civilized society. This right seemed particularly precious in the early 1960s, when the memory of the McCarthy period was still fresh. (The attorneys for Sullivan would later remind the Supreme Court that John Henry Faulk would have had no weapon with which to attack the lies told by *Red Channels* if he had not been able to sue for libel.) The sanctity of libel law was so firmly established that the leadership of the *Times* was seriously considering not appealing. Some argued that the paper should "stick to our established position that we never settle libel cases, we publish the truth, if there's an occasional error we lose, and that's one of the vicissitudes of life."[11]

Herbert Wechsler was surprised by the defeatism he encountered during a meeting with publisher Orville Dryfoos and the top managers at the *Times*. At fifty-two, the Columbia University law professor had appeared frequently before the Supreme Court and had a reputation for original thinking. "He's the kind of person who takes a thought wherever it leads him, refusing to be deflected by where it is going," Marvin E. Frankel, a law school colleague, said. Wechsler urged the *Times* to break new constitutional ground by arguing that the First Amendment does apply to libel. Wechsler recalled:

> As soon as I realized what was involved, my reaction was, first, to give them a sense of how the scope of the First Amendment had been progressively expanded by the Supreme Court in recent years, so that every one of the old shibboleths had gone—the idea that contempt isn't covered by the First Amendment, unlawful advocacy isn't covered—and libel would logically follow.

Wechsler believed that the Court would be willing to take a fresh look at libel law if it was presented with the right case. The *Sullivan* case, which threatened to restrict reporting on a matter of national concern, was the right one, Wechsler told the newspapermen. He acknowledged that the Court would need a strong argument for breaking with tradition, but he thought he had one. He wanted to argue that the *Sullivan* decision threatened to revive the ancient law of seditious libel, a law that permitted the punishment of almost all criticism of government. Congress had passed the Sedition Act in 1798, making it a crime to publish "any false, scandalous and malicious writing" bringing into disrepute the federal government, Congress, or the president. The arrests and prosecutions under the Sedition Act were later widely acknowledged to have been grave injustices, and Congress repaid the fines imposed under the law. Wechsler was convinced that this repudiation of seditious libel could be used to challenge the *Sullivan* decision, becoming the foundation for a broader right to criticize government. Dryfoos withheld judgment during the meeting, but a short time later the lawyer received a telephone call telling him to proceed with the appeal to the Supreme Court.[12]

By the time the *Sullivan* case reached the Supreme Court in January 1964, the threat to free speech had grown even more dire. Not long after Sullivan sued the *Times,* officials in Birmingham, Alabama, had filed a lawsuit over Harrison Salisbury's stories portraying their city as on the verge of civil war over the demands by the civil rights movement. In the spring of 1963, the war erupted when Police Commissioner Eugene ("Bull") Connor unleashed police dogs and fire hoses against demonstrators. Yet Justice William Brennan avoided any mention of recent events in his opinion overturning the libel award against the *Times.* Following the trail blazed by Wechsler in his brief, Brennan reached back to the Sedition Act of 1798 to prove that the right to criticize government was "the central meaning of the First Amendment." He quoted James Madison, the author of the Bill of Rights and a leader of the fight against the Sedition Act. "The people, not the government, possesses the absolute sovereignty," Madison wrote in his *Report on the Virginia Resolutions.* It followed, Brennan observed, that public officials must expect to be abused. "We consider this case against the background of a profound national commitment to the principle that debate on public issues should be uninhibited, robust, and wide-open, and that it may well include vehement, caustic and sometimes unpleasantly sharp attacks on government and public officials," he wrote.[13]

Brennan also quoted Madison to support the view that errors of fact alone were not sufficient to make speech about public officials punishable. "Some degree of abuse is inseparable from the proper use of everything; and in no instance is this more true than in that of the press," Madison had written. Since "erroneous statement is inevitable in free debate," Brennan argued, "it must be protected if the freedoms of expression are to have the 'breathing space' that they 'need to survive.'" The problem with truth as a defense against a libel charge is that facts are often uncertain and that uncertainty can cause both individuals and newspapers to engage in self-censorship: "Under such a rule, would-be critics of official conduct may be deterred from voicing their criticism, even though it is believed to be true and even though it is in fact true, because of doubt whether it can be proved in court or fear of the expense of having to do so." Brennan declared that the only limit on criticism of public officials that could preserve the fullest protection for free speech was a prohibition against statements made with "actual malice"—state-

ments made with the knowledge that they were false or with reckless disregard of the facts indicating whether they were true. The Supreme Court left little doubt in closing the door against libel suits
like Sullivan's. Brennan's opinion was supported by all eight of his
brethren.[14]

While unanimous about the result, several of the justices were
unhappy that Brennan had not endorsed an absolute right to criticize
public officials. Since joining the Supreme Court in 1937, Hugo L.
Black had been the most absolutist in viewing the First Amendment
as a bar to laws restricting speech, including obscenity. Black also
knew the South well. He had been born and raised in Alabama and
had even joined the Ku Klux Klan in the 1920s when that was a good
career move for a young lawyer with political ambitions. (He was
elected to the U.S. Senate in 1927 and served there until his appointment to the Supreme Court a decade later.) The "actual malice" standard would not have stopped the jury in the Sullivan case
from condemning the *Times,* he said.

Nevertheless, the *Sullivan* case represented an enormous step forward in the effort to protect the free speech rights of individuals and
the press. It had shifted the burden of proof in libel cases from the
defendant, who was no longer required to show that everything he
or she had said or written was true, to the plaintiff, who had to
demonstrate that any false statements were made knowingly or reck-
lessly. As a result, it had given dissenters and critics a new freedom
to criticize public officials. This freedom would be of great importance in the coming years as government came under increasing criticism over the war in Vietnam. But the importance of the decision
was already clear to Black. He wrote to Brennan: "You know of
course that despite my position & what I write I think you are doing a wonderful job in the Times case and however it finally comes
out it is bound to be a very long step towards preserving the right to
communicate ideas." First Amendment scholars like Alexander
Meiklejohn were jubilant. "It is an occasion for dancing in the
street," he said.[15]

By the time of the *Sullivan* decision in March 1964, there were many
reasons to celebrate the growth of free speech. The civil rights
movement had used every form of protest to make its point: there
had been boycotts, sit-ins, marches, rallies, and even paid newspaper

advertisements, which were now protected by the First Amendment, thanks to the *Sullivan* decision. The example of thousands of men, women, and children fighting for equal rights at the risk of their lives inspired admiration throughout the country, and no more so than among the students who were flooding the nation's colleges and universities as a result of the postwar baby boom. Students in the North organized demonstrations of their own. In San Francisco, students from the University of California at Berkeley sat down in the lobby of the Sheraton Palace Hotel in a successful effort to force the hiring of more African American employees. Others picketed branches of the chain stores that were the targets of sit-in demonstrations in the South. The bravest students went South themselves, joining the Freedom Ride in 1961, which challenged the segregation of interstate travel, and participating in the effort to register black voters during the Freedom Summer of 1964. The northerners were frequently attacked. In June 1964, Michael Schwerner and Andrew Goodman, two white civil rights workers from New York, and their colleague, James Chaney, an African American from Mississippi, were killed by the Ku Klux Klan in Mississippi.

Many of the students who went South were natural rebels like Tom Hayden. When he entered the University of Michigan in 1957, he discovered an institution that offered its students few rights. He was appalled when several students were expelled for allegedly throwing food at a housemother during a fracas in the dormitory cafeteria. The incident had begun as a protest over a requirement that men wear shirts and ties, and the students had been disciplined without a hearing. "It was a system of absolute arbitrary authority," Hayden recalled. "I couldn't understand it—no due process, no hearings." Hayden's political career began with an effort to draw attention to the case, but his interest was soon drawn to larger problems—civil rights, the very hot cold war with its threat of instant annihilation, and the rise of a mass society that appeared to crush individualism and undermine democracy. He met other students who shared his view that radical action was necessary. Some of them were the children of left-wing parents, but students of all political backgrounds were showing a new interest in politics. At its 1960 convention, the National Student Association declared that the role of the student involves a commitment to an education process that extends beyond classroom training. It involves also the attainment of knowledge and the development of skills and habits of mind and action necessary for responsible participation in the affairs of government and society on all levels—campus, community, state, national, international.[16]

Hayden and a small group of students went further. They believed that students could be a major force for social change. In June 1962, they gave full voice to this belief at a convention of the two-year-old Students for a Democratic Society (SDS). "Students are breaking the crust of apathy and overcoming the inner alienation that remain the defining characteristics of American college life," SDS declared in a sixty-three-page manifesto. It called for the birth of a "participatory democracy" that would make it possible for every individual to achieve independence and find "a meaning in life that is personally authentic." Drafted by the twenty-two-year-old Hayden, "The Port Huron Statement" convinced the fifty-nine members of SDS who participated in the convention that they were going to change the world. "It was exalting," one participant recalled. "It felt like the dawn of a new age."[17]

SDS's dream of a national reform movement driven by students appeared to be coming true. Students had lost patience with the efforts of college authorities to restrict their political activities. Clark Kerr, the chancellor of the University of California at Berkeley, had decreed that a campus group "may not be affiliated with any partisan, political or religious groups, nor have as one of its purposes the taking of positions with reference to the off-campus political, religious, economic, international or other issues of the time." His ban had forced student activists to confine their efforts to recruit new members to a narrow strip of sidewalk that was believed to be public property just outside one of the main entrances to the campus. In September 1964, administrators discovered that the sidewalk actually belonged to the university and ordered the activists to remove their literature tables. Students were outraged. They suspected the administration of attempting to curb their efforts to pressure local employers to hire more African Americans. But the curb on political activity affected conservative students, too. The College Young Republicans and University Youth for Goldwater joined the Young

Democrats, SDS, and the Young People's Socialist League in protesting the ban on campus advocacy.[18]

The students organized the United Front and announced that they would oppose the restrictions on their right of free speech by bringing the tactics of the civil rights movement to the Berkeley campus. Administrators got their first taste of southern protest on October 1 when they attempted to arrest Jack Weinberg, a civil rights worker who had set up a literature table directly in front of the administration building, Sproul Hall. As the police grabbed him, Weinberg went limp, forcing the officers to carry him through an excited crowd of 200 to 300 students. Someone yelled, "Sit down!" The crowd instantly obeyed, and the police found themselves and their patrol car surrounded. Soon thousands of students were crowding around to see what was happening and sitting down to join the protest. Mario Savio, a twenty-two-year-old transfer student, asked if he could address the students from the top of the car and was told to remove his shoes. There, in stocking feet, Savio emerged as the leader of the student protest that was soon calling itself the Free Speech Movement. Savio was a Catholic who had been shaped by the liberal views of Dorothy Day, the Catholic Worker Movement, and liberation theology. He was also a veteran of the Freedom Summer. "We were going to hold a rally," Savio told the crowd. "We didn't know how to get the people. But we've got them now thanks to the University." Later, he met with administrators and negotiated a truce that ended a thirty-hour standoff, releasing both Weinberg and the patrol car.[19]

Over the next two months, Savio and other student leaders would repeatedly provoke the administration into overreaction, including the expulsion of eight demonstrators. On December 2, Savio addressed a large crowd outside Sproul Hall:

> There is a time when the operation of the machine becomes so odious, makes you so sick at heart, that you can't take part; you can't even tacitly take part, and you've got to put your bodies upon the gears and upon the wheels, upon the levers, upon all the apparatus and you've got to make it stop. And you've got to indicate to the people who run it, to the people who own it, that unless you're free, the machine will be prevented from working at all! Now no more talking. We're going in singing "We Shall Overcome." Slowly, there are a lot of us.

With that, Savio led a large crowd of students inside, packing all four floors of the building. Early the next morning, the police moved in and carried out eight hundred of them, making it the biggest arrest of students in American history. Although student support for the protest grew in the wake of the Sproul Hall arrests, the outcome of the struggle was uncertain until administrators made the final mistake of having Savio seized and dragged away as he attempted to speak at an event sponsored by the university. The next day the faculty met to consider endorsing the demands of the Free Speech Movement. It was rainy and the campus was fogbound, but thousands of students gathered outside the building to listen on loudspeakers as the faculty debated. They roared their approval when the teachers voted 824-115 to support the Free Speech Movement. As the professors left the building and walked through the crowd, many of the students were crying, and so were some of their professors. "I kept pinching myself that this place was real," one of the protesters recalled. "The world seemed deeply good." A week later, the administration capitulated, granting the students all the rights guaranteed by the First Amendment.[20]

In late 1964, there still seemed to be every reason to be optimistic about the prospects for social change. The nation had been traumatized by the assassination of John F. Kennedy a year before, but the new president, Lyndon Johnson of Texas, had broken decisively with the reactionary leadership of the South, declaring a "war on poverty" that would tap the idealism of young Americans by creating programs like Volunteers in Service to America (VISTA) and sending them into poor communities across the country to battle illiteracy, unemployment, and inadequate public services. The new president had also shown that he could get things done by breaking a filibuster to pass the Civil Rights Act of 1964 in June. However, there was a shadow over the dreams for the future. In August, North Vietnamese naval boats fired on an American destroyer in the Gulf of Tonkin, and Johnson ordered a retaliatory air strike. He also sought an authorization from Congress "to take all necessary measures to repel any armed attack against forces of the United States and to prevent further aggression" and to support any nation in the South East Asia Treaty Organization, which included South Vietnam, "requesting assistance in defense of its freedom." With the Gulf of Tonkin Resolution in hand, Johnson proceeded to steadily escalate American involvement in the civil war between North and South Vietnam. After a bombing campaign against North Vietnam failed to produce negotiations, he authorized the dispatch of 40,000 troops in April 1965. By the end of 1966, nearly 400,000 Americans soldiers were fighting in Vietnam.

Opposition to the war also grew quickly. Many of the leaders of the student movement felt sympathy for the anticolonial movements around the world that were seeking to throw off the corrupt and antidemocratic regimes that had been installed by colonial powers. They saw Ho Chi Minh, the Communist leader of North Vietnam, as a patriot trying to reunite his country following decades of colonial rule. But for many protesters opposition to the war was more personal. Men over the age of eighteen who were not attending college were subject to the military draft and could be sent to fight in Vietnam. In March 1965, the first protest occurred at the University of Michigan, where more than 3,000 students and teachers participated in a "teach-in" on the war. The next month, SDS organizers were surprised when more than 20,000 people turned out for a Washington demonstration. They had underestimated the breadth of the opposition to the war. Six months later, more than 100,000 people participated in antiwar protests around the country.

Antiwar protesters immediately ran into opposition. The Senate Internal Security Committee, which had made a name for itself during the McCarthy era, was delighted to find a new target. A committee report claimed that the demonstrators were controlled by "communist and extremist elements who are openly sympathetic to the Vietcong and openly hostile to the United States." Where they could, defenders of war tried to punish their opponents. Marchers were hit with eggs and paint, and sometimes assaulted. The Georgia House of Representatives took a less violent but no more subtle approach by refusing to allow Julian Bond, a civil rights worker and pacifist who had criticized the war, to take his seat in the legislature. In Des Moines, Iowa, John Tinker, fifteen, and his thirteen-year-old sister, Beth, were suspended by their school principals for wearing black armbands protesting the war.

Johnson himself worried that the protests might trigger another conservative witch hunt. "We are confronted with a dilemma . . . as a result of the extremes of McCarthyism. . . . You immediately become a dangerous character or suspect if you express strong feelings about our system," Johnson said at a cabinet meeting. "I don't want us to get into that dangerous situation. I love this system." But by 1966, he had become convinced that only Russian manipulation could explain the growth of the antiwar movement. In 1967, he encouraged the Central Intelligence Agency to begin spying on the dissenters in an effort to uncover their links to foreign agents.[21]

There is more than one way to suppress dissent. During World War I, the government banned antiwar publications and jailed war critics. By the mid-1960s, the growing legal protections for free speech made a similar government crackdown impossible. The Supreme Court had drawn an important line in the sand when it declared in the *Yates* case, announced on Red Monday in 1957, that the First Amendment protects the advocacy of revolution unless "those to whom the advocacy is addressed [are] urged to *do* something, now or in the future, rather than merely to *believe* in something." But the government could still attempt to do secretly what it was barred from doing publicly. Even after the *Yates* case brought an end to the legal assault against the Communist Party, the war against the Communists continued covertly.

There was nothing new about the government's secret efforts to destroy the party. Under the leadership of J. Edgar Hoover, the Federal Bureau of Investigation (FBI) had been installing illegal wiretaps on the telephones of suspected Communists and their sympathizers since at least the 1940s and probably even earlier. Hoover had begun his rise in the Justice Department as one of the architects of the Palmer Raids, but his commitment to the cause of anticommunism was more than office politics. Hoover was born in 1895, nearly in the shadow of the Capitol dome in Washington. The son of a government worker, he grew up with a profound respect for authority, both in the form of government and social tradition, which, in Washington, a southern city, included racial segregation. During his long life, which would include forty-seven years as head of the FBI, Hoover waged an unrelenting war against Communists and any group that he believed was vulnerable to Communist subversion, which in the 1960s would include both the civil rights and the antiwar movement.[22]

Hoover's war was not only unrelenting but also unregulated. Congress had banned wiretapping in 1934, and the Supreme Court reaffirmed its illegality in 1939. But Hoover didn't believe there should be any limit on the government's ability to spy on Communists, Fascists, and other groups that appeared to threaten national security on behalf of foreign powers. Franklin D. Roosevelt and his secretary of state Cordell Hull agreed. At a meeting with the two men in 1936, Hoover said he would need a direct authorization by the State Department before he could begin to monitor the activities of Communist and Fascist groups. "Go ahead and investigate the cock-suckers," Hull reportedly told Hoover. Four years later, after war had erupted in Europe, Roosevelt told Hoover to ignore the Supreme Court's 1939 decision on wiretapping because he was "convinced that the Supreme Court never intended any dictum . . . to apply to grave matters involving the defense of the nation." For the next four decades, Hoover would regard the orders he received from Hull and Roosevelt as the authority to conduct secret surveillance whenever he wanted.[23]

The FBI developed a formidable capacity for spying on American citizens. Wiretapping was augmented by the planting of secret microphones and break-ins, which became so common that they were called "black bag jobs" because of the bags that held an agent's burglar tools. The FBI also built a network of thousands of informants inside the Communist Party and the other organizations it was monitoring. As a result, the FBI was ready and waiting when the second Red Scare began. It had gathered information about tens of thousands of Americans whose political connections raised doubts about their loyalty. It supplied the background reports that cost thousands of government workers their jobs and helped heighten the anti-Red hysteria by feeding information to the congressional investigating committees. Because much of its information had been acquired illegally, the FBI often put it in "blind memos." Printed on plain paper so they could not be attributed to the bureau, these reports were given to federal, state, and local investigators. If people in the 1950s had known the extent of the FBI's spying, " 'McCarthyism' would probably have been called 'Hooverism,' " historian Ellen Schrecker has observed.[24]

When the FBI was occasionally caught in illegal acts, its spokesmen argued that the agents were engaged in intelligence gathering that was necessary to protect the nation's security. But the purpose of the spying was broader than that. The FBI was engaged in a clandestine war against not just enemy spies but the Communist Party and other "subversive" groups, including some that were suspect mainly because of their opposition to the Red Scare. One such group was the National Lawyers Guild, which had been founded in 1936 as a liberal alternative to the American Bar Association. The FBI was suspicious because Communist attorneys had played an important role in founding and sustaining the guild. But many prominent liberals joined the guild, including the governors of two states, several United States senators, and a number of leading African American attorneys, including Thurgood Marshall, the legal director of the NAACP. When the newly formed House Un-American Activities Committee attacked the New Deal as Communist in 1938, many liberals quit the guild to escape the taint of radicalism. However, even after the defections of the later 1930s, it continued to attract prominent liberals who admired its strong criticism of the federal loyalty program and other cold war measures.

The FBI never wavered in its view that the guild was a Communist front. In 1947, it launched a surveillance campaign intended to demonstrate that the guild should be added to the attorney general's list of subversive groups. It began wiretapping the telephone of the guild's Washington office. When the wiretap revealed that the guild was planning to issue a report critical of the FBI, agents broke into the office and microfilmed the report. Alerted by the wiretap to the existence of a revised report, they broke in again and stole that, too. The wiretap also revealed that the guild was planning a press conference to release its report. This enabled the FBI to tip a friendly reporter for one of the country's main wire services, who wrote a story claiming that "a left-wing organization already suspected as a Communist front" was preparing a report designed to "weaken" the FBI and force Hoover from office. When the FBI overheard a conversation setting the date for the press release, it alerted the Justice Department, the White House, and possibly Congressman Richard M. Nixon. Less than a week before the guild press conference, Nixon announced that he was urging HUAC to investigate whether the guild was a Communist front. The announcement captured headlines, overshadowing the guild's press conference. But the FBI still had to deal with the report, which claimed that "on a strictly numerical basis, the FBI may commit more federal crimes than it ever detects." The wiretap was useful here, too. The bureau learned of possible investigations by a U.S. senator and the Illinois Bar Association and was able to head them off.[25]

The FBI's knowledge of the inside workings of dissident groups created an enormous temptation for Hoover and his agents to intervene directly in their affairs and attempt to disrupt them. FBI informants were often in a position to spread lies that would cause internal dissension, sometimes by raising suspicion about the loyalty of key leaders. In 1956, as it became apparent that the Supreme Court was intent on expanding protections for civil liberties that would make it harder to convict Communists, Hoover gave in to temptation and ordered the launch of a full-blown counterintelligence program (COINTELPRO). The program nearly succeeded in wiping out the Communist Party altogether as FBI agents and informants undertook nearly 1,400 actions intended to undermine the morale of their enemies. On one occasion, on learning that a party leader was homosexual, the FBI had him arrested for committing homosexual acts to embarrass the party. It even harassed a Cub Scout den mother by telling her neighbors that she was a Communist; she was forced to resign. The FBI's control over a faction of the Communist Party grew so complete that Hoover considered allowing FBI informants to try to take over the party. It was hardly necessary. By the end of 1957, there were only 3,474 Communists left.

Hoover was so impressed with the results of COINTELPRO that he soon turned it against new targets. In 1961, he targeted the Socialist Workers Party. In 1964, in response to the violence against civil rights workers in the South, he added the Ku Klux Klan and other white hate groups to the list. In 1967, the FBI began to pursue militant African American groups like the Black Panther Party. A year later, COINTELPRO targeted the increasingly violent protests against the Vietnam War.[26]

Violence was becoming a growing problem in the antiwar movement. The optimism expressed by the Free Speech Movement and the "Port Huron Statement" had dissipated by 1968, and antiwar protesters were growing increasingly angry at their inability to end the war. Some radicals began to embrace violence, and the bombing of military training facilities on college campuses grew from ten in the spring of 1968 to eighty-four the following spring. At the same time, a "black power" movement emerged that rejected the nonviolence of mainstream civil rights leaders. Yet the FBI showed no ability to distinguish between dissenters and criminals. The most glaring example of this was its campaign to discredit Martin Luther King.

As a southerner, Hoover had always been hostile to King. But when he learned that one of the civil rights leader's closest advisers had been a high-ranking member of the Communist Party, he ordered King's telephone tapped and bugs planted in his hotel rooms. In the most notorious act of the COINTELPRO era, an assistant director of the FBI sent King an anonymous letter threatening to expose his extramarital affairs. King was in Sweden accepting the Nobel Peace Prize when the letter arrived at the Southern Christian Leadership Council's office, accompanied by a tape consisting of conversations and sounds of sexual activity that had been taped in King's hotel rooms. Not suspecting what it was, Coretta King opened the package and listened to the tape. She called King. "They are out to break me," her husband told her. "They are out to get me, harass me, break my spirit." There appears to be no other explanation, Richard Gid Powers, an authority on the FBI, has concluded. "Some of King's friends thought the purpose was to blackmail King into declining the Nobel Prize. Others thought it was to goad King's wife into divorcing him. Or maybe the plan was to put the thought of suicide in King's mind. How could the FBI have sunk so low?" Powers asked.[27]

The FBI also worked actively to undermine the antiwar movement. On May 23, 1968, a directive went out from Washington to all bureau offices ordering them to

> collect evidence on the "scurrilous and depraved nature of many of the characters, activities, habits, and living conditions representative of New Left adherents," to "show the value of college administrators and school officials taking a firm stand," and to expose "whether and to what extent faculty members rendered aid and encouragement" to the antiwar movement. "Every avenue of possible embarrassment must be vigorously and enthusiastically explored. It cannot be expected that information of this type will be easily obtained, and an imaginative approach by your personnel is imperative to its success."

It turned out that FBI agents could be very imaginative. One tactic was to send anonymous letters about student misbehavior to parents, neighbors, and employers. In the days before the Democratic National Convention in Chicago in August 1968, the FBI succeeded in disrupting plans for housing demonstrators that had been made by antiwar activists. Agents in Chicago submitted 217 forms volunteering housing by people who didn't exist. As a result, many protesters were sent on a wild goose chase, forced to make "long and useless journeys to locate these addresses," according to an FBI memo. "Several became incensed" at the organizers, whom they held responsible. The organizers, in turn, began questioning the value of the legitimate offers of help they had received, which undermined their ability to house everyone they had promised. FBI agents undertook nearly a thousand actions against the Klan and the antiwar and civil rights movements.[28]

The efforts to suppress the civil rights and antiwar movements ultimately failed. Neither the clubs of the Chicago police at the Democratic Convention nor the FBI's dirty tricks were any match for broadly based protest movements. In October 1969, nearly three million Americans participated in antiwar protests around the country, and in November 750,000 gathered in Washington for the largest antiwar protest in American history. Although there was more violence ahead, including the deaths of four students at Kent State University in 1970, the antiwar movement succeeded in forcing the withdrawal of American troops from Vietnam, although not before it cost the lives of over fifty thousand Americans and hundreds of thousands of Vietnamese.

The attacks on the antiwar movement might have been more successful if the Supreme Court had not steadfastly protected protest throughout the Vietnam War. In December 1966, the Court ordered the Georgia legislature to allow Julian Bond to take the House seat that had been denied him because of his opposition to the war. The Supreme Court surprised war critics a year and a half later when it upheld a federal law that made it a crime to burn a draft card, but the 7-1 decision did not lead to a softening of the Court's commitment to the First Amendment. In 1969, it upheld the right of John and Mary Beth Tinker to wear black armbands to school. "It can hardly be argued that either students or teachers shed their constitutional rights to freedom of speech or expression at the schoolhouse gate," Justice Abe Fortas wrote in the majority opinion.

A few months later, the Supreme Court demonstrated just how serious it was about protecting politically provocative speech. In June 1964, Clarence Brandenburg, a member of the Ku Klux Klan, was filmed at a Klan rally as he warned that "it's possible there might have to be some revengeance [*sic*] taken" against the federal government for suppressing "the white, Caucasian race." Brandenburg was convicted, sentenced to one to ten years in jail, and fined $10,000 under an Ohio law that banned speech advocating illegal acts. Although the statute was essentially the same as the one the Supreme Court had upheld in the *Whitney* case in 1927, the Warren Court ruled unanimously in *Brandenburg v. Ohio* that advocating violence or other criminal acts alone was not adequate grounds for banning speech, "except where such advocacy is directed to inciting or producing imminent lawless action and is likely to produce such action." The "clear and present danger" test that Justices Holmes and Brandeis had advocated as a safeguard for free speech since the *Abrams* case in 1919 had finally become the law of the land.[29]

Two weeks after the *Brandenburg* decision, at the conclusion of the Supreme Court's 1968–1969 term, Earl Warren resigned, ending fifteen years of service as chief justice. The impact of the Warren Court on the right of free speech and freedom of the press had been profound. University of Chicago law professor Harry Kalven Jr. tried to measure its impact in late 1968. By that time, the Court had handed down decisions in eighty-nine noteworthy free speech cases. If Zechariah Chafee were still alive, Kalven said, he would have to add a second volume to his classic study *Free Speech in the United States* just to cover them all. The Court had issued landmark decisions in cases that helped end the Red Scare, expanded artistic freedom, and encouraged the growth of civil rights. It had shown "a zest for these problems and a creative touch in working with them." Kalven focused on the key words in Brennan's *Sullivan* opinion—that debate on public issues must be "uninhibited, robust and wide-open": "They express a desire to make a fresh statement about the principles of free speech rather than simply repeat the classic phrases of Holmes in *Abrams* and Brandeis in *Whitney*," he said. "The Court is interested enough to be minting contemporary epigrams—to be making its own."[30]

One of the most important tests for the Supreme Court lay ahead. On June 13, 1971, the *New York Times* began publishing a secret government study of the Vietnam War, which became known as the Pentagon Papers. When Richard Nixon's Justice Department persuaded a judge to block the publication of further installments in the series, the Supreme Court was faced with one of its most difficult decisions. It would have to decide whether the government's asserted interest in protecting national security was more important than freedom of the press and the right of people to have basic information about their government's policies, and it would have to do it in the middle of a war.[31]

The relationship between the Nixon administration and the nation's press was badly frayed even before the Pentagon Papers case. Like many of their fellow countrymen, newspaper and television reporters had grown disillusioned with the Vietnam War. The turning point came in January 1968 when North Vietnam and its Vietcong allies launched an offensive that carried their forces to the doorstep of the American embassy in Saigon and inflicted record casualties, killing more than 1,100 Americans and 2,300 South Vietnamese soldiers. Although the rebels were finally repelled with even larger losses, the Tet offensive proved that the Johnson administration had not been telling the American people the truth. "What the hell is going on," Walter Cronkite, the anchor of the *CBS Evening News,* asked. "I thought we were winning the war." As a result, the Nixon administration inherited a press corps that had begun to talk of "a credibility gap" between what the government was saying about Vietnam and the truth about our involvement there. Of course, Nixon already hated the press. "I must have heard Richard Nixon say 'the press is the enemy' a dozen times," William Safire, a Nixon speechwriter, recalled. Nixon was angered by the skepticism that the *New York Times,* the *Washington Post,* and others in the media expressed toward his plan to end the war. In November 1969, Vice President Spiro Agnew made two speeches accusing the networks, the *Times,* and the *Post* of biased coverage of the administration. He appeared to threaten the networks, whose ability to broadcast depended on licenses from the government. "As with other American institutions, perhaps it is time that the networks were made more responsive to the views of the nation," Agnew said.[32]

The publishers of the *New York Times* and the *Washington Post* knew that publishing the Pentagon Papers was going to cause trouble. The study had been commissioned by Secretary of Defense Robert McNamara in June 1967. Although McNamara was the architect of the American war effort, he had become convinced that the war was unwinnable, and he hoped that a study of American involvement in Vietnam since World War II would explain the policy mistakes that had led the United States into the quagmire. Over the next eighteen months, a staff of thirty-six analysts amassed a forty-seven-volume study that included three thousand pages of historical interpretation and four thousand pages of documents.

One of the authors, Daniel Ellsberg, a national security analyst who had become a passionate critic of the war, was convinced that the Pentagon Papers could end the war. During a two-year stay in Vietnam, Ellsberg had come to believe that America's leaders were being fooled by overly optimistic reports from the field. For example, America's generals claimed they were succeeding in their efforts to turn the fighting over to the South Vietnamese Army (SVA). As proof, they cited the growing number of night patrols undertaken by the SVA. "Everyone in Vietnam knew that there had been no patrols—not one," Ellsberg said. But after reading the Pentagon Papers, Ellsberg concluded that the intelligence estimates given to the president were "remarkably accurate." It was America's leaders who had lied, particularly Johnson, who had promised a swift and successful resolution of the war. For two years, Ellsberg tried to give the Pentagon Papers to antiwar leaders in the Congress, but they were unwilling to accept responsibility for revealing classified information. Finally, he made it available to Neil Sheehan, a reporter for the *Times*.[33]

Both Arthur Ochs Sulzberger of the *Times* and Katharine Graham of the *Post* knew that the Nixon administration might try to punish them for allowing the publication of a secret study that portrayed American policymakers in an unflattering light. Attorneys for the *Times* told Sulzberger that he might be criminally prosecuted under the Espionage Act. The *Post* had just issued stock that might crash if an injunction were issued against it, and the Federal Communications Commission could make trouble when the time came to renew the broadcast licenses of the paper's radio and television stations. Pushing hard in the other direction were the managing editors, the *Times*'s A. M. Rosenthal and the *Post*'s Benjamin C. Bradlee. Both assured their bosses that they were sitting on one of the biggest stories of their lives—a story by government insiders citing government documents that proved the American people had been tricked into a war that had cost tens of thousands of American lives. Although the most politically conservative editor at the *Times,* Rosenthal was ready to quit if Sulzberger killed the series.

Graham also faced the threat of a newsroom revolt. The *Post* had obtained its copy of the Pentagon Papers after the *Times* and was considering whether to proceed with its own series of stories after the government had blocked the *Times.* Bradlee told Graham that the *Post* had a duty to support the *Times* in its fight against censorship. The *Post* reporters complained loudly when they learned that the series might be postponed and that the paper might even notify the Justice Department in advance. "That's the shittiest idea I've ever heard," one of the reporters, Don Oberdorfer, said. Graham decided not to wait, and the first *Post* story based on the Pentagon Papers appeared on June 18, 1971, the day that the *Times* would urge a federal judge in New York to lift his injunction.[34]

The lawyers for the *Times* faced some formidable obstacles as the trial opened in the federal courthouse in Manhattan. The judge, Murray I. Gurfein, had just been appointed by Nixon, and the Pentagon Papers case was his first. In the opening session, Gurfein was obviously unsympathetic toward the *Times.* But the biggest problem the newspaper faced was the government's claim that the release of a forty-seven-volume report that included thousands of pages of classified documents would inevitably harm national security. Ironically, Nixon himself had been inclined to ignore the leak initially, believing that it could only hurt the reputations of the Kennedy and Johnson administrations. But Henry Kissinger, Nixon's national security adviser, had changed his mind by arguing that the leak would weaken the president in the eyes of world leaders. By the time they got to court, the government's lawyers were prepared to argue that the Pentagon Papers revealed secrets that would damage our diplomatic relations, expose the nation's intelligence operations, and provide the enemy with useful information about military planning. During a closed hearing, government experts told Gurfein that the secret study would hamper the effort to obtain the release of American prisoners of war in North Vietnam. The United States was negotiating through other nations, and they would be embarrassed if their role became public. Experts also claimed that the reports would cause Australia, New Zealand, and Thailand to withdraw troops from South Vietnam, slowing the departure of American forces.

Yet the government failed. Gurfein lifted his injunction the next day, June 19, 1971, and when the case reached the Supreme Court just two weeks later, it affirmed his decision. It was not that the judges doubted the government's claims. A majority of the Supreme Court justices said they believed that the Pentagon Papers contained material that would harm the nation, and several said they believed the government could prosecute the *Times* under the Espionage Act. "After examining the materials the Government characterizes as the most sensitive and destructive," Justice Byron White agreed that "revelation of these documents will do substantial damage to public interests." But he and Potter Stewart believed that the government had failed to prove the harm was great enough to justify approving a prior restraint on the press. "I am convinced that the Executive is correct with respect to some of the documents involved," Stewart said. "But I cannot say that disclosure of any of them will surely result in direct, immediate and irreparable damage to our Nation or its people."[35]

The Supreme Court's 6–3 decision was greeted with jubilation by journalists and civil libertarians. It appeared to create a powerful precedent that would protect free speech even in time of war. The words of Judge Gurfein's decision made the point best. "The security of the Nation is not at the ramparts alone," he wrote. "Security also lies in the value of our free institutions. A cantankerous press, an obstinate press, a ubiquitous press must be suffered by those in authority in order to preserve the even greater values of freedom of expression and the right of the people to know." In the 1970s, it appeared that the Supreme Court might become more deferential to government's demand for secrecy when it enjoined a former CIA agent from publishing classified information that had not previously been in the public domain and barred another CIA man from ever writing or speaking about intelligence matters he had learned about during his service without agency approval. But the landmark decision in *New York Times v. U.S.* has stood the test of time. Since the early 1980s, the government has not gone to court to block the publication of information that might be damaging to national security.[36]

The *New York Times* and the *Washington Post* resumed publication of the Pentagon Papers on July 1, 1971. Their revelations fueled a national debate over whether the government of the United States had tricked the American people into an unwinnable war. But the impact of the Pentagon Papers case was even more profound. Just two weeks after the government lost its case in the Supreme Court, Nixon authorized the formation of an investigative unit within the White House and assigned it the job of cracking down on government leakers, starting with Daniel Ellsberg. In September, probably with Nixon's knowledge, the "Plumbers" broke into the offices of Ellsberg's psychiatrist to get information that would help convict Ellsberg, who had been indicted for violating the Espionage Act and theft of government property. The black bag job was only one example of the ways in which Nixon's men now imitated the tactics of the FBI's COINTELPRO program. Undertaking a campaign of what they called "rat-fucking," they engaged in a series of dirty tricks to disrupt the campaigns of Democrats who were vying to oppose Nixon in the 1972 elections.

On June 17, 1972, five members of the Plumbers were arrested in the act of burglarizing the Democratic National Committee offices in the Watergate building in Washington, D.C. It took two years and an intensive investigation by the *Washington Post,* Federal District Court judge John J. Sirica, and committees of the House and Senate to reveal the truth: high officials in the Nixon administration had approved the burglary, and the president himself had joined in covering up their role by authorizing the payment of hush money to the burglars. After Hoover's death in May 1972, the White House also attempted to use FBI director L. Patrick Gray to thwart his agency's investigation. In July 1974, less than two years after Nixon won the election in a landslide, the House Judiciary Committee approved three articles of impeachment. Two stemmed directly from the Pentagon Papers case—the formation of the Plumbers unit and the burglary of Ellsberg's psychiatrist. Nixon resigned on August 8. William Safire later concluded that the Pentagon Papers case helped precipitate Nixon's downfall. "A hatred of the press—a need to stop the leaks and teach the leakers a lesson—caused Nixon to go over the brink," he said.[37]

Almost before the country could breathe a sigh of relief over the end of the Watergate horrors, however, it was shocked by new revelations of government wrongdoing. On December 22, the *New York Times* revealed that the CIA had been engaged in a massive campaign of spying on American citizens. Although forbidden by law to operate in the United States, the CIA had used illegal break-ins, wiretaps, and mail openings to gather information on over ten thousand antiwar protesters and other dissidents. The story was written by Seymour Hersh, a Pulitzer Prize–winning reporter who had uncovered the massacre of Vietnamese civilians by American troops at My Lai. Over the next two weeks, Hersh and other *Times* reporters published thirty-two stories detailing the sins of the agency.

The *Washington Post* joined in, describing the misdeeds of the secret government agency. In January 1975, it reported that the FBI had spied on members of Congress, collecting information about their personal lives. A week later, the *Post* also revealed the first public evidence of the government campaign against Martin Luther King when it reported that the FBI had bugged King's hotel room during the 1964 Democratic convention. But the most sensational story was aired four weeks later. Daniel Schorr, a correspondent for the *CBS Evening News,* had learned that President Ford had told associates that the CIA had participated in assassinations. Unable to confirm it, Schorr decided to confront CIA director William Colby. "Has the CIA ever killed anybody in this country?" he asked. Colby was stunned. "Not in this country," he replied.[38]

Congress worked quickly to follow up the charges made by the press. After years of deferring to the executive branch in matters involving national security, it had been infused with new blood as a result of the first post-Watergate elections. Ten new senators and seventy-five new House members were determined to challenge presidential authority and earn the name of the "fighting ninety-fourth"

Congress. By the end of January, the Senate had established a special committee headed by Frank Church of Idaho and charged it with describing the operations of the "shadow government" created by the intelligence agencies. The Senate Select Committee to Study Governmental Operations with Respect to Intelligence Activities did not disappoint. The first public hearing opened with the revelation that the CIA possessed shellfish toxin and cobra venom that could be used in assassination attempts. Later, the committee confirmed that the CIA had tried at least eight times to kill Fidel Castro and that it had sent a "lethal substance" to agents in the Congo who would have tried to kill the nationalist leader Patrice Lumumba if someone else hadn't murdered him first. The CIA had also played an indirect role in the deaths of three other leaders. In addition, the Church Committee discovered many of the secrets of the COINTELPRO program, including the FBI's effort to blackmail Martin Luther King. The final Church Committee report revealed that the CIA had engaged in nine hundred covert actions since 1961; that its computers contained the names of 1.5 million potentially "subversive" Americans; and that it had spied on 7,000 of them. With the CIA, the FBI had opened 380,000 letters, and it had investigated over 500,000 dissidents without proving that any of them were guilty of committing a crime. Reforms were essential to eliminate the systematic abuse of civil liberties, the report concluded. It recommended nearly two hundred changes in foreign and domestic intelligence gathering.[39]

Some of the most important Watergate reforms were a series of amendments to the Freedom of Information Act passed in November 1974, weeks before the country began to learn of the abuses committed by its intelligence agencies. In 1953, Harold L. Cross, a former counsel for the *New York Herald Tribune,* launched a campaign to establish the public's right to gain access to government information. "Public business is the public's business," Cross declared in the book that became the founding text of the freedom of information movement, *The Public's Right to Know.* Commissioned by the American Society of Newspaper Editors, Cross's book acknowledged that reporters were skilled at obtaining information from public officials. However, few laws actually compelled the disclosure of public information when the officials turned obstinate. In 1955, Congressman John Moss of California took up the fight for a federal bill, which finally became law in 1966.[40]

While the Freedom of Information Act (FOIA) established the principle that the public has a right to government information, it contained numerous exemptions and lacked important enforcement provisions. In October 1974, Congress passed a bill that narrowed the types of documents that could be withheld, imposed a timetable for complying with FOIA requests, and threatened officials with administrative sanctions for wrongfully withholding documents. President Ford and his top advisers, including Chief of Staff Donald Rumsfeld and his deputy, Richard Cheney, believed the measure would disclose military and intelligence secrets and hamper law enforcement. However, Ford's veto of the bill was easily overridden. The strengthened Freedom of Information Act opened the federal government to wide-ranging scrutiny by journalists, scholars, and individual citizens. In 2002, over 2.4 million requests were filed under the Freedom of Information Act. The information was used in more than four thousand news stories.[41]

But giving the people a right to demand information did not solve the immediate problems of reforming the nation's intelligence agencies and restoring trust in the government. The reputations of the FBI and the CIA had been severely damaged by the revelations of the Church Committee. The number of Americans who had a "highly favorable" opinion of the FBI fell from 84 percent in 1965 to 37 percent in 1975. Only 14 percent of the public gave the CIA high marks. President Ford took the first step toward regaining public confidence in February 1976 when he reaffirmed the ban on CIA spying on domestic groups and restricted the National Security Agency to intercepting communications outside the United States. The next month Attorney General Edward Levi imposed strict guidelines prohibiting the FBI to investigate any individual or group on the basis of activities protected by the First Amendment. The FBI could launch a preliminary investigation only when there was evidence of an intent to break the law, and it could not continue for more than ninety days or involve the use of informants, wiretaps, and mail "covers" unless the preliminary investigation had identified "specific and articulable facts" supporting the suspicion of illegal intent. The Justice Department had to approve these investigations in advance and then review them annually to ensure that they were still justified. Congress also took steps to increase its oversight of the nation's intelligence agencies, both foreign and domestic. In May 1976, the Senate created the Select Committee on Intelligence; the House organized its own intelligence committee a couple of months later.[42]

By the late 1970s, Vietnam, Watergate, and the intelligence scandals had helped create a movement for greater openness at all levels of government. State legislatures and local governments passed legislation opening their records to public access for the first time. Many also enacted open meeting laws that strictly limited the amount of public business that could be transacted behind closed doors.

Lawsuits often accomplished what public officials were unwilling to do voluntarily. The police in New York, Chicago, Los Angeles, and Memphis were sued for spying on dissidents in the 1960s. These cases were frequently resolved by agreements that barred similar conduct in the future. Sometimes politicians even took the lead in controlling the police. In 1979, the Seattle City Council responded to the news that its police department had spied on 750 residents by passing an ordinance setting strict limits to the department's intelligence gathering and providing for an auditor to ensure compliance. Appointed by the mayor, the auditor was given the responsibility to review police files, issue reports to the city council, and notify citizens who may have become the victims of illegal investigations. Not surprisingly, the police had opposed the ordinance, but they soon reconciled themselves to it. Although it was not required, the police chief opened his personal safe to the auditor. Even in drizzly Seattle, the sun was shining in.[43]

CHAPTER 8

The Counterattack, 1970–2002

On a December evening in 1976, a Methodist minister in Mississippi was watching television with his family when he suddenly glimpsed his future. The Reverend Donald Wildmon would later say that as he changed channels, he was unable to find a single program that wasn't drenched in sex, violence, or profanity. Believing that God had called him to the fight against "indecency" in the media, Wildmon quit his job as pastor of a small-town church and moved to Tupelo, Mississippi, where he founded the National Federation for Decency. He was not a prepossessing figure. At thirty-eight, he was short, plump, and balding. Even he would have admitted that with his large, thick glasses, he had a great face for radio. But what Wildmon lacked in looks he made up for in political shrewdness and tenacity, qualities that would make him the Anthony Comstock of his age.[1]

At the same time, a thirty-year-old feminist legal scholar was also searching for a path. Catharine A. MacKinnon's father was a lawyer who had been active in Republican politics in Minnesota and had served one term in Congress and five years as U.S. attorney before Richard Nixon made him a federal judge in 1969. But MacKinnon rejected the worldview of her parents and immersed herself in radical politics at Yale University during the early 1970s, fighting racial injustice with the Black Panther Party, protesting the Vietnam War, and joining the new women's movement. Unlike Wildmon, MacKinnon was a charismatic figure—a Joan of Arc to his

Comstock. MacKinnon's most distinctive feature was the long au-
burn hair that she swept to the top of her head like a proper Victorian lady. She didn't sound like one, however. Her language was
sexually explicit and full of scorn for the oppressors of women, especially those who argued that women who participated in the production of "adult" magazines and films did so voluntarily. "Forget
the realities of women's sexual/economic situation. When women
express our free will, we spread our legs for the camera," MacKinnon
said. She was also a powerful speaker whose hair would often slip
from its pins, falling into her handsome, angry face as she delivered
a clarion call for action. After she graduated from Yale Law School
and began teaching, her female students adored her and were ready
to follow her anywhere. In 1983, she would lead them into battle
against pornography.[2]

In just a few short years, these obscure individuals would pose
one of the gravest threats to First Amendment rights since the Mc-
Carthy period. They didn't do it alone. Wildmon and MacKinnon
rode a great conservative wave that began in the 1960s. After decades
out of power, conservatives finally were able to nominate one of
their own for president in 1964, Barry Goldwater. They were not
discouraged by Goldwater's landslide defeat but redoubled their or-
ganizational efforts, exploiting the deep divisions created in American society by the civil rights and antiwar movements. A longing for
a return to traditional American values helped elect Richard Nixon
in 1968.

Wildmon and MacKinnon also benefited from the shock that
many people felt at the rapid proliferation of sexual and violent material in the media. The motion-picture code that the movie industry had imposed on itself in the 1930s had finally been replaced. In
1966, Jack Valenti, a former aide to Lyndon Johnson, became president of the Motion Picture Association of America (MPAA), the
successor to the association that Will Hays had headed. Valenti disliked the code. "There was about this stern, forbidding catalogue of
'Dos and Don'ts' the odious smell of censorship," he recalled. "I determined to junk it at the first opportune moment." In 1968, the
MPAA joined with the National Association of Theater Owners in
launching a rating system that gave parents advance warning about
the amount of sex and violence in particular films. (Some filmmak-

ers would later claim that the "voluntary" rating system was not without its censorial elements because many theaters would not book a film with an "X"—later "NC-17"—rating.) Although television and radio remained regulated industries and the threat of being punished for violating standards of broadcast decency had not disappeared, they also began to relax the self-imposed guidelines that restricted content. The television networks developed dramas, situation comedies, and soap operas depicting characters who were divorced, unfaithful, and even pregnant and unwed. At the same time, sexually explicit material was increasingly entering the mainstream. Hugh Hefner had gotten the ball rolling in 1953 with the founding of *Playboy* magazine. By the 1960s, men's magazines were available on newsstands and in drugstores in many parts of the country. "Hard-core" pornography depicting sex acts was sold in adult bookstores and exhibited in movie theaters in most large cities.[3]

In 1967, concern over the proliferation of sexually explicit material led Congress to create a commission to study the problem. The overwhelming majority of those who voted to establish the National Commission on Obscenity and Pornography hoped that it would prove that pornography was harmful. It was given a budget of $20 million, which it used to commission original scientific research on the effects of sexually explicit material. But the experiment backfired. The test results convinced twelve of the seventeen commission members that obscene material was not harmful to adults, and they recommended legalizing it. Nixon condemned the report. "The warped and brutal portrayal of sex in books, plays, magazines and movies, if not halted and reversed, could poison the wellspring of American and Western culture and civilization," he said. The U.S. Senate agreed, voting 60 to 5 to repudiate the report.[4]

Nixon was able to create a Supreme Court that would endorse his hard line. The resignations of Justices Abe Fortas, Earl Warren, Hugo Black, and John Harlan made it possible for him to appoint four new members to the Court in three years, Warren Burger, Harry Blackmun, Lewis Powell, and William Rehnquist. Burger became the new chief justice. The appointments gave the conservatives the upper hand when the Supreme Court accepted five obscenity cases during its 1972–1973 term. William Brennan, the author of the *Roth* decision, which declared that obscenity is not protected by the

First Amendment, had become convinced that it was impossible to ban obscene material without suppressing sexually explicit speech that had serious value. But he was now in the minority. In a 5–4 decision, the Nixon appointees joined in significantly expanding the definition of "obscenity" by narrowing the exemption for material with redeeming social value and authorizing local communities to apply their own standards in defining "obscenity." The 1973 decision in *Miller v. California* made it possible for the first time for a jury in a conservative community to send someone to prison for producing or distributing material that would not be judged obscene elsewhere.

Donald Wildmon's epiphany occurred three years after the *Miller* decision. He knew change was in the air. But his National Federation for Decency struggled, and Wildmon's wife had to get a job to help the venture survive. The problem was how to clean up television with only fourteen hundred members. Clearly, boycotts of TV programs would not work: the number of people who would turn off their sets at any one time would never be large enough to register in the ratings. But religious groups had recently used the threat of a boycott to chase advertisers away from a new satire, *Soap*. In the spring of 1978, Wildmon announced that his supporters would boycott Sears until it withdrew sponsorship of three shows at the top of his hit list—*Three's Company, Charlie's Angels,* and *All in the Family.* Wildmon used his handful of supporters to maximum effect by staging demonstrations outside Sears stores in several parts of the country and in downtown Chicago in front of the Sears Tower itself. The boycott worked. While denying it was acting under pressure, Sears canceled its ads on *Three's Company* and *Charlie's Angels.*

Wildmon was on to something, but he needed help. In December 1980, he traveled to Lynchburg, Virginia, to enlist the Reverend Jerry Falwell, one of the most powerful ministers in the country. Falwell, a TV evangelist and the founder of the Liberty Baptist College, had just launched a campaign to persuade Christians to enter the battle for political righteousness. At a Washington press conference the year before, he had announced the formation of a new group, Moral Majority, to "fight the pornography, obscenity, vulgarity, profanity" that he claimed had taken over the public schools. During the Lynchburg meeting, Wildmon urged Falwell to join the fight to purify television. "The networks don't care about your moral values, but they do care about this," Wildmon said, holding up a dollar bill. "Great," Falwell said. "Let's go with it." Wildmon was exultant as he returned to his motel room. "Now I have the numbers," he recalled thinking. "Now I have the clout. After three years of wandering in the wilderness, I've found a road to the Promised Land."[5]

Two months later, in February 1981, Wildmon announced that two hundred organizations had formed the Coalition for Better Television (CBTV). In addition to Moral Majority, it had the support of Phyllis Schlafly, the founder of Eagle Forum, the organization that led the opposition to the Equal Rights Amendment, and Concerned Women of America. Those three groups alone had over three million members. Theoretically, these supporters would join in boycotting advertisers who sponsored the worst programming on television. The targets of the boycott were to be selected following three months of monitoring by four thousand members of the coalition. The monitors would rate the offending shows on the basis of "sex incidents per hour," scenes of violence, and uses of profanity.

Advertisers quailed at the threat of the impending boycott. Four months later, Wildmon told a reporter for the Associated Press that the CBTV crusade was having a major impact. "I've talked with six advertisers in the last week who have pulled 150 commercials off the air," he said. His most important convert was Owen B. Butler, the chairman of Procter and Gamble, the company that spent more on television annually than any other—nearly $500 million. In a speech to the Academy of Television Arts and Sciences, Butler announced that his company had withdrawn advertising from fifty television shows over the previous year. The threat of a boycott had been so successful that the boycott itself was called off. With Falwell and Schlafly looking on, Wildmon announced at a press conference that the boycott was no longer necessary because advertisers had promised CBTV officials that they would help restore moral values in television. But he warned that the CBTV still might institute a boycott if the new fall shows were objectionable.[6]

It was no surprise that a minister was leading a new crusade against television. Donald Wildmon was the latest in a long line of conservative clerics to warn of the dangers of corrupting art. But no one expected a feminist to become a leader in the antipornography movement. Catharine MacKinnon herself would not have predicted it. She was a radical and a feminist. The women's movement was such a powerful influence that MacKinnon postponed work on her Ph.D. in political science to enter Yale Law School, where she resolved to do something about the fact that the law had "nothing whatever to do with the problem of sexual inequality as it's experienced by women." On graduating from law school, MacKinnon started teaching Yale's first women's studies course. As a feminist, MacKinnon opposed censorship. She knew very well that Emma Goldman, Margaret Sanger, Mary Ware Dennett, and other feminist heroines had been prosecuted under the Comstock censorship law.[7]

MacKinnon changed her mind about censorship when the heady optimism of the early days of the new women's movement began to wane. Feminists suffered a number of serious defeats in the late 1970s. Only four years after giving women the right to abortion, the Supreme Court limited the effect of its ruling by declaring that the government could not be compelled to pay for the abortions of poor women. The fight for the Equal Rights Amendment was foundering. To many, it seemed that the women's movement itself was on the verge of collapse. It was during this period of disillusion that some feminists began to insist that violence against women was a bigger obstacle to sexual equality than child-rearing practices or job discrimination. Many feminists believed that sexually explicit material reinforced sexist attitudes, and a growing number were becoming convinced that it also incited rape. In 1976, Los Angeles feminists forced the removal of a billboard that used a picture of a battered woman to advertise the Rolling Stones' new album, *Black and Blue*. Three years later, Women against Pornography was formed in New York, launching the feminist antipornography movement.

MacKinnon was baffled by the failure of women to rally to her vision of feminism. The women's movement was uncovering new evidence every day that the problem of violence against women was far bigger than crime statistics indicated, but women were unmoved. In the face of all the facts, "the view that basically the sexes are equal in the society remains unchallenged and unchanged," MacKinnon insisted. Why was feminism on the ropes at the very moment when it should have been reaping a whirlwind of female anger? MacKinnon became convinced that pornography blinds women to their oppression by making sexual abuse seem normal. It brainwashes them.

> In pornography, there it is, in one place, all of the abuses that women had
> to struggle so long even to begin to articulate, all the unspeakable abuse:
> the rape, the battery, the sexual harassment, the prostitution, and the sex-
> ual abuse of children. Only in pornography it is called something else:
> sex, sex, sex, sex, and sex, respectively. Pornography sexualizes rape, bat-
> tery, sexual harassment, prostitution, and child sexual abuse; it thereby
> celebrates, promotes, authorizes and legitimizes them.

As a result, she argued, women actually desire sexual subordination.
"Men's power over women means that the way men see women
defines who women can be," she said. MacKinnon had rejected censorship because it had been used to oppress women. But she now believed that it could be a force for change: suddenly, it seemed that
only censorship could free the minds of women.[8]

The City of Minneapolis gave MacKinnon the opportunity to act
on her new convictions. In the fall of 1983, the city zoning commission was seeking ways to contain the spread of adult bookstores and
theaters. MacKinnon and Andrea Dworkin, who were teaching a
course on pornography at the University of Minnesota, were invited
to testify. The commissioners got more than they asked for. Dworkin
was a leader of the feminist antipornography movement. An iconoclast
who wore overalls to express her contempt for fashions that emphasized sex appeal, she blasted the commission for compromising with
the pornographers and told them that their definition of "pornography" was too narrow. "Women do not just encounter this degradation
in what you are calling adult bookstores. It's in supermarkets; it's in
all kinds of places that we go," Dworkin said. But the Supreme Court
had declared that sexually explicit material was protected by the First
Amendment unless it was obscene. MacKinnon offered the politicians a way out of this dilemma. She suggested that hearings might be
held at which experts would establish how pornography harms
women. Once the harm was proved, it could be shown that pornography was not speech at all but a form of sex discrimination that could
be banned as a violation of the civil rights of women. At least one
commission member who was also a member of the city council
thought the proposal a stroke of genius and agreed to introduce a bill
to pay MacKinnon and Dworkin for drafting an ordinance.[9]

The two women needed only five weeks to prepare the legislation that was submitted to the Minneapolis City Council. It authorized any woman to sue the producer or distributor of a pornographic work for "trafficking in pornography." "Pornography" was defined as "the sexually explicit subordination of women, graphically depicted, whether in pictures or words," and included one or more of nine elements:

> women . . . presented dehumanized as sexual objects, things or commodities; . . . presented as sexual objects who enjoy pain or humiliation; . . . presented as sexual objects who experience sexual pleasure in being raped; . . . presented as sexual objects tied up or cut up or mutilated or bruised or physically hurt; women's body parts are exhibited . . . such that women are reduced to those parts; women . . . presented as whores by nature; . . . presented being penetrated by objects or animals . . . presented in scenarios of degradation, injury, abasement, torture, shown as filthy or inferior, bleeding, bruised or hurt in a context that makes these conditions sexual.[10]

The MacKinnon-Dworkin ordinance was passed by the city council following a brief but bitter fight. With the help of between 100 and 200 active supporters, MacKinnon and Dworkin organized a campaign that forced the bill through the council. They handpicked the witnesses at a public hearing into the alleged harmfulness of sexually explicit material. Asked why critics of this view had not been allowed to testify, MacKinnon denied that there was another side to this issue. "Andrea Dworkin and I did not waste city council's resources with outdated and irrelevant data and investigations," she said. When Dworkin did debate the ordinance with a representative of the Minnesota Civil Liberties Union, her supporters booed the opposition. As the council began consideration of the ordinance, it came under heavy pressure from the activists. "We were lobbied very hard," council member Barbara Carlson, a feminist who opposed the ordinance, recalled. "You couldn't go to the bathroom without being lobbied. And we were hearing from people in California—movie stars. . . . We were just hysterical with this whole thing. . . . Their behavior toward anyone who dared to have an opposing view was appalling." When conventional methods of pressure didn't seem adequate, MacKinnon's supporters staged sit-down protests in the council chamber, which led to a number of arrests.

The ordinance was finally approved on a 7-6 vote following a last-minute switch by one member of the council. Mayor Donald Fraser vetoed the ordinance, but five months later the Indianapolis City Council overwhelmingly approved a nearly identical measure, and the mayor there enthusiastically signed it into law.[11]

Within minutes of its enactment in Indianapolis, the new law was challenged by the American Booksellers Association, the Association of American Publishers, magazine wholesalers and distributors, and a librarians' group, the Freedom to Read Foundation, who feared that it would result in the suppression of mainstream books, magazines, and movies. The plaintiffs argued that the terminology of the ordinance was inherently vague. Words like "pornography," "subordination," "graphic," "sexually explicit," "sexual objects," "humiliation," "abasement," "inferior," "conquest," "postures of servility or submission," and "women . . . being penetrated by objects" were subject to different interpretations. The ordinance could be applied to many popular movies, including *Dressed to Kill, 10, Swept Away, Last Tango in Paris*; books like John Updike's *Witches of Eastwick,* Anaïs Nin's *The Delta of Venus,* Ian Fleming's James Bond novels, and many of the books by best-selling authors like Sidney Sheldon, Judith Krantz, and Harold Robbins. The American Civil Liberties Union filed a supporting brief that argued that the definition of "pornography" was broad enough to include classics like *Tom Jones* and *The Arabian Nights,* and works by feminists Kate Millet and Susan Brownmiller. It could even be used to censor books that Andrea Dworkin had written, the ACLU said.

Three months later, U.S. District Court judge Sarah Evans Barker issued a decision in the case. Barker, who had recently been appointed by President Ronald Reagan, didn't disagree with the Indianapolis City Council's view "that pornography and sex discrimination are harmful, offensive and inimical," or that "some legislative controls are in order." But she rejected MacKinnon's argument that "pornography" is not speech and dismissed the contention that women were incapable of protecting themselves from either participating in or being victimized by it. As defined by the ordinance, "pornography" was clearly speech and therefore protected by the First Amendment. For that reason alone, the ordinance must fall, Barker said. She added another:

It ought to be remembered by defendants and all others who would support such a legislative initiative that, in terms of altering sociological
patterns, much as alteration may be necessary and desirable, free speech,
rather than being the enemy, is a long-tested and worthy ally. To deny
free speech in order to engineer social change in the name of accomplishing a greater good for one sector of our society erodes the freedoms
of all and, as such, threatens tyranny and injustice for those subjected to
the rule of law.

In the months ahead, as Indianapolis appealed Barker's decision,
many prominent feminists would announce their opposition to the
Indianapolis ordinance for the same reason. Nobody needed the
First Amendment more than feminists, they argued.[12]

MacKinnon was not the only antipornography crusader to encounter disappointment at this time. In late 1981, Wildmon decided
that a television boycott would be necessary after all. But Jerry Falwell disagreed. "Our feeling is that the networks have made a
significant effort to clean up their act," a spokesman for Falwell explained. The desertion by the Moral Majority forced Wildmon to
change his plans. Without the $2 million that Falwell had promised,
he could not buy the advertising he needed to target offending companies. Wildmon abandoned the proposed boycott of advertisers
and announced a boycott against RCA, the owner of NBC. Nine
months later, RCA reported that its third-quarter earnings were
$47.6 million, a $152 million increase over the previous year, when
it had shown a loss. Wildmon's critics celebrated the failure of his
boycott. Actor Tony Randall, whose show *Love, Sidney* was a target
of the National Federation for Decency, dismissed his nemesis as
"that ignorant, cynical, Bible-thumping ass in Mississippi."[13]

But Wildmon and MacKinnon were just getting started. It
helped to have friends in high places. In 1980, Wildmon and other
conservative activists had strongly supported the presidential candi-
dacy of Ronald Reagan because they believed that he would take
steps to curb sexually explicit material. They were disappointed
when during his first term Reagan focused almost exclusively on
economic and defense policies. Soon after Reagan's reelection,
Wildmon and his allies visited the president and persuaded him to
act. The result was the creation of the Attorney General's Commission on Pornography in 1985. Appointed by Attorney General Ed-

win Meese, the Meese Commission became an important vehicle for the views of Wildmon, MacKinnon, and other leaders of the antipornography movement. With a few exceptions, the commission was stacked with people who supported vigorous enforcement of the obscenity laws. The chairman was Henry Hudson, a former prosecutor who had made his reputation by prosecuting adult bookstores and movie theaters.

Wildmon did not waste his opportunity. At a public hearing in Los Angeles in October 1985, he told the Meese Commission that it must attack not only organized crime, reputed to be the biggest producer of "hard-core" obscenity, but also major corporations that were involved in the sale of nonobscene, First Amendment–protected material with sexual content. "The general public usually associates pornography with sleazy porno bookstores and theaters," Wildmon said. "However, many of the major players in the game of pornography are household names." Wildmon then proceeded to name them. The Southland Corporation, the owner of the 7-Eleven convenience store chain, was at the top of his list. Wildmon had launched a boycott of the chain the previous year in an effort to force it to stop selling *Playboy* and *Penthouse* magazines. He alleged that 22 other corporations were involved in "pornography distribution," including CBS, Time, Ramada Inns, RCA, and Coca-Cola. The list also included 3 national distributors of magazines, 11 chain stores, including Rite Aid and Dart Drug Stores, and a chain of video stores, National Video.[14]

Wildmon's testimony before the Meese Commission became national news when the commission sent a letter to the corporations on his list, informing them that they had been identified as distributors of "pornography" during testimony before the commission and inviting them to reply to the charge. Instead, several lawsuits were filed to force the commission to withdraw its letter. The American Booksellers Association, the Council for Periodical Distributors Associations, the Magazine Publishers of America, *Playboy,* and *Penthouse* accused the commission of attempting to pressure corporations to withdraw First Amendment–protected material. Threatening to identify them as pornographers amounted to putting them on a blacklist, they charged. A federal judge ordered the commission to retract the letter and barred it from issuing any lists of retailers.

Critics of the Meese Commission attempted to discredit it by pointing to Wildmon's role in inspiring the commission's letter. But supporters noted that the commission had support from both sides of the political spectrum, including the noted feminist Catharine MacKinnon. MacKinnon had given her usual flashy performance during testimony before the commission in Chicago—"biting off her words as if they were bottlecaps," according to Steve Chapman, a *Chicago Tribune* columnist. Chapman paid close attention to the words of a woman who had swayed the city councils of two major cities. "Serious people are obliged to take her seriously," he said.

> This isn't easy, given her fundamental absurdities. In the status quo, she claims, "the pornographers have credibility and rights and women do not." Pornography, she insists, merely "institutionalize(s) a subhuman, victimized, second-class status for women." She says her approach will be found constitutional if, for a change, the law is applied "as if women are human beings."

The Meese Commission embraced MacKinnon. It endorsed the Indianapolis ordinance despite the fact that a three-judge appeals court panel had unanimously upheld Barker's decision. It also thoroughly assimilated MacKinnon's language, condemning "non-violent materials depicting degradation, domination, subordination or humiliation." Not surprisingly, MacKinnon hailed the commission's work. "Today could be a turning point in women's rights," she said when the final report was released.[15]

The conservative antipornography groups certainly saw the Meese Commission report as a turning point. "No longer can the media or anyone else say that those opposing pornography are 'extreme right-wing fundamentalists,'" the Reverend Jerry Kirk, executive director of the National Coalition Against Pornography, wrote in August 1986. The fight had been "mainstreamed":

> Pornography is not a conservative or liberal issue. It is an issue for everyone who cares about the well-being of children, women, men and families. For some, it is a religious issue. For others, it is a moral issue. But for everyone, pornography is a public safety issue: the safety of our children from sexual abuse and molestation, our women from rape and degradation and our families from disease and disintegration.

Wildmon sought to appeal to this broadened constituency in 1988 by changing the name of his organization from the National Federation for Decency to the American Family Association (AFA). By 1992, the AFA's budget had grown by 40 percent to $7 million.[16]

Retailers quickly adjusted to the change in the political climate. The Southland Corporation, already embarrassed by the Wildmon boycott, decided not to wait for the commission's final report. Soon after receiving the commission's letter threatening to identify it as a distributor of pornography, it ordered its 4,500 7-Eleven stores to stop selling *Playboy* and *Penthouse* and recommended that 3,600 franchise stores do the same. Other Wildmon targets soon followed Southland's example. Within months, 6 of the chains that had received the Meese Commission letter and 34 smaller chains also decided to pull *Playboy* and *Penthouse*. By August 1986, 17,000 stores no longer carried the magazines. The removal of *Playboy, Penthouse,* and other men's magazines from stores across the country had a domino effect, leading retailers in some parts of the country to drop other controversial magazines, including magazines about rock and roll music, several teen magazines, the swimsuit issue of *Sports Illustrated,* and issues of *American Photographer* and *Cosmopolitan.*

Legislators and prosecutors around the country also jumped on the antipornography bandwagon. The commission had made a number of recommendations to the states, including raising penalties for the sale of obscene material. There was a surge in the number of obscenity bills being introduced in legislatures throughout the country. While the Meese Commission was still holding hearings, the North Carolina legislature passed a toughened obscenity law in late 1985. On May 29, 1986, prosecutors put it to the test, descending on the offices of PHE, Inc., one of the country's largest mail-order distributors of sexually explicit material. Between thirty and forty members of a joint state and federal task force swarmed into the building expecting to catch PHE employees engaged in illegal acts. They demanded to see the studios where "sex videos" were made. What they found instead was one hundred employees performing the mundane duties of order-taking and fulfillment. "They acted like it was a drug raid, and I guess we were a real disappointment to them," PHE's director of operations, Skip Loy, said. "I had to tell the officers, I said, there's no videos produced here. We just got things in boxes." Three months later, PHE and its owner, Philip D. Harvey, were indicted on nine counts of obscenity.[17]

Recordings also became a target. In 1985, at the urging of the Parents Music Resource Center, a group created by Elizabeth "Tipper" Gore, the wife of Tennessee senator Al Gore, the Senate Commerce Committee held hearings on the increasingly graphic sexual and violent content in rap and other popular forms of music. The music industry agreed to put warning labels on recordings that parents might find objectionable, but some law enforcement officials were not satisfied. In June 1988, Tommy Hammond, a record store owner in Alabama, was convicted of selling an album by the group 2 Live Crew. The sheriff of Broward County, Florida, warned retailers that they would face arrest for selling albums by 2 Live Crew. Not even museums were immune in the campaign against indecency. In 1990, Cincinnati museum director Dennis Barrie was prosecuted for obscenity and child pornography for exhibiting works by photographer Robert Mapplethorpe. Barrie was acquitted, and Hammond's conviction was reversed on appeal. But prosecutors had sent a clear message to retailers to watch their step.

The efforts of local prosecutors paled beside the ambition of a new division of the Justice Department, the National Obscenity Enforcement Unit (NOEU). Created at the recommendation of the Meese Commission, NOEU had been placed in the hands of a religious zealot, H. Robert Showers. Showers professed his Christianity loudly, even signing some of his official memos "Yours Truly in Christ." He opposed not just obscenity but all sexual material. Showers once told an attorney who represented a distributor of sexually explicit material that "almost anything that depicted any kind of nudity, particularly front nudity, male and female, and any sex act, was immoral and obscene." Under Showers, NOEU was openly sympathetic to antipornography groups like the Bay Area Citizens against Pornography, whose materials linked pornography with "Satanism." Thus, it was not a surprise when the Justice Department announced in July 1988 that it was launching a campaign, Operation PostPorn, to target the fourteen largest mail-order distributors of sexual material. Although the stated goal was to punish the companies for distributing obscene material, Justice Department officials made it clear to the owners of these businesses that they would not permit them to distribute even constitutionally protected material like *Playboy* and *The Joy of Sex*.[18]

Operation PostPorn employed a new weapon in the war on indecency. In 1985, Brent Ward, the U.S. attorney in Utah, had proposed to Meese that the Justice Department indict distributors of sexually explicit material in several jurisdictions at the same time. The goal, Ward said, was to "test the limits" of the companies' endurance by confronting them with enormous legal costs as well as compounding the jail time and fines that their owners potentially faced. "Multiple, simultaneous prosecutions at both federal and local levels . . . carry the potential to undermine profitability to the point that survival of the obscenity enterprises will be threatened," Ward explained. There was one problem. The *United States Attorney's Manual* specifically discouraged simultaneous multiple prosecutions because of the "unfairness associated with [them]." The legal system is supposed to guarantee the right of the accused to defend him- or herself during a trial. But who would risk going to trial when the potential fines were ruinous and jail terms rivaled those handed out to murderers? Nevertheless, the manual was rewritten to allow multiple prosecutions, although only in obscenity cases. Ward's prediction was quickly confirmed. Few of the distributors were prepared to fight. Although two made a brief effort to defend themselves, they soon joined at least five others in reaching a settlement with the Justice Department in which they agreed to close their businesses.[19]

The chilling effect of obscenity prosecutions was deepened by the activity of groups such as the American Family Association. The Meese Commission report had offered encouraging words to antipornography activists. Acknowledging that law enforcement could do nothing to curb the sale of sexually explicit material that was not obscene, the report advised people to use their First Amendment right to protest the sale of this material; picketing, distributing leaflets, and engaging in economic boycotts were all legitimate ways in which citizens could suppress material that they disliked. The AFA did not need prodding. Its most active local leaders, such as David Caton of Tampa, engaged in robust protests. Beginning in 1987, Caton led an imaginative campaign to drive men's magazines out of Florida. When demonstrations outside the businesses that sold the magazines failed to force their removal, Caton picketed the homes of the business owners and distributed flyers and "door-hangers" informing the neighbors that the smut peddler next door was promoting sexual abuse. He wrote the wife of one company owner and sent a letter to the local YMCA demanding the man's removal from its board of directors. Members of the Florida AFA visited video stores and convenience stores to ensure that they were complying with the law regulating the display of sexual material. Caton announced plans to send representatives to observe obscenity trials, where they would wear large red badges to demonstrate their support for the prosecution. Although Caton did not succeed in eliminating men's magazines even in Tampa, his harassing tactics led Waldenbooks, Playboy, and other businesses to sue him, creating a new controversy over whether they were violating his First Amendment rights.

While convenience stores took the brunt of these attacks, bookstores faced protests too. In the fall of 1988, two men entered the Bookman, a small bookstore in Grand Haven, Michigan, a resort community of twelve thousand on the banks of Lake Michigan. They approached Mary Dana, who owned the store with her husband, Jim, and identified themselves as members of the local AFA. They asked her to stop selling *Playboy* and *Penthouse* magazines, handing her a letter that strongly suggested that they had the support of the local police and that they would urge the police to prosecute the store if their demands were not met. Dana told the AFA "negotiating team" that the store would not remove the magazines. The Bookman was targeted in the next issue of the local AFA newsletter, and the Danas soon began to receive mimeographed cards from people who threatened to boycott the store unless it stopped selling "pornography." The Danas remained firm. "We believed that it was our job as booksellers to provide the full range of reading material to the community within the limits of the law," Jim Dana said later. "We were not going to remove anything."[20]

By the end of 1988, media companies had grown weary of the attacks by censorship groups. Many were frightened. It was the perfect atmosphere for Donald Wildmon to launch another assault on television. Even at the height of his fame in the late 1980s, Wildmon was not a household name, but he didn't need to be. His effectiveness lay in his ability to threaten advertisers with the charge of promoting immorality. In December, he created a new group, Christian

Leaders for Responsible Television (CLeaR-TV), and announced that it would boycott the worst advertiser at the conclusion of the sweeps period in May. The threat had an immediate effect: Kimberly-Clark and Tambrands announced they would not advertise on the show *Married . . . with Children*; Ralston Purina Company, General Mills, and Domino's Pizza canceled their ads on *Saturday Night Live*. Pepsi bowed to Wildmon's demand that it sever its connection with the singer Madonna because one of her music videos, *Like a Virgin,* used religious imagery that offended him. Wildmon's blast at a movie dramatization of the *Roe v. Wade* case, which the critics praised for its even-handed treatment of the abortion controversy, cost NBC as much as $1 million in lost advertising revenue.

In early 1989, Wildmon opened a new front in his war against indecency. He had learned that the National Endowment for the Arts (NEA) had provided funding for an exhibit that included a photograph entitled *Piss Christ*. The photograph, by Andres Serrano, depicted a crucifix submerged in a jar filled with the artist's urine. Wildmon immediately began a campaign against the NEA claiming that the tax dollars of the American people were being spent to support "pornographic, anti-Christian 'works of art.' " He sent a reproduction of the Serrano photograph to every member of Congress. Many were horrified. New York senator Alfonse D'Amato tore up the photograph on the Senate floor and denounced the NEA for funding "shocking, abhorrent art." Wildmon's attack was a smashing success. Congress barred the NEA from giving grants to artists whose work "might be deemed obscene." Artists successfully challenged the restriction as well as a second law requiring the NEA chair to ensure "respect for the diverse beliefs and values of the American people." But Congress continued to require the NEA to uphold "general standards of decency" when awarding grants.[21]

Groups like the ACLU, Freedom to Read Foundation, Media Coalition, National Coalition against Censorship, and People for the American Way worked hard to contain the threat posed by Wildmon, MacKinnon, and their supporters. They testified against bad legislation, filed lawsuits to challenge censorship laws, and undertook a number of important public relations initiatives. One of the most lasting efforts began in 1982, when librarians and booksellers celebrated the first Banned Books Week, which remains the only national event celebrating the freedom to read. The ACLU assigned one of its smartest spokesmen, Barry Lynn, to challenge the Meese Commission. A United Church of Christ minister who had given up the pulpit to attend law school, Lynn dogged the heels of the commission as it traveled from city to city, pointing out its flaws to the local press. The National Coalition against Censorship held a national conference, "The Meese Commission Exposed," during which leading writers and artists warned against the dangers of censorship. After Wildmon's attack on the NEA, both the ACLU and People for the American Way aggressively campaigned against censorship in arts funding. The ACLU created the Arts Censorship Project to coordinate its efforts.

More money was poured into the fight. The budget of Media Coalition, a media trade group that fought censorship legislation, tripled during the 1980s. The American Booksellers Association was particularly aggressive in beefing up its ability to respond to censorship threats. Throughout the 1980s, booksellers had strongly opposed the growing pressure for censorship. In 1986, they joined magazine wholesalers and distributors in founding Americans for Constitutional Freedom to oppose the recommendations of the Meese Commission. But in February 1989, their concern reached a new level when Iran's Ayatollah Ruhollah Khomeini issued a *fatwa* calling for the execution of Salman Rushdie, the author of *Satanic Verses,* a novel that many Muslims considered blasphemous. A number of bookstores around the world were firebombed, including two in Berkeley, California. The ABA responded to the crisis by establishing a task force on free expression that recommended the creation of a new organization, the American Booksellers Foundation for Free Expression. Arts organizations responded similarly to the crisis over the NEA, creating the National Campaign for Freedom of Expression to oppose content restrictions on NEA grants.

The anticensorship groups depended heavily on volunteers. Throughout the 1980s, publishers, librarians, booksellers, record and video store owners, writers, artists, and concerned citizens spoke out against censorship. They fought challenges to books in their local library, mounted displays during Banned Books Week, and wrote or joined amicus briefs in censorship cases. When the Meese Commission held its hearing in New York, it was picketed by women dressed as Keystone Kops who wore buttons identifying them as the "Sex Police." In 1990, two booksellers, an artist, and the owner of a mail-order business selling sexually explicit material won victories that helped turn the tide against the censorship forces.

By the summer of 1989, Jim and Mary Dana were beginning to believe that the threat of an economic boycott against their bookstore by members of the American Family Association had passed. The postcard campaign against them had finally ended in the spring, and AFA members had stopped writing regular letters to the local newspaper. Jim Dana was hoping that the local AFA chapter had folded for lack of interest when he read in the newspaper that the city council had given the AFA permission to hold an antipornography rally in the city's waterfront stadium. AFA members also persuaded the county commissioners to pass a resolution calling on citizens to join a letter-writing campaign and an economic boycott aimed at businesses that sold "pornography." The fight quickly became bitter. A member of the Danas' church who was also a customer published a letter to the editor in the local newspaper condemning them for profiting from the sale of pornography. Jim Dana attempted to defend himself, but the letters page was flooded with condemnations. "I was feeling beleaguered, angry and helpless," he said later.[22]

The Danas were not the only Michigan retailers in trouble. The Michigan AFA had been working hard to pass new legislation at the state level. Legislators had introduced twelve obscenity bills that covered everything on the Meese Commission's wish list and more. There was a new definition of "obscenity" that was significantly broader than the one approved by the U.S. Supreme Court. There were also draconian penalties for the sale of obscene material, including four years in jail and a fine of $100,000 for a first offense, and a bill inspired by the MacKinnon ordinance. When Jim Dana testified against the legislation, the hearing room was overflowing with antipornography activists, who booed him and the lobbyist for the ACLU. The committee unanimously approved the legislation and sent it to the Senate floor.

Dana returned home determined to mobilize his community against the legislation. He had already taken several steps to build local support for his store in the battle with the AFA, including offering a petition that simply said the signers did not want other people deciding what they could read. After the hearing, he added language condemning the legislation. A newsstand down the street started offering the petition, too, and the video store joined the campaign. Soon individuals, including teachers and librarians, began to circulate the petition among their friends. The Danas sent a letter to the people who had signed their petition urging them to write to or phone their legislators. Dana also issued a call to booksellers throughout the state to meet for the purpose of organizing opposition to the censorship package. A dozen booksellers created the Michigan Booksellers Association, which would eventually represent more than 140 bookstores.

National groups representing booksellers, publishers, librarians, and video store owners eagerly joined the Michigan battle. As defenders of free speech, they worried about the most extreme proposals, including the change in the definition of "obscenity" and third-party liability. But they also saw the Michigan legislation as an opportunity to undertake a public campaign. The AFA had achieved its victories by threatening to denounce advertisers, retailers, legislators, and even members of Congress as "pro-pornography." But the anticensorship groups believed that if they could frame the issue as a fight for free speech, identifying the AFA as "pro-censorship," they could win public support. In December 1989, Oren J. Teicher, the executive director of Americans for Constitutional Freedom (ACF), wrote a memo outlining a direct mail campaign to kick off the Michigan fight. Besides defeating bad legislation, the campaign would assist in "developing tactics that will be of value in subsequent campaigns," Teicher said. The opening gun was fired on February 15, 1990, when ACF mailed twenty-five thousand letters to Michigan residents urging them to lend their names to the fight against the censorship package.[23]

Wildmon seemed to have little to fear. He was riding high on the success of his attack on the National Endowment for the Arts, and in April he discovered another NEA grant that he was sure he could turn to his advantage. One of his supporters had sent him the catalog for an exhibition that had opened in January at Illinois State University in Normal, Illinois. The works were by a young artist, David Wojnarowicz, who was not nearly as successful as Robert

Mapplethorpe or Andres Serrano, Wildmon's first targets. Wojnarowicz, who worked in a variety of mediums, had made only $15,000 from the sale of his works in 1988 and $34,000 in 1989. But in other ways, Wojnarowicz was an ideal target. He was homosexual and appeared hostile to religion. One of the works in the Illinois exhibition showed Jesus injecting heroin into his arm. In addition, Wojnarowicz had incorporated small, sexually explicit images into several of his collages. The university had used a $15,000 grant from the NEA to help pay for the exhibition. Wildmon didn't need to know anything more. He had the sexually explicit images enlarged, and he incorporated them along with the image of the drug-abusing Christ into a pamphlet titled *Your Tax Dollar Helped Pay for These "Works of Art."* In an envelope that carried the warning "Caution —Contains Extremely Offensive Material," Wildmon mailed his pamphlet to 523 members of Congress, 3,230 Christian leaders, 947 Christian radio stations, and 1,578 newspapers.[24]

Wildmon reaped the anticipated windfall of publicity, but he also got something he didn't expect—a legal fight. Wojnarowicz had been an angry young man even before Wildmon held him up to national ridicule. Art had helped him overcome a troubled youth, part of which he had spent homeless, prostituting himself to live. AIDS was killing his friends at a rapid rate. Then, in 1989, he learned that he also had the AIDS virus. His anger at government officials for not doing more to fight the disease was clear in many of the works that were shown in the Illinois exhibition. It was why the exhibit was called Tongues of Flame. Now, he had a new target for his anger. Wojnarowicz sued Wildmon in U.S. District Court in New York for defamation and copyright infringement and sought a court order blocking further distribution of the pamphlet. Wojnarowicz charged that Wildmon had turned his art into "banal pornography" by taking eleven sexually explicit images from larger works and representing them as the artworks themselves. In June, Judge William C. Conner dismissed Wojnarowicz's libel and copyright claims on First Amendment grounds. But he condemned Wildmon's pamphlet as a violation of a New York artists' rights law, which prohibits the mutilation of original works of visual art. "Defendants' distribution of a pamphlet, suggesting that plaintiff's work consists of sexually explicit images, has irreparably harmed plaintiff's professional and personal reputation," Conner declared. He issued an injunction blocking further distribution of the pamphlet and ordered Wildmon to communicate corrective information to everyone who had received it. Wojnarowicz failed in his effort to win significant damages. The judge awarded him only $1 because Wojnarowicz could not prove that Wildmon's attack had hurt the sale of his works. But he had won an important victory. He had shown that Wildmon could be stopped. Only three weeks later, the antipornography movement suffered a serious loss when another determined man succeeded in stripping the federal government of its most potent weapon in the war against indecency.[25]

Phil Harvey, the owner of PHE, Inc., had been engaged in a desperate struggle with law enforcement since 1987, when he was indicted on state obscenity charges in North Carolina. Despite his acquittal, federal authorities had continued to threaten him with prosecution. He was one of the main targets of the Justice Department's multiple-prosecutions strategy, and the government expected him to fold under the threat of a long jail term and heavy fines. But Harvey was different from the distributors who quit. For them, selling sexually oriented material was a business. Harvey had entered the business in 1970 as an outgrowth of his interest in family planning. He had become interested in the issue of population growth during the five years he spent in India distributing food as part of the CARE program. Convinced that only birth control would improve the standard of living in underdeveloped countries, he returned to the United States to study family planning administration. As part of his graduate work, he had started a business distributing condoms by mail. At a time when condoms were still difficult to obtain, PHE filled a real need, and business boomed. As the company began to experiment with other kinds of products, including sexually oriented books, magazines, and videos, Harvey and his employees discussed how far they wanted to go. "'Do we want to do this?' was a question that came up frequently," Harvey recalls. The answer was clear, particularly when PHE employees considered the alternative of working for the tobacco companies that dominated the local economy. "The difference, strongly felt by many employees at PHE, is that our products do not harm, and indeed, seem to be of real benefit," Harvey said.[26]

Harvey was principled, but he was also cautious. Bruce Ennis, a

Washington attorney and former legal director of the ACLU, urged him to go on the offensive, filing a civil suit to challenge the constitutionality of the multiple-prosecutions strategy and expose the government's ulterior motive of suppressing legally protected sexual material. However, Harvey's legal team in North Carolina urged him not to do anything to anger the government as they negotiated an agreement that they hoped would forestall further indictments. That strategy was abandoned in early 1990, when the Justice Department announced that it was going to bring another mail-order retailer to trial in Virginia, North Carolina, and two districts in Alabama over an eight-week period. Harvey and his lawyers concluded that he would be next. In March, PHE sued the Justice Department in federal court in Washington, accusing government attorneys of conspiring to suppress the sale of legal material with sexual content and attempting to coerce him into abandoning his First Amendment rights. On July 23, Judge Joyce Hens Green agreed, declaring the multiple-prosecution strategy unconstitutional and enjoining the government from prosecuting Harvey in more than one place at a time. She also agreed that the government was engaged in a conspiracy to suppress the sale of legally protected material.

Meanwhile, the antipornography movement in Michigan had stalled. A new group, the Michigan Intellectual Freedom Coalition, was beginning to roll out a public campaign whose centerpiece was a petition drive being conducted in bookstores, video stores, and theaters throughout the state. To support the petitions, the coalition produced an anticensorship trailer starring author and radio personality Garrison Keillor. Keillor had recently testified in Congress on behalf of the NEA, and part of his testimony was used for the trailer. "My ancestors were Puritans who came here from England in 1648," Keillor said as the trailer began. "I'm a Puritan myself and I see a lot every day that is offensive to me but like most Americans I oppose censorship and suppression—it's wrong and it just never works. . . . Censorship can't eliminate evil, it can only kill freedom." By July, the Keillor trailer was showing in more than two hundred theaters, and over five hundred video stores were displaying it as a segment on a tape of coming attractions. Forty thousand people signed the petition in a matter of months. In October, the Michigan Intellectual Freedom Coalition declared victory when the state legislature recessed without approving any new obscenity laws.[27]

The issue of pornography and women's rights almost immediately reasserted itself, however. In 1986, the U.S. Supreme Court had rejected Indianapolis's final appeal in *American Booksellers Assn. v. Hudnut,* summarily affirming the decisions in the lower courts. Nevertheless, in February 1991, Senator Robert Dole of Kansas introduced the Pornography Victims' Compensation Act, authorizing the victim of a sex crime to sue the producer and distributor of material that is both "sexually explicit" and "violent" if the material was "a proximate cause" of the crime. The MacKinnon ordinance was broader than the Pornography Victims' Compensation Act, but the provisions of the federal bill were still breathtaking. Like the MacKinnon ordinance, it targeted speech that was protected by the First Amendment, making producers and distributors of legal works liable for the crimes committed by others. Random House, which had just published Brett Easton Ellis's controversial novel *American Psycho,* could be sued by the victim of an assault "inspired" by the book, as could the retailer who sold it to the attacker. The shift of responsibility from the criminal to the publisher or bookseller was symbolized by a provision allowing the criminal himself to testify on what role the "pornographic" material had played in his crime. In April, Senator Mitch McConnell of Kentucky introduced an even broader version of the bill, omitting the requirement that the material be violent.

Despite the radicalism of the Pornography Victims' Compensation Act, its prospects for passage appeared good. An antipornography bill had passed in each of the previous election years, and to many veteran lobbyists it seemed that Congress would approve the bill in time for the 1992 elections. Media groups responded strongly. Eighteen trade associations presented a legal memo to the Senate Judiciary Committee demonstrating that third-party liability was a drastic departure from legal tradition, which would weaken the ability of the courts to hold criminals responsible for their crimes. However, opposition only strengthened the bill at first. McConnell introduced a substitute measure on the eve of a committee hearing in July that applied only to obscene material. Since a majority of the committee members were cosponsors, its approval seemed certain.

A number of media groups dropped their objections to the Pornography Victims' Compensation Act after it was narrowed to apply only to obscene material, but booksellers, publishers, librarians, magazine wholesalers and distributors, and video retailers remained strongly opposed. Knowing that the line between obscene and nonobscene is vague and shifting, they feared that the threat of third-party liability would lead retailers to stop selling any work that might trigger a lawsuit, including books, magazines, and videos that had serious literary and artistic merit. Soon, they discovered that members of the Judiciary Committee agreed with them, particularly its chairman, Senator Joseph Biden of Delaware. More surprising was the support they received from a Republican from Colorado, Hank Brown. Brown came under heavy pressure from Focus on the Family, a conservative group that was headquartered in Colorado Springs. However, both he and Biden were determined to introduce amendments that would minimize the chilling effect of the law. They raised questions during hearings that defeated hopes for a quick victory and gave critics of the bill a chance to organize.

In September 1991, Americans for Constitutional Freedom released *Sense and Censorship,* a pamphlet that argued there is no credible scientific evidence that sexually explicit material causes violence against women. The same argument was made humorously in a *New York Times* op-ed in January 1992. Written by Joe Teller, the normally silent half of a comedy team, Penn and Teller, the piece burlesqued the notion that "if we stop showing rape in movies people will stop committing it in real life":

> Give us a break! When one pays $7 to go into a theater to see big pictures moving on a wall, one does not have to be a mental giant to realize you are watching a movie. It makes you wonder how they explain the millions of people who saw "Psycho" without stealing bankrolls or bumping off blondes.

When people started laughing at the Pornography Victims' Compensation Act, its opponents knew they had a chance to kill it.[28]

The death blow was delivered not by media groups or a growing chorus of editorial writers but by feminists. Since 1983, Catharine MacKinnon and her followers had tried to portray themselves as representing the views of most feminists, but anticensorship feminists had fought back. In the Indianapolis case, a group called the Feminist Anti-Censorship Task Force filed an important amicus brief. Other feminists protested that the issue of pornography was distracting women from the fight against the real sources of sexual inequal-

ity in American society, and warned against the danger of making a
political alliance with conservatives who obviously opposed the major goals of the women's movement. The fight against the Pornography Victims' Compensation Act revealed that many American
feminists remained strongly opposed to censorship. While the national board of the National Organization of Women did not take a
position on the bill, five state chapters, including New York and
California, announced their opposition. In February 1992, the Ad
Hoc Committee of Feminists for Free Expression sent a letter to the
Judiciary Committee signed by 180 prominent women, including
Betty Friedan, Adrienne Rich, Judy Blume, Nora Ephron, Erica
Jong, Susan Isaacs, and Jamaica Kincaid. "[S. 1521] scapegoats speech
as a substitute for action against violence," the letter read. "Rape,
battery and child molestation are vicious crimes that this nation
should take every measure to eliminate. But S. 1521 will do crime
victims more harm than good."[29]

The Pornography Victims' Compensation Act was finally approved by the Judiciary Committee in June, but its fate had been
sealed. Not even MacKinnon was supporting it. In fact, she had
never endorsed the bill because it was confined to obscenity, and
she had always argued that the definition of harmful material should
include all sexually explicit material depicting the subordination
of women. Nevertheless, the failure of the Pornography Victims'
Compensation Act marked the final defeat of MacKinnon's effort to
convert the women's movement to censorship. The letter of the
Feminists for Free Expression closed with words that were clearly
addressed to MacKinnon and her followers:

> It is no goal of feminism to restrict individual choices or stamp out sex-
> ual imagery.... It is the right and responsibility of each woman to read,
> view or produce the sexual material she chooses without the interven-
> tion of the state "for her own good." We believe genuine feminism en-
> courages individuals to make these choices for themselves. This is the
> great benefit of being feminists in a free society.

MacKinnon was unrepentant. "The law of equality and the law of
free speech are on a collision course in this country," she wrote in
1993, ten years after she introduced her antipornography ordinance.

But her legal theory had been discredited, and her political influence had been greatly diminished.[30]

The antipornography movement still possessed one powerful issue—child protection—and in 1996 it used the strong popular support for keeping kids safe to pass two bills that seriously threatened free speech. The Communications Decency Act (CDA) was the first effort by Congress to censor the burgeoning Internet. The nation's lawmakers had little understanding of the complexities of this new electronic medium, which almost overnight had grown from a small network of computer "geeks" into a vast shopping mall. The Internet was also an outlet for an enormous amount of information provided by government, universities, and nonprofit groups. The miracle of this new medium was its interactivity, its ability to bring people all over the world together through e-mail, automated mailing lists, and chat rooms. Congress didn't understand any of this, but it had heard that children were being exposed to sexually explicit material on the Internet, and that was all it needed to know. It banned the posting of any "indecent" or "patently offensive" material anywhere that minors could see it. The Supreme Court made short work of the CDA, ruling in a near-unanimous decision in 1997 that the law was unconstitutional because it forced the removal of material that adults were entitled to see.[31]

The second law involved child pornography and was a far more difficult target. The Supreme Court had approved laws banning the sale of child pornography in 1982 to prevent children from being used in the production of sexually explicit material. But the Child Pornography Prevention Act that was introduced in 1996 went far beyond what the Supreme Court had approved in that case, *Ferber v. New York*. It banned any material that appeared to depict minors engaged in sexual conduct, including movies in which adults portrayed minors; drawings and paintings of minors; and any work that showed the breast or buttocks of a female minor. In a hearing by the Senate Judiciary Committee, Judith F. Krug, the director of the American Library Association's Office for Intellectual Freedom, objected that the bill would outlaw an enormous amount of First Amendment–protected material. Adults had appeared as minors in hundreds of films involving sexual conduct or nudity, including *Cleopatra, The Last Picture Show, Midnight Cowboy, The Prime of Miss Jean Brodie, Car-*

rie, and *Equus.* Depictions of nude children in art ranged from an ad
for Coppertone suntan lotion in which a little girl's bathing suit is
being pulled down by a dog to classic works of art by Donatello,
Correggio, Titian, Degas, and Picasso. There were flashes of the
naked breasts or buttocks of minors in many films, including Zef-
firelli's *Romeo and Juliet* and Louis Malle's *Pretty Baby.* Although the
bill's sponsors agreed to remove the ban on breasts and buttocks as
well as to exempt classic art, the version of the Child Pornography
Prevention Act that was approved by Congress remained a dangerous
departure from the *Ferber* standard.[32]

It was only a matter of time before antipornography activists
seized upon the expanded definition of child pornography. In August 1997, Randall Terry, a political organizer who had made a reputation in the antiabortion movement, announced that he would
lead a campaign to force the nation's biggest bookstore chains to stop
selling the works of Jock Sturges, an acclaimed photographer who
often took pictures of nude people, including minors. Sturges's work
did not portray sexual conduct, but Terry and his supporters considered almost any picture of a nude child pornographic. They held
demonstrations at more than twenty bookstores around the country. In New York City, Dallas, Denver, Omaha, and Kansas City,
the demonstrators entered the bookstores and destroyed copies of
Sturges's books. At the same time, Focus on the Family urged its
members to pressure the police to file child pornography charges
against their local Barnes and Noble and Borders stores. The tactic
worked. In Tennessee, Barnes and Noble was indicted for displaying
material that is "harmful to minors" because it sold Sturges's books
in a place where minors could see them. In Alabama, the chain was
charged with the sale of child pornography. Barnes and Noble and
Borders refused to stop selling the books, but the potentially chilling effect of a broad definition of child pornography was becoming
clear. In 2002, the Supreme Court declared the Child Pornography
Prevention Act unconstitutional in a 7-2 decision. Justice Anthony
Kennedy's majority opinion marked the emergence of the Court's
strongest defender of First Amendment rights since the retirement of
William Brennan.

Free speech advocates did not have high hopes for Kennedy
when Ronald Reagan appointed him to the Supreme Court in 1988.
A former law professor, he had been a conservative on the gener-

ally liberal Ninth Circuit Court of Appeals. His first Supreme Court decision involving First Amendment rights seemed to confirm the conventional wisdom when he joined the majority in affirming the constitutionality of expanding the federal Racketeer Influenced and Corrupt Organization (RICO) law to include obscenity offenses, increasing the penalties that could be imposed. Two years later, Kennedy again voted with the majority in upholding a restriction on nude dancing, rejecting the claim that it was a form of artistic expression and therefore entitled to First Amendment protection. Yet, less than a year after joining the Court, Kennedy had also joined in a surprising and controversial decision that upheld the right of protesters to burn the American flag.

In 1994, Kennedy demonstrated that he was willing to lead the opposition to censorship measures. In the case of *Alexander v. U.S.,* the court was asked to decide whether the mandatory forfeiture provision of the RICO law could be applied to obscenity crimes. The majority upheld a lower-court order that forced Ferris J. Alexander to surrender his interest in the businesses that had been convicted of obscenity offenses as well as $9 million in illegal profits. Kennedy was concerned. While he had not opposed the increase in fines and jail terms available under RICO, the forfeiture penalty gave the government the power to close a business that was disseminating ideas that it disliked. Kennedy said that this appeared to be exactly what the Meese Commission had wanted when it recommended the use of RICO to the states. "The Court's decision is a grave repudiation of First Amendment principles," he wrote. "This ominous, onerous threat undermines free speech and press principles essential to our personal freedom."[33]

Kennedy's opinion in the case challenging the Child Pornography Prevention Act, *Ashcroft v. Free Speech Coalition,* began with a review of the history of the 1982 *Ferber* case. By upholding a law banning the production and sale of all material that depicted a minor engaged in sex acts or "lascivious" display of their genitals, the Supreme Court had created a new exception to the First Amendment. Whatever artistic merit these works might contain was outweighed by the harm done to the children who were used to produce them, the Court declared in *Ferber.* At the time, the Association of American Publishers and others warned that removing First Amendment protection from these materials threatened the ability of producers and distributors to disseminate works of serious value that dealt with the subject of youth and sexuality, including sex education material. But the Court rejected this argument, stating that for these purposes producers could use adults who appeared to be children. The Child Pornography Prevention Act (CPPA) flew in the face of this distinction between real child pornography and material that only appeared to depict children.

Kennedy reaffirmed that the central purpose of *Ferber* was protecting children from being harmed in the production of sexually explicit material. By extending the scope of the laws to include images of people who appear to be minors, Congress had exceeded its authority to protect children and censored an idea. "The statute proscribes the visual depiction of an idea—that of teenagers engaging in sexual activity—that is a fact of modern society and has been a theme in art and literature throughout the ages," Kennedy wrote. He noted that there had been at least forty film treatments of the story of Romeo and Juliet, some of which implied that the teenagers (Juliet is only thirteen) had sex. Kennedy also pointed out that the last two films to win the Academy Award for Best Picture, *American Beauty* and *Traffic,* had depicted sexual conduct by teenagers. Under the provisions of the CPPA, however, everyone involved in the production of these films could be sentenced to fifteen years in jail. "With these severe penalties in force, few legitimate movie producers or book publishers, or few other speakers in any capacity, would risk distributing images in or near the uncertain reach of this law," Kennedy said.[34]

Kennedy's opinion leaned heavily on the precedents that the Supreme Court had established over the previous five decades to protect speech with sexual content. The government argued that sexually explicit material was being used to seduce children. But Kennedy observed that the Supreme Court had ruled in 1957 that government cannot ban publications because of their tendency to "incite minors to violent or depraved or immoral acts" because doing so "would reduce the adult population . . . to reading only what is fit for children." The government had also insisted that it was necessary to curb this material because it incited pedophiles. But there was no proof of this, Kennedy said. As a result, the law ran afoul of a 1969 case that declared that government "cannot constitutionally premise legislation on the desirability of controlling a person's private thoughts." Kennedy added his own summary of the principle that the Supreme Court had defined and defended in its First Amendment cases. "The right to think is the beginning of freedom, and speech must be protected from the government because speech is the beginning of thought," he said. Supporters of the law complained loudly. In 2002, Donald Wildmon and his allies were still feared by some. Sixteen years after the Meese Commission, 7-Eleven and many other convenience store chains still didn't carry *Playboy* and *Penthouse*. But Kennedy's opinion was compelling evidence that the thirty-year-old effort to restore the government's role in protecting its citizens from "immoral" media had failed.[35]

9/11

The day was as gloomy as the mood of the nation. Yet we arrived in Washington on April 26, 2002, full of hope that we could draw attention to the rapidly proliferating threats to free speech in the wake of the devastating terrorist attacks on September 11, 2001. We were disappointed that it was rainy. We were forced to cancel our plan to hold the event outdoors, with a clear view of the Capitol in the background—for the television cameras that we hoped would appear. Instead, we met in a huge and dimly lit hearing room in the Hart Senate Office Building, which was one of the buildings that had been temporarily closed by the anthrax attacks in the fall. But we still had confidence in our plan. We would hold a press conference sponsored by some of the most prominent free expression groups in the country, including the ACLU, the National Coalition against Censorship, and People for the American Way, as well as a number of smaller groups, including my own, the American Booksellers Foundation for Free Expression. The news conference was scheduled to mark a significant occasion. On April 26, the USA Patriot Act, a law that gave the federal government broad new powers to conduct secret surveillance, was six months old.[1]

We didn't miss a thing in our planning. We had drafted a statement that provided a detailed overview of the new dangers to free speech. We had worked to secure important speakers, including the executive director of the Reporters Committee for Freedom of the Press, who we felt sure would help draw reporters alarmed by government restrictions on their efforts to cover the detention of more than one thousand Muslim men as well as the war in Afghanistan. Representative Patsy Mink of Hawaii would speak of her fear that the country was on a path leading to civil liberties abuses similar to the internment of Japanese Americans during World War II. We felt our strongest draw would be Wisconsin senator Russ Feingold, the man who had risked his political career by casting the sole vote against the Patriot Act in the Senate. We were encouraged when, several days before the press conference, the *Baltimore Sun* published an editorial based on our statement. The editorial asked exactly the right question. "If the heinous acts of Sept. 11 prompt us to abandon the very liberties essential to our democracy, what are we fighting for?" it read. But the editorial turned out to be our main achievement. When the press conference started, we could see only one reporter. There was no coverage in any major newspaper the next day. After all our hard work, we weren't just disappointed—we were embarrassed.[2]

But appearances were deceiving. By late April 2002, there was a growing concern around the country that in responding to the 9/11 attacks, the federal government was sacrificing civil liberties to national security, committing the same mistake it had made during World War I, World War II, and the cold war. It had already stirred the ghost of the Palmer Raids by pulling more than one thousand Muslim men off the streets and holding them incommunicado. Yet the worst civil liberties abuses were avoided. Although the administration of George W. Bush would repeatedly threaten civil liberties by seeking ever-broader powers to fight terrorism, it would be opposed by scores of individuals and organizations that were determined to strike a balance between individual freedom and national security. Unknown to us as we met in the cavernous room in the Hart Building, a grass-roots movement had been born on January 7, 2002, when the city council in Ann Arbor, Michigan, passed a resolution declaring its intention to protect the due process and equal protection rights of the immigrants living in their community. Twenty-two other cities would pass civil liberties resolutions by the end of the year. The battle moved on to the national stage in 2003 as legislation amending the worst features of the USA Patriot Act was introduced in Congress. The campaign to reform the Patriot Act came to a climax in late 2005, when differences over adding civil liberties protections created a deadlock between the House and the Senate. By then, we had won the battle for the public's attention. Hundreds of thousands of Americans were actively opposing the threats to free speech.

In the days after the 9/11 attacks, Americans were transfixed by the sight of the collapsing World Trade Center as it was endlessly re-broadcast on television. Residents of New York and Washington also heard the sounds of fighters patrolling overhead. In the subways, soldiers stood guard with automatic weapons. Vermont senator Patrick Leahy, the chairman of the Senate Judiciary Committee, would later recall the mood of the people he encountered as he took long walks around the Capitol in an effort to collect himself. "I saw the same faces as I did when I was a law school student [in Washington] and President Kennedy had been killed," Leahy said. "I saw the same shock, and I wanted to make sure our shock didn't turn into panic." But Leahy was having a difficult time controlling his own emotions. On the day of the attacks, he watched a F-16 fighter fly low over the city. "I was just thinking how angry I was," he recalled.[3]

Most Americans shared Leahy's anger and wanted to strike back at the terrorists. This meant not only supporting American troops as they fought to overthrow the Taliban in Afghanistan but attacking anyone who questioned the national security policies of President George W. Bush. Bush's approval rating in the polls, which had languished since the disputed 2000 election, now stood at close to 90 percent, and those who didn't understand—or ignored—the dramatic swing in the country's mood soon suffered for it. Comedian Bill Maher outraged many Americans when he said on his television show that piloting airliners into the World Trade Center was braver than firing missiles into Afghanistan. But far less offensive remarks had similar consequences. Editors at two weekly newspapers were fired for columns and editorials accusing Bush of cowardice because he did not immediately return to Washington after the attacks. "The opinion piece . . . was not appropriate to publish during this time our country and our leaders find themselves in," the publisher of the *Texas City Sun* explained in a front-page editorial.[4]

The mood was ugly on college campuses as well. On the morning of the 9/11 attacks, Richard Berthold, a history professor at the University of New Mexico, jokingly told his class, "Anyone who can blow up the Pentagon gets my vote." Some of his students were horrified, and so were university administrators. They promptly suspended him. "It was a stupid thing to say," Berthold quickly acknowledged. But conservative critics thought the problem went considerably deeper than bad jokes. They had long believed that the nation's colleges and universities had become a haven for left-wing academics, and a number of professors seemed to confirm this in commenting on the attacks. "[The terrorist attack] was no more despicable than the massive acts of terrorism...that the U.S. government has committed during my lifetime," a journalism professor at the University of Texas at Austin said. A mathematics professor at the City University of New York charged that "the ultimate responsibility lies with the rulers of this country, the capitalist ruling class."[5]

Conservative groups took advantage of the public mood by attacking dissenters as disloyal. In November, the American Council of Trustees and Alumni (ACTA) denounced professors as "the weak link in America's response to terrorism" because they were pointing "accusatory fingers, not at the terrorists, but at America itself." They published a report that listed 117 allegedly anti-American statements made on college campuses in recent weeks, including the statements by the professors at the University of Texas and City University of New York. The report also cited calls for building "bridges and relationships, not simply bombs and walls," and for creating an international tribunal to try Osama bin Laden. Wasima Alilkhan of the Islamic Academy of Las Vegas was added to the list for saying "ignorance breeds hate." Several months later, a new group, Americans for Victory over Terrorism, expanded the list of people "who are attempting to use this opportunity to promulgate their agenda of 'blame American first'" to include legislators, authors, and columnists. Even former president Jimmy Carter made the list for criticizing President Bush's use of the phrase "axis of evil" as "overly simplistic and counter-productive." "We do not wish to silence people," William Bennett, the leader of the new group, insisted. But those on the receiving end of the criticism disagreed. "Their aim is to enforce a particular party line," Eric Foner, a Columbia University professor, said, referring to the American Council of Trustees and Alumni study. "Now they're seizing upon this particular moment and the feeling that they're in the driver's seat to suppress the expression of alternative points of view." Hugh Guterson, one of the professors on the list, accused ACTA of creating a new blacklist. "It has a little whiff of McCarthyism," he said.[6]

As in the past, the greatest threat to free speech came not from individuals or private groups but from government. From its inception, the administration of George W. Bush had been strongly inclined toward expanding the power of the executive branch in ways that undermined First Amendment rights. Dick Cheney, the new vice president, had served as an assistant to President Gerald Ford and had long believed that the post-Watergate reforms had critically weakened the presidency. "For the 35 years that I've been in this town, there's been a constant, steady erosion of the prerogatives and the powers of the president of the United States, and I don't want to be a part of that," Cheney told an NBC interviewer in January 2003. The measures that opened government to greater public scrutiny were clearly part of the problem. As one Bush administration insider observed, it was "a matter of theology that we the people have made the White House too open and too accountable." Cheney acted on this conviction in 2001 when the Government Accountability Office, the investigating arm of Congress, asked him to reveal whether any representatives of the oil industry were participating in meetings of the energy task force that he chaired. Cheney refused to comply on the grounds that the president and his staff have "a zone of autonomy in obtaining advice." The early months of the Bush administration also saw a struggle over the Presidential Records Act, a 1978 law that provided that with the exception of material affecting national security, all presidential records would be released to the public twelve years after the end of an administration. Ronald Reagan's papers were to become public in January 2001, but the Bush administration delayed their release while it crafted an executive order that would potentially severely restrict public access by giving both the sitting president and former presidents greater discretion to withhold documents.[7]

The 9/11 attacks gave the Bush administration a powerful rationale for expanding government secrecy, and it acted quickly to cloak crucial aspects of its newly declared "war on terrorism." It refused to release any information about the more than one thousand Muslim men that it had arrested in the days after the attacks. Guilty of nothing except being citizens of Arab countries, the men were arrested without warning, disappearing into jails all over the United States, where they were sometimes beaten by prison guards who sought revenge against the "terrorists." None was charged with terrorism. Nevertheless, the Justice Department refused to allow them to contact their families or hire lawyers. It also barred the press from attending the administrative hearings that would determine whether the men were expelled from the United States. On October 12, Attorney General John Ashcroft encouraged federal officials to embrace secrecy, not just in national security matters but in all of their affairs. In a memo to the heads of all federal departments and agencies, Ashcroft explained that while the administration was committed to "full compliance" with the Freedom of Information Act (FOIA), it was "equally committed to protecting other fundamental values that are held by our society," including "safeguarding our national security, [and] enhancing the effectiveness of our law enforcement agencies." Therefore, federal officials should give "full and deliberate consideration of the institutional, commercial and personal privacy interests that could be implicated by disclosure" before releasing documents. They should also not worry about being second-guessed when they decided to deny FOIA requests. "You can be assured that the Department of Justice will defend your decisions unless they lack a sound legal basis," Ashcroft concluded.[8]

By mid-October, the attorney general was fast emerging as the leader of the effort to expand the government's power to fight terrorism. Ashcroft had been Bush's most controversial cabinet choice. He was a skilled politician who had been attorney general and governor of Missouri and had served one term in the Senate, but his record on civil liberties and civil rights was not strong. As attorney general of Missouri, he had once sued the National Organization for Women for boycotting Missouri over its failure to pass the Equal Rights Amendment. The courts rejected his suit because it threatened free speech. But it was his opposition to a plan to integrate the St. Louis schools and his attacks on abortion rights that led more than two hundred national groups to oppose his nomination to head the Justice Department. Forty-two senators voted against his confirmation. For the first eight months of Ashcroft's tenure, this lack of support seemed to inhibit him. But the 9/11 attacks gave Ashcroft an opportunity to assert himself as a key player in the government's effort to protect the American people from further attacks. He believed that the attacks had changed the mission of law enforcement in the United States. Government could no longer wait until a crime had been committed to begin an investigation. "Al Qaeda wants to hit us and hit us hard. We have to use every legal weapon available to protect the American people from terrorist attacks," Ashcroft said. Within hours of the attacks, when he was still in hiding with the other members of the government, Ashcroft had ordered his lawyers to draft legislation giving the government new powers to fight terrorism. What emerged was a 342-page bill titled "Uniting and Strengthening America by Providing Appropriate Tools Required to Intercept and Obstruct Terrorism Act." The title was awkward because the authors wanted to create an appealing acronym—the USA Patriot Act.[9]

The Patriot Act contained miscellaneous provisions that amended dozens of existing laws. Most of them were not controversial. There was no serious disagreement about the necessity for improving airport security, tightening visa regulations and controls over biochemical agents, strengthening the money-laundering laws to deny financing to terrorist groups, and modernizing electronic surveillance laws that had been written prior to the widespread use of cellular telephones, computers, e-mail, and the Internet. There was also a consensus that the laws that prevented the sharing of information between the nation's foreign intelligence and law enforcement agencies needed to be modified. When the Central Intelligence Agency (CIA) was created in 1947, Congress attempted to prevent it from spying on Americans by denying it law enforcement powers in the United States. After the Church Committee revealed that the CIA had spied on antiwar groups, the ban on domestic surveillance was reaffirmed, and strict rules limited information sharing by the FBI and CIA, creating a barrier that was further reinforced by bureaucratic infighting. As a consequence, the results of the grand jury investigation of Osama bin Laden in the wake of the bombing of

American embassies in Africa were never made available to the CIA, which might have used the information to track Al-Qaeda agents in the months before the 9/11 attacks. The Patriot Act eliminated the obstacles to intelligence sharing in terrorism investigations.

However, civil libertarians were alarmed by other provisions of the Patriot Act. The Supreme Court had declared that Americans could not be punished for belonging to a political party that advocates violence. The Patriot Act did not withdraw this right from citizens, but it stripped it from noncitizens, making them subject to deportation for belonging to or providing material support to a "terrorist organization," which it defined as any group of two or more persons that has threatened to use violence. Although in 1990 Congress had repudiated the practice of excluding foreigners on the basis of their political views, the Patriot Act denied entry to aliens who "endorse or espouse terrorist activity" and gave the attorney general authority to arrest any immigrant that he certifies as a "suspected terrorist." In addition, the Patriot Act seemed to carry information sharing too far, removing all safeguards against the possibility that the CIA might once again become deeply involved in monitoring political activity in the United States.[10]

The Patriot Act also increased the power of the government to engage in secret searches. In the wake of the Church Committee investigation, reformers had succeeded in passing the Foreign Intelligence Surveillance Act (FISA) in 1978. The law recognized that the FBI needed the authority to conduct wiretapping and secret searches in pursuit of foreign agents engaged in spying in the United States. In the past, the FBI had simply assumed it had this authority. However, FISA required the FBI to apply to a secret court, the Foreign Intelligence Surveillance Court, composed of federal judges who would review its applications to ensure that the primary purpose of the spying was to deter foreign espionage and not to evade the safeguards involved in normal criminal investigations. In a criminal investigation, the government has to demonstrate that there is "probable cause" to believe that a person is engaged in criminal activity before it can obtain a search warrant or wiretap. Under FISA, however, it is necessary to show only that the person who is targeted is the "agent of a foreign power." The Patriot Act expanded the FBI's access to FISA warrants by eliminating the requirement that the collection of foreign intelligence is the "primary purpose" of an investigation. In the future, it would be able to engage in wiretapping and secret searches as long as foreign intelligence gathering was "a significant purpose." As a result, the FBI would be free to use secret surveillance in a criminal case even when it could not establish probable cause. The power to conduct secret searches was augmented by a provision of the Patriot Act that allows the government to postpone notification when a search is conducted in a criminal case if notification would "seriously jeopardize" the investigation.[11]

One of the most chilling provisions of the Patriot Act made it possible for the FBI to seize vast amounts of personal data about American citizens in the dragnet that it was deploying for terrorists. Section 215 authorized the FBI to seek warrants from the FISA Court to seize "any tangible things" that it needed "for an authorized investigation . . . to protect against international terrorism or clandestine intelligence activities." The FBI already had the power to force the disclosure of records by travel-related businesses. Section 215 extended this authority to all organizations, nonprofit and charitable groups as well as businesses, and to any individual person. While government has long enjoyed the right to issue subpoenas, it normally has to show probable cause. Under Section 215, however, the government was required to prove only that the records were "sought for" a terrorism or espionage investigation. In addition, there was no necessity to show that the target of the order was suspected of any crime, much less terrorism. The only limitation was that the records could not be sought for a citizen or permanent resident "solely upon the basis of activities protected by the First Amendment." Finally, the whole process of securing the records was cloaked in secrecy: the FBI requested the order from the secret FISA Court, and the order contained a gag provision that prevented the recipient from revealing its existence to anyone other than a person whose assistance was necessary to provide the documents. It was not even clear whether the recipient could consult a lawyer. But even if a lawyer was called, there seemed no other option than to comply. Section 215 made no provision for challenging the order in court.[12]

Despite the radical nature of some of the Patriot Act's provisions, the attorney general demanded immediate passage of the legislation. "The American people do not have the luxury of unlimited time in erecting the necessary defenses to future terrorists acts," Ashcroft told the House Judiciary Committee on September 24, 2001. While as anxious as the attorney general to protect the American people, some members of Congress refused to rubber-stamp his bill. Senator Leahy, the Democratic chairman of the judiciary committee, was willing to waive the formal committee process and negotiate the legislation directly with the Justice Department. But he insisted on a number of concessions to protect civil liberties, including an agreement to assign a judge to oversee information sharing between the CIA and the FBI. On the House side, the judiciary committee quickly made a number of changes in the bill and voted unanimously to send it to the floor. One of the most important concessions in the House was made at the insistence of Majority Leader Richard Armey, a Texas Republican, who proposed that the sixteen most controversial sections of the Patriot Act be subject to a four-year "sunset." This would give Congress a chance to amend them or let them expire if they proved to be troublesome.[13]

As the negotiations progressed, Ashcroft grew increasingly impatient. He also began to wonder whether the Justice Department itself hadn't given too much away. On October 2, he met with Leahy and told him that he was withdrawing from the agreement that his negotiators had reached with members of Leahy's staff. Leahy was stunned. Only the night before, he had assured Senate Majority Leader Tom Dashle that Ashcroft had signed off on the deal. "John, when I make an agreement, I make an agreement," Leahy said. "I can't believe you're going back on your commitment." Ashcroft was not only dissatisfied with the deal but was unwilling to negotiate further. Not long after leaving Leahy's office, he criticized Congress for delaying the approval of the Patriot Act. "I think it is time for us to be productive on behalf of the American people," he said. "Talk won't prevent terrorism." Senator Orrin Hatch, a Utah Republican who was standing at Ashcroft's side, agreed. "It's a very dangerous thing. It's time to get off our duffs and do something," he said. Nine days later, on the one-month anniversary of the 9/11 attacks, the Senate approved the Patriot Act by 98-1. Meanwhile, the House leadership had endorsed the idea of adding the sunset provision but rejected the changes approved by the House Judiciary Committee. It sent the administration's bill to the floor, where it was approved by

357-66. The minor differences between the two bills were quickly reconciled, and two weeks later, on October 26, the bill was signed by President Bush.[14]

The passage of the Patriot Act was accomplished with nearly unprecedented speed. Indeed, critics of the bill insisted that it had been approved with unseemly haste. "It is virtually certain that not a single member of the House read the bill for which he or she voted," charged David Cole and James X. Dempsey in their book *Terrorism and the Constitution.* One House member who voted against the bill later claimed that his copy had just reached his desk when the vote was called. It was "still warm" from the copying machine, he said. Ashcroft had won the battle. He now possessed the weapon that he claimed was indispensable to preventing future terrorism on American soil. "Like the smart bombs, laser-guided missiles and predator drones employed by our armed forces to hunt and kill al Qaeda in Afghanistan, the Patriot Act is just as vital to targeting terrorists who would kill or cripple our people and destroy our freedom at home," Ashcroft said. But at what cost, asked Russ Feingold, the sole Senate opponent of the Patriot Act. "Congress will fulfill its duty only when it protects *both* the American people and the freedoms at the foundation of American society," he said on the floor of the Senate. "So let us preserve our heritage of basic rights. Let us practice as well as preach that liberty. And let us fight to maintain that freedom that we call America." Ashcroft had won the battle to pass the Patriot Act, but the war over civil liberties was just beginning.[15]

Three days after the 9/11 attacks, representatives of dozens of civil rights and civil liberties groups had jammed the conference room on the ground floor of the American Civil Liberties Union office in Washington. The crowd spilled outside into an adjoining garden; others listened from the hallway, sitting on the staircase that led to the offices above. "I had never seen that kind of turnout in 25 years," Laura Murphy, the director of the ACLU's national office, said later. Morton Halperin, a former ACLU official, had expressed what was in the minds of many of his colleagues in an e-mail on the day after the attacks. "There can be no doubt that we will hear calls in the next few days for Congress to enact sweeping legislation to deal with terrorism," he wrote. "This will include not only the secrecy provision, but also broad authority to conduct electronic and other surveillance and to investigate political groups." Halperin proposed to convene a meeting of concerned groups as soon as possible to begin preparing a defense of civil liberties. "We should not wait," he said. The response to Halperin's call demonstrates how large and diverse the civil liberties community had become by the turn of the twenty-first century. During the meeting at the ACLU, a new group was formed, In Defense of Freedom Coalition, and work began on a ten-point statement that was released the following week. "We need to consider proposals calmly and deliberately with a determination not to erode the liberties and freedoms that are at the core of the American way of life," the statement read. More than 150 religious, civil rights, and civil liberties groups endorsed it. They included groups who had been fighting for civil liberties for many years, like the Quakers, as well as newer organizations that specialized in the civil liberties and privacy issues created by digital communication. Many of the groups were liberal, but there were also a significant number of libertarian organizations. Three hundred law professors joined in endorsing the coalition statement.[16]

Inevitably, however, people who feared a repetition of the civil liberties abuses of the past looked to the ACLU for leadership. With a $50 million budget and a staff of five hundred, the ACLU was by far the largest civil liberties group in the country. It also had offices in all fifty states. In the immediate aftermath of the attacks, the ACLU offered a measured response to the hundreds of reporters who called hoping for dramatic quotes about the new threat to civil liberties. "Some ... have questioned whether the ACLU has made as much noise as it should," the *New York Times* reported. There were also questions about whether the new executive director, Anthony D. Romero, who had started his job only a week before 9/11, was up to the task. Later, while acknowledging that the ACLU had "refused to engage in speculation about the loss of our liberty," Romero would defend the decision to pursue a two-pronged approach, supporting the war against terrorism while insisting on respect for civil liberties. "We were calling on Congress to be deliberate and thoughtful as it considered new legislation. And my organization was practicing what it preached," Romero explained. The ACLU called its new campaign "Safe and Free in Times of Crisis."[17]

Whatever hope the ACLU may have had that it would be able to negotiate with the Bush administration quickly faded. On October 26, the day the Patriot Act was signed into law, Romero and members of his staff met with FBI director Robert S. Mueller III in an effort to get answers about the hundreds of detainees who were being held by the government. Mueller's refusal to discuss any details of the detentions convinced Romero that the ACLU had to pursue a more aggressive strategy. A few days later, it joined with several other groups to file a request for the information under the Freedom of Information Act. It also began drafting a letter to the embassies of ten Arab countries, offering to help them secure the release of their countrymen. "We are particularly interested in highlighting instances of abuse by our government and in developing a systematic litigation to challenge its unconstitutional practices," it read. Some of the ambassadors were unfamiliar with the ACLU and were perplexed that an American organization would offer to sue its government on their behalf. But the ACLU's position was crystal clear to the attorney general. On December 6, in an appearance before the Senate Judiciary Committee, he blasted civil libertarians. "We need honest, reasoned debate, and not fear-mongering," Ashcroft said.

> To those who pit Americans against immigrants and citizens against noncitizens, to those who scare peace-loving people with phantoms of lost liberty, my message is this: Your tactics only aid terrorists, for they erode our national unity and diminish our resolve. They give ammunition to America's enemies, and pause to America's friends. They encourage people of good will to remain silent in the face of evil.

In the ACLU's opinion it was Ashcroft who was telling people to shut up, and it blasted back. Laura Murphy, the director of the national office, accused Ashcroft of "a blatant attempt to stifle growing criticism of recent government policy" and of "equating legitimate political dissent with something unpatriotic and un-American."[18]

Ashcroft's attack on civil libertarians only encouraged opposition to the administration's policies. A grass-roots movement was beginning to stir in isolated spots around the country. In November, the Bill of Rights Defense Committee had been formed in Northampton, Massachusetts, to press the city council to pass a resolution committing "local law enforcement [to] continue to preserve residents' freedom of speech, religion, assembly and privacy . . . even if requested or authorized to infringe upon these rights by federal law enforcement acting under new powers granted by the USA PATRIOT Act." By the time Northampton approved the resolution in May 2002, the councils in Ann Arbor (Michigan), Denver (Colorado), and Amherst and Leverett (Massachusetts) had passed similar statements. Four more towns approved resolutions in the next eight weeks, including Cambridge, Massachusetts, and Boulder, Colorado. While the origins of the movement clearly lay in college towns with large liberal constituencies, the Bill of Rights Defense Committee believed that its message had broad appeal and began to offer information and advice to activists in communities throughout the country. The ACLU quickly realized the movement's potential. In October 2002, it announced that it was expanding its "safe and free" campaign. It would encourage the movement to pass local and state legislation "prohibiting local law enforcement participation in repressive Administration initiatives." It also began running a thirty-second television commercial that urged people to "look what John Ashcroft is doing to our Constitution."[19]

The civil libertarians faced an uphill struggle, however. The fear of a new attack was strong, and public opinion polls showed overwhelming support for the administration's policies. One of the major obstacles was the lack of an obvious and imminent threat to civil liberties that was capable of arousing a large number of Americans. There were certainly threats: the danger of detention without charge; the plan to try suspected terrorists in military tribunals that did not offer sufficient legal safeguards for the rights of the innocent; and the Justice Department's announcement that it would monitor the conversations between terrorist suspects and their attorneys. But these dangers did not directly affect most American citizens. Nor was there a loud outcry in May when the Justice Department announced that it would loosen the restrictions on surveillance that had been imposed on the FBI in 1976, allowing the government to monitor political and religious groups without demonstrating that there was any reason to believe they were engaged in criminal activity. However, the Patriot Act was a natural target. It contained two sections that an average citizen might find truly alarming: Section 213, which allowed the government to conduct secret searches in any criminal investigation, delaying notification for a "reasonable" period; and Section 215, which authorized the issuance of a search order for "any tangible things" in a terrorism investigation. In the coming months, the so-called sneak-and-peek warrants would generate a great deal of controversy, prompting the House of Representatives to try cutting off federal funding for such searches. But it was Section 215 that attracted the most publicity. In part, this was because it deeply worried two large groups—the nation's librarians and booksellers.

The librarians had already had a bad experience with the FBI. In June 1987, two FBI agents approached a clerk at Columbia University's Mathematics and Science Library and requested information about foreigners who used the library. They were overheard by a reference librarian, who told them that they must speak with Paula Kaufman, the director of academic information services. Kaufman refused to help them. "I explained that we were not prepared to cooperate with them in any way, described our philosophies and policies respecting privacy, confidentiality and academic freedom and told them they were not welcome here," Kaufman wrote in a letter to the American Library Association's Intellectual Freedom Committee. An investigation by the ALA revealed the Columbia librarians were not the only ones approached by the FBI. In 1973, the FBI had launched a Library Awareness Program in an effort to identify potential Soviet agents who were attempting to gain access to "sensitive" but unclassified information, including the names of technical experts whom it might attempt to recruit as spies. Although the FBI had focused on libraries in New York City, it also contacted librarians in ten other states. Librarians around the country were alarmed that the government was attempting to turn them into informers and had apparently succeeded in obtaining information from some of their colleagues. Their outrage grew in 1989 when they learned through a Freedom of Information Act request that the FBI had investigated more than one hundred librarians to determine whether they were acting at the behest of the Soviet government in working to discredit the Library Awareness Program. To help restore confidence in the confidentiality of library records, state library associations launched a highly successful campaign to pass state privacy laws banning the release of library records except in compliance with a court order.[20]

The moment of truth for booksellers came more than a decade later. In March 1998, Kenneth Starr, a special prosecutor investigating possible crimes by President Bill Clinton, subpoenaed two Washington bookstores in an effort to identify books purchased by Monica Lewinsky, a White House intern who had a sexual relationship with Clinton. Booksellers were surprised by the subpoena. No one could remember a bookseller ever being subpoenaed. They were also alarmed because Starr's subpoena revealed that, like librarians, they possessed a lot of information about their customers' reading preferences. This had not been a problem prior to the invention of computerized inventory systems. By 1998, however, almost every bookstore used computers that were capturing the names of books purchased with a credit card or check. Both of the subpoenaed booksellers, Kramerbooks and Afterwords and Barnes and Noble, challenged Starr's subpoenas on the grounds that they violated the First Amendment and would make customers afraid to purchase books that might meet with the government's disapproval. The case was mooted only a few months later when Lewinsky agreed to voluntarily turn over her book purchase records as part of an immunity deal that she struck with Starr. However, the issue of protecting the privacy of bookstore records emerged again in 2000 when the Denver police obtained a warrant to search one of the country's leading independent bookstores, Tattered Cover, in an effort to identify books that had been sent to a suspect in a drug case. The case generated national attention and another lawsuit. In 2002, the Colorado Supreme Court voted unanimously to suppress the warrant and required that all future efforts to obtain bookstore records in the state must be preceded by a hearing at which the booksellers would have an opportunity to argue against the issuance of a subpoena.

The Tattered Cover case was still under way when I first learned about Section 215 of the Patriot Act. James X. Dempsey of the Center for Democracy and Technology was describing the provisions of the Patriot Act in September 2001 to members of the Free Expression Network, a loose association of groups that meets quarterly to discuss First Amendment issues. He discussed Section 215, then commonly referred to as the "business records" section, and was preparing to move on when I asked him for a clarification. Until then, I had never heard of the Foreign Intelligence Surveillance Court. Was he saying that this secret court could force a bookstore or library to turn over records without the government having to demonstrate that the person was suspected of a crime? Was it true that the order could not be legally challenged and that the bookseller or librarian could not even reveal the existence of the order to my group or any other civil liberties organization? I was stunned when Dempsey confirmed that the Patriot Act would strip booksellers and librarians of the ability to do anything to protect reader privacy. We had no way of knowing how aggressively the government intended to use this new power, but our recent experience made us worry. Five days after President Bush signed the Patriot Act into law, we notified members of the American Booksellers Association of the implications of Section 215. We told them that while the law did not explicitly recognize a right to consult an attorney when they received an order, we believed that they retained that right and offered to help them secure counsel. However, we added a caveat: because of the gag order, they must not tell us why they were requesting legal assistance. We promised to continue to fight for reader privacy. After our failed news conference in April 2002, however, we were at a loss to know what we were going to do next.

The first hopeful sign appeared in Vermont in the fall of 2002. In October, the executive board of the Vermont Library Association approved an open letter to the state's congressional delegation, urging the repeal of the provisions of Section 215 that threatened reader privacy. Drafted on behalf of both librarians and booksellers, the letter was then circulated for signatures and eventually received the endorsement of forty-five libraries and twenty-nine bookstores. "Our professions are founded on principles that encourage the free expression of ideas and the right of a citizenry to access those ideas free of censorship, violations of privacy, or the threat of government intrusion," the letter read. "We consider ourselves front-line defenders of the First Amendment." The librarians and booksellers urged their legislators to take steps to avoid the civil liberties abuses that had occurred during national emergencies in the past. "Let us do what is right so that Americans will look back at this time with pride, rather than shame." Specifically, they requested legislation that would repeal the provisions of Section 215 that "cast a wide net of suspicion and surveillance over the community of readers, researchers, and information seekers." Although the odds of success for such a legislative appeal are always small, there seemed to be some hope that Senator Leahy might respond. In July, he had asked the Justice Department to report on the implementation of the Patriot Act, including its impact on libraries. But the response that came from Washington a few weeks after the letter was sent, came not from Leahy but from the state's only representative in the House, Bernie Sanders.[21]

In some ways, Sanders's interest was a surprise. Although he was one of the sixty-six members of the House who voted against the Patriot Act, Sanders had not taken an active interest in civil liberties issues during his eleven years in Congress. At sixty-one, he was a veteran legislator who was serving his sixth term in the House. "Sanders is a tall, angular man with a messy head of gull-white hair and a circa-1977 set of big framed glasses," a *Rolling Stone* reporter observed in 2005. "Minus the austere congressional office, you might mistake him for a physics professor or a journalist of the Jimmy Breslin type." Sanders was serious. His major interest throughout his political career had been the economic issues that have the most direct impact on the lives of middle- and working-class Americans. He had been born in Brooklyn, New York, to parents who never stopped worrying about how they were going to stretch the salary of his father, a paint salesman. As a student at the University of Chicago, he became an admirer of the Socialist Eugene Debs. "It has never made sense to me...that a tiny clique of people should have incredible wealth and power while most people have none," Sanders explained in his autobiography. His radical egalitarianism eventually propelled him into third-party politics in Vermont, where he ran for several statewide offices before being elected mayor of Burlington in 1981.[22]

In other ways, however, Sanders's decision to make himself a leader in the fight to amend the Patriot Act made perfect sense. It isn't easy being a Socialist in Vermont. Sanders discovered that there was little patience for long-winded analyses of the problems of capitalism. He developed a laserlike focus on the nuts-and-bolts problems brought to his attention by his constituents. "We could never forget about taking care of the basics," Sanders said. He could not look away when the librarians and booksellers of his state asked for his help. Once engaged, Sanders was a fighter. From the beginning, he had chosen to advance his political ambitions the hard way, and he relished the opportunity to challenge the Bush administration in a new arena. With a bookseller and a librarian at his side, Sanders announced on December 20 that he would lead the fight to amend Section 215. "This is a crashing, crushing attack on basic rights in this country, and it's got to be opposed," Sanders said. "I will do everything in my power in the Congress, working in a nonpartisan way with other concerned members, to strip this very dangerous language from the bill."[23]

The nation's mood had begun to shift by the time Sanders made his announcement in December 2002. The Bush administration had unveiled two domestic surveillance programs that made the American people nervous about government threats to their privacy. Operation TIPS, a plan to enlist workers in the transportation and public utilities industries in a national terrorist watch, raised the prospect that citizens would be spied on by their mail carriers and meter readers. A Pentagon program, Total Information Awareness (TIA), proposed to build an enormous database containing all of the personal information that was available through the Internet, creating a fear that Big Brother would indeed be watching. TIPS and TIA were so widely condemned that Congress was able to assert itself for the first time against antiterrorism measures, successfully blocking both programs. In December, a *USA Today* opinion poll showed that there had been a dramatic shift in sentiment about civil liberties. A year earlier, 53 percent of those polled had answered "no" to the question "To prevent terrorism, should the government violate your civil liberties?" When the same question was asked in September, 62 percent said "no." This new concern could also be measured in the growing membership of the ACLU, which had increased by more than 20 percent over the past year and now stood at 330,000.[24]

As a result, critics of the Patriot Act began to believe that the time had come to win the changes they were seeking. In January 2003, the American Library Association told Congress that "sections of the USA PATRIOT Act are a present danger to the constitutional

rights and privacy rights of library users" and urged changes to the
sections that "abridge the rights of inquiry and free expression." It
also urged its sixty-four thousand members "to defend and support
user privacy and free and open access to knowledge and information." It was in this atmosphere of hopefulness that Bernie Sanders
introduced the Freedom to Read Protection Act (H.R. 1157) in
March. The bill exempted bookstore and library records from Section 215. This meant that the FBI would once again be required to
obtain a subpoena for any information it sought from booksellers
and librarians and that those requests could be challenged in court.
Even before the bill had been filed, Sanders had received strong editorial support from both the *Nashville Tennessean* and the *Los Angeles Times.* "Rep. Bernie Sanders, an independent from Vermont,
doesn't believe that Uncle Sam should have access to your reading
list. And he's right," the *Tennessean* wrote. "What the provision will
inevitably do is make every library patron or bookstore customer
think twice before selecting their reading material." Over the next
two weeks, the *Detroit Free Press, Honolulu Advertiser,* and *Providence
Journal Bulletin* also endorsed H.R. 1157. The bill began to pick up
legislative support. When it was introduced, it was cosponsored by
Sanders, Ron Paul of Texas, a libertarian Republican, and twenty-
three Democrats. By the end of June, H.R. 1157 had been endorsed
by 118 House members, including 13 Republicans.[25]

There were other signs of dissent that the Bush administration
could not ignore. There had been a dramatic increase in the number
of cities and towns passing anti–Patriot Act resolutions. Twenty-two
communities had passed resolutions by the end of 2002. Another
nineteen acted in January 2003 alone. In February, a public interest
group obtained a copy of an eighty-six-page bill drafted by the Justice Department that would have enhanced many of the government's powers under the Patriot Act. The revelation that there was a
"Patriot II" in the works probably speeded the passage of more resolutions. More than twenty local governments added their names to
the anti–Patriot Act list in each month during the spring. In April,
Hawaii became the first state to pass a resolution. The administration
could try to ignore the local resolutions, dismissing them as the
protests of a handful of "liberal" towns, but it had to face facts when
the Republican House of Representatives expressed its disapproval of

a key provision of the Patriot Act. In July, the House voted 309–118 to approve an amendment barring the Justice Department from using any of its funds to conduct the secret searches authorized by Section 213. The amendment was later dropped, but Attorney General John Ashcroft was concerned that the critics of the Patriot Act were gaining ground. A month after the House vote, he announced that he would undertake a national speaking tour to build support for the Patriot Act.

Ashcroft had his work cut out for him. Just as he was hitting the road, a Gallup poll revealed that concern about the threats to individual rights stood at its highest level since the 9/11 attacks. More than two-thirds of those polled said the government should not take further steps to prevent terrorism if they would violate civil liberties. But the attorney general had a well-conceived plan. Before invitation-only audiences that included large numbers of uniformed law enforcement officers, he extolled the administration's record. "We are winning the war on terrorism," he said in more than a dozen speeches and in interviews with local television stations. A Gallup poll taken in November showed that Ashcroft's campaign may have slightly increased support for the government. However, the sound of applause seemed to make the attorney general overconfident; in a speech to the National Restaurant Association on September 15, he once again attacked critics of the government's antiterrorism policies, and this time he named one:

> Unfortunately, at this moment Washington is involved in a debate where hysteria threatens to obscure the most important issues.... According to these breathless reports and baseless hysteria, some have convinced the American Library Association that under the bipartisanly enacted PATRIOT Act, the FBI is not fighting terrorism. Instead, agents are checking how far you've gotten in the latest Tom Clancy novel.... The law enforcement community has no interest in your reading habits.... The hysteria is ridiculous.

The ALA reacted angrily to Ashcroft's speech. "We are deeply concerned that the attorney general should be openly contemptuous of those who seek to defend our Constitution," Carla Hayden, the ALA president, said. Press criticism may have caused Ashcroft to regret his remarks, for several days later he did something that he had been resisting for more than a year, authorizing the Justice Department to reveal the number of times it had used Section 215. In fact, it had never been used, a spokesman said.[26]

Despite Ashcroft's best efforts, the movement to curb the government's antiterrorism powers continued to grow, and a significant amount of the support for change was coming from conservatives who normally saw eye-to-eye with the attorney general. There was a natural affinity between libertarian conservatives and civil libertarians on some issues, including privacy. The American Conservative Union, Eagle Forum, and the Free Congress Foundation had all participated in the In Defense of Freedom statement issued by the civil liberties community in the days after 9/11. Two of the most conservative House members, Majority Leader Dick Armey of Texas and Georgia representative Bob Barr, tried to curb some of the worst excesses of the Patriot Act and the law creating the Department of Homeland Security. "When the history of the response to September 11 is written, it will record that evangelical and libertarian conservatives . . . did more to defend liberty than mainstream liberal Democrats," journalist Jeffrey Rosen wrote in 2002.[27] But Barr and Armey soon left Congress, and Rosen acknowledged that they had no apparent successors. Then, in October, Senator Larry Craig, a conservative Republican from Idaho, and Senator Dick Durbin, an Illinois Democrat, introduced the Safety and Freedom Ensured (SAFE) Act (S. 1709). The SAFE Act was broader than the Freedom to Read Protection Act. It added protections for all records sought under Section 215, narrowed the authority to engage in "sneak and peek" searches, and addressed a number of other civil liberties problems created by the Patriot Act. In the months ahead, libertarians would play an active role in the coalition of groups that the ACLU would assemble to push S. 1709.

The book and library community was also increasing its support for reforming the Patriot Act. In February 2004, the American Library Association, the American Booksellers Association, and PEN American Center, an authors' group, launched the Campaign for Reader Privacy. (The Association of American Publishers joined a short time later.) The purpose of the group was to rally support for the Freedom to Read Protection Act and Senator Russ Feingold's

Library, Bookseller and Personal Data Privacy Act. It announced that it was starting a petition campaign in bookstores and libraries with the goal of collecting one million signatures in support of restoring the safeguards for reader privacy that had been eliminated by the Patriot Act. Even the sponsors recognized that collecting one million signatures was an ambitious goal. As publicly funded institutions, libraries were understandably reluctant to been seen taking a stand on a partisan political issue. Many booksellers were worried about alienating customers who supported the Bush administration. But the booksellers who put out the petitions discovered that their customers were eager to sign them. "Customers were like, 'The FBI can do that?' People just sign it right and left," a bookseller in Muncie, Indiana, reported. Booksellers who pasted a copy of the petition on their front door found that it was drawing people inside. "It's not just our customers," one of them explained. "People are just walking in and signing." Within three months, 120,000 signatures were collected by more than four hundred booksellers in thirty-eight states. The Campaign for Reader Privacy also received the strong support of book and library associations as well as many of the biggest companies in the business. Forty associations representing virtually every bookstore, library, and writer in the country as well as eighty-one companies, including Barnes and Noble Booksellers, Borders, Random House, and Simon and Schuster, endorsed a statement supporting changes in Section 215.[28]

In July, Bernie Sanders put the strength of the reform movement to the test. The Republican leadership of the House of Representatives refused to hold a hearing on the Freedom to Read Protection Act, but it could not stop him from seeking to add it as an amendment to the appropriations bill that funded the Justice Department. On July 8, he forced a vote on the amendment, which barred the department from using any funds appropriated in the act to seek a court order for bookstore and library records under Section 215. At that point, H.R. 1157 had more than 145 cosponsors, giving the amendment a good chance of passage. The White House warned that the president would veto the appropriations bill if it included the Sanders amendment. In opening the debate in the House, Sanders assured his colleagues that they could protect civil liberties without undermining the war on terrorism. "While we fight terrorism vigorously, we must do it in a way that does not undermine the basic constitutional rights of the American people," he said. If his amendment was approved, government would still be able to search bookstore and library records, but it would have to obtain a search warrant or grand jury subpoena, ensuring judicial review by the regular courts. Connecticut Republican Christopher Shays was scornful in his reply. A letter from the Justice Department had been read into the record that asserted that a member of a terrorist group affiliated with Al-Qaeda had used a library computer to access the Internet as recently as the previous winter and spring. "We are trying to amend the Patriot Act because some librarians find it offensive that we may want to go in and find out who a terrorist talks with when they use a computer," Shays said. Secrecy was essential if the FBI was going to disrupt terrorist plans. "And we are going to tie their hands behind their backs anyway and say we have to let a terrorist know first before we break into a terrorist cell," he added.[29]

Yet the White House veto threat, the revelation that terrorists were using library computers, and the arguments of Shays and his supporters were not enough to defeat the Sanders amendment. Initially, it appeared to have passed (219-210). However, as the fifteen-minute deadline for the vote approached, some of the Republican supporters of the amendment began to switch their votes under heavy pressure from party leaders. As time expired, Democrats began shouting for the vote to be closed, but the Republican leaders continued to twist arms for another twenty-three minutes. As cries of "Shame, Shame!" and "Democracy!" were heard on the floor, the Republicans switched nine votes, creating a tie that killed the amendment. Although disappointed, Sanders was not discouraged. "People are waking up to the fact that the government can walk into their libraries . . . and monitor their reading habits," he said.[30]

The battle over civil liberties was also being fought in the courts. Although cases were filed by many different civil rights, press, and advocacy groups, once again the ACLU and its state affiliates played a dominant role in the legal struggle. In the five years after 9/11, they launched more than eighty lawsuits, covering a wide range of issues, including detention, the use of torture, racial profiling and discrimination, domestic spying, illegal search and seizure, and government secrecy. The largest category of First Amendment cases concerned the clash between authorities and people protesting the use of American troops in Afghanistan and Iraq. In 2003, the ACLU challenged a policy that kept antiwar protesters penned in "free speech zones" far removed from the site of speeches by the president and other members of the administration. The policy was implemented by police in more than a dozen cities at the request of the Secret Service. The ACLU also litigated a wide variety of local ordinances that limited protests on the pretext of preserving public order and defended the right of free expression for individuals, including a police officer who criticized his department's antiterrorism training.

One of the individuals who needed help was Bretton Barber, a high school junior in Dearborn Heights, Michigan. Barber was sent home from school in February 2003 for wearing a T-shirt with a picture of President Bush and the words "International Terrorist." Although a teenager, Barber was no political novice. "I wore the T-shirt to express my antiwar sentiment," said Barber, who had attended several antiwar demonstrations in the previous month. More significant, he had joined the ACLU the year before. His first call for help went to the ACLU, but he did not delay in asserting his constitutional rights when he was not immediately able to contact someone. Instead, he went on the Internet and reread the U.S. Supreme Court decision in *Tinker v. Des Moines Independent School District,* the case that upheld the right of students to wear armbands protesting the Vietnam War. Then, he called his principal:

> She immediately asked if I was familiar with the Supreme Court case, *Tinker v. Des Moines.* I said I was very familiar with it. She said it happened in 1969. I said no, it happened in 1965, but it got decided in 1969. Then she quoted directly from the dissenting opinion, to say that the school has the right to control speech. I knew that wasn't how the case came out, but I didn't argue with her.

Barber's ACLU attorneys did the arguing for him. They convinced a federal judge that the T-shirt did not threaten to cause any disruption in the school, which was the only legitimate grounds for banning it. "I haven't decided when I'll wear the shirt again, but now I have the confidence of knowing that I have the right to wear it," Barber said.[31]

In one of the most potentially significant First Amendment cases, the ACLU challenged the constitutionality of Section 215 in a lawsuit filed in Detroit in July 2003. It charged that the fear of being secretly monitored through searches under Section 215 had caused a dramatic decline in membership and donations at the nation's mosques. "Our clients have every reason to believe that in 21st century America they will be subject to new abuses of power under the Patriot Act," ACLU attorney Ann Beeson said.[32]

Many of these cases failed. Despite some success in the lower courts in challenging the government's refusal to reveal whom it had detained and its ban on press coverage of immigration hearings involving the detainees, the appeals courts generally sustained the administration's claim of broad power to meet the national security threat. The trend was disappointing to those who had hoped that the growth of civil liberties would prevent a recurrence of the abuses that had occurred in previous national emergencies. At a conference of federal judges, one speaker urged the participants to take a strong stand in protecting individual rights and noted that they had been granted lifetime tenure for the purpose of withstanding popular pressure. "Look, lifetime tenure isn't that important," a judge replied. "We're human beings and we don't like to be criticized." Judicial caution hurt the effort to get the government to provide an accounting of its use of Section 215. The ACLU filed two Freedom of Information Act lawsuits in an effort to force the government to reveal whether it was secretly searching bookstore and library records. However, a district court judge ruled that even the *number* of searches could be legitimately withheld under the national security exemption in the law. The case in Detroit also went nowhere. The judge had still not issued a decision when the Patriot Act was reauthorized almost three years later.[33]

Yet, slowly, the courts began to assert themselves. While the ACLU had little luck in challenging the use of "free speech zones," it succeeded in many of the cases that it brought over local efforts to restrict free speech. Sometimes even the threat of legal action was enough to vindicate First Amendment rights. In June 2004, an FBI agent visited a library in rural Washington State seeking the identity of someone who had written an apparent threat in the margin of one of the library's biographies of Osama bin Laden. "If the things I'm doing is [*sic*] considered a crime, then let history be a witness that I am a criminal. Hostility toward America is a religious duty and we hope to be rewarded by God," the note read. The book had been delivered to the FBI by a library patron who thought the language should be investigated. Library officials informed the FBI that it would not release any patron information without a subpoena. Further investigation by the library's lawyer revealed that the marginalia in the book were nearly identical to a statement that bin Laden had made several years earlier. When the FBI insisted that it still wanted the information and obtained a subpoena, the library asked a judge to suppress it on First Amendment grounds. "If public libraries just start passing records out to [the] FBI, we might as well just lock our doors," Library Director Joan Airoldi explained. The case never went to trial, however, because the FBI dropped its demand for the information.[34]

In September 2004, the ACLU won its first major victory against the Patriot Act. Section 505 authorized the FBI to use administrative subpoenas called National Security Letters (NSLs) to obtain electronic records from telephone companies and Internet-service providers. Like Section 215 orders, NSLs could not be challenged in court and imposed a gag on recipients. Unlike Section 215, however, the FBI did not require the permission of the Foreign Intelligence Surveillance Court before issuing an NSL. As a result, the number of NSLs grew rapidly. In 2005, the FBI served more than nine thousand NSLs in investigating 3,501 United States "persons"—either citizens or permanent resident aliens. One Internet-service provider who received an NSL decided to take a chance. Although the law did not authorize legal challenges and even made it doubtful that it was okay to seek legal counsel, he asked the ACLU to join him in fighting the NSL. The gag order made this extremely difficult. At one point, the government made the ACLU censor its own Web site by removing information about when briefs were due.[35]

The decision was worth the trouble, however. U.S. District Court judge Victor Marrero struck down the entire section. Because the law required Internet-service providers to surrender the names of their customers and their "transactional records," NSLs could easily be used "to compile elaborate dossiers on Internet users," including "a log of e-mail addresses with whom a subscriber has corresponded ... the anonymous message boards to which a person logs on or posts, the electronic newsletters to which he subscribes and the advocacy websites he visits." It was unconstitutional to give the FBI so much authority without any judicial oversight, Marrero declared. In addition, permanently barring recipients from discussing their NSLs was a prior restraint and therefore violated the First Amendment. Marrero stayed his decision while the government appealed. However, his ruling could not have been more timely. Congress was preparing to reauthorize the Patriot Act in 2005, and Marrero had sent a strong message that important parts of it needed fixing.[36]

When the reauthorization process began in the spring of 2005, however, it was the supporters of the Patriot Act who appeared to have the upper hand. Late in 2003, it had seemed that dissatisfaction with the Patriot Act might make it an issue in the 2004 presidential campaign. During the Iowa caucuses in December, Massachusetts senator John Kerry, the eventual Democratic nominee, called for "replacing the Patriot Act with a new law that protects our people and our liberties at the same time." However, a Gallup poll in April 2004 showed that Americans remained deeply concerned by the threat of terrorism. More than 60 percent of them approved of the Bush administration's antiterrorism policies. They also supported the Patriot Act by a more than two-to-one margin. The critics of the Patriot Act also found themselves without their favorite whipping boy. Although John Ashcroft had indicated to the president his willingness to continue as attorney general, he was replaced by the more politic Alberto Gonzales, the White House counsel. The political climate seemed to worsen in June when the Senate Intelligence Committee approved a bill expanding the FBI's surveillance authority even further, allowing it to issue its own administrative subpoenas whenever it thought it was necessary in a terrorism investigation.[37]

Concern among civil libertarians had grown to such a point by June that some were fearful about the prospects for another vote on Bernie Sanders's Freedom to Read Amendment. Having come so close to victory the year before, Sanders was determined to try again.

Once again, the White House tried to stop him, announcing that the president would veto the appropriations bill that funds the Commerce, Justice, and State Departments if Sanders succeeded in attaching his amendment to it. This time the president's threat failed. On June 15, the House approved the Sanders amendment by a vote of 238-187. Thirty-eight Republicans joined all but one of the Democrats—Dan Boren of Oklahoma—in voting for the measure. The vote on the Freedom to Read Amendment thrilled the critics of the Patriot Act, but it was only a symbolic victory because the amendment was later removed when conferees reconciled the differences between the bills passed by the House and Senate. A more significant development occurred six weeks later when the Senate unanimously approved a Patriot Act reauthorization bill that included important new safeguards for civil liberties. The most important provision narrowed the FBI's authority to seek records under Section 215. It would no longer be permitted to request all records that it considered relevant but must demonstrate to the FISA court judge that the records pertained to a suspected terrorist or someone known to the suspect. The Senate bill also allowed the recipient of a Section 215 order or National Security Letter to challenge it in court and gave NSL recipients the right to challenge the gag order. Although the Senate bill did not go as far as the SAFE Act, civil libertarians embraced it as a significant improvement over both the Patriot Act and the reauthorization bill that had already been approved by the House.

There were even more remarkable days ahead. A conference committee met to reconcile the differences between the House and Senate bills and produced a bill that deeply disappointed those who were seeking significant changes in the Patriot Act. The House quickly approved the conference report, and its passage in the Senate seemed certain. However, when things appeared darkest, four Republican senators announced that they would support a filibuster to block approval of the bill until additional civil liberties safeguards were added. Larry Craig of Idaho had sponsored the SAFE Act, the Senate bill supported by civil libertarians. On December 15, Craig joined two cosponsors of the SAFE Act, Lisa Murkowski of Alaska and John Sununu of New Hampshire, and Chuck Hagel of Nebraska in voting against the motion to bring the reauthorization bill to the floor. With their support, the Democrats defeated the motion, 52 to 47. Because Congress was preparing to adjourn and the temporary provisions of the Patriot Act were set to expire at the end of the year, the administration was forced to agree to a five-week extension. Booksellers, librarians, and other Patriot Act critics were jubilant. They believed that they were on the verge of winning the fight they had been waging for over three years. But the battle ended with a whimper, not a bang. During the congressional recess, the Republicans who had joined the filibuster reached an agreement with the White House to support the bill in return for several changes that did not include the requirement that searches be limited to the records of suspected terrorists. "Key members of the Senate have now caved, agreeing to renew these provisions in exchange for only minimal improvements," the *New York Times* wrote in an editorial. Critics of the Patriot Act spoke out strongly against the "compromise." "Although some have claimed that the compromise language includes new protections for library patrons, those alleged protections are illusory," Michael Gorman, the president of the American Library Association, said. While vowing to fight on, the ACLU acknowledged its "profound disappointment."[38]

The disappointment was understandable, for the "concessions" that had been made by the White House were indeed minor considering that the government retained the right to secretly search the records of people who were not suspected of criminal conduct. Yet the focus on the "White House compromise" obscured the fact that a number of safeguards had been added to the reauthorization bill at each stage of its progress through the House and Senate. While none was as important as limiting FBI searches to suspected terrorists, taken together, they represented a significant improvement in the Patriot Act. For example, the House had agreed to require the director of the FBI to personally authorize all bookstore and library searches under Section 215, providing some protection against overzealous agents in the field. Even more significant was the explicit recognition that people who receive Section 215 orders and National Security Letters have the right to consult an attorney and to challenge them in court. The ACLU and other critics correctly noted that the right to challenge these secret orders is undermined by a number of restrictions. However, people who can consult an attorney and challenge the government are far less likely to surrender records than those who think they have no choice. By the same token, the fact that bookstores and libraries can get a court to review the government's demands should act as another deterrent to FBI agents who may be inclined to seek records they don't really need. The reauthorization bill began to strip away some of the secrecy cloaking government surveillance as well. Recipients of NSLs and Section 215 orders can now challenge the gag order that accompanies them. The reauthorization bill makes it easy for the government to maintain the gag by asserting that secrecy is necessary to protect the national security, but the gagged party can file challenges every year until the gag is lifted, meaning that at least some of the orders will eventually be made public.

One of the most important safeguards in the reauthorization bill is expanded congressional oversight over the operation of the Patriot Act. John Ashcroft's refusal to share the most basic information about how the Justice Department was using its expanded powers frustrated even sympathetic members of Congress. Booksellers and librarians were particularly incensed by his unsupported claim that revealing the total number of bookstore and library searches somehow threatened national security. The reauthorization bill specifically addressed the latter problem, requiring the Justice Department to provide annual reports of the number of bookstore and library searches. Congress also required a report of the number of NSLs issued every year. Finally, the reauthorization bill ordered the Justice Department's inspector general to prepare an audit of the "effectiveness and use, including any improper and illegal use, of the investigative authority" exercised by the FBI under the Patriot Act. Among other things, the audit is supposed to show how effectively the FBI has guarded the privacy of the records that it has obtained as well as the extent to which the information has been used in its operations and criminal proceedings. During the legislative fight over reauthorization, critics of the Patriot Act questioned whether the inspector general could be objective enough to undertake a meaningful review. However, the inspector general's report on the department's handling of detainees in the immediate aftermath of the 9/11 attacks confirmed that many abuses had occurred. Taken together, the Patriot Act reforms approved by Congress at least began the process of establishing accountability for the government's secret powers.[39]

While it did not achieve all of its legislative goals, the Patriot Act reform movement did succeed in its effort to make civil liberties a central issue in debate over the war on terrorism. As our unsuccessful press conference in April 2002 demonstrated, this was by no means inevitable. The fear of new attacks was a serious impediment. So was the fact that the president's party controlled both houses of Congress, giving it the power to deny critics of the president's policies an opportunity to hold hearings on the Freedom to Read Protection Act, the SAFE Act, and other reform measures. Civil libertarians responded by reaching out directly to the American people. The ACLU's success was reflected in the continued strong growth in its membership, which had reached 400,000 by the fall of 2006, a 40 percent increase since September 11, 2001. The Bill of Rights Defense Committee's campaign persuaded more than four hundred local communities and eight state legislatures to pass resolutions announcing their concern about the threat to civil liberties. Booksellers and librarians mobilized their customers and patrons. As a result, the Bush administration repeatedly failed to expand its surveillance powers. Congress rejected the TIPS and TIA programs, and the efforts to pass a Patriot II and to give the FBI the power to issue administrative subpoenas were both stillborn. The administration did succeed in making fourteen of the sixteen temporary provisions of the Patriot Act permanent. However, it wanted to make them all permanent and was forced to accept a four-year extension of Sections 215 and 206, which expanded the government's wiretapping authority. It is possible that the electoral victories that gave the Democrats control of Congress in November 2006 will lead to further changes in the Patriot Act in 2007 or 2008.

There were other reasons for optimism about free speech in 2006. Although Congress had been the center stage for the civil liberties fight during the reauthorization of the Patriot Act, other important institutions were at work—the American press and the courts, both of which contributed significantly to the campaign to strengthen individual rights. Many civil libertarians had despaired over the failure of the press to be more aggressive in its coverage of the federal government in the wake of the 9/11 attacks. They remembered the bravery that the *New York Times,* the *Washington Post,* and CBS had displayed in covering Vietnam and Watergate. Since 9/11, however, the American press seemed to have succumbed to the notion that it is unpatriotic to criticize the government as it covered terrorism at home and new American wars abroad. While the flag waving of the Fox News Channel was difficult to bear, there was a special bitterness toward the *Times,* which many blamed for flawed reporting that helped the administration justify the invasion of Iraq. (The *Times* later acknowledged that its reporting about Iraqi weapons of mass destruction had depended too heavily on Iraqi exiles who were hostile to the regime of Saddam Hussein.)[40]

Beginning in 2004, however, the press began to display a new aggressiveness. In April 2004, a CBS News program, *60 Minutes II,* revealed the mistreatment of prisoners at the Abu Ghraib prison in Iraq. In 2005, the *Washington Post* uncovered the existence of a system of secret Central Intelligence Agency prisons that were being used to circumvent American laws, and ABC News detailed the harsh interrogation tactics used by CIA officers. On December 16, the *New York Times* reported that the National Security Agency (NSA) had been wiretapping American citizens without warrants since 2002. In May 2006, an NSA program to collect the telephone records of millions of Americans was exposed by *USA Today.* Not surprisingly, these stories angered the administration, leading some officials to suggest the possibility of prosecuting reporters who revealed national security secrets. The revelations also generated more debate about threats to civil liberties and prompted the ACLU and the Electronic Frontier Foundation to challenge the NSA spying in court.

At the same time, the administration was facing a serious challenge to its authority in the courts. Since 9/11, it had claimed enormous power to conduct the war on terrorism, including the right to do almost anything it wanted with "enemy combatants," including holding them in secret prisons and subjecting them to "waterboarding" and other forms of torture during interrogation; denying them access to the American courts; and trying them for war crimes in military tribunals that did not provide the rights required by the Geneva Convention. The president claimed this authority under a

2001 congressional resolution giving him the power to use military force against Al-Qaeda as well as the war-making powers granted to him by the Constitution. This claim was soon challenged by several of the men held as enemy combatants, including two American citizens, José Padilla and Yaser Hamdi. Considering the history of deference that the Supreme Court has shown for executive authority during times of crisis, it would not have been surprising if the justices had sought some compromise with the administration. Instead, in June 2004, they rejected the president's claim that enemy combatants were not entitled to ask the courts to review their detention. In an eloquent 8-1 decision in the case of *Hamdi v. Rumsfeld,* Justice Sandra Day O'Connor, writing one of the last opinions before her retirement, declared that a citizen who is held as an enemy combatant must have the opportunity to rebut the claims of the government in court. O'Connor told the government it was making the mistake that governments so frequently make during times of war. "It is during our most challenging and uncertain moments that our Nation's commitment to due process is most severely tested; and it is in those times that we must preserve our commitment at home to the principles for which we fight abroad," O'Connor wrote. She also reproved the government for arguing that the judiciary had "a heavily circumscribed role" during wars and other national emergencies. "We have long since made clear that a state of war is not a blank check for the President when it comes to the rights of the Nation's citizens," she wrote.[41]

The Supreme Court's decision in *Hamdi* sent a message to the federal courts that they must act to protect civil liberties. Judge Marrero was the first to heed the call when he overturned the NSL section of the Patriot Act three months later. A second NSL case became public in August 2005 when the ACLU challenged the FBI's effort to force a Connecticut library consortium, Library Connection, to provide information about a patron who had used one of its computers in February. The case seemed star-crossed from the beginning. First, the FBI was confronting four very determined librarians—Barbara Bailey, Peter Chase, George Christian, and Janet Nocek. They were well aware that the NSL section had been declared unconstitutional by Judge Marrero. Although they were willing to consider complying with a court order that had been issued by a judge, they refused to turn over records just because the FBI was demanding it. Then, while requiring that the librarians and the ACLU strictly observe the NSL gag order, the government did not properly censor its own documents, inadvertently revealing the names of Peter Chase and Library Connection. In September, U.S. District Court judge Janet C. Hall ordered the government to lift the gag on the plaintiffs. They hoped to be able to speak out in time to influence the debate over the reauthorization of the Patriot Act. But the Justice Department appealed Judge Hall's decision, and the gag stayed in place until the government dropped the case in the spring of 2006. At a press conference in May, George Christian, the executive director of Library Connection, said he regretted not being able to participate in the Patriot Act debate. "The fact that I can speak now is a little like being permitted to call the fire department only after a building has burned to the ground," he said.[42]

In August 2006, another judge, Anna Diggs Taylor of the U.S. District Court in Detroit, delivered an even bigger blow to the administration. Taylor had been assigned the ACLU lawsuit challenging the government's NSA spying program. Suing on behalf of a group of journalists, lawyers, and scholars who had extensive contacts in Muslim countries, the ACLU argued that warrantless wiretapping was having a chilling effect on freedom of speech by making Muslims abroad unwilling to speak with Americans on the telephone. In her decision, Taylor noted that Congress had explicitly created the Foreign Intelligence Surveillance Court to ensure that all government wiretapping was overseen by the courts. Once again, the government argued that the president possessed the authority to engage in warrantless wiretapping based on the congressional resolution and his "inherent powers." Citing *Hamdi,* Taylor rejected the president's claim. "There are no hereditary Kings in America and no powers not created by the Constitution," she declared.[43]

On September 11, 2006, the fifth anniversary of the 9/11 attacks, the American people were clearly ambivalent over the Bush administration's national security policies. They were far more concerned about the threat of terrorism than the threat to civil liberties. A Gallup poll taken in August 2006 showed that 82 percent of the respondents were convinced that there would be a suicide attack on

American soil in the next five years. It is not surprising that they expect their government to take active steps to protect them and that nearly 60 percent express support for the Patriot Act. However, it is also true that by a two-to-one margin the American people oppose taking any additional measures that violate civil liberties and that the number of people who believe the administration has gone too far has grown steadily and now stands at 41 percent. In addition, polls show that people are evenly divided over allowing government to search bookstore and library records, the wisdom of wireless wiretapping, and the NSA's program of collecting the telephone records of millions of Americans.[44]

The surprise in the poll numbers is not that people are ambivalent. It would be foolish not to fear terrorism in the wake of the bombings that were carried out by Al-Qaeda agents or sympathizers in Madrid in 2004 and in London the following year. The latest Gallup poll was taken after the August 2006 arrest of twenty-four people in England who were suspected of planning to blow up as many as ten airplanes in flight. What is remarkable is that notwithstanding the very real danger of terrorism, the support for civil liberties is as high as it is. Many Americans are clearly worried about repeating the mistakes that we have made in the past. They include a group of law students at the University of Montana who in late 2005 launched a campaign to win pardons for seventy-five men and three women who were convicted during World War I under the state sedition law, which banned speech that criticized the government. A law professor had suggested the idea after reading a book about the sedition cases by a colleague in the journalism department, Clemens P. Work. Not all of the students were enthusiastic in the beginning. "At first, I wasn't sure it was important to exonerate these people," one said. "But the more I thought about it, I realized that in the context of today's world, it's important to reaffirm the foundation of free speech." In May 2006, Montana governor Brian Schweitzer issued the pardons. "Across this country, it was a time in which we had lost our minds," Schweitzer told the relatives of the convicted during a ceremony in the statehouse rotunda. "So today in Montana, we will attempt to make it right. In Montana, we will say to an entire generation of people, we are sorry. And we challenge the rest of the country to do the same."[45]

The support for free expression involves more than the redress of past abuses. It also reflects the emergence of a constituency for free speech. Some of its supporters are members of minority groups who have experienced oppression directly or people who have seen its effect on friends and family. Governor Schweitzer's grandparents were German-speaking immigrants from Russia who arrived in Montana only a few years before the use of German was banned and German-language school books burned in patriotic bonfires during World War I. Other free speech supporters work for the growing number of civil liberties groups that have been founded since the 1950s. Journalists and their associations have long played an important role in the fight for press freedom and open government. Clemens Work, the author of the book about the Montana sedition cases, is both a former reporter for *U.S. News & World Report* and a former deputy director of a journalists' group, the Reporters Committee for Freedom of the Press. Finally, numerous professional and trade associations lobby actively on free speech issues. While the book and library community has taken a leading role, representatives of the other media groups have weighed in on issues affecting their members. One of the most beleaguered groups in recent years has been the video-game industry, which has been forced to challenge many laws banning the sale to minors of games with violent content. (The courts have repeatedly struck down these laws as violations of the First Amendment.)

Perhaps the best explanation for the expansion of free speech is that over the last century we have learned that it will survive only if we continue to cultivate it. The First Amendment was the law of the land for many years before it became an effective shield for dissent. The people of Montana during World War I saw no inconsistency between their belief in free speech and imprisoning people for saying things they disliked. The founding of the ACLU in 1920 was the critical first step toward making our professions about free speech mean something. Yet the labors of the activists alone would never have been enough if the Supreme Court had failed to recognize its responsibility for protecting the First Amendment, not only from the federal government but from the depredations of state legislatures, mayors, police chiefs, and sheriffs. The willingness of judges to look beyond the extreme and inflammatory opinions of the plaintiffs before them to the principle involved has placed free speech at the center of our constitutional system. Nor did the courts work alone. Although Congress acted as an oppressor during the McCarthy era, it has also approved critical reforms like the Freedom of Information Act that have strengthened free speech.

In the end, however, free speech depends on the courage of the individuals who fight for their rights. "Liberty lies in the hearts of men and women; when it dies there, no constitution, no law, no court can save it," Judge Learned Hand wrote in 1944. We are fortunate to live in a country that includes many brave souls. They have made freedom of speech one of the glories of American civilization.[46]

ACKNOWLEDGMENTS

I can testify to the existence of a free expression community from personal experience. In 1982, I was a graduate student working nights in the check-return department of a large commercial bank in New York City. When I spotted a want ad from a "First Amendment trade association," I applied for a part-time position with Media Coalition, a group of businesses that defend the right to produce and distribute material protected by the First Amendment, including works with sexual content. When I went to work for Media Coalition, I was hoping for an interesting but not too demanding job that would pay my bills while I wrote my dissertation. But the 1980s produced a cultural counterrevolution that attempted to roll back the free speech victories that had been won since 1920. My job quickly became full-time, and I have been working in this field ever since. In 1998, I was hired by the American Booksellers Foundation for Free Expression (ABFFE), a group that was organized by the American Booksellers Association (ABA) in the wake of the "culture wars."

My largest debt in writing this book is owed to the many friends and colleagues in the free speech community who have helped educate me. At the head of the list are Michael A. Bamberger, the general counsel of Media Coalition, Oren J. Teicher of the American Booksellers Association, Judith F. Krug of the American Library Association, and Burton Joseph, special counsel to *Playboy*. Joan Bertin of the National Coalition Against Censorship (NCAC) is both a wise adviser and a good friend. I am also very grateful for the counsel of David Horowitz of Media Coalition and my colleagues in the Free Expression Network.

There would be little for free speech advocates to do if individuals were unwilling to fight when someone violates their First Amendment rights. I have had the privilege of meeting many free speech heroes and heroines over the years, but I have worked most closely with booksellers. Joyce Meskis, the owner of the Tattered Cover Book Store in Denver, has been an inspiration to me, her city, and her industry. Chuck and Dee Robinson of Bellingham, Washington, Jim and Mary Dana of Grand Haven, Michigan, and Rhett and Betty Jackson of Columbia, South Carolina, have all fought for free speech in their communities. The members of the ABFFE board of directors have taken time from business and family to ensure that booksellers continue to play an important role in the free speech community.

I have been buoyed by the encouragement of a number of friends who gave me their comments on the manuscript: Betsy Burton of The King's English Bookshop in Salt Lake City, Marjorie Heins of the Free Expression Policy Project at the Brennan Center for Justice, Joan Bertin and Svetlana Mincheva of NCAC, and Len Vlahos of ABA.

I consider myself very fortunate to have gained the ear of Tom Hallock at an early stage in this project. The associate publisher of Beacon Press, Tom believed that this was the right book for a publishing house that put its future at risk by publishing the full text of the Pentagon Papers in 1971. He brought my proposal to the attention of director Helene Atwan, who has significantly improved the manuscript while helping me complete it far more quickly than I had thought possible.

My agent, Anne Depue, played an important role in framing the book. Dan Cullen and Mary Chris Welch, my old friends, held my hand throughout.

Because this book was written while I still clung tightly to my day job, I depended heavily on the research assistance of Mary Phillips-Sandy and Alexis Wolff. Thanks to Patricia O'Toole for helping me find them.

It is not surprising that I became interested in civil liberties. I come from a family of exhibitionists and loudmouths. In college, my parents, Joseph Finan and Sally Seidman, studied acting. My father went into radio, and for most of his career, he was a talk show host in Cleveland and Denver. My mother was active in Democratic Party politics and served on the board of the Colorado ACLU. My sons, Samuel and Alexander, show every sign of carrying on our loudmouth tradition. As kids, they took great joy in testing my commitment to free speech. My wife, Patricia Willard, is no big mouth, but she is a writer, which is why she let me write another book after the first one took decades. I could never have gotten the job done without her enthusiasm for the book and its author.

Introduction

1. Eric Lichtblau, "At F.B.I., Frustration over Limits of Terror Law," *New York Times,* December 11, 2005.
2. *Abrams v. U.S.,* 250 U.S. 616 (1919), 630; *Annals of Congress,* 4th Cong., 2nd sess., 934.

Chapter 1: Ground Zero

1. National Popular Government League, *To the American People: Report upon the Illegal Practices of the United States Department of Justice* (Washington, DC: National Popular Government League, May 1920; repr., New York: American Civil Liberties Union, May 1920), 18.
2. Ibid., 11–12; Stanley Coben, *A. Mitchell Palmer: Politician* (New York: Columbia University Press, 1963), 219–21; Robert K. Murray, *Red Scare: A Study in National Hysteria, 1919–1920* (Minneapolis: University of Minneapolis Press, 1955; repr., New York: McGraw-Hill, 1964), 196–98 (page numbers refer to the reprint edition).
3. Coben, *A. Mitchell Palmer,* 215.
4. "Statement by Emma Goldman," October 27, 1919, Emma Goldman Papers, University of California at Berkeley, available at http://sunsite.berkeley.edu/Goldman/Exhibition/plea.html.
5. *Abrams v. United States,* 250 U.S. 616 (1919), 630.
6. Geoffrey R. Stone, *Perilous Times: Free Speech in Wartime from the Sedition Act of 1798 to the War on Terrorism* (New York: W. W. Norton, 2004), 94–108.
7. David Rabban, "The Free Speech League, the ACLU, and Changing Conceptions of Free Speech in American History," *Stanford Law Review* 45, no. 47 (November 1992): 53.
8. Harry N. Scheiber, *The Wilson Administration and Civil Liberties* (Ithaca, NY: Cornell University Press, 1960), 5, 6, 11, n. 1.
9. Paul L. Murphy, *World War I and the Origin of Civil Liberties in the United States* (New York: W.W. Norton, 1979), 76, 78.
10. Rabban, "Free Speech League," 106.
11. Robert C. Cottrell, *Roger Nash Baldwin and the American Civil Liberties Union* (New York: Columbia University Press, 2000), 640.
12. Thomas A. Maik, *The Masses Magazine (1911–1917): Odyssey of an Era* (New York: Garland Publishing, 1994), 195–96; *Masses Publishing Co. v. Patten,* 244 F 535 (S.D.N.Y. 1917); decision reversed, 246 F 24 (2nd Cir. 1917).
13. Scheiber, *Wilson Administration,* 33, 34.

14. Murphy, *World War I*, 173.

15. Stone, *Perilous Times*, 171.

16. *Debs v. U.S.*, 249 U.S. 211 (1919).

17. James R. Mock and Cedric Larson, *Words That Won the War: The Story of the Committee on Public Information, 1917–1919* (Princeton, NJ: Princeton University Press, 1939), 64; Stone, *Perilous Times*, 172–73; Murphy, *World War I*, 132.

18. Donald Johnson, *Challenge to American Freedoms: World War I and the Rise of the American Civil Liberties Union* (Lexington: Mississippi Valley Historical Association, University of Kentucky Press, 1963), 65; Murphy, *World War I*, 128–29.

19. Johnson, *Challenge to Freedoms*, 63.

20. "Reminiscences of Roger N. Baldwin," Oral History Collection, Columbia University, 16–17, 19.

21. Ibid., 14.

22. Cottrell, *Roger Nash Baldwin*, 20.

23. Ibid., 21.

24. Lucile Millner, quoted in Cottrell, *Roger Nash Baldwin*, 34.

25. Ibid., 30–31.

26. "Reminiscences of Baldwin," 153.

27. Ibid., 4.

28. Ibid., 168.

29. Samuel Walker, *In Defense of American Liberties: A History of the ACLU* (New York: Oxford University Press, 1990), 37.

30. Quoted in Cottrell, *Roger Nash Baldwin*, 54, 59.

31. Ibid., 55.

32. Quoted in Johnson, *Challenge to Freedoms*, 20.

33. Walter Nelles, *A Liberal in Wartime: The Education of Albert DeSilver* (New York: W. W. Norton, 1940), 137.

34. Ibid., 66–67.

35. "Bigelow Denounces Outrages on Labor," *New York Call*, January 14, 1918, 1; "Bigelow Tells of Beating," *New York Times*, January 14, 1918, 11.

36. Walker, *In Defense of American Liberties*, 37.

37. Nelles, *Liberal in Wartime*, 149; Walker, *In Defense of American Liberties*, 38; Lucille Milner, *Education of an American Liberal: An Autobiography* (New York: Horizon Press, 1954), 72–73.

38. Cottrell, *Roger Nash Baldwin*, 81.

39. Johnson, *Challenge to Freedoms*, 75–76; Nelles, *Liberal in Wartime*, 148–49.

40. Johnson, *Challenge to Freedoms*, 76.

41. Ibid., 78.

42. *Shaffer v. United States*, 255 F 886 (9th Cir. 1919), 887–89, quoted in Stone, *Perilous Times*, 171.

43. *Schenck v. United States*, 249 U.S. 52 (1919).

44. Zechariah Chafee Jr., "Legislation against Anarchy," *New Republic* 19, no. 246 (July 23, 1919): 381–82.

45. Stone, *Perilous Times*, 168.

46. Murphy, *World War I*, 199.

47. Ibid., 83.

48. Jonathan Prude, "Portrait of a Civil Libertarian: The Faith and Fear of Zechariah Chafee, Jr.," *Journal of American History* 60, no. 3 (December 1973): 637.

49. Edward D. Re, *Freedom's Prophet: Selected Writings of Zechariah Chafee, Jr., University Professor, Harvard Law School* (New York: Oceana Publications, 1981), 17.

50. Ibid., 227.

51. Zechariah Chafee Jr., "Freedom of Speech," *New Republic* 17, no. 211 (November 16, 1918): 67–68.

52. Richard Polenberg, *Fighting Faiths: The Abrams Case, the Supreme Court and Free Speech*

(New York: Viking Penguin, 1987; repr., New York: Penguin Books, 1989), 219–20 (page citations refer to the reprint edition).

53. Ibid., 221.

54. Ibid., 236.

55. *Abrams v. U.S.,* 250 U.S. 616 (1919), 628.

56. Polenberg, *Fighting Faiths,* 241.

57. "Hughes Urges Reseating of 5 Socialists," *New York Tribune,* January 10, 1920, 1.

58. "The Red Hysteria," *New Republic* 21, no. 269 (January 28, 1920): 250–51; "Prating Patriots Worse Than Reds," *New York World,* January 13, 1920, 1.

59. Quoted in Henry Moskowitz, ed., *Progressive Democracy: Addresses and State Papers of Alfred E. Smith* (New York: Harcourt, Brace, 1928), 276.

60. Ibid., 278.

61. Ibid., 281.

Chapter 2: Mob Rule, 1921–1930

1. David A. Corbin, ed., *The West Virginia Mine Wars: An Anthology* (Charlestown, WV: Appalachian Editions, 1990), 71–72.

2. Arthur Warner, "Fighting Unionism with Martial Law," *The Nation,* October 12, 1921, 395.

3. Ibid.; Heber Blankenhorn, "Marching through West Virginia," *The Nation,* September 14, 1921, 288.

4. John Haynes Holmes, *Is Violence the Way Out of Our Industrial Disputes?* (New York: Dodd, Mead, 1920), xvi.

5. American Civil Liberties Union [henceforth ACLU], *The Fight for Free Speech,* first annual report (New York, September 1921), 7, 15.

6. Graham Adams Jr., *Age of Industrial Violence, 1910–1915: The Activities and Findings of the United States Commission on Industrial Relations* (New York: Columbia University Press, 1966), 216–17.

7. U.S. Commission on Industrial Relations, *Final Report and Testimony* 11:10844, 10841.

8. Ibid., 10873.

9. Ibid., 10875, 10894.

10. Paul L. Murphy, *The Meaning of Freedom of Speech: First Amendment Freedoms from Wilson to FDR* (Westport, CT: Greenwood Publishing, 1972), 160.

11. William Allen White, *The Autobiography of William Allen White* (New York: Macmillan, 1946), 612, 613–14; "Memphis Editor Held; Injunction Violator," *New York Times,* September 5, 1922, 2; Murphy, *Meaning of Freedom,* 162–63.

12. Murphy, *Meaning of Freedom,* 160–61.

13. Robert C. Cottrell, *Roger Nash Baldwin and the American Civil Liberties Union* (New York: Columbia University Press, 2000), 95.

14. Ibid., 106,108.

15. Samuel Walker, *In Defense of American Liberties: A History of the ACLU* (New York: Oxford University Press, 1990), 47.

16. Donald Johnson, "The American Civil Liberties Union: Origins, 1914–1917" (PhD diss., Columbia University, 1960), 306–8.

17. Ibid., 316–17; "Twelve Union Leaders Arrested in Mingo," *New York Times,* July 9, 1921, 11.

18. Johnson, "American Civil Liberties Union," 329.

19. Arthur Garfield Hays, *Let Freedom Ring* (New York: Boni and Liveright, 1928), 102.

20. Ibid., 105–6, 109.

21. Adams, *Age of Industrial Violence,* chap. 1 passim; Martin Zanger, "Politics of Confrontation: Upton Sinclair and the Launching of the ACLU in Southern California," *Pacific Historical Review* 38 (1969): 387.

22. Zanger, "Politics of Confrontation," 388–89.

23. Ibid., 391–93; Murphy, *Meaning of Freedom,* 158.

24. Zanger, "Politics of Confrontation," 400–404.

25. Martha Glaser, "Paterson, 1924: The ACLU and Labor," *New Jersey History* 94, no. 4 (Winter 1976): 160–62; Murphy, *Meaning of Freedom*, 152.

26. ACLU, *"Unlawful Assembly" in Paterson* (New York: ACLU, 1925), 8; Murphy, *Meaning of Freedom*, 131.

27. Murphy, *Meaning of Freedom*, 122, 132; ACLU, *The Fight for Free Speech* (New York: ACLU, September 1921), 15.

28. Kenneth T. Jackson, *The Ku Klux Klan in the City, 1915–1930* (New York: Oxford University Press, 1967), 11–12, 236.

29. David M. Chalmers, *Hooded Americanism: The History of the Ku Klux Klan* (New York: Watts, 1981; repr., Durham, NC: Duke University Press, 1987), 33; Jackson, *The Ku Klux Klan in the City*, 11; Waldo Roberts, "The Ku-Kluxing of Oregon," *Outlook*, March 14, 1923, 490.

30. Jackson, *The Ku Klux Klan in the City*, 168, 171, 177, 179.

31. Albert DeSilver, "The Ku Klux Klan," *The Nation*, September 14, 1921, 8.

32. Chalmers, *Hooded Americanism*, 200; Roberts, "The Ku-Kluxing of Oregon," 491; Walker, *In Defense of American Liberties*, 58.

33. "Why Kansas Bans the Klan," *Literary Digest* 75 (November 11, 1922): 13; "For Chicago Klan Inquiry," *New York Times*, December 5, 1922, 3; Jackson, *The Ku Klux Klan in the City*, 176–77.

34. *New York Times*, quoted in "Why Kansas Bans the Klan," *Literary Digest* 75 (November 11, 1922): 13; Paula Eldot, *Governor Alfred E. Smith: The Politician as Reformer* (New York: Garland Publishing, 1983), 333; "Ku Klux Klan Openly Defies New Law," *New York Times*, May 28, 1923, 2.

35. Walker, *In Defense of American Liberties*, 61–62.

36. Murphy, *Meaning of Freedom*, 188.

37. Norman Hapgood, ed., *Professional Patriots* (New York: Albert & Charles Boni, 1928), 7, 21.

38. Ibid., 14, 15, 19.

39. Ibid., 16–17.

40. ACLU, *The Gag on Teaching* (New York: ACLU, 1931), 11–15, 18–20.

41. Ibid., 12–13, 18–20; Murphy, *Meaning of Freedom*, 209–11.

42. ACLU, *Gag on Teaching*, 11; Murphy, *Meaning of Freedom*, 212.

43. Edward J. Larson, *Summer for the Gods: The Scopes Trial and America's Continuing Debate over Science and Religion* (1997; Cambridge, MA: Harvard University Press, 1998), 82.

44. Ibid., 55.

45. Ibid., 39; ACLU, *The Tennessee Evolution Case* (New York: ACLU, July 1925), 3.

46. ACLU, *Tennessee Evolution Case*, 1; ACLU, *Gag on Teaching*, 8–10; Larson, *Summer for the Gods*, 82–83.

47. Quoted in Larson, *Summer for the Gods*, 112.

48. Ibid., 112, 142; Walker, *In Defense of American Liberties*, 73.

49. Larson, *Summer for the Gods*, 143, 146, 102.

50. Ibid., 221.

51. L. Sprague de Camp, *The Great Monkey Trial* (Garden City, NY: Doubleday, 1968), 333.

52. Ibid., 334–35; Larson, *Summer for the Gods*, 179.

53. Charles Evans Hughes, "Liberty and Law," *American Bar Association Journal* 11 (September 1925): 564–66.

54. Murphy, *Meaning of Freedom*, 204; *Congressional Record*, vol. 67, pt. 2 (December 19, 1925–January 18, 1926), 1925.

55. Walker, *In Defense of American Liberties*, 59; "A Remarkable Organization," *St. Louis Post-Dispatch*, June 13, 1926, 2B; "Civil Liberty," *New York World*, May 17, 1927, 12; ACLU reply, "From the Civil Liberties Union," *New York World*, May 18, 1927, 12.

56. Murphy, *Meaning of Freedom*, 192–93.

57. Ibid., 195–200, 203; "Blacklists Spur Patriot Bodies to Bar Speakers," *New York World*,

February 16, 1928, 13; Sherwood Eddy, "The American Legion and Free Speech," *Christian Century* 45 (March 1, 1928): 277–78.

58. Carrie Chapman Catt, "An Open Letter to the D.A.R.," *Woman Citizen* 12, no. 2 (July 1927): 12; Murphy, *Meaning of Freedom,* 201, 204.

59. Murphy, *Meaning of Freedom,* 202; *New York Times,* May 1, 1928, 26.

Chapter 3: Banned in Boston

1. "Arbuckle Acquitted in One-Minute Verdict," *New York Times,* April 13, 1922.

2. David A. Yallop, *The Day the Laughter Stopped: The True Story of Fatty Arbuckle* (New York: St. Martin's Press, 1976), 253; Andy Edmonds, *Frame Up! The Untold Story of "Fatty" Arbuckle* (New York: William Morrow, 1991), passim.

3. Robert Sklar, *Movie-Made America: A Cultural History of American Movies* (New York: Random House, 1975; rev. ed., New York: Vintage Books, 1994), chap. 8 passim; Daniel Czitrom, "The Politics of Performance: Theater Licensing and the Origins of Movie Censorship in New York," in Francis G. Couvares, ed., *Movie Censorship and American Culture* (Washington, DC: Smithsonian Institution Press, 1996), 16–43; *Mutual Film Corp. v. Industrial Commission of Ohio,* 236 U.S. 230 (1915), 244.

4. Morris Ernst and Pare Lorentz, *Censored: The Private Life of the Movie* (New York: Jonathan Cape and Harrison Smith, 1930), 49–50.

5. Ibid., 41–42, 72–73, 84–86.

6. National Council on Freedom from Censorship, *What Shocked the Censors: A Complete Record of Cuts in Motion Picture Films Ordered by the New York State Censors from January 1932 to March 1933* (New York: National Council on Freedom from Censorship, 1933), 96, 98; Ernst and Lorentz, *Censored,* 17; Leonard J. Leff and Jerold L. Simmons, *The Dame in the Kimono: Hollywood, Censorship and the Production Code from the 1920's to the 1960's* (London: Weidenfeld and Nicolson, 1990), 15.

7. Ernst and Lorentz, *Censored,* 6–9, 69–70.

8. Yallop, *The Day the Laughter Stopped,* 243.

9. Paul S. Boyer, *Purity in Print: The Vice-Society Movement and Book Censorship in America* (New York: Charles Scribner's Sons, 1968), 11; Sklar, *Movie-Made America,* 126–27; *Los Angeles Times,* August 10, 1921, sec. 2, p. 14.

10. Czitrom, "Politics of Performance," 29; "600 Theaters Here Exclude Arbuckle," *New York Times,* September 14, 1921, 3.

11. Boyer, *Purity in Print,* 31; Yallop, *The Day the Laughter Stopped,* 182.

12. Heywood Broun and Margaret Leech, *Anthony Comstock: Roundsman of the Lord* (New York: Albert & Charles Boni, 1927), 80–81; Watch and Ward Society, quoted in Boyer, *Purity in Print,* 20–21.

13. Helen Lefkowitz Horowitz, *Rereading Sex: Battles over Sexual Knowledge and Suppression in Nineteenth-Century America* (New York: Alfred A. Knopf, 2002), 369–85.

14. Broun and Leech, *Anthony Comstock,* 18, 217; Horowitz, *Rereading Sex,* 382–84; Boyer, *Purity in Print,* 5.

15. Horowitz, *Rereading Sex,* chaps. 18 and 19 passim; Boyer, *Purity in Print,* 12.

16. Ellen Chesler, *Woman of Valor: Margaret Sanger and the Birth Control Movement in America* (New York: Simon & Schuster, 1992), 34–38, 63–65.

17. Ibid., 22–29, 57–65.

18. Ibid., 97–99.

19. Broun and Leech, *Anthony Comstock,* 249; Chesler, *Woman of Valor,* 128–30, 140–41.

20. Boyer, *Purity in Print,* 30, 33–35.

21. Ibid., 69–70.

22. Ibid., 79, 83–85; B. L. Reid, *The Man from New York: John Quinn and His Friends* (New York: Oxford University Press, 1968), 449.

23. Boyer, *Purity in Print,* 46–48, 77–78.

24. Jay A. Gertzman, *Bookleggers and Smuthounds: The Trade in Erotica, 1920–1940*

(Philadelphia: University of Pennsylvania Press, 1999), 105; Henry F. Pringle, "Comstock the Less," *American Mercury* (January 1927): 60; Boyer, *Purity in Print*, 83.

25. Boyer, *Purity in Print*, 102–5, 121, and chap. 5 passim.

26. "The Worst Bill Yet," *New York Times*, April 18, 1923, 20.

27. "Ford Tells How to Purge Books," *New York Times*, March 18, 1923, sec. XX, 2; "Likely to Railroad Clean Book Bill," *New York Times*, April 19, 1923, 1.

28. Boyer, *Purity in Print*, 155–56.

29. Henry Holt, quoted in "Plan Laid to Censor All New Literature," *New York Times*, August 4, 1922, 1; "The Censorship Situation," *Publishers Weekly*, April 28, 1923, 1323.

30. Boyer, *Purity in Print*, 31–32, 171–72.

31. "Reply to Mr. Hutchinson by Arthur Proctor," *Publishers Weekly*, May 26, 1923, 1623; Boyer, *Purity in Print*, 113–15.

32. "'Clean Book' Bill Dies in Senate," *New York Times*, May 3, 1923, 1; Boyer, *Purity in Print*, 118–19.

33. Boyer, *Purity in Print*, 120–22, 127.

34. Charles Angoff, "Boston Twilight," *American Mercury* (December 1925): 444.

35. Boyer, *Purity in Print*, 176.

36. Terry Teachout, *The Skeptic: A Life of H. L. Mencken* (New York: HarperCollins, 2002), 226; "Editor Defies Watch and Ward," *Boston Globe*, April 6, 1926, 6; Boyer, *Purity in Print*, 175–81.

37. "Both Heard in Mencken Case," *Boston Herald*, April 7, 1926, 10; Boyer, *Purity in Print*, 179–80.

38. Boyer, *Purity in Print*, 183–187.

39. Ibid., 188; "Oppose Book Censorship," *New York Times*, May 13, 1927, 28.

40. Boyer, *Purity in Print*, 184; Zechariah Chafee Jr., *The Censorship in Boston* (Boston: Civil Liberties Committee of Boston, 1929), passim.

41. "Ridicule Book Censorship at Forum Dinner," *Boston Herald*, April 17, 1929, 1.

42. Boyer, *Purity in Print*, 203; Walker, *In Defense of American Liberties*, 82.

43. "Enemies of Society," *New Republic* 58, no. 753 (May 8, 1929): 318; Walker, *In Defense of American Liberties*, 85.

44. Walker, *In Defense of American Liberties*, 85; Boyer, *Purity in Print*, 204; Chafee, *Censorship in Boston*, 21–22.

45. Boyer, *Purity in Print*, 196–98.

46. Ibid., 198.

47. Ibid., 209, chap. 8 passim.

48. "Assails Exclusion of Remarque's Book," *New York Times*, July 29, 1929, 26.

49. *Congressional Record*, October 11, 1929, 4445–46.

50. Ibid., 4454; Boyer, *Purity in Print*, 238.

51. Willard Johnson, ed., *Laughing Horse: A Symposium of Criticism, Comment and Opinion on the Subject of Censorship* (Taos, NM: Willard Johnson, February 1930; repr., New York: Kraus Reprint Corp., 1967), 20.

52. Boyer, *Purity in Print*, 268.

53. Judge Woolsey's opinion was reprinted in James Joyce, *Ulysses* (New York: Random House, 1961), x.

Chapter 4: The Court Takes a Hand

1. "Holmes Assails Whalen," *New York Times*, July 1, 1929, 23.

2. "Walker Warns Reds Stern Curb Awaits Lawless Outbreaks," *New York Times*, March 4, 1930. 1.

3. "Reds Battle Police in Union Square," *New York Times*, March 7, 1930, 1, 2; James R. Barrett, *William Z. Foster and the Tragedy of American Radicalism* (Urbana: University of Illinois Press, 1999), 165.

4. ACLU, *Police and Official Lawlessness against Communists in New York* (New York:

ACLU, 1930) 7; "Reds Boring into Business, Schools and City Bureaus, Whalen Warns," *New York Times,* March 9, 1930, 2.

5. " 'Red Scare' Protest Issued by Liberals," *New York Times,* May 19, 1930, 18.

6. ACLU, *Blue Coats and Reds* (New York: ACLU, 1929), 3, 9, 10.

7. Paul L. Murphy, *The Meaning of Freedom of Speech: First Amendment Freedoms from Wilson to FDR* (Westport, CT: Greenwood Publishing, 1972), 222–28, 239–44; ACLU, *Justice—North Carolina Style* (New York: ACLU, 1930), 10, 13; ACLU, *The Kentucky Miners Struggle: The Record of a Year of Lawless Violence* (New York: ACLU, 1932), 3.

8. W. A. Swanberg, *Dreiser* (New York: Charles Scribner and Sons, 1965), 383–89; ACLU, *The Kentucky Miners Struggle,* 9.

9. *Congressional Record,* 71st Cong., 1st sess., March–May 1929, pt. 1, p. 356.

10. Murphy, *Meaning of Freedom,* 242–43.

11. Fred W. Friendly, *Minnesota Rag: The Dramatic Story of the Landmark Supreme Court Case That Gave New Meaning to Freedom of the Press* (New York: Random House, 1981; repr., New York: Vintage Books, 1982), 66–68.

12. Ibid., 71, 75.

13. Ibid., 23, 45–46.

14. Ibid., 78–79.

15. Ibid., 21, 64–65, 89.

16. Ibid., 88.

17. Murphy, *Meaning of Freedom,* 254–56, 367, n. 32.

18. Ibid., 257; *Gitlow v. New York,* 268 U.S. 652 (1925), 658, 669.

19. *Whitney v. California,* 274 U.S. 357 (1927), 372; *U.S. v. Schwimmer,* 279 U.S. 644 (1929), 650.

20. *Gitlow v. New York,* 673.

21. *Whitney v. California,* 377; *U.S. v. Schwimmer,* 655.

22. *Milwaukee Leader,* quoted in Murphy, *Meaning of Freedom,* 232–33; "Fighting Freedom's Battle," *Trenton Times,* March 2, 1931, quoted in ACLU, *Still the Fish Committee Nonsense! The Answer of the Press to the Fish Committee Proposals to Outlaw Free Speech for Communists* (New York: ACLU, 1932), 7.

23. Friendly, *Minnesota Rag,* 93, 104.

24. Ibid., 105, 103.

25. Ibid., 119–20; *Gitlow v. New York,* 666.

26. *Stromberg v. California,* 283 U.S. 359 (1931), 369.

27. Friendly, *Minnesota Rag,* 129.

28. Ibid., 126–27.

29. *Near v. Minnesota,* 283 U.S. 697 (1931), 713, 718–19

30. Quoted in "The Supreme Court's Shift to Liberalism," *Literary Digest* 109 (June 13, 1931): 8.

31. Irving Bernstein, *The Lean Years: A History of the American Worker, 1920–1933* (Boston: Houghton Mifflin, 1960), 398–99; Jerold S. Auerbach, *Labor and Liberty: The La Follette Committee and the New Deal* (Indianapolis: Bobbs-Merrill, 1966), 211.

32. ACLU, *Liberty under the New Deal* (New York: ACLU, 1934), 3; Auerbach, *Labor and Liberty,* 27, 211.

33. "Hague Carries His CIO Fight to the Nation," *Washington Post,* January 7, 1938, sec. X, 3; "Mayor Hague Says He Will Keep Up Fight to Bar Red 'Elements' from Jersey City," *New York Times,* December 10, 1937, 16; Dayton David McKean, *The Boss: The Hague Machine in Action* (New York: Houghton Mifflin, 1940), 196, 228.

34. *Lovell v. City of Griffin, Georgia,* 303 U.S. 444 (1938); *Hague v. Committee for Industrial Organization,* 307 U.S. 496 (1940), 516; Zechariah Chafee Jr., *Free Speech in the United States* (Cambridge, MA: Harvard University Press, 1954), 429.

35. Auerbach, *Labor and Liberty,* 205.

36. *Thornhill v. Alabama,* 310 U.S. 88 (1940), 102, 105.

Chapter 5: The Second Red Scare

1. "Murphy Sworn in at the White House," *New York Times,* January 3, 1939, 3; Sidney Fine, *Frank Murphy: The New Deal Years* (Chicago: University of Chicago Press, 1979), 90.

2. Sidney Fine, *Frank Murphy: The Detroit Years* (Ann Arbor: University of Michigan Press, 1975), 164, 166.

3. "Reminiscences of Roger N. Baldwin," Oral History Collection, Columbia University, 138; Fine, *The Detroit Years,* 11–12, 18.

4. Fine, *The Detroit Years,* 69, 396–97.

5. Frank Murphy to Morris L. Ernst, January 9, 1939, quoted in Sidney Fine, *Frank Murphy: The Washington Years* (Ann Arbor: University of Michigan Press, 1984), 79; "'Civil Rights' Unit Set Up by Murphy," *New York Times,* February 4, 1939, 2; J. Woodford Howard Jr., *Mr. Justice Murphy: A Political Biography* (Princeton, NJ: Princeton University Press, 1968), 205; *Unity Magazine,* March 1939, quoted in Jerold S. Auerbach, *Labor and Liberty: The La Follette Committee and the New Deal* (Indianapolis: Bobbs-Merrill, 1966), 208.

6. Howard, *Mr. Justice Murphy,* 210.

7. Ibid., 206–10.

8. Ellen Schrecker, *Many Are the Crimes: McCarthyism in America* (Boston: Little, Brown, 1998), 15; Samuel Walker, *In Defense of American Liberties: A History of the ACLU* (New York: Oxford University Press, 1990), 115, 120–23; Geoffrey R. Stone, *Perilous Times: Free Speech in Wartime from the Sedition Act of 1798 to the War on Terrorism* (New York: W. W. Norton, 2004), 245; Shawn Francis Peters, *Judging Jehovah's Witnesses: Religious Persecution and the Dawn of the Rights Revolution* (Lawrence: University of Kansas Press, 2000), 72.

9. Peters, *Judging Jehovah's Witnesses,* 23.

10. Ibid., 26.

11. Ibid., 55, 65–66.

12. Ibid., 8, 10, 34, 84.

13. Stone, *Perilous Times,* 255.

14. Ibid., 257, 264–66, 272–75; Walker, *American Liberties,* 136.

15. Stone, *Perilous Times,* 278–79.

16. *Jones v. Opelika,* 316 U.S. 584 (1942), 623–24; *West Virginia State Board of Education v. Barnette,* 319 U.S. 624 (1943), 642; Peters, *Judging Jehovah's Witnesses,* 254; Stone, *Perilous Times,* 280–83.

17. Walker, *In Defense of American Liberties,* 168–69.

18. Henry Steele Commager, ed., *The Documents of American History Since 1898,* vol. 2, 9th ed. (Englewood Cliffs, NJ: Prentice-Hall, 1973), 527.

19. Ellen Schrecker, *The Age of McCarthyism: A Brief History with Documents* (Boston: Bedford Books of St. Martin's Press, 1994), 212.

20. Schrecker, *Many Are the Crimes,* 15, chap. 2 passim.

21. Ibid., 31.

22. Schrecker, *Age of McCarthyism,* 38–39, 151–54.

23. Stone, *Perilous Times,* 252; Schrecker, *Age of McCarthyism,* 174.

24. "Paraders, Watchers in May Day Event Fewer than in '49," *New York Times,* May 1, 1949, 1, 3.

25. Stone, *Perilous Times,* 360.

26. Schrecker, *Age of McCarthyism,* 84; *Many Are the Crimes,* 97; Ellen W. Schrecker, *No Ivory Tower: McCarthyism and the Universities* (New York: Oxford University Press, 1986), passim.

27. Schrecker, *Many Are the Crimes,* 330; *Age of McCarthyism,* 217–23; John Henry Faulk, *Fear on Trial* (New York: Simon & Schuster, 1964; repr., Austin: University of Texas Press, 1983), 92, 96–97 (page citations are to the reprint edition).

28. Schrecker, *Many Are the Crimes,* 324; Stone, *Perilous Times,* 365; Schrecker, *Age of McCarthyism,* 223.

29. Stone, *Perilous Times,* 332, 336, 378, 390–91.

30. Harry S. Truman, "Veto of Internal Security Act, Sept. 22, 1950," in Schrecker, *Age of McCarthyism,* 194–95.

31. Walker, *In Defense of American Liberties,* 198; William R. Tanner and Robert Griffith, "Legislative Politics and 'McCarthyism': The Internal Security Act of 1950," in Robert Griffith and Athan Theoharis, eds., *Specter: Original Essays on the Cold War and the Origins of McCarthyism* (New York: Franklin Watts, 1974), 183–86.

32. Schrecker, *No Ivory Tower,* 94; Walter P. Metzger, "Ralph F. Fuchs and Ralph E. Himstead: A Note on the AAUP in the McCarthy Period," *Academe* 72, no. 6 (November–December 1986): 29–30; Schrecker, *Age of McCarthyism,* 85–86; *Many Are the Crimes,* 303.

33. Walker, *In Defense of American Liberties,* 183.

34. Ibid., 131, 139–42, 155–58.

35. Eric Bentley, ed., *Thirty Years of Treason: Excerpts from Hearings before the House Committee on Un-American Activities* (New York: Viking Press, 1971), 1948.

36. Walker, *In Defense of American Liberties,* 194.

37. Stone, *Perilous Times,* 419; William O. Douglas, "The Black Silence of Fear," *New York Times Magazine,* January 13, 1952, 24.

38. Stone, *Perilous Times,* 384.

39. A. M. Sperber, *Murrow: His Life and Times* (New York: Freundlich Books, 1986), 417.

40. Ibid., 415–16.

41. Ibid., 436–38.

42. Norman Mailer, "The White Negro: Superficial Reflections on the Hipster" (1956), quoted in Stone, *Perilous Times,* 419.

43. Faulk, *Fear on Trial,* 195, 205.

44. Ibid., 206, 230, 271.

45. James W. Ely Jr., Joel B. Grossman, and William M. Wiecek, eds., *The Oxford Companion to the Supreme Court* (New York: Oxford University Press, 1992), 87; *Yates v. United States,* 354 U.S. 298 (1957), 324–25; *Watkins v. United States,* 354 U.S. 178 (1957), 202.

46. Stone, *Perilous Times,* 422; Schrecker, *Many Are the Crimes,* 371–73; Faulk, *Fear on Trial,* 274.

Chapter 6: The Fight for Artistic Freedom, 1945–1966

1. "600 Pupils Hold Burial Rites for 2000 Comic Books," *Washington Post,* October 27, 1948, 1; "Catholic Students Burn Up Comic Books," *New York Times,* December 11, 1948, 18; "Comic Criminals to Burn," *New York Times,* January 7, 1948, 23.

2. Helen Lefkowitz Horowitz, *Rereading Sex: Battles over Sexual Knowledge and Suppression in Nineteenth-Century America* (New York: Alfred A. Knopf, 2002), 382–83.

3. James C. N. Paul and Murray L. Schwartz, *Federal Censorship: Obscenity in the Mail* (New York: Free Press of Glencoe, 1961), 69–72.

4. Hugh Merrill, *Esky: The Early Years at Esquire* (New Brunswick, NJ: Rutgers University Press, 1995), 32, 109–10.

5. Edward de Grazia, *Girls Lean Back Everywhere; The Law of Obscenity and the Assault on Genius* (New York: Random House, 1992), 210, 211, 222.

6. Morris L. Ernst and Alexander Lindey, *The Censor Marches On: Recent Milestones in the Administration of the Obscenity Law in the United States* (New York: Doubleday, 1940; repr., New York: Da Capo Press, 1971), 115–17, 126 (page numbers refer to the reprint edition); Robert Sklar, *Movie-Made America: A Cultural History of American Movies* (New York: Random House, 1975; rev. ed., New York: Vintage Books, 1994), 173–74 (page numbers refer to the reprint edition).

7. Sklar, *Movie-Made,* 174; Frank Walsh, *Sin and Censorship: The Catholic Church and the Motion Picture Industry* (New Haven, CT: Yale University Press, 1996), 244–46.

8. William B. Lockhart and Robert C. McClure, "Literature, the Law of Obscenity, and the Constitution," *Minnesota Law Review* 38, no. 4 (1954): 310–11, 317–18.

9. Ibid., 314–15; William B. Lockhart and Robert C. McClure, "Censorship of Obscenity: The Developing Constitutional Standards," *Minnesota Law Review* 45, no. 5 (1960): 14–15.

10. James Gilbert, *A Cycle of Outrage: America's Reaction to the Juvenile Delinquent in the 1950s* (New York: Oxford University Press, 1986), 37, 75.

11. Bradford W. Wright, *Comic Book Nation: The Transformation of Youth Culture in America* (Baltimore: Johns Hopkins University Press, 2001), 92–93; Gilbert, *Cycle of Outrage,* 99, 101–2.

12. Fredric Wertham, "The Comics ... Very Funny!" *Saturday Review of Literature,* May 29, 1948, 27, 29; Wright, *Comic Book Nation,* 155.

13. Wright, *Comic Book Nation,* 97–98; Amy Kiste Nyberg, *Seal of Approval: The History of the Comics Code* (Jackson: University Press of Mississippi, 1998), 37.

14. Wright, *Comic Book Nation,* 166.

15. Ibid., 172–73.

16. Ibid., 176.

17. Louise S. Robbins, *Censorship and the American Library: The American Library Association's Response to Threats to Intellectual Freedom, 1939–1969* (Westport, CT: Greenwood Press, 1996), 14–15, 64, 71, 74.

18. Ibid., 12–13, 15–16.

19. Ibid., 35–36, 39.

20. Ibid., 37; Louise S. Robbins, *The Dismissal of Miss Ruth Brown: Civil Rights, Censorship and the American Library* (Norman: University of Oklahoma, 2000), 72, 92, 163.

21. Robbins, *Censorship and the American Library,* 52, 76.

22. Ibid., 77, 189, 192; American Library Association, *Intellectual Freedom Manual,* 7th ed. (Chicago: American Library Association, 2006), 228.

23. Robbins, *Censorship and the American Library,* 80, 82, 188.

24. John Costello, *Virtue under Fire: How World War II Changed Our Social and Sexual Attitudes* (Boston: Little, Brown, 1985), 260; Wardell B. Pomeroy, *Dr. Kinsey and the Institute for Sex Research* (New York: Harper & Row, 1972), 282, 343.

25. Leonard J. Leff and Jerold L. Simmons, *The Dame in the Kimono: Hollywood, Censorship and the Production Code from the 1920's to the 1960's* (London: Weidenfeld and Nicolson, 1990), 136.

26. James R. Petersen, *The Century of Sex:* Playboy's *History of the Sexual Revolution, 1900–1999* (New York: Grove Press, 1999), 201; Gay Talese, *Thy Neighbor's Wife* (Garden City, NY: Doubleday, 1980), 84.

27. Allen Ginsberg, *Collected Poems, 1947–1980* (New York: Harper & Row, 1984), 126; Barry Miles, *Ginsberg: A Biography* (New York: Simon & Schuster, 1989; repr., London: Virgin Publishing, 2000), 194 (page citations refer to the reprint edition); *Roth v. United States,* 354 U.S. 476 (1957), 487.

28. *Winters v. New York,* 333 U.S. 507 (1948), 519; *Joseph Burstyn, Inc. v. Wilson,* 343 U.S. 495 (1952), passim; *Butler v. Michigan,* 352 U.S. 380 (1957), 383.

29. Hunter R. Clark, *Justice Brennan: The Great Conciliator* (New York: Birch Lane Press, 1995), 63, 68, 71.

30. Lockhart and McClure, "Censorship of Obscenity," 19; De Grazia, *Girls Lean Back,* 300, 302–3.

31. *Roth v. United States,* 354 U.S. 476 (1957), 481, 484, 489; De Grazia, *Girls Lean Back,* 193.

32. *Roth v. United States,* 487–88.

33. Lockhart and McClure, "Censorship of Obscenity," 32n. 158; "Obscenity in Court," *Washington Post,* June 30, 1957, E4; Harry Kalven Jr., "The Metaphysics of Obscenity," *The Supreme Court Review* (Chicago: University of Chicago Press, 1960), 10.

34. *Kingsley Pictures Corp. v. Regents,* 360 U.S. 684 (1959), 688; Lockhart and McClure, "Censorship of Obscenity," 42–43, 47.

35. E. R. Hutchinson, *Tropic of Cancer on Trial: A Case History of Censorship* (New York: Grove Press, 1968), 16, 25; De Grazia, *Girls Lean Back,* 370.

36. Anthony Lewis, "The Most Recent Troubles of 'Tropic of Cancer': A Chapter in Censorship," *New York Times Book Review,* January 21, 1962, 5.

37. *Jacobellis v. Ohio,* 378 U.S. 184 (1964), 187, 189–90, 197.

38. Ibid., 192, 194–95.

39. Hutchinson, *Tropic of Cancer On Trial,* 244.

Chapter 7: Let the Sunshine In

1. Taylor Branch, *Parting the Waters: America in the King Years, 1954–63* (New York: Simon & Schuster, 1988; repr., New York: Touchstone, 1989), 138 (page citations refer to the reprint edition).

2. Ibid., 138–40.

3. Ibid., 140–41; Gerome Ragni and James Rado, "Aquarius" and "The Flesh Failures (Let the Sunshine In)"; *Hair* opened on Broadway on April 29, 1968.

4. Numan V. Bartley, *The Rise of Massive Resistance: Race and Politics in the South During the 1950's* (Baton Rouge: Louisiana State University Press, 1969), 117; Gertrude Samuels, "The Silent Fear in Little Rock," *New York Times Magazine,* March 30, 1958, 78.

5. Bartley, *Massive Resistance,* 82.

6. "Alabama Judge Refuses to Set Aside $100,000 Fine Levied against NAACP," *Washington Post,* July 31, 1956, 1.

7. "Bills Aimed at NAACP Stir Va. Assembly Fight," *Washington Post,* September 11, 1956, 28; "Arkansas Loses in NAACP Case," *New York Times,* June 9, 1959, 31.

8. Harry Kalven Jr., *The Negro and the First Amendment* (Columbus: Ohio State University Press, 1965), 66; *NAACP v. Button,* 371 U.S. 415 (1963), 429, quoted in Kalven, *The Negro,* 82.

9. "Heed Their Rising Voices," *New York Times,* March 29, 1960, 25.

10. Anthony Lewis, *Make No Law: The Sullivan Case and the First Amendment* (New York: Random House, 1991), 25.

11. Ibid., 107.

12. Ibid., 104, 107.

13. *New York Times v. Sullivan,* 376 U.S. 254 (1964), 270, 273, 274.

14. Ibid., 271–72, 279.

15. Lewis, *Make No Law,* 150, 152, 154.

16. James Miller, *"Democracy in the Streets": From Port Huron to the Siege of Chicago* (New York: Simon & Schuster, 1987), 49.

17. Ibid., 124–25.

18. Ibid., 45–46.

19. David Lance Goines, *The Free Speech Movement: Coming of Age in the 1960s* (Berkeley, CA: Ten Speed Press, 1993), 168.

20. Ibid., 361; Margot Adler, "My Life in the Free Speech Movement: Memories of a Freshman," in Robert Cohen and Reginald E. Zelnick, eds., *The Free Speech Movement: Reflections on Berkeley in the 1960's* (Berkeley: University of California Press, 2002), 125.

21. Geoffrey R. Stone, *Perilous Times: Free Speech in Wartime from the Sedition Act of 1798 to the War on Terrorism* (New York: W. W. Norton, 2004), 441, 442.

22. *Yates v. United States,* 354 U.S. 298 (1957), 318–19.

23. Richard Gid Powers, *Broken: The Troubled Past and Uncertain Future of the FBI* (New York: Free Press, 2004), 168; Richard Gid Powers, *Secrecy and Power: The Life of J. Edgar Hoover* (New York: Free Press, 1987), 237.

24. Ellen Schrecker, *Many Are the Crimes: McCarthyism in America* (Boston: Little, Brown, 1998), 203.

25. Percival R. Bailey, "The Case of the National Lawyers Guild, 1939–1958," in Athan G. Theoharis, ed., *Beyond the Hiss Case: The FBI, Congress, and the Cold War* (Philadelphia: Temple University Press, 1982), 138–39, 142.

26. Powers, *Broken,* 235–36.

27. Ibid., 246–47.

28. Ibid., 279; David Cunningham, *There's Something Happening Here: The New Left, the Klan, and FBI Counterintelligence* (Berkeley: University of California Press, 2004), 54.

29. *Tinker v. Des Moines School District,* 393 U.S. 503 (1969), 506; *Brandenburg v. Ohio,* 395 U.S. 444 (1969), 444–45, 447; Stone, *Perilous Times,* 521–23.

30. Harry Kalven Jr., " 'Uninhibited, Robust, and Wide-Open': A Note on Free Speech and the Warren Court," *Michigan Law Review* 67, no. 2 (1968): 302.

31. Ibid.

32. Stone, *Perilous Times,* 453; David Rudenstine, *The Day the Presses Stopped: A History of the Pentagon Papers Case* (Berkeley: University of California Press, 1996), 94; "Transcript of Address by Agnew Criticizing Television on Its Coverage of the News," *New York Times,* November 14, 1969, 24.

33. Peter Schrag, *Test of Loyalty: Daniel Ellsberg and the Rituals of Secret Government* (New York: Simon & Schuster, 1974), 34, 44.

34. Rudenstine, *The Day the Presses Stopped,* 132.

35. *New York Times v. United States,* 403 U.S. 713 (1971), 729, 731.

36. *United States v. New York Times Company et al.,* 328 F. Supp. 330–31 (S.D.N.Y. 1971).

37. Ibid., 344.

38. Kathryn S. Olmsted, *Challenging the Secret Government: The Post-Watergate Investigations of the CIA and the FBI* (Chapel Hill: University of North Carolina Press, 1996), 65.

39. Ibid., 107, 175.

40. Harold L. Cross, *The People's Right to Know: Legal Access to Public Records and Proceedings* (New York: Columbia University Press, 1953), xiii.

41. George Kennedy, "How Americans Got Their Right to Know," www.johnmossfoundation.org/foi/kennedy.htm; National Security Archive, "Veto Battle 30 Years Ago Set Freedom of Information Norms," www.gwu.edu/ ~nsarchiv/NSAEBB/NSAEBB142/index.htm.

42. Powers, *Broken,* 314.

43. Samuel Walker, "The Politics of Police Accountability: The Seattle Police Spying Ordinance as a Case Study," in Erika S. Fairchild and Vincent J. Webb, eds., *The Politics of Crime and Criminal Justice* (Beverly Hills, CA: Sage Publications, 1985), 144–57.

Chapter 8: The Counterattack, 1970–2002

1. Christopher M. Finan and Anne F. Castro, "The Rev. Donald E. Wildmon, 1977– 1992" (New York: Media Coalition, 1992), passim, www.mediacoalition.org/reports/ Wildmon%20report.pdf.

2. Catherine A. MacKinnon, *Feminism Unmodified: Discourses on Life and Law* (Cambridge, MA: Harvard University Press, 1987), 136; Christopher M. Finan, "Catharine A. MacKinnon: The Rise of a Feminist Censor, 1983–1993" (New York: Media Coalition, 1993), passim, www.mediacoalition.org/reports/Macreport3.pdf.

3. Jack Valenti, "How It All Began," www.mpaa.org/Ratings_HowItAllBegan.asp.

4. Richard M. Nixon, "Statement about the Report of the Commission on Obscenity and Pornography," October 24, 1970, available at www.presidency.ucsb.edu/ws/index.php? pid=2759&st=obscenity&st1=.

5. Harry F. Waters, George Hackett, and Jeff B. Copeland, "The New Right's TV Hit List," *Newsweek,* June 15, 1981, 101.

6. Irvin Molotsky, "Groups Set Aside Boycott of TV Sponsors," *New York Times,* June 30, 1981.

7. Fred Strebeigh, "Defining Law on the Feminist Frontier," *New York Times Magazine,* October 6, 1991, 31.

8. MacKinnon, *Feminism Unmodified,* 171, 172.

9. Andrea Dworkin, Testimony, Minneapolis Zoning Commission, October 18, 1983, 2; transcript in author's possession.

10. Donald A. Downs, *The New Politics of Pornography* (Chicago: University of Chicago Press, 1989), 114–15.

11. Ibid., 86, 89.

12. *American Booksellers Assn. v. Hudnut,* 598 F. Supp. 1316 (1984), 1327, 1337.

13. Tony Schwartz, "A Boycott of TV Advertisers Is Again Threatened," *New York Times,* January 28, 1982; Tony Randall, quoted in *Time,* March 7, 1983, 120.

14. Donald E. Wildmon, "Pornography in the Family Marketplace," attached as an addendum to letter from Alan Sears, Executive Director, Attorney General's Commission on Pornography, to various corporations; letter and addendum in author's possession.

15. Steve Chapman, "Perspective," *Chicago Tribune,* July 31, 1985, 15; John Leo, "Pornography: The Feminist Dilemma," *Time,* July 21, 1986, 21.

16. Jerry Kirk to C. Fred Fetterolf, August 13, 1986; letter in author's possession.

17. Philip D. Harvey, *The Government v. Erotica* (Amherst, NY: Prometheus Books, 2001), 27.

18. ACLU, "Above the Law: The Justice Department's War against the First Amendment" (December 1991), 6.

19. Jim McGee, "U.S. Crusade against Pornography Tests the Limits of Fairness," *Washington Post,* January 11, 1993, A1.

20. Interview with Jim Dana, undated, 3; in author's possession.

21. *Insight,* July 2, 1990, 14; Marjorie Heins, *Sex, Sin and Blasphemy: A Guide to America's Censorship Wars* (New York: New Press, 1993), 131–36.

22. American Booksellers Foundation for Free Expression, *Free Expression* (American Booksellers Foundation for Free Expression, Autumn 1991), 5.

23. Oren J. Teicher, "Proposal for a Michigan Anti-Censorship Campaign," December 13, 1989, 4 (typescript, in author's possession).

24. *Wojnarowicz v. American Family Assn.,* 745 F. Supp. 130 (S.D.N.Y. 1990) Excerpts available at www.csulb.edu/%7Ejvancamp/doc6.html.

25. Ibid.

26. Harvey, *Government v. Erotica,* 39.

27. Garrison Keillor, "Garrison Keillor Anti-Censorship Video" (script in author's possession).

28. Joe Teller, "Movies Don't Cause Crime," *New York Times,* January 17, 1992.

29. Ad Hoc Committee of Feminists for Free Expression to members of the U.S. Senate Judiciary Committee, undated [February 1992], 1; in author's possession.

30. Ibid., 2; Catharine A. MacKinnon, *Only Words* (Cambridge, MA: Harvard University Press, 1993), 71.

31. *Reno v. ACLU,* 521 U.S. 844 (1997).

32. *New York v. Ferber,* 458 U.S. 747 (1982).

33. *Alexander v. U.S.,* 509 U.S. 544 (1993), 1.

34. *Ashcroft v. Free Speech Coalition,* 535 U.S. 234 (2002).

35. Ibid.

Chapter 9: 9/11

1. The other sponsors of the press conference were Electronic Frontier Foundation, Electronic Privacy Information Center, Feminists for Free Expression, First Amendment Project, Online Policy Group, Peacefire, PEN American Center, and Washington Area Lawyers for the Arts.

2. "On Gag Rules, Spy Tools and Freedom of Speech," *Baltimore Sun,* April 22, 2002, 10.

3. Robert O'Harrow Jr., "Six Weeks in Autumn," *Washington Post,* October 27, 2002, W06.

4. Quoted in Bill Carter and Felicity Barringer, "A Nation Challenged: Speech and Expression; In Patriotic Time, Dissent Is Muted," *New York Times,* September 28, 2001, 1.

5. David Glenn, "The War on Campus," *The Nation,* December 3, 2001,

www.thenation.com/doc/20011203/glenn; Jerry L. Martin and Anne D. Neal, "Defending Civilization: How Our Universities Are Failing America and What Can Be Done About It" (American Council of Trustees and Alumni, revised and expanded, February 2002), 4.

6. Emily Eakin, "On the Lookout for Patriotic Correctness," *New York Times,* November 24, 2001, 15; Jim Lobe, "The War on Dissent Widens," *AlterNet,* March 12, 2002, www.alternet.org/story/12612/.

7. Andrew Rudalevige, *The New Imperial Presidency* (Ann Arbor: University of Michigan Press, 2005), 186–87, 189, 191, 211.

8. John Ashcroft to Heads of All Federal Departments and Agencies, "Freedom of Information Act," October 12, 2001, www.fas.org/sgp/foia/ashcroft.html.

9. Nancy V. Baker, *General Ashcroft: Attorney at War* (Lawrence: University of Kansas Press, 2006), 73–74.

10. David Cole and James X. Dempsey, *Terrorism and the Constitution: Sacrificing Civil Liberties in the Name of National Security,* 2nd ed. (New York: New Press, 2002), 153, 158.

11. Ibid., 160–61.

12. USA Patriot Act, sec. 215, amending 50 U.S.C. 1862 and 1863.

13. Baker, *General Ashcroft,* 150; O'Harrow, "Six Weeks in Autumn."

14. O'Harrow, "Six Weeks in Autumn."

15. Cole and Dempsey, *Terrorism,* 151; Baker, *General Ashcroft,* 74; *Congressional Record,* October 25, 2001, S11022.

16. O'Harrow, "Six Weeks in Autumn"; In Defense of Freedom Coalition, "In Defense of Freedom," www.indefenseoffreedom.org.

17. Lynda Richardson, "Public Lives; Liberty and Justice, With an Emphasis on All," *New York Times,* January 8, 2002, B2; Anthony D. Romero, "ACLU Insists on Need to Be Safe and Free," February 6, 2002, www.aclu.org/natsec/emergpowers/14390prs20020206.html.

18. "A Nation Challenged: Excerpts from Attorney General's Testimony before Senate Judiciary Committee," *New York Times,* December 7, 2001, B6; Laura W. Murphy, "ACLU Appalled by Ashcroft Statement on Dissent; Calls Free Speech 'Main Engine of Justice,'" December 10, 2001, www.aclu.org/freespeech/protest/10916prs20011210.html.

19. "Northampton City Council Resolution," May 2, 2002, www.bordc.org/detail.php?id=12; ACLU, "ACLU Mobilizes Members and Supporters Nationwide to Keep America 'Safe and Free,'" Oct. 16, 2002, www.aclu.org/safefree/general/17663prs20021016.html.

20. Joan Starr, "Libraries and National Security: An Historical Review," *First Monday,* 9, no. 12 (December 2004), http://firstmonday.org/issues/issue9_12/starr; Robert D. McFadden, "FBI in New York Asks Librarian Aid in Reporting on Spies," *New York Times,* September 1 , 1987, 1; David Johnston, "Documents Disclose F.B.I. Investigations of Some Libraries," *New York Times,* November 7, 1989, 1.

21. Vermont Library Association, "USA PATRIOT Act Letter," October 21, 2002, www.vermontlibraries.org/patriot.html.

22. Mike Taibbi, "Four Amendments and a Funeral," *Rolling Stone,* August 10, 2005, www.rollingstone.com/politics/story/7539869/Four_amendments_a_funeral; Bernie Sanders and Huck Gutman, *Outsider in the House* (London: Verso, 1997), 16.

23. Sanders and Gutman, *Outsider in the House,* 64; Adam Silverman, "Sanders Seeks to Repeal Part of Patriot Act," *Burlington Free Press,* December 21, 2002, 1B.

24. "ACLU Membership Surges in Post–9/11 World," *USA Today,* December 11, 2002, A1.

25. "Reading over Your Shoulder," *The Tennessean,* January 25, 2003; American Library Association, "Resolution on the USA PATRIOT Act and Related Measures That Infringe on the Rights of Library Users," January 29, 2003, www.ala.org/ala/washoff/WOissues/civilliberties/theusapatriotact/alaresolution.htm.

26. Darren K. Carlson, "Far Enough? Public Wary of Restricted Liberties," Gallup poll, Jan-

uary 20, 2004, www.galluppoll.com/content/?CI=10324; Eric Lichtblau, "Ashcroft's Tour Rallies Supporters and Detractors," *New York Times,* September 8, 2003; Federal Document Clearing House, "Attorney General Ashcroft Delivers Remarks at National Restaurant Assn.'s Annual Public Affairs Conference, Sept. 15, 2003"; American Library Association, "American Library Assn. Responds to Attorney General," September 16, 2003, www.ala.org/template.cfm?Section=archive&template=/contentmanagement/contentdisplay.cfm&ContentID=44012.

27. Jeffrey Rosen, "Civil Right," *New Republic* 227, no. 17 (October 21, 2002): 15.

28. "Customers Eager to Lend a Hand to Reader Privacy Campaign," *Bookselling This Week,* February 19, 2004, www.news.bookweb.org/freeexpression/2247.html; "Forum Makes for 'Excellent Day' for Great Lakes Booksellers," *Bookselling This Week,* April 1, 2004, www.news.bookweb.org/news/2387.html; "Book and Library Community Statement Supporting the Freedom to Read Protection Act (H.R. 1157), the Library and Bookseller Protection Act (S. 1158) and the Library, Bookseller and Personal Data Privacy Act (S. 1507)," *Bookselling This Week,* February 17, 2004, http://news.bookweb.org/freeexpression/2235.html.

29. *Congressional Record,* July 8, 2004, H5439, H5350.

30. Eric Lichtblau, "Effort to Curb Scope of Antiterrorism Law Fails," *New York Times,* July 9, 2004.

31. Tamar Lewin, "High School Tells Student to Remove Antiwar Shirt," *New York Times,* February 26, 2003; ACLU, "Judge Rules in Favor of Michigan Student's Right to Wear Anti-War T-Shirt to School," October 1, 2003, available at www.aclu.org/freespeech/youth/11405prs20031001.html.

32. ACLU, "PATRIOT Act Fears Are Stifling Free Speech, ACLU Says in Challenge to Law," November 3, 2003, www.aclu.org/safefree/patriot/18418prs20031103.html.

33. Jeffrey Rosen, "Privacy Pleas," *New Republic* 228, no. 20 (May 26, 2003): 20.

34. "Jittery Patron Calls FBI after Reading Note in Bin Laden Bio," *Library Journal,* October 4, 2004, www.libraryjournal.com/article/CA458088.html.

35. Assistant Attorney General William E. Moschella to J. Dennis Hastert, April 28, 2006, www.fas.org/irp/agency/doj/fisa/2005rept.html.

36. *Doe v. Ashcroft,* no. 04-CIV-2614 (S.D.N.Y. September 29, 2004), 79–80, available at www.nysd.uscourts.gov/rulings/04CV2614_Opinion_092904.pdf.

37. Peter Wallsten, "Politics of Patriot Act Turn Right for Bush," *Los Angeles Times,* April 25, 2004.

38. "Another Cave-in on the Patriot Act," *New York Times,* February 11, 2006; American Library Association, "ALA President Michael Gorman Responds to Senate PATRIOT Act Reauthorization Vote," March 1, 2006, available at www.ala.org/template.cfm?Section=archive&template=/contentmanagement/contentdisplay.cfm&ContentID=118686; ACLU, "Senate Adopts Patriot Act Reauthorization without Necessary Reforms," March 2, 2006, available at www.aclu.org/safefree/general/24348prs20060302.html.

39. USA PATRIOT Improvement and Reauthorization Act of 2005 (H.R. 3199), Section 106A; the ACLU underlined the importance of the changes in the law in October 2006 when it withdrew its legal challenge to Section 215. "While the reauthorized Patriot Act is far from perfect, we succeeded in stemming the damage from some of the Bush administration's most reckless policies," said Ann Beeson, the ACLU's associate legal director. Edward L. Cardenas, "ACLU Drops Patriot Act Suit," *Detroit News,* October 28, 2006, www.detnews.com/apps/pbcs.dll/article?AID=/20061028/METRO/610280349/1003.

40. "The Times and Iraq," *New York Times,* May 26, 2004.

41. *Hamdi v. Rumsfeld,* 542 U.S. 536 (2004).

42. Frank Eltman, "Connecticut Librarians Bitterly Decry Gag Order in Patriot Act Case," Associated Press, May 30, 2006, www.boston.com/news/local/connecticut/articles/2006/05/30/conn_librarians_bitterly_decry_gag_order_in_patriot_act_case/.

43. *ACLU v. National Security Agency,* no. 06-CV-10204 (E.D.MI, August 17, 2006), 40, available at www.mied.uscourts.gov/eGov/taylorpdf/06%2010204.pdf.

44. Joseph Carroll, "Public Divided on Whether Wiretapping Was Justified," Gallup poll, January 12, 2006, available at www.galluppoll.com/content/?ci=20887&pg=1; "Civil Liberties," Gallup poll, June 1, 2006, available at www.galluppoll.com/content/?ci= 5263&pg=1; Lydia Saad, "Most Americans Say Lives Not 'Permanently Changed' by 9/11," Gallup poll, September 11, 2006, available at www.galluppoll.com/content/ Default.aspx?ci=24439&VERSION=p.

45. Maurice Possley, "Jailed for Their Words," *Chicago Tribune,* December 28, 2005; Charles S. Johnson, "Pardon the Delay," *Helena Independent-Record,* May 4, 2006, available at www.helenair.com/articles/2006/05/04/helena_top/a01050406_04.txt%20; Clemens P. Work, *Darkest before Dawn: Sedition and Free Speech in the American West* (Albuquerque: University of New Mexico, Press, 2005).

46. Learned Hand, *The Spirit of Liberty* (New York: Alfred A. Knopf, 1974), 189–90.